MIGRATION AND THE INTERNATIONAL LABOR MARKET, 1850–1939

International migration has long been a topic of debate. In the West, questions concerning its causes and consequences have always influenced policy. As a result much has been written on the historical role of immigration, although this has largely focused on social rather than economic history.

Migration and the International Labor Market, 1850–1939 redresses this imbalance and puts the emphasis firmly on economic issues. This volume concentrates on the two central aspects of international migration – the forces which cause it and its economic impact. The contributors are drawn from a wide range of countries representing both the Old and the New Worlds. Each of them examines and tests the validity of migration theories in the historical setting. In some cases migration is viewed from a comparative perspective – an approach which is facilitated by new data on internationally comparable real wages. The authors also look at the responsiveness of migration from different countries to international wage differentials and the degree of international labor market integration. A number of chapters go on to examine the impact of migration on real wage growth and economic convergence between original and destination countries. These issues remain at the heart of debates over international migration policy. This analysis, therefore, not only sheds light on historical experience but helps inform the current debate.

Timothy J. Hatton is Reader in Economics at the University of Essex. He has written widely on aspects of labor markets 1850–1950. His recent work has concentrated on issues of labor market performance with international and interregional migration.

Jeffrey G. Williamson is Laird Bell Professor of Economics at Harvard University. He is a distinguished authority on cliometrics and has written extensively on economic history and development.

MIGRATION AND THE INTERNATIONAL LABOR MARKET, 1850–1939

Edited by Timothy J. Hatton and Jeffrey G. Williamson

London and New York

First published 1994
by Routledge
11 New Fetter Lane, London EC4P 4EE

Simultaneously published in the USA and Canada
by Routledge
29 West 35th Street, New York, NY 10001

Typeset in Garamond by Solidus (Bristol) Limited

Printed and bound in Great Britain by
Biddles Ltd, Guildford and King's Lynn

British Library Cataloguing in Publication Data
A catalogue record for this book is available from the British Library

Library of Congress Cataloging in Publication Data
Migration and the international labor market, 1850–1939 / edited by Timothy J.
Hatton and Jeffrey G. Williamson
p.   cm.
Includes bibliographical references and index.
ISBN 0–415–10768–7   ISBN 0–415–10769–5 (pbk.)
1. Alien labor–history. 2. Emigration and immigration–Economic aspects. 3. Labor
market–History.
I. Hatton, T.J. II. Williamson, Jeffrey G., 1935– .
HD6300.M54   1994
331.6'2'09–dc20   94–3975
CIP

CONTENTS

FIGURES

FIGURES

TABLES

CONTRIBUTORS

Dudley Baines is Reader in Economic History at the London School of Economics and Political Science, London, England.

George R. Boyer is Associate Professor of Labor Economics at Cornell University, Ithaca, New York, USA.

Riccardo Faini is Professor of Economics at the University of Brescia, Italy.

Henry A. Gemery is Pugh Family Professor of Economics at Colby College, Waterville, Maine, USA.

Alan G. Green is Professor of Economics at Queen's University, Kingston, Ontario, Canada.

Timothy J. Hatton is Reader in Economics at the University of Essex, Colchester, England.

Marvin McInnis is Professor of Economics at Queen's University, Kingston, Ontario, Canada.

Kevin O'Rourke is Lecturer in Economics at University College, Dublin, Ireland.

David Pope is a professor in the Division of Economics and Politics, Research School of Social Sciences, Australian National University, Canberra, Australia.

Pierre Sicsic is an economist at the Centre de Recherche, Banque de France, Paris, France.

Alan M. Taylor is Assistant Professor of Economics at Northwestern University at Evanston, Illinois, USA.

CONTRIBUTORS

Alessandra Venturini is Professor of Economics at the University of Florence, Italy.

Jeffrey G. Williamson is Laird Bell Professor of Economics at Harvard University, Cambridge, Massachusetts, USA.

Glenn Withers is Professor of Economics at La Trobe University, Melbourne, Australia, and Director of the Australian Government's Economic Planning Advisory Council, Canberra.

ACKNOWLEDGEMENTS

Drafts of these papers were first presented at the Villa Serbelloni, Bellagio, Italy where the authors whose work appears in this volume met jointly with a group led by Peter Scholliers and Vera Zamagni. We are grateful to Professor Zamagni, not only for insightful comments on all the papers presented at Bellagio, but also for handling local arrangements so ably. The Rockefeller Foundation has our deepest gratitude for supplying a delightful environment for what turned out to be a productive conference. We are also deeply grateful to The North Atlantic Treaty Organisation's Advanced Research Workshop programme which provided finance, without which the conference would not have been possible.

The manuscripts were processed mainly at Harvard where Ann Flack played her usual cheerful and competent secretarial and editorial role. It is also a pleasure to acknowledge the work of Alan Jarvis and Rebecca Garland of Routledge in expediting the publication of this volume.

Finally, the editors gratefully acknowledge the National Science Foundation which helped finance much of the research underlying the papers in this volume which list one or both of us as authors.

TJH, Colchester, Essex
JGW, Cambridge, Massachusetts
May, 1994

Part I

INTRODUCTION

1

INTERNATIONAL MIGRATION 1850–1939

An economic survey

Timothy J. Hatton and Jeffrey G. Williamson

International migration has long been a topic of debate. Questions concerning its causes and consequences have always been prominent in policy debate in North America, South America, Australasia, and more recently in Europe, where they have reached a heightened pitch. Why do some countries produce more migrants than others and why does the intensity of migration vary over time? How well do different migrant groups assimilate into the host country and to what extent do they suffer disadvantages compared with, and segmentation from, natives? Do immigrants rob jobs from natives? What impact do they have on wage rates and living standards in the host country? Does emigration improve the lot of those left behind?

These questions certainly help focus the current debate, and history is a good place to look for answers. Indeed, these questions have provoked a very large historical literature, most of which has focused on the mass migrations which took place during the century prior to the First World War. Yet when Frank Thistlethwaite (1960) wrote his influential survey more than thirty years ago, he reported that the existing literature had focused disproportionately on the consequence of migration (particularly in the United States), neglecting the causes (particularly in Europe). After three decades, this imbalance is now reversed. Furthermore, recent research often loses sight of two fundamental questions: what are the economic forces which cause international migration? – and what is its economic effect?

The chapters in this volume focus on these two questions, and break new ground along the way. Several of them take a comparative approach, exploring differences in migration experience across countries and regions. Several of them examine the emigration experience of southern Europe, countries which have been studied less intensively than the rest of Europe – a fact lamented some years ago by John Gould (1979: 624). Furthermore, rarely has the literature examined the effects of interwar economic conditions and restrictive policies on the flow of immigrants and their economic impact, compared with pre-1913 years. Here again several of the chapters break new ground. Perhaps most important of all, a number of the chapters assess quantitatively the economic impact of migration on emigrating and immigrating countries. These studies are provocative and pioneering. They also offer a link to another flourishing literature – economic convergence – by assessing the contribution which migration has made to relatively slow growth in rich countries and relative fast growth in poor countries.

This introduction outlines the major features of international migration in the period from 1850 to 1939, synthesizing recent and earlier research findings into what we believe is a new picture of international migration. Our treatment is thematic. This allows us to highlight what we believe are similar economic forces operating in different economic environments, countries and time periods. This approach allows us to place the contributions in a wider perspective, to point to the areas where more research needs to be done, and to stress those insights that are especially relevant to current policy debate.

THE DIMENSIONS OF INTERNATIONAL MIGRATION

In the century following 1820, about 50 million Europeans set sail for labor-scarce New World destinations, magnitudes big enough to be called "mass migrations." About three-fifths of these went to the United States. Earlier migration from labor-abundant Europe had been a mere trickle as with emigrations from labor-abundant India and China. The only comparable intercontinental migration was that of black slaves from Africa to the Americas and the Caribbean. Indeed, it was only in the 1840s that the number of Europeans emigrating to the United States exceeded the number of Africans, and it was not until the 1880s that the cumulative European immigration exceeded that of African (Eltis 1983: 225).

European intercontinental emigration is plotted in the upper portion of Figure 1.1. In the first three decades after 1846, the figures averaged about 300,000 per annum; in the next two decades, the figures more than doubled; and after the turn of the century they rose to over a million per annum. The European sources also changed dramatically. In the first half of the century, the dominant emigration stream was from the British Isles followed by Germany. A rising tide of Scandinavian and other northwest European flows joined these streams by mid-century. Southern and eastern Europe joined the flow in the 1880s. This new emigrant stream accounted for most of the rising total in the late nineteenth century. It came first from Italy, Spain and Portugal, but it was joined by Austria–Hungary, Russia and Poland after the 1890s.[1]

The overwhelming majority went to the Americas. Figure 1.2 plots this immigration from 1846 to the quotas: the pattern closely replicates the total intercontinental emigration in Figure 1.1.[2] Migration to the Americas was

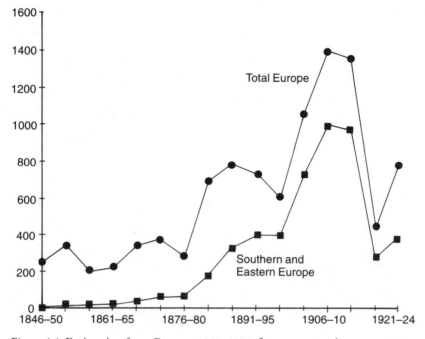

Figure 1.1 Emigration from Europe, 1846–1924, five-year annual averages (000's)

dominated by the United States, but there were significant flows to South America after the mid-1880s, led by Argentina and Brazil, and to Canada after the turn of the century. A small but persistent stream also linked the United Kingdom to Australasia and South Africa.

Very important migrations also took place between countries within Europe, although these flows are less precisely measured. For example, the overwhelming bulk of Belgian emigrants went to France and the Netherlands, while as late as the 1890s more than half of all Italian emigrants went to destinations in Europe (chiefly France and Germany). There were also significant migrations within the New World such as that from Canada across the border to the United States, although, as Marvin McInnis demonstrates in Chapter 7, the precise magnitudes are still being refined.

These mass migration statistics typically refer to gross rather than net flows. The distinction becomes increasingly important as the upward trend in gross emigration is partially offset by an even steeper rise in return migration later in the century. United States authorities estimated that between 1890 and 1914 return migration was 30 percent of the gross inflow. It varied greatly by nationality; nearly half among Italians and Spaniards but only 5 percent among Russians. Other New World countries had high rates of return migration; between 1857 and 1924, return migration from Argentina (Italians and Spaniards) was 47 percent of the gross inflow. The high rate

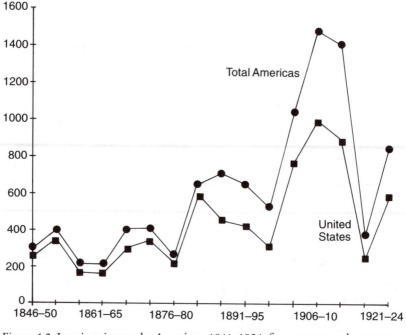

Figure 1.2 Immigration to the Americas, 1846–1924, five-year annual averages
(000's)

of return migration among Italians represented a growing trend towards temporary, often seasonal, migration, a phenomenon later to be called the "flight of the birds of passage."

For most purposes, the migrant flow relative to country populations is a more relevant statistic than absolutes. Table 1.1 reports European emigration rates per decade per thousand of population and they include intra-European migration where data are available. These gross rates exaggerate the net movements, but they document broad orders of magnitude none the less. Rates exceeding 50 per thousand were not uncommon for Britain, Ireland, Norway, and several southern European countries at the end of the century. Table 1.2 reports some New World immigration rates. These are even larger than the Old World emigration rates. Migration rates like this imply significant economic effects on sending and receiving labor markets even if we allow for the rising trend of return migration.

Who were these migrants?

Early-nineteenth-century migrant streams were often led by farmers and artisans from rural areas traveling in family groups intending to acquire land and settle permanently at the frontier. But as Europe industrialized, the migrants from any given country were increasingly drawn from urban areas and non-agricultural occupations, though many still had rural roots (Walker 1964; Kero 1974; Hvidt 1975; Carlsson 1976; Swierenga 1976). For example,

6

Table 1.1 European emigration rates by decade (per 1000 mean population)

Country	1851–60	1861–70	1871–80	1881–90	1891–1900	1901–10
Austria–Hungary	2.9	10.6	16.1	47.6	—	—
Belgium	—	—	—	8.6	3.5	6.1
British Isles	58.0	51.8	50.4	70.2	43.8	65.3
Denmark	—	—	20.6	39.4	22.3	28.2
France	1.1	1.2	1.5	3.1	1.3	1.4
Germany	—	—	14.7	28.7	10.1	4.5
Ireland	—	66.1	141.7	88.5	69.8	—
Netherlands	5.0	5.9	4.6	12.3	5.0	5.1
Norway	24.2	57.6	47.3	95.2	44.9	83.3
Sweden	4.6	30.5	23.5	70.1	41.2	42.0
Switzerland	—	—	13.0	32.0	14.1	13.9
Finland	—	—	—	13.2	23.2	54.5
Italy	—	—	10.5	33.6	50.2	107.7
Portugal	—	19.0	28.9	38.0	50.8	56.9
Spain	—	—	—	36.2	43.8	56.6

Source: Ferenczi and Willcox (1929: 200–1).

Table 1.2 New World immigration rates by decade (per 1000 mean population)

Country	1851–60	1861–70	1871–80	1881–90	1891–1900	1901–10
Canada	99.2	83.2	54.8	78.4	48.8	167.6
United States	92.8	64.9	54.6	85.8	53.0	102.0
Cuba	—	—	—	—	—	118.4
Argentina	38.5	99.1	117.0	221.7	163.9	291.8
Brazil	—	20.4	41.1	72.3	33.8	—

Source: See Table 1.1.

emigrants from Britain in the 1830s, a country which at that time had already undergone a half century of industrialization, were mainly from non-farm occupations (Erickson 1990: 25). However, the increasing importance of less industrial southeast Europe as an emigrant source actually raised the emigrant proportion from rural Europe and lowered their average skills and literacy (Lindert 1978: 243).

By the late nineteenth century, migrants were typically young adults. Only 8 percent of the immigrants entering the United States between 1868 and 1910 were over 40 years old and another 16 percent were under 15. Thus, the "mass" migrants exhibited very high labor-participation rates. The migrant flow was also dominated by males: they accounted for 64 percent of all United States' immigrants between 1851 and 1913, and for more than three-quarters of the emigrants from Spain and Italy.[3] Emigrants tended to be single and emigrated as individuals rather than in family groups, although a significant minority were young couples with small children. In short, the migrants carried a very low dependency burden with them. The typical migrant was also unskilled, although this was less true for Australasia than for North America. No doubt this was due in part to the fact that he was young, but it also reflected his limited educational and occupational background.

This evidence suggests that those who emigrated had the most to gain from the move, and were likely, therefore, to be the most responsive to labor market conditions. By emigrating when young they were able to reap the gains over most of their working lives. By moving as single individuals they were able to minimize the costs of the move, including earnings forgone in passage and during job search. Costs were reduced even further by the assistance of friends and relatives in the destination countries. Since the emigrants were typically unskilled, they also had little technology- or country-specific human capital invested and hence stood to lose few of the rents from such acquired skills (except for language).

This picture reinforces the notion that economic forces were uppermost in migration decisions and that most migrants moved in the expectation of a more prosperous and secure life for themselves and their descendants. A few moved to escape religious or political persecution, and others did so in convict chains (such as the early "migrants" to Australia). But most moved to escape European poverty. And most moved under their own initiative without either government pressure or assistance, although Australia and Brazil offer good counter-examples. As the technology of transport and communication improved, the costs and uncertainty of migration fell, and overseas migration came within reach of an increasing portion of the European population for whom the move offered the most gain. These forces accompanied by European famine and revolution gave rise to the first great surge of mass emigration in the 1840s.

DETERMINANTS OF MIGRATION

As Table 1.1 indicates, emigration rates ranged from over 50 per thousand per decade from countries like Ireland and Norway to a mere 2 per thousand from France. Why did emigration rates vary so widely? And why was there an upward trend in the Italian and Portuguese emigration rates, while it was downwards for Germany and Sweden after the 1880s? One of the main challenges facing scholars has been to explain why emigration rates were not always highest from the poorest countries, whose populations would have gained most from the move, and why emigration rates often rose from low levels as successful economic development took place at home (Easterlin 1961; Tomaske 1971; Williamson 1974b; Massey 1988; Baines 1991: Ch. 2). Can the various emigration rates in Table 1.1 be explained by a common economic framework, or does instead the explanation lie with non-economic factors and country-specific idiosyncratic events?

We explored these questions recently using pooled European emigration rates averaged across decades for eleven countries (Hatton and Williamson 1994). Similar results are also presented in Chapter 3, which focuses specifically on the experience of the Latin countries. Our findings support the view that emigration rates across countries and through time can be explained by a common framework and by reference to a surprisingly small number of economic and demographic variables. The main findings follow.

First, the ratio of home to receiving country wages had a significant negative impact on emigration. While consistent with conventional theory, earlier studies, constrained by lack of comparative data on real wages (a constraint now released: Williamson 1994), had been unable to isolate this effect adequately. Second, the rate-of-natural-increase-lagged-twenty-years had a powerful effect on emigration rates, just as Richard Easterlin (1961) forcibly argued thirty years ago. This demographic effect stimulated emigration directly by raising the share of the population in the prime emigration age group, or by reducing the ability to acquire land, rather than simply indirectly by lowering the domestic wage. Third, emigration increased as the proportion of the labor force in agriculture fell. While this effect was never very strong, it does support the argument of Massey (1988) and a number of earlier writers who have seen industrialization as breaking ties with the land and leading to increased labor mobility (Semmingsen 1960: 152-3; Thistlethwaite 1960: 38).

There is also strong evidence of persistence in emigration rates as reflected in two variables: the emigration rate in the previous decade and the stock of previous emigrants living abroad. These variables reflect the important pull of earlier migrants – the "friends and relatives" or "chain migration" effect stressed by many historians. The first of the two variables may also reflect the lagged adjustment of expectations, but both proved to be very important and significant: for example, every additional thousand of past emigrants induced an additional twenty emigrants to leave each year. There is independent evidence supporting this powerful influence. Among all European immigrants arriving in the United States in 1908-9, 94.7 percent said they were joining friends and relatives (US Immigration Commission 1910: 59). Furthermore, many European emigrants traveled on tickets which were pre-paid in the destination country. These accounted for 30 percent of Finnish emigrants after 1890, for 50 percent of Swedish emigrants in the 1880s, for 40 percent of Norwegian emigrants in the 1870s and 25 percent of Danish emigrants in the 1880s and 1890s (Kero 1991: 191; Hvidt 1975: 129).

Some observers have argued that the typical pattern in northwest Europe was that emigration started from low levels, rose to a peak and then declined (Akerman 1976: 25, 32). A long-run inverse "U" shape can be identified in the emigration histories of a number of countries in northwest Europe. The upswing of the emigration cycle usually coincided with industrialization and rising real wages at home. Since this successful development often reduced the gap between real wages at home and abroad, how can we account for the simultaneous upswing in the emigration rate, much like that which has been observed for Mexico, Central America, the Middle East and Asia since the 1950s? For the typical late-nineteenth-century emigrating country, we argue that demographic forces, industrialization and the mounting stock of previous emigrants abroad all served to drive up the emigration rate in early stages of industrialization. As these forces weakened, the narrowing gap between home and foreign wages began to dominate and emigration receded (Hatton and Williamson 1994). Emigration passed through a life cycle in the late nineteenth century, and we think that an economic–demographic model can account for it remarkably well.

An alternative argument stresses that emigration was constrained in its early stages by the poverty of potential emigrants and their inability to save (or borrow) enough to finance a passage to the New World despite the strong economic incentive to do so. The friends and relatives effect would also have been relatively weak given the small stock of previous emigrants abroad. As industrialization took place in the home country, real wage rates rose and the constraint on migration was gradually released. More and more migrants were able to finance the move and, in contrast with conventional theory, the home wage and the emigration rate rose together.

Can either argument be used to explain why the poorer countries of southern and eastern Europe joined the mass emigration so late and why their emigration rates rose so steeply to 1913? Our own analysis in Chapter 3 suggests that the forces driving emigration in Italy, Spain and Portugal were identical to those operating in northwest Europe. Although their emigration rates were higher than would have been predicted by the experience of northwest Europe, the Latins responded to demographic and economic forces in remarkably similar ways. However, Riccardo Faini and Alessandra Venturini (Chapter 4) argue that income constraints were important to Italian emigration. Estimating time series regressions for emigration to three destinations, they find that domestic income per capita had a positive effect (even controlling for the income gap between source and destination) and that the rise in income explained nearly a third of the emigration surge from 1900 to 1913.

Another argument is sometimes advanced: that access to information is crucial in the early stages of emigration. John Gould (1980b) found that there were vast differences in emigration intensity within any given country, and that these tended to narrow over time, presumably as knowledge of opportunities diffused. As other localities followed the leaders, the country-wide emigration rate rose. The fact that emigration rose first around booming ports, along expanding trading routes and from well-placed islands, is consistent with the information hypothesis, but it is also consistent with the importance of transport costs, with rising real wage conditions at home, or with the effects of chain migration. Dudley Baines (1991 and Chapter 2) believes the former and thus suggests that regional variations in emigration rates may not be explained by reference solely to economic and demographic variables.

The few studies which have investigated the determinants of local emigration rates have obtained mixed results: there is no strong evidence linking emigration rates to economic and demographic variables (Norman 1976; Baines 1986), although it must be said that the available data are often inadequate and that explicit multi-variate models have not often been applied. Some systematic patterns have been identified none the less. A prominent feature associated with areas of heavy emigration in mid-century northwest Germany was a well-developed cottage linen industry, interlinked with agriculture (especially seasonally). Such "proto-industrial" areas had higher rates of natural increase than other rural areas. They were also vulnerable to rising factory competition, and thus had increasing problems absorbing the natural increase (Kamphoefner 1976: 182). The rise of large estates in the East Elbian region converted agricultural workers to wage laborers, restricting their opportunities to acquire smallholdings and stimulating out-migration (Walker 1964: 164).

Late-nineteenth-century rural Ireland offers much stronger support for the influence of economic and demographic variables at the local level (Hatton and Williamson 1993). While large agricultural employment shares were correlated with high emigration rates between Irish counties, a higher share of landholdings below 5 acres reduced emigration. The gap between the wage in destination countries and the county wage, and the incidence of poverty (the proportion on poor relief and the proportion of poor quality housing), both had the expected positive effect on emigration. Average family size also had a strong positive effect on the emigration rate. These results for Ireland may not be typical of what would be found if similar studies were performed for other countries and for two reasons. First, information about opportunities was fully diffused by the 1880s, and most Irish men and women had friends or relatives who had emigrated previously. Second, there were few opportunities to migrate to rapidly growing industrial centers within Ireland (except around Belfast).

The analysis is made more complicated where migration alternatives were more plentiful (see Baines, Chapter 2). For one thing, measurement is influenced by the size of the region and by the economic arbitrariness of administrative or even international boundaries within Europe. Typically, there were large and often transient movements across boundaries in both directions but net flows were almost always from rural to urban and from low-wage to high-wage areas. There is a growing body of evidence that net movements were positively related to real wage gaps and inversely related to distance from place of origin. Migrants from the surrounding rural hinterland were often drawn into booming urban centers thus suppressing overseas emigration; the opposite was true for more remote rural areas. But several

11

Scandinavian studies have shown that movement to the city was often the first step in overseas migration (Carlsson 1976; Semmingsen 1972). Local cities and overseas destinations were competing alternatives and emigration was often simply rural–urban migration on an international scale (Thomas 1972).

Migrants from a given locality often followed a well-trodden path to specific overseas locations. Thus, more than 90 percent of Dutch emigrants from the province of Zuid settled in the communities of Patterson in New Jersey, Nordeloos in Michigan, Pella in Iowa and South Holland in Illinois (Swierenga 1991: 150). As the "friends and relatives effect" would suggest, the stock of past immigrants from the sending area was an important influence on the location of new immigrants. None the less, studies which have analyzed the intended destinations of immigrants arriving in the United States show clearly that state per capita income was important to the location decision (Gallaway, Vedder and Shukla 1974; Dunlevy and Gemery 1977, 1978). This influence, and the subsequent mobility of immigrants, produced a growing diaspora for all nationalities within the United States.

While persistence characterized emigration in the late nineteenth century, it was continuously modified by changing economic conditions in the receiving countries. But to what extent did emigrants view New World destinations as closely competing options? As Alan Taylor argues in Chapter 5, the international labor market was segmented so that migrant streams split along different racial, national and cultural lines. Emigrants from southern Europe flowed chiefly to countries such as Argentina, Brazil and Cuba, even though their incomes would have been higher in the United States, Canada or Australia. While they were officially excluded from Australia they could have emigrated to North America. It has been argued that the barriers to upward mobility facing Latin emigrants were greater in the United States than in Argentina and thus that there was more return migration from the former (Baily 1983; Klein 1983). The segmentation of international labor markets is not yet fully understood, leaving some important questions unanswered for the late nineteenth century. For example, in the case of Italy why did those going to North America come largely from the South, and why did those going to South America come largely from the North? Why did an increasing share of Italians go the United States?

FLUCTUATIONS IN MIGRANT FLOWS

One of the most prominent features of nineteenth-century emigration is its sharp year-to-year fluctuation. The pioneering studies of Harry Jerome (1926) and Dorothy Thomas (1941) examined the relationship between migration and business cycles. Jerome found that the timing of United States immigration was determined chiefly by the American business cycle and that conditions in the sending countries had only a minor influence. In contrast,

Thomas found that domestic conditions were important in determining the timing of Swedish emigration, and sometimes decisively so. A sizable econometric literature has grown up since these pioneers wrote, much of which was admirably surveyed by Gould (1979).

The earlier studies were preoccupied with assessing the relative strength of "pull" abroad and "push" at home. There has been little consensus as to how these terms should be defined; our strong preference would be to reserve them to describe the underlying labor market fundamentals (Williamson 1974b). The discussion instead typically dwells on whether the coefficients on variables representing conditions abroad are larger or more significant that those representing conditions at home. Using that criterion, the literature has reached no consensus: pull abroad is found to have mattered most in some studies (Kelley 1965; Gallaway and Vedder 1971; Richardson 1972), while push at home is found to have mattered most in others (Wilkinson 1970; Quigley 1972; Magnussen and Sigveland 1978).

Two types of variables have typically been included to represent conditions at home and abroad. These are prospective earnings, proxied either by GNP per capita or the average wage, and employment opportunities proxied by unemployment or some other cyclical variable. Allen Kelley (1965), Harry Richardson (1972) and David Pope (1981a, 1981b), all concluded that wages were not important but that unemployment rates were central, especially the unemployment rate in the receiving country. By contrast, Maurice Wilkinson (1970), Thorvald Moe (1970) and John Quigley (1972) found highly significant coefficients on absolute or relative wages. As Gould (1979) pointed out, where adequate proxies for both wages and unemployment rates are included the latter usually dominate. Alternatively, Pope (1981a) combined employment rates and wage rates to form expected income variables along the lines originally suggested by Michael Todaro (1969).

The battle between the proponents of push and pull is really a false one. It makes little sense to consider the prospective emigrant as acting solely in response to conditions at home or abroad; emigration decisions must surely have been based on some comparison between the two. In the absence of an explicit model, however, it is impossible to infer that asymmetry between the estimated coefficients necessarily violates the postulate that emigrants rationally chose between the alternatives facing them. Similarly, it can hardly have been unemployment alone that mattered since we almost always observe net migration flowing towards those countries with the higher wage rates. Some of these problems arise essentially because the specifications used are *ad hoc*.

A more recent approach is to develop a migration model from micro-foundations assuming heterogeneity across individuals who are risk averse and face uncertainty about the probability of employment (Hatton 1993). In such a world, the foreign employment rate might be expected to take on a larger coefficient than that on the home employment rate (if there is a greater uncertainty about employment prospects abroad) and a larger coefficient than that on the wage gap. Furthermore, since emigrants are presumed to be concerned with the present value of their future earnings stream, they can be expected to form an estimate based on past experience. This fact can account for the success of the lagged dependent variable in econometric analysis, often the most significant variable in these earlier studies (Gould 1979: 659). Additional dynamics enter the model on account of the timing decision: even though it might be worth while (in present value terms) to emigrate this year, it may be better still to wait a year (Burda 1993; O'Connell 1993).

Models along these lines have been estimated for emigration from the United Kingdom 1879–1913 (Hatton 1993) and Ireland 1876–1913 (Hatton and Williamson 1993). The results for the United Kingdom strongly support the model, especially the role of the foreign employment rate and the wage gap. They also indicate large short-run effects arising from changes in employment rates, particularly at the destination. In the long run, an increase in the overseas employment rate by 10 percent (for example, a fall in the unemployment rate from 10 percent to 1 percent) increased the annual emigration rate from the United Kingdom by 4 per thousand while a 10 percent rise in the foreign to home wage ratio raised the emigration rate by 2.2 per thousand. Similar results were obtained for Ireland alone where the long-run effects of a 10 percent increase in the foreign relative to the home wage ratio raised the emigration rate by 2.4 per thousand. In both cases, employment rates dominated short-run fluctuations in emigration but trends were determined largely by secular changes in the wage ratio. The long-run convergence of the Irish real wage on that of destination countries accounted for a fall of the emigration rate of about 4 per thousand between 1876–80 and 1909–13.

Can similar models explain time series emigration rates from other countries? In Chapter 3, we apply a restricted version of the model to emigration from Portugal, Spain and Italy for the period before the First World War. The results indicate again that variations in foreign activity had powerful effects on timing while the wage ratio was a more important influence on long-run trends. A 10 percent rise in the foreign to domestic wage ratio raised intercontinental emigration by between 0.5 and 1 per thousand per annum. These wage effects are broadly consistent with those obtained from cross-sectional analysis, but are smaller than those obtained for the United Kingdom and Ireland. Thus, the argument that Latin Old World countries provided a more elastic emigrant supply to Latin America – an extension of the familiar labor surplus model (Lewis 1978; Díaz-Alejandro 1970) – is not borne out by the evidence.

This important finding is also borne out when viewed from the perspective of the receiving countries. In Chapter 5, Taylor applies the same approach to the immigration rates of Italians and Spaniards to Argentina and the British to Australia. Observers such as Díaz-Alejandro (1970) argued that Argentina faced a very elastic supply of emigrants. Taylor finds, however, that the emigrant supply to Argentina was no more elastic than that to Australia. The main reason why the immigration rate to Argentina was so much higher than to Australia in the years before the First World War was that the wage gap between the Latin countries and Argentina was much larger than that between Britain and Australia.

WERE MIGRANTS COMPLEMENTS OR SUBSTITUTES FOR NATIVES?

In his famous book *The Uprooted*, Oscar Handlin argued that late-nineteenth-century American immigrants were poorly assimilated. He argued that they were largely from rural peasant backgrounds and were unable to adapt easily to American labor markets. They faced cultural and economic barriers which were only overcome after several generations. They crowded into ghettos, segmented from the rest of society, suffering poverty, squalor and disease.

Handlin's thesis has been severely criticized in the four decades since 1951 (see the excellent summary in Cinel 1982: 10–14). Perhaps this is not surprising, since *The Uprooted* was not based firmly on quantitative evidence nor did it offer explicit comparisons between foreign city immigrants and native American city immigrants as Pierre Sicsic does for France in Chapter 6. The new view paints a more benign picture. It argues that immigrants were able to adapt to American labor markets and that the clash of cultures was not nearly as sharp as Handlin suggested. By gathering in ethnic communities, they were able to maintain some of their traditions, culture and customs while gradually integrating into American life. Furthermore, immigrant communities had positive benefits. Social networks provided a structure for mutual aid. This included information and access to jobs in a manner more effective than was true even for native American blacks moving up from the South (Briggs 1978; Bodnar 1985).

While Handlin argued that immigrants had difficulty gaining access to jobs, the evidence that the foreign-born suffered higher unemployment than the native-born is weak at best. The US Commissioner of Labor survey for 1901 reported that the average unemployment rate for foreign-born household heads was 10.1 percent as compared with 8.3 percent for the native-born. This was due both to slightly higher unemployment incidence and slightly longer durations, a finding confirmed more recently by a detailed analysis of 1910 Census data (Margo 1990a: 56). However, such differences as these seem to be explained almost entirely by differences in the two groups' occupations (Keyssar 1986: 79–89).

As evidence of occupational discrimination, some writers have quoted official statistics showing that male immigrants had earnings as low as two-thirds of the native-born.[4] When one controls for human capital endowments, however, the wage gap between native- and foreign-born becomes much smaller and sometimes evaporates entirely. Robert Higgs (1971) found little difference in the predicted earnings of native- and foreign-born after controlling for literacy and ability to speak English. Using different controls, Paul McGouldrick and Michael Tannen (1977) found a 5–10 percent difference between immigrants from southeast Europe and the native-born; and similar results were reported by Joan Hannon (1982a, 1982b) – about 7 percent – and by Barry Eichengreen and Henry Gemery (1986) – about 6 percent. Although these results suggest that immigrant earnings were lower largely because of their more modest skill endowments, they also received somewhat lower returns to their skills.

For immigrants who acquired their skills in America, earnings over the life cycle converged towards those of the native-born although the catching up was much more modest for those who acquired their skills prior to arrival (Hannon 1982a, 1982b; Eichengreen and Gemery 1986; Hanes 1991). Differences in earnings largely reflected differences in occupational attainment and slower upward mobility seems to have limited immigrant catch up. Stephen Thernstrom (1973), for example, found that Boston immigrants had less upward mobility than the native-born, especially among the Irish and Italians. It was particularly difficult for many of the immigrant groups to break out of manual occupations, even after a generation or more. Thus, nineteenth-century American immigrant convergence seems to have been slower than that observed among American immigrants in the postwar period, although the latter has been subject to a lively debate (Chiswick 1978; Borjas 1985). Perhaps access to the better jobs was limited by prejudice, and perhaps inability to speak English was one proxy for such prejudice. Perhaps – but inability to speak English can account for some, but not all, of the initial disadvantage. The Irish, for example, did not fare any better than the Italians.

If their skills were sufficiently lower, or if the labor market was sufficiently segmented, immigrants might not have been close substitutes for native labor as a whole even though they might have been close substitutes for unskilled parts of the labor force. This is an important issue for determining the impact of immigration on native-born wages and living standards. It is an issue that formed the background to much of the immigration debate prior to the First World War. The same debate rarely emerged in the Old World where, by inference, emigrants must have been viewed as close substitutes for those who stayed behind. We focus therefore on the labor markets facing immigrants in the New World.

There have been few efforts to explore directly the degree of substitutability between native and immigrant labor in the late nineteenth century. James Foreman-Peck (1992), however, has performed such a test for United States manufacturing in 1890. He estimated a translog production function treating immigrant and native labor as separate factors of production. His results show that these two types of labor were not complements: bigger immigrant supplies did not increase the marginal product of native labor. Foreman-Peck's results are consistent with the earlier observations of McGouldrick and Tannen (1977) who found no differences in the productivity performance of New England and southern textile industries despite the fact that the former employed immigrants while the latter did not.

Immigrant labor competed directly on almost equal terms with native labor in unskilled occupations. Nevertheless, immigrants tended to concentrate in different occupations than native-born, although it must be said that the most relevant comparison – with native American immigrants from the countryside – is rarely made (but see Sicsic for France in Chapter 6). Different immigrant groups often dominated certain occupations. Thus, while Italians accounted for only 4.2 percent of the US population in 1900, they accounted for 55 percent of the male barbers and hairdressers, 97 percent of the bootblacks, 34 percent of the shoemakers, 18 percent of the masons and 16 percent of the peddlers (Baily 1983: 285). Immigrants as a whole were much more evenly distributed across occupations, although they were still concentrated in relatively unskilled jobs. While it might seem likely that immigrants tended to bid down the wage in the occupations and industries where they were concentrated, there is little direct evidence on this point. Few such studies exist, and for good reason: to the extent that immigrants crowded into certain occupations, they displaced native and "older" immigrant labor, who then migrated to other occupations.

Given the relatively high occupational and spatial mobility in late-nineteenth-century America, immigration was more likely to have affected unskilled relative to skilled wages economy-wide rather than simply lowering wages in those unskilled groups or cities where the immigrants clustered. Between the mid-1890s and the First World War, the wage gap between the skilled and unskilled grew. This trend has frequently been associated with the flood of "new" immigrants, but some doubt has been shed recently on the view that an unskilled immigrant glut was mainly responsible for the rising wage gap. The widening pay gap in manufacturing was also driven by rapid technical change in manufacturing, and consequently unbalanced derived demand growth favoring skilled labor (Williamson and Lindert 1980: 208–9, 236). Furthermore, the urban unskilled labor pool was fed not only by foreign immigrants but by a rural influx which was highly sensitive to both urban employment conditions and wage rates (Hatton and Williamson 1992a). For the same years, David Pope and Glenn Withers find in Chapter 12 that the skill composition of immigration in Australia directly influenced the wage gap between skilled and unskilled; the greater the proportion of skilled immigrants, the lower the skill premium. Perhaps the absence of an elastic labor supply from rural areas heightened this effect for Australia compared with the US.

Can the impact of immigration be observed through differential wage effects across cities or regions? Most US immigrants went initially to major cities on the East Coast, but a substantial number traveled directly to inland cities such as Pittsburgh, Chicago and Milwaukee, and many more followed subsequently. The simple correlation between wages and immigration rates is positive reflecting the immigrants' choice of destination. But Claudia Goldin (1993) has recently found a negative correlation between *changes* in the immigrant share of the labor force and *changes* in the real wage across US cities between 1890 and 1914. Such results suggest that an immigrant glut lowers wages, but they probably understate the economy-wide impact. The explanation lies with the high geographic mobility of the American population, not to mention the post-immigration mobility of the immigrants themselves (Ferrie 1992). Internal labor mobility tends to dissipate immigrant-induced wage gaps across localities. Cross-section estimates are thus likely to be downward biased; we need other methods to measure the economy-wide impact of immigration on wages.

MIGRATION AND THE NATIONAL ECONOMY

Is migration a good thing or a bad thing and for whom? The debate is at least as old as the Industrial Revolution, appearing first in Britain and then repeatedly among the followers. As Michael Greenwood and John McDowell (1986: 1745–7) point out, it certainly has a long history in the United States. The debate reached a crescendo in 1911 after the Immigration Commission had pondered the problem for five years. The Commission concluded it was a bad thing, contributing to low wages and poor working conditions. But what about the sending countries? The migrants and their children clearly benefited, but what about those they left behind? The 1954 Irish Commission on Emigration concluded that a century of mass emigration had had a positive effect on Irish wages. In the words of the Commissioners: "With regard to those who remained at home, emigration . . . has reduced the pressure of population on resources . . . and thus helped to maintain and even to increase our income per head"(1954: 140).

Did the mass migrations reduce wage gaps between poor and rich countries raising real wages in the poor emigrating countries and lowering real wages in the rich immigrating countries? Historical correlations between rates of population increase and the real wage are unlikely to offer any clear answer to these questions. True, there is an inverse correlation for the years 1870–1913, and a good share of those population growth rate differentials were due to migration. Up to 1913, immigration accounted for 50 percent of Argentina's, 32 percent of the USA's and 30 percent of Australia's population increase (Taylor 1992a: Table 1.1; Williamson 1974a: 248). Emigration reduced Swedish population increase by 44 percent between 1871 and 1890 (Karlstrom 1985: 155, 181).

In the absence of increasing returns, and in the presence of a given technology and at least one fixed factor, all comparative static models in the classical tradition predict that migration tends to make labor cheaper in the immigrating country and scarcer in the emigrating country, especially in the short run when dynamic responses can be ignored. A simple partial equilibrium analysis of the immigrant-absorbing labor market is presented in Figure 1.3. Suppose that domestic labor supply S_N is augmented by an exogenous influx of European immigrants ($\bar{M}$, "pushed" by the malthusian devil), and the domestic labor market is given sufficient time to surmount domestic wage rigidity. What real wage decline is required to induce firms to hire the immigrant-augmented labor force? The figure shows a decline in the real wage from $w_E(t)$ to $w'_E(t)$ as the economy shifts down the labor demand curve. The more inelastic the labor demand curve, the more dramatic the decline in the domestic wage. Some recent work using a general equilibrium approach suggests that aggregate labor demand elasticities in late-nineteenth-century America were quite high, but that they fell sharply around the turn of the century (Williamson 1982: 273).

The position of the labor demand curve in Figure 1.3 is fixed by endowments and technology. This characterization is obviously inappropriate for a fast-growing America that absorbed the immigrants while

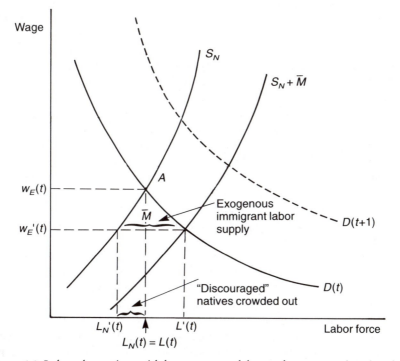

Figure 1.3 Labor absorption, with homogeneous labor and exogenous immigration

undergoing capital accumulation, land settlement, structural change and technical progress. Suppose these buoyant growth conditions are characterized by $D(t+1)$ in Figure 1.3. Assuming constant wage elasticities on D and S_N, the impact of the immigrant influx on employment and the real wage along $D(t+1)$ is exactly the same as before along $D(t)$. What is different about this case, however, is that upward shift in labor demand. This suggests it may be difficult to observe the impact of immigration on the wage unless we can control for the impact of other forces shifting the labor demand curve.

What about possible crowding out effects on the supply side? High native labor supply elasticities would imply "discouraged" workers being crowded out of the labor force as native labor was displaced by immigrants at their occupational and locational points of entry and as this displacement spread through the labor market economy-wide. If native labor supplies were very elastic, only small real wage declines would have been necessary to accommodate the immigrants. Some groups in America – women, blacks and off-farm migrants – were marginalized by immigrant competition in the major urban centers (Thomas 1972: Ch. 5; Hatton and Williamson 1992b). However, this argument relates largely to the displacement of potential internal migrants and others characterized by elastic labor supply; the aggregate native labor supply curve for the economy as a whole would have been a lot less elastic.

Perhaps immigrants robbed locals of jobs in another sense. If wage adjustment was sticky or delayed an immigrant-induced shift in the labor supply curve would create unemployment, especially when the labor demand curve was relatively stable. After all, calls for immigration restriction have almost always been loudest during times of high unemployment whether in America in the 1890s or in Germany in the 1990s. This question has been prominent in Australian debate and it has been addressed recently by David Pope and Glenn Withers (1993). Using annual data for 1860–1980, they estimate a simultaneous equations model of Australian immigration and unemployment. While the unemployment rate was found to be a powerful determinant of immigration, the long-run effects of immigration on unemployment appear to have been negligible. Pope and Withers interpret the result as reflecting immigrant-induced demand responses which shifted out the derived demand for labor at the same time – in a sense, immigrants brought their jobs with them.

There is, however, another interpretation of the Pope and Withers finding. In a well-functioning labor market, the effect on unemployment should have been only transitory; in the long run the effect should have been felt instead through lower wages. It is the wage that is central to the debate and this is the issue they address in their contribution to this volume (Chapter 12). Here they estimate a model of the real wage and immigration on annual data for 1861–1913. The result indicates a *positive* effect of immigration on the real wage, both in the short run and the long run. Although the effects are small, their results suggest nevertheless that immigration did not lower the wage. This Australian result contrasts with those for the US which reveal a positive relationship between emigration and the real wage (Geary and Ó Gráda 1985). These two contrasting studies certainly need reconciliation.

An alternative approach is to use computable general equilibrium (CGE) models which allow for the full set of interactions within the economy, but which do not account for possible dynamic effects. A few recent efforts have used these models to assess the impact of migration on sending and receiving regions. The early-nineteenth-century Irish migration to Britain offers one such example (Williamson 1990: Ch. 6): Irish immigration raised the British labor force by 6 percent between 1821 and 1851, and its impact, according to a CGE model, was to make the British wage 4.1 percent lower in 1851 than it would have been in the absence of immigration. The impact of immigration on the late-nineteenth-century US labor force was larger: an early CGE application estimated that immigration from 1870–1910 reduced the wage in 1910 by 9.9 percent compared with the no-immigration case (Williamson 1974a).

An emigration example is offered by Sweden. In the early 1880s, Knut Wicksell argued that emigration would solve the pauper problem which blighted labor-abundant and land-scarce Swedish agriculture at that time. The challenge that Wicksell laid down to more empirically oriented economists has only recently been taken up. Urban Karlstrom (1985: 155) used a CGE to estimate that the real wage in Sweden was 9.4 percent higher in 1890 than it would have been in the absence of twenty years of emigration after 1870.

Two contributions to this volume provide new estimates of the impact of emigration from Britain and immigration to the United States in the four decades after 1870 (O'Rourke, Williamson and Hatton, Chapter 10) and for emigration from Ireland from the 1850s to 1908 (Boyer, Hatton and O'Rourke, Chapter 11). The US impact is large: the labor force reduction as a result of a hypothetical total ban on immigration after 1870 would have raised the 1910 wage by 24.7 percent. Absence of emigration from Britain would have lowered its wage in 1910 by a slightly more modest 19 percent. An absence of Irish emigration after 1851 would have led to a population as much as 2.2 times its actual level in 1911, and the wage would have been a massive 34 percent lower.

These huge differences in population and labor force would, of course, have led to profound changes in the structure of output and employment and to the returns of other factors of production, like land and capital. It is the latter which should alert us to a problem: one of the least plausible assumptions in this kind of counterfactual exercise is that the capital stock in the immigrant or emigrant countries would itself have remained unchanged in response to these dramatic differences in labor force growth. When the CGE models assume no international capital mobility, they show that rental rates on capital would have decreased dramatically in the New World and increased dramatically in the Old World in the event of no migration. Yet we know that international capital flows were very large in the late nineteenth century with Britain at the center. Furthermore, the international capital market was highly integrated, probably as highly integrated as it is today (Edelstein 1982; Zevin 1992). Thus, it seems likely that much of the capital which "chased after labor" to the New World would have stayed home had international migration been suppressed.

Since capital chased after labor, the effect of the mass migrations on the real wage in sending and receiving countries was attenuated. In immigrant-receiving countries, capital inflows would have muted the rise in the return to capital; in emigrant-sending countries, capital outflows would have muted the fall in the return to capital; more capital in the immigrating country would have raised the marginal product of labor attenuating the fall in the real wage; and less capital in the emigrating country would have attenuated the rise in the real wage. The two chapters which employ the CGE methodology in this volume offer alternative estimates of the impact of migration assuming that capital was, first, perfectly mobile internationally and second, perfectly immobile internationally. In the former case, the return to capital is fixed by the world market rate. For the United States, the capital inflow accompanying immigration mitigated the fall in the wage so that in the no-migration case the real wage would have been about 9 percent higher, a third of the immobile capital case but still sizable. For Britain, absence of emigration after 1870 would now have reduced the wage by a bit less than 7 percent, also a more modest effect compared with the capital immobility case but still significant. For Ireland, the capital inflows would have reduced the no-emigration after 1851 fall to 11 percent, which is only a third of the estimate without capital mobility, but, again, still sizable.

The moral of the story is that international capital mobility reduced the effects of mass migration on wages and living standards. Yet the impact of mass migrations were still substantial. Why? It was due to the fact that there were immobile factors which mattered a lot in the late nineteenth century, namely land and natural resources. We shall return to this explanation below.

FACTOR MARKETS, COMMODITY MARKETS AND ECONOMIC CONVERGENCE

The literature on economic convergence has reached enormous proportions: started by Alexander Gerschenkron (1952), Moses Abramovitz (1979, 1986) and Angus Maddison (1982, 1991), it has flourished under the recent leadership of William Baumol (Baumol *et al.* 1989) and Robert Barro (1991; Barro and Sala-I-Martin 1991). It has also generated a "new growth theory" in which human capital accumulation and endogenous technical progress plays a richer role. Few of the economists working on convergence have paid serious attention to history. Even the economic historians among them have paid little attention to the contribution which international commodity, labor and capital market integration has played in the process. Instead, their focus has been on technical change and human capital formation.

Most of the recent attention has been on the period since 1950, but there was also a substantial per capita income and real wage convergence in the late nineteenth century. A recent paper by one of the present authors (Williamson 1994) constructed a purchasing-power, parity-adjusted, urban-unskilled real-wage database for 15 countries over the very long run. The 1870–1913 period underwent a real wage convergence similar in magnitude to the better-known convergence after the Second World War. Perhaps most interesting, however, is the finding that most of the late-nineteenth-century real-wage convergence can be attributed to an erosion in the real-wage gap between the Old and New Worlds, and not to any significant convergence within the Old World or within the New World. Around 1870, real wages in the labor scarce New World were much higher than in the labor abundant Old World – 136 percent higher. By 1895, real wages in the New World were 100 percent higher, and in 1913 they were about 87 percent higher. The Old World caught up quite a bit with the New between 1870 and 1913.

How much of this real-wage convergence can be accounted for by international migration between the Old World and New? It must have made some contribution since migrations were serving to lower real wages in the New World and to raise them in the Old, compared with a world with no migration. The orders of magnitude may, at first sight, seem too small to account for much of the overall gap between the Old World and New (especially when assessed under conditions of international capital mobility). But appearances can be misleading: it is not just the effect of emigration on sending-country wages or of immigration on receiving-country wages that matters, but rather these two effects taken together; and it is not the effect of migration on absolute wage levels that matters, but rather its impact on the convergence between poor and rich.

Consider the example offered by the two most important countries on either side of the Atlantic: Britain and the US. American real wages were 67 percent higher than the British in 1870, while 62 higher in 1910. The Anglo-American convergence was more modest than between the Old and New World more generally, but it *was* a convergence, notwithstanding the oft-repeated tales of American industrial success and British industrial failure. The estimates from the CGEs with no migration but with capital mobility suggest that the Anglo-American wage gap would have *increased* from 67 to 89 percent over the forty years after 1870 rather than decline as it did to 62 percent (O'Rourke, Williamson and Hatton, Chapter 10). The implications of mass migration for Irish–American convergence is similar. Boyer, Hatton and O'Rourke (Chapter 11) offer a "best guess" estimate that about one-quarter of the Irish–American real-wage convergence between 1858 and

1908 can be explained by Irish emigration, while Williamson (1993) uses their finding to infer that about half of the Irish–American convergence is explained by mass migration, Irish and non-Irish.

For other New World/Old World pairs of countries with greater degrees of convergence and lower migration rates, the contribution of migration to overall convergence would be less although still substantial. We are not yet in a position to judge the overall contribution of mass migration to real-wage convergence between the Old World and the New, but even when we are, there will still be room for other factors contributing to convergence. We shall consider three of these in what follows: changing factor endowments per worker, differing rates of technical progress and commodity price convergence.

The standard model of economic growth (Solow 1957) emphasizes the rate of capital deepening in accounting for differences in real wage and per capita income growth between countries. Since economists have recently given renewed emphasis to capital deepening, it seems appropriate to ask whether differing rates of capital deepening were a key ingredient accounting for late-nineteenth-century real wage convergence as well. Evidence from five countries suggests not. The US experienced faster capital-deepening from 1870 to 1913 than any of the European countries, although Germany, Sweden and Italy all experienced greater capital-deepening than Britain (Wolff 1991; Hatton and Williamson 1992b: Table 6; Maddison 1992). Perhaps it was not the rate of capital-deepening as a whole but rather investment in machinery that mattered (de Long 1992; de Long and Summers 1991). However, this seems to have been a less important factor before 1914 than after.

A more important reason for real-wage convergence between Old World and New had to do with land and natural resource endowment. Since increases in capital and labor were applied to these resources at far greater rates in the New World than in the Old, labor's marginal product should have fallen relatively and that of land and natural resources should have risen relatively. These events would have been consistent with the writings of David Ricardo, John Stuart Mill and other classical economists; they would predict a fall in the wage–land rent ratio in the New World relative to the Old. New evidence dramatically supports this view, and econometric analysis confirms that these factor price ratios were being driven in part by trends in land–labor ratios (O'Rourke, Taylor and Williamson 1993). The New World was relatively abundant in other resources too, particularly minerals, and these were important to America's rise to industrial supremacy just prior to the First World War (Wright 1990; Nelson and Wright 1992). Thus, to the extent that the effective supply of these resources was expanded by discovery and exploitation, the New World was able to stay ahead industrially at least until such resources were easily tradable at low transport costs.

What about differing rates of technical progress? This has long been seen as the key factor driving postwar economic convergence as follower countries benefited from technological diffusion from the leaders. It has also long been a major theme in European economic history (Gerschenkron 1952; Landes 1969; Pollard 1981). Clearly improved techniques were important contributors to catching up but, in the words of Moses Abramovitz (1986), "social capability" can limit the speed of catching up. Alternatively, and in the words of the new endogenous growth literature, catching up in poor countries is conditioned by the accumulation of human capital (Lucas 1988; Barro 1991; Mankiw *et al.* 1992).

The effects of technical progress on the returns to different factors of production depend not just on its overall rate but also on its factor-saving bias. Since industrial output makes little use of farmland, industrialization tends to be land saving, raising instead the relative demand for labor and capital. Industrialization should, therefore, tend to raise the wage–land price ratio (hereafter called the wage–rental ratio). Accordingly, more rapid industrialization in Europe compared with Argentina or Australia should have raised the European wage–rental ratio by more. Such events should have contributed to factor price convergence. This prediction would be reinforced if productivity advance in the late-nineteenth-century New World was labor-saving and land-using, as the induced innovation hypothesis would suggest (Hayami and Ruttan 1971) and as economic historians generally believe (Habbakuk 1962; David 1974; Williamson and Lindert 1980). The prediction would be further reinforced if productivity advance in the Old World was land-saving and labor-using, as we also generally believe. Late-nineteenth-century evidence seems to offer strong support for these predictions: productivity advance had a strong negative effect on the wage–rental ratio in the New World but a strong positive effect in the Old World (O'Rourke, Taylor and Williamson 1993).

One form of technical progress that was particularly important for real-wage convergence between Old World and New was transport innovation in railroads and ocean shipping. Douglas North (1958) called the decline in freight costs "radical," and the primacy of technical change in the fall of ocean shipping costs has been affirmed by Knick Harley (1988) and of railroad shipping costs by Albert Fishlow (1966). The effect was to reduce dramatically the commodity price gaps between Liverpool and Chicago (O'Rourke and Williamson 1992). Between 1870 and 1912 the grain price in Liverpool fell from 60.2 percent above to 14.2 percent above the Chicago price, and there were dramatic declines as well in meat and animal fats, iron and cotton. That is, these events produced a late-nineteenth-century commodity price convergence, if not quite equalization.

Ever since Eli Heckscher was writing in 1919 and Bertil Ohlin in 1924, it has been argued that under certain circumstances commodity price equalization tends to produce factor price equalization. Indeed, it can be argued that trade is a substitute for factor mobility. Under the Heckscher–Ohlin theorem, labor-scarce, land-abundant countries should export land-intensive commodities while land-scarce, labor-abundant countries should export labor-intensive commodities. Recent evidence strongly supports the Heckscher–Ohlin theorem, finding that late-nineteenth-century trade patterns were largely dictated by relative factor abundance (Crafts and Thomas 1986; Wright 1990; Estevadeordal 1992). It follows that the trade-induced changes in relative factor demands should have tended to equalize factor prices across countries.

Heckscher and Ohlin were motivated precisely by the convergence of commodity prices which they thought they observed in the late nineteenth century and which has now been more clearly documented. But until recently there had been no assessment of its quantitative impact on real wages. Using CGE models for Britain and America we are now able to assess its likely impact (O'Rourke and Williamson 1992; O'Rourke, Williamson and Hatton, Chapter 10); commodity price convergence served to erode the Anglo-American real-wage gap by 19 percentage points between 1870 and 1910 (assuming international capital immobility). Of course, by eroding the wage gap commodity price convergence led to lower rates of intercontinental migration than otherwise, a response which tended to offset the commodity-price-convergence effect a bit. Even allowing for such migration responses, commodity price convergence still accounted for a 13 percentage point convergence in the real wage. These Anglo-American results are supported by econometric analysis explaining wage–rental ratio trends for a wider range of countries, although its effects were weaker in those European countries which sought to protect agriculture with tariffs, including, ironically, the Scandinavian countries whose experience motivated Heckscher and Ohlin in the first place (O'Rourke, Taylor and Williamson 1993).

The moral of the story is this: migration of labor and capital did produce economic convergence between the New World and the Old in the late nineteenth century. But other forces were at work too, sometimes offsetting the effects of migration and sometimes reinforcing it. These additional forces were: the fuller utilization of natural resources in the New World as more capital and labor were applied to them; the differential effects of technical progress and particularly its factor-saving bias; and the commodity price convergence which resulted from the collapse in freight rates. Together these forces were serving to integrate the world economy and to produce convergence in real wages and per capita incomes. In 1914, this convergence process came to an abrupt halt.

ECONOMIC DIVERGENCE: THE INTERWAR PERIOD

From the First World War until the 1950s, economic convergence ceased. The effects of the First World War were long lasting and caused a severe setback to both the belligerent and the neutral nations. More pertinent still, international migration fell to a fraction of its prewar level, capital movements were severely restricted, and commodity trade was suppressed first by high shipping costs early in the interwar period and then later by rising protection during the Great Depression.

To many observers, the single most important change in conditions governing migration was the postwar imposition of immigration controls in the United States. A literacy test was imposed in 1917 and this was followed by ever more restrictive measures: the Emergency Quota Act of 1921, the Immigration Act of 1924 and the National Origins Act of 1929. Why were these laws enacted? James Foreman-Peck (1992) has argued that the countries which remained open to immigration in the nineteenth century were either those which did not have liberal governments (pro-labor, with a wide franchise) or which remained European dominions. The United States fits neither of these characterizations and hence the question is not so much why it imposed restrictions from 1917 onwards but why such measures were not adopted earlier. One of the present authors argued some time ago that the answer lay with the growth in labor demand, which slowed down late in the nineteenth century, and with the elasticity of labor demand, which declined (Williamson 1982). More recently, Claudia Goldin (1993) has argued that the nativist and pro-restriction lobbies were made up of a shifting balance of fragile coalitions. These included employers groups, organized labor and a variety of movements ranging from anti-Catholics to nativists influenced by the eugenics movement (Jones 1992: Ch. 9).

Restriction voices became louder in cyclical slumps, such as the 1890s, when both capitalists and organized labor united in opposing immigration. After all, these may have been times when immigration fell off, but they were also times of high unemployment. From the 1890s onwards, congressional bills for restriction were repeatedly placed before Congress, but until 1917 they were defeated (often very narrowly, it should be said). Were the causes of the final triumph of restriction economic in nature? Certainly the 1910 Report of the Immigration Commission dwelt at length on the economic effects of immigration before recommending the literacy test. Furthermore, Goldin (1993) has found that the voting pattern of representatives on whether to override President Wilson's veto of the literacy test was related to the change in the local wage between 1907 and 1915: those from regions with the greatest increase in the wage were more likely to vote in favor of the status quo. There is also evidence that the absorptive capacity of the American labor market declined around the turn of the century so that any increase in an immigrant-swollen labor supply would have caused a greater fall in the wage than previously (Williamson 1982).

The literacy test would have reduced prewar immigration by about a quarter, the Immigration Act of 1921 would have cut it by about a half, the 1924 Act by about three-quarters and the 1929 Act by about four-fifths

(Goldin 1993: 8). Yet, from 1921 onwards total American immigration consistently fell below the quota. Why? The quotas did bind for some nationalities, a likely result given that they were based on national origin percentages enumerated in the 1910 census.[5] For the regions of "new" immigration (south and east Europe), the quota was only 3 percent of the annual average arrivals from 1910–14 (Kirk 1946: 85): thus their quotas were filled. For those nationalities from north and west Europe, their numbers fell way below their quotas. The reasons why the "old" migrants rarely filled their quotas should be clear. First, the rates of natural population increase in western Europe fell dramatically between 1870 and 1910, particularly in those countries of major emigration such as Britain and Germany. In addition, those migrant flows were cut back by First World War deaths and injuries among males in the prime emigrating age group (Winter 1985: 75). In addition, the friends and relatives effect had probably been weakened by the virtual cessation of immigration and the breakdown in communications during the War. On the other hand, American real wages rose relative to most European countries between 1914 and 1925.

In Chapter 9, Henry Gemery suggests several other reasons why potential European migrants would have been deterred from emigrating to the United States after the War. These include the advent of social insurance (as in Britain and Ireland), the reduction of emigrant subsidies (as in Italy), and the outright prohibition of emigration from the newly established Soviet Union. Moreover, Gemery finds that models which successfully explain immigration in the late nineteenth century fail for the interwar years. Only fluctuations in American unemployment seem to influence immigration. Given that immigrants seem to have fared less well in the American labor market after the War, this may reflect the increased importance of job access. It is also likely, though impossible to quantify, that the quotas deterred immigration by signaling a new and more negative American attitude toward migrants.[6]

The importance of the change in American policy is indicated by the fact that immigration to other New World countries fell by less than that to the United States. Although immigration to Australia, Canada and Argentina was lower in the 1920s than in the 1900s, in each case it was higher than in the 1890s. In contrast, US immigration in the 1920s was lower even than the 1890s. Some migrants may have been channeled to other destinations in the face of the quotas. This substitution must have been limited, since otherwise one might have expected a boom in the emigration of quota-constrained southern and eastern Europeans to Latin America: no such boom is observed. Thus, there was either diminishing pressure to emigrate from these countries, or worsening economic conditions in Latin America were deterring potential migrants, or both. Destinations in Europe also provided an alternative outlet as inter-European migration revived – mainly to France. Thus more than half of the 1.3 million Italian emigrants in the 1920s moved within Europe, overwhelmingly to France (Kirk 1946: 108).

British emigration to the Dominions was given official encouragement through subsidies under the Empire Settlement Act of 1922. However, Pope (1981a, 1985) has argued that such subsidies did not fully compensate for the rise in the real costs of passage, even to Australia where the largest grants were given. Although these countries did not adopt blanket quotas as in the United States, they did adopt more selective immigration policies involving two main features. First, they limited or discouraged immigration from southern and eastern Europe, and second, they provided selective incentives to agricultural workers and potential rural settlers. A selective immigration policy was introduced in Canada after the Immigration Act of 1910; it sought to direct migrants to settlement in the booming prairies. As Alan Green shows in Chapter 8, this policy seems to have reversed the prewar trend of rising wage rates in the prairies relative to the eastern provinces.

As Sicsic shows in Chapter 6, immigration accounted for the bulk of the labor force increase in France from 1911 to 1926, notwithstanding the increasingly tight regulation of immigration. But the force of regulation was to direct immigrants into certain industries so that the occupational composition of immigrants diverged increasingly from that of internal migrants. In contrast, the contribution of immigration to US labor force growth fell sharply from the prewar period to the 1920s and then further in the 1930s. In Chapter 9, Gemery provides new estimates of this immigration contribution in the interwar period. He also finds that the fall in the immigrant contribution to the urban labor force in the 1920s was largely compensated by internal rural–urban migration.

The Great Depression was the *coup d'état* for the age of mass migrations, at least until the late twentieth century. International migration ebbed to a small fraction of its prewar level. Perhaps this is not surprising since the major recipient countries suffered more severe depressions than did most European countries (Eichengreen and Hatton 1988: 10). In addition, employment conditions in receiving countries had always been central in determining the timing of European emigration. So it is not surprising that the Great Depression severely reduced the flow of emigrants, so severely that the United States immigration from most countries fell below the quota. However, the fall in immigration undoubtedly attenuated the New World slump in unemployment. Without the precipitous decline in immigration, the unemployment crisis in the New World would have been very much worse. Indeed, their "guest worker" effect had been at work for decades prior to the quotas (Keyssar 1986: 79; Tyrrell 1991: 147). During slumps, fewer chose to emigrate and more emigrants chose to return, thus muting the impact of the decline in jobs on those unemployed. During booms, the opposite forces were at work.

USING THE PAST TO INFORM THE PRESENT

This chapter has only briefly outlined how the mass migrations worked to forge increasingly powerful links between national labor markets prior to the break-up of the global labor market during the interwar years, but it suggests a remarkably close correspondence between late-nineteenth-century and post-Second World War experience. Sufficiently close, in fact, to suggest that this past could be used to inform the present.

Since the 1940s, the world has slowly begun to recover most of the forces of integration that bound together the world economy prior to 1914 – or at least that portion of the world economy which included the current members of the OECD club. The evolution of the EC, GATT negotiations, Kennedy Rounds and even NAFTA have all served to create commodity price convergence, increasing foreign trade shares and specialization. The world commodity market integration that was destroyed after 1914 has been recovered by 1994. International capital markets collapsed during the Great Depression, and capital transfers were transacted primarily by government authorities until the private capital market boom of the 1970s. By the 1990s, world capital markets have become as well integrated as they were in the 1890s.

This slow recovery of late-nineteenth-century commodity and factor market conditions has also been manifested by mass migrations. As Gemery's Table 9.1 (this volume) shows, net immigration accounted for about a third of the total population increases in the US prior to 1910; between the wars it averaged below a tenth; by the 1970s it was 40 percent, higher than it was in any decade prior to 1913. It remained high in the 1980s. Although Europe has not undergone quite the same increase in the immigrant share, none the less the foreign-born numbers have become very significant there too. It would be unwise to assign all of this late-twentieth-century rise in the level of mass migration to supply conditions in poor sending regions, but it is hard to resist that conclusion given what history tells us. Poor agrarian countries did not send out emigrants in large numbers to rich countries in the nineteenth century. Nor did poor countries send out many emigrants during decades of early industrialization at home. Poor countries *did* send out emigrants in very large numbers after industrialization at home had had a few decades to make its impact felt. And as these poor emigrant latecomer countries reached newly-industrialized-country status, their emigration rates fell. Thus, it is hardly surprising that Mexican emigration to the US – illegal and legal – was only a trickle until the 1950s, or why it has remained such a problem for America until the present, and why the problem will disappear in the near future. Other poorer, but industrializing, latecomers will continue to supply those emigrants well into the next century, at least if late-nineteenth-century experience is any guide. The supply will be manifested by continued problems with illegal immigrants in North America and Europe, and it will be manifested by increased demands by the poor from the South of the Pacific Rim to gain entrance to labor markets in rich Japan.

As the late twentieth century recovered the level of late-nineteenth-century mass migrations to the United States, the "quality" of the immigrants has declined, replicating the same downward "quality" drift that led at least in part to the quotas and other restrictions of this century. It is a great irony that the US has become a country full of new low-skilled immigrants, when the Dillingham Commission concluded almost a century ago that restrictions would be necessary to stem the tide of "low-quality" immigrants. Indeed, does not current American policy reinforce those trends? A notable divergence between US experience, on the one hand, and Canadian and Australian experience, on the other, suggests that this may have been so.

What impact have both of these events had – rising immigrant numbers and declining immigrant "quality"? America only recently became aware of rising inequality across the 1980s; it has been going on for a bit longer, but the rising inequality tide seems to have surged over the past decade, so much so that much of the income-leveling achieved since 1929 has been lost. Furthermore, the US has undergone a much-publicized productivity slow-down since the 1960s. What role have the more recent mass migrations played in this process? Is the correlation between rising inequality and productivity slowdown on the one hand, and rising mass migrations on the other, spurious? Many modern economists seem to think so, believing that immigration has had only modest impact on the US economy. However, we suspect that their micro studies have looked for evidence in the wrong place. The macro-CGE models used for the late nineteenth century suggest quite different results. We suspect the same would be true for the late twentieth century, especially if the focus were placed on convergence. But, generally, economists interested in the convergence of poor countries on rich have rarely assessed the contribution of international migration to the process. Economic convergence has been dramatic since the 1950s. Economic convergence was also dramatic in the half-century or so up to 1913. Much of the convergence prior to 1913 was due to the mass migrations. Is there reason to suspect that the same has not been true for the late twentieth century? We think not.

Convergence in the late nineteenth century was also driven by commodity market integration, that is, by pronounced trends toward commodity price equalization. As Heckscher and Ohlin predicted some time ago, the surge in world trade after 1850 or so contributed to factor price equalization and thus convergence. Indeed, in some cases the contribution was profound and equal to that of labor migration. Has the world trade boom since 1950 – the recovery of those pre-1913 conditions – made the same contribution to convergence? We do not yet have the studies which answer that question, but it seems likely to be in the affirmative. Since trade and migration are, at least in theory, partial substitutes, history suggests that policy-makers would be well served to keep that property of substitution in mind when debating and implementing trade and migration policy in the 1990s. Some commentators would suggest that this indeed may be the case for many who supported the ratification of NAFTA.

These then are some of the lessons of late-nineteenth-century history which inform the present. The rest of this book supplies the details on precisely how that history unfolded between 1850 and 1939.

NOTES

1 These statistics are derived mainly from records of emigration and cover a limited, though increasing, number of countries over time. The countries included in the lower graph for southern Europe are: Austria–Hungary, Poland, Russia, Italy, Portugal, Spain and Malta.

2 The immigration statistics tend to produce larger totals than the emigration statistics. Hence, totals for immigration in the Americas are similar to those for all European intercontinental emigration despite the fact that the European totals include such destinations as Australia, New Zealand and South Africa.

3 Females formed a higher proportion of the emigrants from a few countries like Ireland, where they accounted for 48 percent betwen 1851 and 1913.

4 One of the few statistics quoted by Handlin was that (about 1900) "for every hundred dollars earned by native wage earners, the Italian born earned eighty-four, the Hungarians sixty-eight, and other Europeans fifty-four" (1951: 76). However, figures from the US Commissioner of Labor and the US Immigration Commission indicate that southern and eastern Europeans generally earned about 15 percent less than natives (Hill 1970: 109).

5 The Quota Act of 1921 limited the number of alien immigrants from each European country to 3 percent of that nationality living in the United States in 1910. In 1924, the quota was reduced to 2 percent of each nationality enumerated in the 1890 census, and in 1929 the proportion was reduced further to produce a total annual quota of 150,000.

6 William Marr (1977) has found some evidence that the quotas deflected some British emigrants away from the United States to other destinations despite the fact that British immigration to the United States was always below the quota.

Part II

WHY DID THEY MIGRATE?

2

EUROPEAN LABOR MARKETS, EMIGRATION AND INTERNAL MIGRATION, 1850–1913

Dudley Baines

In this chapter I raise some general questions about migration – both within Europe and overseas – and the development of national and international labor markets. I discuss the causes of migration – i.e. the proximate causes – the relation between economic development, industrialization and migration rates and the relation between European internal migration patterns and European emigration.

THE CAUSES OF MIGRATION

Discussions about the causes of migration, both in contemporary economies and in the past, can usually be placed into one of two categories. In one formulation the decision to migrate depends on the migrant's expected relative income, which is the difference between the present value of an individual's expected lifetime income if he or she migrates and the present value if he or she does not migrate, discounting for the cost of moving and for the uncertainties inherent in migration. This view of the cause of migration implies that spatial income differentials would predict migration rates.

Three things are important. First, the costs of migration are not negligible and would include income forgone as well as direct travel costs. (Because transport was slow in the nineteenth century, forgone income was considerable and could exceed the cost of the passage.) Hence, migrants must have access to funds. Funding may be provided by other people, however, including, for example, migrants who have already left. Second, an individual does not have to migrate permanently to increase his or her lifetime income. Temporary migration has the same effect. Third, we may define "income" very widely so that it includes non-material benefits. The release of a young person from family control could be a motive for emigration, for example. (Historically, this might be an important reason for female migration.)

35

There is an alternative formulation in which the migration decision depends on access to *information* about economic and social conditions in the places to which migrants might be able to go. The information could cover incomes, employment opportunities, housing conditions, etc. Obviously, all migration must depend on information, but in this formulation, information is an *independent* cause of migration. The implication is that the greater the amount of (relevant) information that is available the greater migration there will be, holding income differences constant. The information hypothesis underlies many historical accounts of emigration. It has often proved difficult to explain nineteenth-century emigration rates from cross-section data – e.g. from incomes and other variables in the places from which the emigrants came. Many historians have implicitly accepted that information was an independent cause of emigration. There is a problem, however. We have no way of measuring the flow of information that is independent of the emigration flow itself since the experience of previous migrants was the most important source of information for most nineteenth-century emigrants.[1] This means that the information hypothesis is difficult to test.

It has proved possible to model nineteenth-century internal migration in some countries from cross-section data. The studies showed that the effect of internal migration was to move people from places of low to places of high income. In other words, the pattern confirmed the relative income hypothesis. One reason why the relative income effect explains internal migration better than emigration patterns may be that many internal migrants traveled relatively short distances. This would mean that the variance in the information available to the individual migrant was probably low. This is less likely to be true of the information available to emigrants.

INTERNAL MIGRATION AND EMIGRATION: DEFINITIONS

Unfortunately, the units of analysis commonly used in migration history may not be the appropriate ones. It is usual to define migration across a national border as "emigration" and movement within a national border as "internal migration." If the emigrants crossed the Atlantic, for example, these definitions present no difficulty, but within Europe many of the national boundaries were arbitrary from the viewpoint of migration. For example, workers who moved from the eastern Netherlands to Germany in the late nineteenth century, which was mainly towards the Ruhr, were measured at the border by the Dutch government and classed as "emigrants." But the workers were crossing regularly (and at least annually) in both directions (Stokvis 1992). In other words, the labor markets of the eastern Netherlands and the Ruhr must have been partially integrated. If this was the case, we are observing internal migration, which happened to be measured because it crossed a national boundary. On the other hand, historians usually class migration from Ireland to Britain in the nineteenth century as "emigration."[2] It is more realistic to consider migration from Ireland to Britain as "internal." It occurred within the same nation-state and within labor markets that were highly integrated.

MIGRATION AND THE ECONOMIC DEVELOPMENT OF EUROPE, 1800–1914

We would expect internal migration rates to have been high in the nineteenth century. The structural changes that were occurring had implications for the location of industry. The growth in the use of coal as a power source, for example, meant that some industries were able to achieve large cost advantages by locating on the coalfields – i.e. the coalfields conferred an absolute advantage on these industries. Other industries located near the coalfields to obtain external economies – i.e. the location had a comparative advantage. A new set of industrial towns was created with a high demand for labor. This demand for labor could not be met by the natural increase in their population, particularly at nineteenth-century urban mortality levels. An opening was created for migration to these cities at least in the initial stages of their growth.

The industrial town was the new feature of nineteenth-century urban growth and of nineteenth-century internal migration patterns. The rate of urbanization in Europe was positively correlated with the rate of industrialization. The urban population of Germany grew by more than nine times in the nineteenth century and that of Britain by more than eight times, a phenomenon which could not have occurred without migration.[3] But, as we know, urbanization was a complex process. Moreover, the urbanization of Europe began long before industrialization and continued into the nineteenth century in all countries whether they were early or late industrializers. The urban population of France grew by more than 300 percent in the nineteenth century while total French population grew by about 40 percent, for example. In Spain, the figures are about 300 percent and 70 percent respectively (De Vries 1990: 45–7.) Obviously, many of the characteristics of the pre-industrial migration patterns remained.

In general, the capital cities (in both early and late industrializing countries) grew faster than that of the country in which they were located. This was partly because the capital cities were important industrial areas – as in the case of London, Berlin and Paris – but also because most capital cities had comparative advantages in commercial and domestic services, just as they had in the eighteenth century. Thirty-six percent of the growth in commercial services in Britain from 1851–1911, occurred in London, for example (Lee 1979). And the relatively high demand for domestic services in the large cities partly explains the high levels of female rural–urban migration (Hohenberg and Lees 1985: 210, 228–9). The combined effect of the economic changes was that the proportion of the European population that was urban rose from about 12 percent in 1800 to about 19 percent in 1850 and 41 percent in 1910 (Bairoch 1988: 216).[4]

The counterpart of migration to the urban areas was an outflow from nearly all the rural areas of the European countries. The reasons for rural–urban migration (and rural emigration) are complex but it has often been possible to relate rural out-migration to the difference between rural and urban incomes. This was confirmed in a study of migration patterns in England and Wales, 1861–1900, which found that relative wage levels were a significant determinant of the pattern and timing of migration (Baines 1986: 239–41, 247–8, 317–23).[5] Sicsic reached a similar conclusion about French migration which overturned a long-held view that the French peasantry were immobile (Sicsic 1992; see also Chapter 6). It is important to remember that rural out-migration was caused by more than the relative decline of agriculture. Urbanization meant that the demand for industrial labor suffered a relative decline in the rural areas. The effect of this may be seen in England and Wales. Four and a half million people (net of returns) left the rural areas (very strictly defined[6]) between 1841 and 1911. In the same period, the agricultural labor force declined by only about 0.75 million. Data for rural occupations are always difficult to interpret because of dependants and because many people were part-time industrial workers but the implication is that less than half of the out-migrants from the rural areas of England and Wales came from agriculture (Cairncross 1949: 82–6).

The majority of migrants – both rural and urban – moved over relatively short distances. This was one of Ravenstein's "laws of migration" which were described in his famous papers of 1885 and 1889. And there is ample evidence that many people traveled only short distances from many countries, including Germany, Britain, France and Sweden.[7] There were many important exceptions to the pattern of short distance movement, however (Ravenstein 1885 and 1889; Pounds 1985: 140; Redford 1976; Moch 1983: 45, 55; Hohenberg 1974: 488; Fridlizius 1979: 130).

There is some evidence that rural–urban migrants traveled further than rural–rural migrants and that migrants to the larger towns traveled greater distances. There were two reasons for this. The surrounding areas (the so-called urban influence field) had higher out-migration rates. And the larger towns attracted relatively more migrants from a greater distance. The British pattern was examined by Anderson. He took a clustered sample from the 1851 census. More than three-fifths of the migrants in the urban areas were living more than 26 km from their place of birth compared with only one-third of the migrants in the rural areas. But four-fifths of the migrants to London had come from more than 26 km (Anderson 1990: 8, 11). London attracted nearly as many migrants (1.25 million) between 1841 and 1911 as the eight largest industrial towns and the coalfields combined (1.54 million) (Cairncross 1949: 82–6). Migration to Paris followed a similar pattern. In the nineteenth century, migrants came to Paris from the whole of France, except the southeast and Languedoc, whilst Marseilles and Lyons had much smaller catchment areas (Chatelain 1971: 28–9; Hohenberg 1974: 472, 485–6).[8] Similarly, by the 1907 census, a third of the migrants resident in the Ruhr industrial towns and 40 percent of the migrants in Berlin were long-distance migrants from eastern Germany, many of whom were ethnic Poles. Nearly 300,000 of the 6.7 million who had been born in northeast Germany and who had not emigrated were enumerated in Berlin in 1907 and nearly 400,000 in the Rhineland or Westphalia (Köllman 1971: 102; Bade 1987: 62). The implication of these patterns is that urban demand determined the rate and timing of rural–urban migration.

There has been some controversy concerning the way migrants moved towards the cities. There is often only one observation of a migrant's provenance – for example, his or her place of birth. It is difficult to tell if the predominant moves were stepwise – i.e. from a rural area to a small town and then to a larger town – or whether the intermediate moves were more likely to be random. The distinction is important because if the migration pattern was stepwise the implication would be that the predominant moves were rural–urban. The dominant direction of migration would then be clear and we would be justified in using rural–urban wage differentials to explain it. The evidence about serial migration is mixed. Weber thought that migrants went directly to towns. Redford thought that in Britain at least migration followed a wave-like motion where one group of in-migrants replaced another. There is a detailed study of Preston in the mid-nineteenth century which showed that the migrants had followed many (mainly short distance) moves that appeared to be random before they arrived in what was the dominant town in the area. (A study of Malmö in 1836 and 1855 came to similar conclusions.) We do not know enough about the way that migrants reached the cities. In turn, this means that it is not proven that rural–urban moves predominated (Anderson 1971: 25; Fridlizius 1990: 129).

TRANSIENCE

A characteristic of nineteenth-century migration was extreme transience. The direction of the net migration flows conceals a very large number of countervailing moves. Data are available for German cities from the early 1880s. They show average annual in-migration rates into the urban areas of about 14 percent and out-migration rates of about 11 percent in 1881 rising to 18 percent and 16 percent respectively in 1912. That is, 18 percent of the population of the towns had taken up residence in that year and 16 percent of the population had left (Langewiesche and Friedrich 1987: 89–91; Hochstadt 1981: 452). (Simple arithmetic will show that these rates of population turnover must be caused by transience and not by high in- and out-migration rates of different groups of people.) Studies of individual cities, such as Dusseldorf and Duisberg show much higher transience with gross migration rates exceeding 25 percent (Bade 1987: 91; Hohenberg and Lees 1985: 255).[9] Comparable rates may be found in other countries.[10] Transience means that there was a high rate of labor turnover, of course, which affects the way that we look at migration. If transience was common, a relatively large proportion of the labor force would have experience of an urban labor market. This would include a large proportion of the rural labor force, which, in turn, would probably affect the expectations of people in the rural areas. In other words, because transience was common, migration increased the information that people had about urban wages and conditions.

TEMPORARY MIGRATION

The term "temporary migration" is frequently used to mean something different to transience. Temporary migrants, in this sense, were people who moved regularly to the same destination and returned to the same starting point, often annually, many of whom crossed national frontiers. One important source of temporary migrants was the mountainous regions of France, Spain and northern Italy (Viazzo 1989; Houston and Withers 1990). There were 1 million foreign temporary workers in France in the second half of the nineteenth century, a half of whom were Italian, and by the early twentieth century a further 1 million in northern Germany, most of whom had come from Poland (Bade 1987: 70; Pounds 1985: 79–80, 200; Hohenberg and Lees 1985: 255; Chatelain 1971). The original purpose of temporary migration was connected with the harvest but by the nineteenth century harvest migration had peaked and increasing numbers of temporary migrants worked in construction and in industrial occupations. Moreover, the building of railways in eastern and southern Europe substantially increased the number of temporary migrants (Nugent 1992: 87). (There is little evidence of "peasant immobility.") In other words, it was the development of eastern and southern Europe that increased the migration rate, not its "backwardness."

The most important new development was the growth of temporary *emigration*. By the early twentieth century temporary emigration from the southern European countries was common and in many areas was more important than the temporary internal migration which it had superseded. By this time, very little of the temporary emigration was driven by the harvest and it was mainly urban.

MIGRATION RATES

The structural changes in the European economies – for example, the increased concentration of industrial production – would suggest that internal migration rates were higher in the later nineteenth century than earlier. Migration rates may have been exceptionally high in the period but it is difficult to prove. Historically high migration rates (around 15 percent per annum) have been observed before there was significant industrialization in many countries.[11] And, as I have suggested, the characteristics of industrial and pre-industrial migration appear to have been rather similar. The main reason that gross migration rates were high in both periods was transience. (In pre-industrial western Europe, a high proportion of young women entered domestic service at some time although usually for only short periods. Other reasons for pre-industrial migration were marriage and apprenticeship (Flinn 1981: 65–75; Houston and Withers 1990: 93).) The second continuity is that short distance moves were very important, both in the late nineteenth century and in pre-industrial Europe. For example, 70 percent of an English village in Bedfordshire in 1782 had been born outside the village but only a half of them had been born further than 8 km away. Similarly, 76 percent of the migrant marriage partners in Crulai, in Normandy, 1690–1789, came from parishes closer than 10 km (Schofield 1970: 261, 264; Poussou 1970: 25). There were also many examples of organized temporary migration before industrialization. Lucassen identified seven temporary "migration systems" that were flourishing in 1800 involving 300,000 harvest workers (Lucassen 1987: 108–9).[12] Finally, the characteristic movement towards the larger cities (particularly the capital cities) was a feature of both periods. The non-industrial Italian cities were large receivers of migrants in both the eighteenth and nineteenth centuries, for example. Moreover, just as in the later nineteenth century the pattern of rural–urban migration can be explained by income differentials (see De Vries 1984: 215ff; De Vries 1990: 59). It is, of course, true that rising agricultural productivity (and food imports) in the nineteenth century removed an important constraint on the size of the agricultural population. But agricultural productivity was also growing in the pre-industrial period and potentially releasing migrants. Moreover, pre-industrial productivity had constrained the relative size of the urban and rural populations – i.e. it had constrained net migration. High mobility levels (i.e. high gross migration rates) were not incompatible with the constraint that a large number of people had to work on the land.

The main effect of the industrialization of Europe was to change the destination of migrants. The industrial town provided a new destination, as I have said, but the most important change was that an increasing proportion of the population went overseas. In other words, a much greater proportion of European migrants were going overseas, which means that the growth of emigration from Europe is prima facie support for the information flow hypothesis.

If both net and gross migration rates were determined partly by the amount of information available to prospective migrants we would expect that internal migration rates would have continued to rise into the twentieth century since most of the changes in the economy should have made information more readily available. Yet in some countries we observe an inverted U-shaped profile. Migration rates rose to the late nineteenth century and then fell. As we have seen, migration into and out of German cities – measured by change of residence – rose from about 12.5 percent per annum in the early 1880s to about 17 percent per annum just before the First World War. They then fell to about 9 percent in the 1920s, 7 percent in the 1950s and 5.5 percent in the 1970s.[13] There is some evidence from other countries, including Sweden and Switzerland, which points generally in the same direction (Hochstadt 1981: 453, 455; Hohenberg and Lees 1985: 255; Langewiesche and Lenger 1987: 91). On the other hand, the only British data of comparable quality until very recently (which come from the late 1940s when it was necessary to register a change of address) show gross migration rates between local authority areas of around 20 percent per annum (Newton and Jeffery 1951: 18).

It is not obvious why gross internal migration rates have been falling in some countries in the twentieth century. The gap between "rural" and "urban" wages has narrowed, of course. Or perhaps more accurately the differences between "urban" and "rural" areas have narrowed. But this would affect net migration rates rather than gross. If gross migration rates are low in the later twentieth century it is probably because transience has fallen. Both the labor and housing markets are probably less open than they were in the late nineteenth century, and the education of children (i.e. the location of schools) is a more important consideration.

We can look at this differently, however. If internal migration has become more difficult, *ex ante* migration rates will not have been declining as fast as *ex post* migration rates. An inverted U-shaped pattern over time may not sufficiently account for changes in the objective difficulty of migration. *Ex ante* migration rates may have remained high.

THE MEASUREMENT OF MIGRATION RATES

It is difficult to be dogmatic about changes in gross migration rates because there are serious problems in the measurement of migration. Historical migration estimates are based on a variety of sources including apprenticeship records, vital data, population counts and certificates given to migrants by local authorities. Data that are a proxy for a continuous population register are extremely rare (Hollingsworth 1970: 89–94). The most commonly used data that are systematically used to measure migration historically are population counts. Census counts are the most important of these. If vital data (birth and death rates) are available population counts can be manipulated to show the net balance of migration over a period.[14] But the result of this calculation is only a residual which measures the net effect of migration over a period not the actual number of moves.

Virtually all the migration estimates based on historical material are very sensitive to the size of the population under consideration, and to a lesser extent to the geographical area involved. Migration estimates are also very sensitive to the length of the period chosen. Since there are always countervailing moves, some gross moves will always be concealed. The observed migration rate out of a large area will be less than that out of a small area since the boundaries are smaller relative to the population size. Similarly, the observed migration rate will be inversely related to the period under consideration. On the other hand, the main problem with historical emigration data is not under-recording but over-recording. Most countries counted outgoing passengers and there was relatively little clandestine emigration in the nineteenth century because most emigration was approved or tolerated by the European governments. But most of the European data do not distinguish emigrants from other passengers. Nor do they normally measure return migration (Baines 1991: 17–20).

There is an analytical problem because the observed internal migration rates are unlikely to be an unbiased sample of the actual migration flows. For example, there are likely to have been more countervailing moves to the urban areas than to the rural areas and we can be fairly sure that urban migration rates are systematically understated compared with rural migration rates. For example, net migration of natives of the 18 most urban counties in England and Wales to other counties, 1861–1900, has been estimated as something under 7 percent per decade. Net migration of natives of the 34 most rural counties was 10 percent per decade. (The difference is not an artifact of the age distribution.) But there was virtually no systematic difference between urban and rural emigration rates, where the size effect is irrelevant (Baines 1986: 158, 231–5, 243). In other words, there is no evidence that rural–urban emigration rates were higher than urban emigration rates in England in the nineteenth century.[15] If this were generally true it would mean that as countries became more urban, observed migration rates would increasingly be understated, which may account for some of the apparent fall in internal migration rates in the twentieth century.[16]

THE EFFECT OF MIGRATION ON URBAN POPULATION GROWTH

In the eighteenth century, all European cities had a negative rate of natural increase. Deaths exceeded births. Urban population growth depended entirely on migration (Wrigley 1990: 103; De Vries 1984: 179). By the middle of the nineteenth century, most western European cities, including Paris, Berlin and London, had positive natural increase. But the southern and eastern European cities did not achieve positive natural increase until the 1870s at the earliest. For most of the nineteenth century, all the population growth of Naples, Rome, Odessa, Prague and St. Petersburg was caused by migration. In most western European cities, on the other hand, migration was directly responsible for less than half of the urban growth in the second half of the century.[17]

A simple calculation of the relative shares of migration and natural increase can be misleading, however. In the first place, the contribution of migration depends on the population growth rate itself. (In two cities with identical birth and death rates, the proportion of the growth caused by migration will be greater in the city with the highest population growth overall.) Second, in-migrants were composed disproportionately of young adults which leads to significant age-structure effects on birth and death rates. In-migration had the effect of increasing the natural growth rate which in turn increased the proportion of urban growth caused by natural increase. Williamson estimated that in-migration doubled the natural growth rate of British cities in the middle years of the nineteenth century (Williamson 1990: 8–45).[18] This effect cannot operate in the long run, however. Young adult migrants would have had both high life expectancy and a high birth rate which would have increased the native population in the medium run. Hence, at a constant rate of in-migration, age-structure effects could not operate over the long run in Britain (Williamson 1990: 47–51). There are similar cases offered by experience on the Continent. For example, in Prussian cities in 1905, 72.4 percent of the population aged over 15 were migrants, but of the large population aged 15 and under 77.6 percent were natives (Laux 1989: 132). Finally, calculations of the relative importance of migration and natural increase depend on a more or less arbitrary definition of the starting point, since most of the urban population were ultimately descended from migrants. In the long run, the effect of migration was to determine where children were born – i.e. where the natural increase of the population would occur.

EUROPEAN EMIGRATION

There were large differences in the incidence of emigration within Europe. Three-quarters of the emigrants came from only six countries. Of the 51.7 million emigrants recorded between 1815 and 1930, 22 percent (11.4 million) came from Britain, 19 percent (9.9 million) from Italy, 14 percent (7.3 million) from Ireland, 9 percent (4.8 million) from Germany (and its constituent states), and 12 percent (6.2 million) from Iberia. Less than a quarter of the emigrants came from Scandinavia, France, the Low Countries, Russia and eastern Europe.

The destinations of European emigrants were rather more limited. Ninety-five percent went to five countries: 32.6 out of 54 million went to the USA, 7.2 million went to Canada (although many subsequently went to the USA),[19] 3.5 million to Australia, 4.3 million to Brazil and 6.4 million to Argentina (Ferenczi and Willcox 1931: 230–1; Mitchell 1983: 139–47). The main reason for the discrepancy between the 51.7 million recorded "emigrants" and the 54 million recorded "immigrants" in the same period is that the data measure passengers and, hence, include people who were not emigrants. Movement within and between European countries was almost certainly greater although, as we have seen, the measurement and definition of internal migration is problematic.

There were marked annual fluctuations in emigration rates which tended to be common to all countries, peaking in 1854, 1873, 1883, 1907 and 1913 (Ferenczi and Willcox 1929, 1931: 236–88). This meant, in effect, that once a country had entered the phase of large-scale emigration, fluctuations in its emigration rate tended to run in common with those of other countries. The implication is that economic conditions in the receiving countries – which, as we have seen, were dominated by the USA – were important in the timing decision. To return to the explanatory hypotheses, the common pattern of emigration rates between European countries can only mean that a large proportion of emigrants could obtain up-to-date information about conditions in some country to which emigrants customarily went.

THE RELATIVE INCIDENCE OF EMIGRATION

The relative incidence of emigration from individual countries depends on whether we consider the nineteenth and early twentieth centuries as a whole or as shorter periods. Italy, for example, only had heavy emigration in the four decades leading up to the First World War. If, arbitrarily, we consider only the highest four decades of emigration from each country in the period, we would find that the greatest incidence was in Ireland with an annual average rate of emigration per thousand of population of 12.9, followed by Norway 7.1, Scotland 6.6, Italy 5.1 and England and Wales 4.7. The countries with the lowest incidence of emigration measured by the annual average per thousand were France 0.2, Belgium 0.5, and the Netherlands 0.7 (Baines 1991: 8–11). It is important to note that high rates of emigration continued – except for the actual years of the war – into the 1920s, although by that time, there were severe restrictions on immigration into some countries, notably the USA. A large fall occurred in European emigration in the depression of the 1930s which affected many of the destination countries very severely. (See Gemery, Chapter 9.)

The almost universal unit for which data were collected was the nation-state. But it is not clear that the nation-state is the appropriate unit of measurement. It is a commonplace of emigration history that emigration was a regional phenomenon. A third of all Finnish emigrants (1860–1930) came from one province which had an emigration rate of three and a half times the national average. Half of all emigrants from Austria–Hungary (1881–1910) came from Galicia which had an emigration rate of ten times the national average. These are just the extreme cases of a widespread phenomenon

(Chmelar 1973: 319; Kero 1974: 60). Ethnicity was one reason for the high variance in regional emigration rates. Most emigrants from Russia were ethnic Poles or Jews, for example. But ethnicity is not the main reason. There were very wide regional variations in emigration rates from England, which was ethnically homogeneous.

To date, the quantitative analyses of regional emigration differentials have had mixed results. Provincial emigration rates in Denmark in the late nineteenth century were found to be negatively correlated with average income in the provinces (Hvidt 1975: 38–40). But studies of emigration rates from Swedish provinces could not relate emigration rates and economic and social conditions (Carlsson 1976: 114–48). And these results have been confirmed by detailed studies of individual Swedish communities (Teder-brand 1972: 307; Rondhal 1972: 273). And a study of emigration from English and Welsh counties (1860–1900) also failed to find any systematic relationship between emigration rates and economic conditions (Baines 1986: 166–77).[20]

The reason that it has proved difficult systematically to relate regional emigration rates to economic and social variables may be because the variance in the incidence of emigration within the region was high. The "region" is unlikely to be a sufficiently sensitive unit but only a proxy for a more discrete unit such as the village or the family. Hence, the available data are insufficiently disaggregated.

In the absence of systematic evidence, the persistence of high regional emigration rates has usually been explained by path dependency – the effect of previous emigration on the decision to emigrate. It is obvious that path dependency must have been important. Remittances from previous emigrants could finance more emigration. (American and Scandinavian evidence suggests that by the late nineteenth century 30–40 percent were traveling on pre-paid fares, although the proportion in the earlier nineteenth century would have been much less (Brattne 1976: 276; Kero 1974: 177–8).) Information about the labor market or transport arrangements would reduce uncertainty. Finally, path dependency is confirmed by the well-known tendency for immigrants to concentrate in particular localities, such as the Norwegian communities in Iowa or the Italian neighborhoods in New York. The existence of the ethnic ghetto has been taken to be prima facie evidence of "chain migration." This must be partly true, but not all emigrants, even those from southeast Europe, entered an ethnic ghetto. Moreover, recent work in urban history has shown that the ghettos were rarely ethnically homogeneous (Baines 1991: 66–70; Bodnar 1985: 175; Vecoli 1986: 268; Zunz 1982: 59–87). Path dependency cannot explain early emigration, of course, and quite often the initial reason for an emigration stream was random when compared with the reasons for emigration at a later stage. Religious dissidents were very important in early-nineteenth-century emigration from Germany and Scandinavia, for example (Hvidt

1975: 148–55; Norman and Rundblom 1972: 53–61; Walker 1964: 78–80, 112–14).

Changes in the variance of regional emigration rates within a country could be assumed to depend on the strength of the relative income effect compared with the strength of path dependency. If the path dependency effect dominated, the variance in regional emigration rates would not tend to fall over time. Hence, if the variance in regional emigration rates was falling it would imply that the effect of economic and social conditions was becoming relatively more important than path dependency. Trends in the dispersion of regional emigration rates are difficult to interpret but they seem to have narrowed in Sweden, Finland and (marginally) in Italy. They do not seem to have narrowed in Norway, Portugal and England (Norman and Rundblom 1985: 65–7; Brettell 1986: 86–7; Baines 1986: 285–98). The relative importance of path dependency remains an open question.

RETURN MIGRATION

It is thought that about 30 percent of Europeans who emigrated between 1815 and 1914 returned (Gould 1979: 609). The causes of return migration are very complex but it had two main characteristics. Return migration rates rose through the period. And, in general, return migration was higher to southern and eastern Europe than to northern and western Europe. For example, over the period as a whole about 20 percent of Scandinavians returned. Nearly 40 percent of English emigrants returned in the fifty years before the First World War – although the rate before then had been much lower. In the early twentieth century, 40–50 percent of Italians and 30–40 percent of Portuguese, Croats, Serbs, Hungarians and Poles returned (Baines 1986: 135–8; Brettell 1986: 84; Hvidt 1975: 187; Gould 1980a: 609; Krajlic 1985: 406; Palairet 1979: 44–9; Puskas 1986: 223; Tederbrand 1972: 359; Virtanen 1979: 395). The measurement of return migration rates presents some difficulties since inward migrants could be returning for the second or third time. The estimates above are the true rate of return – the proportion of the number of individual emigrants who returned. In other words, these data are consistent with recorded return migration rates from Argentina of 43.3 percent (1857–1914) and from the USA of 52.5 percent (1908–14) (Nugent 1992: 35).

We can establish with reasonable certainty from internal evidence that the majority of the southern and eastern European emigrants who returned were intentional temporary emigrants. The proportion of males was very high and higher than it had been from northern and western Europe. Most important, the proportion of males among the returners was higher again. This is consistent with the view that the decision to return home was made before they left Europe. These particular emigrants are best described as target earners who were working overseas to acquire capital to use in Europe or to supplement the family income in Europe. As we have said, temporary emigration was not a new phenomenon. In some areas, such as northern Italy, it was only the second stage of a history of temporary migration to other parts of Europe which it had either replaced or supplemented.

The emigrants from northern and western Europe in the earlier period were more likely to "settle" and more likely to travel in a family group. It is not clear, however, that the so-called "new" emigrants from southern and eastern Europe had different *motives* to those of the so-called "old" emigrants. In the late nineteenth century, successful temporary emigration depended on a high demand for unskilled labor in the urban areas of the overseas countries and a fall in the cost and increase in the quality of transport, conditions which only occurred from the later nineteenth century when emigration from Europe was dominated by the south and east. In the earlier part of the century when emigration was dominated by northern Europe, returning was very difficult.[21] We cannot say that the earlier emigrants did not return because they did not intend to. What we do know is that returns to Britain increased markedly in the 1870s, which was the first decade in which it was possible for all British emigrants to cross the Atlantic reliably and comfortably by steamship (Baines 1986: 75–87).

URBANIZATION, INTERNAL MIGRATION AND EMIGRATION

The relationship between European economic growth and emigration has been controversial. In one formulation the main source of emigrants is the rural areas. The emigrants come from the less dynamic sectors of the economy; these could be the agricultural regions. This view has been associated with the idea of the "proletarianization" of much of European agriculture in the nineteenth century (Bade 1987: 67–8; Gjerde 1985: 16–24, 37–9; Morawska 1985: 25; Walker 1964: 165–6; Zubrzycki 1953: 252). Examples of the effect of the decline in non-agricultural incomes may be found in the histories of Polish and Irish emigration (Collins 1982: 77; Mokyr 1983: 281, 290–2; Zubrzycki 1956: 77).

We might also expect that emigrants came from the declining industrial (or sometimes proto-industrial) areas. For obvious reasons this would not apply to southern and eastern Europe, but there are examples of emigration from declining industrial areas in Britain and North Rhein–Westphalia (Erickson 1989 and 1990; Kamphoefner 1986; Van Vugt 1991: 560).

If emigration was the alternative to rural–urban migration the emigration rate would be determined by the ability of the cities – the more dynamic sectors – to absorb the "surplus" rural population. This is the implication of the Brinley Thomas model which relates European, particularly British emigration, to "long-swings" in European and overseas investment. In the first phase, investment (in infrastructure and housing) in the European cities was relatively high, internal migration was relatively high and emigration was relatively low. In the second phase, investment in Europe was relatively low, internal migration was relatively low and emigration was relatively high. Brinley Thomas's analysis rests on an assumption that most European internal migration was rural–urban and that the emigrants came from the rural areas. For obvious reasons most European emigrants did come from the rural areas, but that rural emigration rates exceeded urban is not proven. (In Britain, urban emigration rates were higher than rural.) The idea of the "long-swing" has also attracted serious criticism. That there were marked fluctuations in the rate of overseas investment and in emigration is beyond doubt, but the internal dynamics of the "long swing" itself have been severely disputed (Thomas 1954: 92, 124–5, 175; Thomas 1972: 45–54). The implication of the Brinley Thomas model is that the emigration rate would fall as the rate of urbanization and industrialization increased.[22] According to this view, the fall in emigration from eastern Germany after the 1880s was caused by industrialization and, particularly, the demand for labor in the Ruhr (Bade 1985: 124–5; Bade 1987: 141; Bairoch and Goertz 1986: 291; Köllman 1971: 61; Walker 1964: 89–91).

Urbanization was not universally associated with falling emigration rates, however. Emigration from Britain, for example, which was the most urbanized and industrialized country, did not fall in the nineteenth century. A study of internal migration in England and Wales (1861–1900) confirmed that the attraction of the cities was a powerful influence on the rate of rural–urban migration. But emigration from the rural areas could not be related to the attraction of the cities. In other words, rural–urban migration and rural emigration were not alternatives. The geographical pattern of emigration does not accord with the relative income hypothesis, at least in the period 1861–1900 when the geographical origins of English emigrants can be established (Baines 1986: 175–7, 213–49). Studies of Swedish migration patterns in the same period have reached similar conclusions (Carlsson 1976: 128–34; Ostregren 1986: 132; Rondhal 1972: 273; Tederbrand 1972: 307).

STAGE EMIGRATION

The implication that rural–urban migration and emigration were substitutes implies that emigration rates from the urban areas would be lower than from the rural areas. Yet studies of several countries have shown that in the late nineteenth century urban emigration rates were higher than rural emigration rates. The countries include Denmark, Finland, Norway and Britain (Baines 1986: 143–7; Hvidt 1975: 41, 52; Kero 1974: 54; Semmingsen 1972: 53).

These data do not disprove the rural provenance of most of the emigrants. Studies of Scandinavian cities have shown that 25–50 percent of urban emigrants had not been born in the cities from which they left. More than a half of the emigrants from Bergen in the period 1875–94 and 75 percent of those from Stockholm from 1880–93 had not been born there (Semmingsen 1960: 154; Nilsson 1973: 365). What Scandinavian historians have called "urban influence fields" have been identified for most of the larger Scandinavian cities and St Petersburg. These cities drew large numbers of migrants from the surrounding rural areas, of which many subsequently emigrated (Hvidt 1975: 58; Kero 1974: 54; Norman and Rundblom 1988: 81; Rondhal 1972: 269; Rundblom and Norman 1976: 134–6). The smaller towns did not have "urban influence fields" and emigration from the surrounding rural areas would be expected to be higher. The question is complicated by gender differences. In some countries, women were more likely to move internally than men, and in Sweden, for example, it is also likely that a disproportionate number of women were stage emigrants (Norman and Rundblom 1988: 79).[23]

Because of stage emigration the distinction between "rural" and "urban" emigration is a difficult one. Ultimately, it rests on the *intentions* of the rural–urban migrants. If the internal migrants intended to emigrate when they *originally* left the rural areas, then the decision to emigrate must have been made in a rural environment and they were, in effect, rural emigrants. If the decision was made in an urban environment they were, in effect, urban emigrants. For obvious reasons it is impossible to know whether the rural-born emigrants had already decided to emigrate at the point when they left the rural areas. Nor do we know if there was any systematic relationship between migration and emigration. That is, in an economy where transience was common, which, if any, of the internal moves made emigration more probable? For example, did a rural–urban move increase the probability of emigration compared with an urban–urban or a rural–rural move?

The study of emigration from Stockholm (1880–1893) showed that 75 percent of the emigrants from the city had not been born there. But nearly half of the emigrants from Stockholm had lived in the city for at least five years before they left. Hence, if we consider that the period of residence is an adequate proxy for the environment in which the decision to emigrate was taken, most of the emigrants from Stockholm were effectively urban (Nilsson 1973: 310). A study of a small industrial town in northern Sweden came to similar conclusions (Tederbrand 1972: 308). Unfortunately, outside Sweden the data are rarely sufficient to allow the extensive nominal record linkage that is necessary and there are very few comparable studies. There is, however, an English study based on census and vital registration data rather than nominal record linkage. Three types of emigrants were distinguished; rural-born emigrating from rural areas, urban-born emigrating from urban areas and rural-born emigrating from urban areas. An upper bound of rural–urban stage emigration was estimated by assuming that a move from a rural to an urban area doubled the propensity to emigrate. The study showed that two-thirds of all English and Welsh emigrants between 1861 and 1900 came from urban areas. Moreover, no more than a third of the emigrants from the urban areas can have been born in the rural areas. The implication is that the majority of emigration decisions were taken in an urban environment, and, in the main, by people who had lived in cities all their lives. Stage migration in the Scandinavian sense was rare in England. For example, three-quarters of the emigrants from London had been born in London. In comparison, three-quarters of the emigrants from Stockholm had not been born there (Baines 1986: 259–1, 264–5; Nilsson 1973: 310).

CONCLUSION

The causes of both internal migration and emigration were very complex and, because they involve human motivation, are difficult to explain whether we use qualitative or quantitative analysis. I will confine my remarks to those factors which affect the quantitative analysis of migration patterns.

The first complication concerns the availability of data. We find it easier to explain emigration than internal migration because, on the surface, it is easier to observe. We are able to explain fluctuations in emigration rates because we have time-series data for emigration, normally annually. But even here there are problems. Because we do not normally know the annual return migration rate we do not know the annual net movement of emigrants. The second problem is that we rarely have cross-section data which are of comparable quality. Hence, the regional incidence of emigration has proved particularly difficult to explain.

Emigration is easier to measure than internal migration because we observe a far larger proportion of overseas moves than internal moves. (The distinction between "emigration" and "internal migration" can sometimes be difficult, however.[24]) Nor can we be sure that the internal moves that we do observe are the most important moves or an unbiased sample of all the internal moves. The net effect of internal moves – i.e. the net balance of migration – is usually easy to establish. (This may also include the effect of emigration, of course.) We may consider that a net balance of migration is the appropriate variable. If we do we are implicitly assuming that the one lifetime move that we observe is the most important. But it would be important to know, for example, whether emigrants had been more internally mobile than non-emigrants. The relevant variable would then be the total number of moves that the individual had made before emigrating. Data to test this hardly exist.

The second reason why we cannot adequately relate internal and overseas migration is that we may be unsure about where the prospective emigrants were living when they made the decision to leave. If the majority of the decisions to emigrate were taken in the rural areas, urban wage levels may not be appropriate variables with which to explain emigration rates. Urban wages would only be appropriate if we were certain that the decision to emigrate was taken in the urban areas or with the knowledge of urban wage rates. If stage migration was common we are left with serious uncertainties.

Unless more disaggregated and community level data become available the many gray areas in our understanding of European migration will probably remain for the foreseeable future.

NOTES

1 The commonest variable used to proxy the "friends and relatives" effect (as it is often called) in models of emigration has been the stock of emigrants in the destination country.

2 The Registrar-General published data from 1876 which showed migration from Ireland to Britain but, even on a basis of net migration, these data are probably understated by a factor of at least two. The under-recording of gross migration is greater (Ó Gráda 1975: 147).

3 Between 1800 and 1890 the population of the geographical area of Germany grew by 102 percent, but the urban population grew by 931 percent. The figures for England and Wales were 834 percent and 222 percent, respectively. The urban threshold is defined as a population of more than 10,000. Calculated from De Vries (1984: 45–7).

4 The definition of "Europe" excludes Russia. Its inclusion would reduce the figures to 10.9 percent, 16.4 percent and 32.9 percent in 1800, 1850 and 1910, respectively (Bairoch and Goertz 1986: 289). (Note that the urban threshold here is 5000 rather than 10,000 as in footnote 3 above. The change in basis makes very little difference to the results.)

5 There are serious boundary errors in the British census in the nineteenth century which make the results of some studies problematic (e.g. Friedlander and Roshier 1966; Greenwood and Thomas 1973; Vedder and Cooper 1974). Baines has corrected for boundary changes (1986: 96–7, 123–4).

6 Cairncross, following earlier work by Welton, calculated the total urban population in all urban districts, boroughs, etc., of more than 2,000 people. The rural areas were the residuals (Cairncross 1949).

7 The German census of 1907 showed that the great majority of migrants to the German cities, of more than 50,000 population came from the *Land* on which the city was located or from the neighboring *Land* (Köllman 1969: 97).

8 Migration rates to Paris were highest from the neighboring departments. Sixty-two percent of migrants to Lyons had been born in the same or adjacent departments – i.e. 38 percent could be considered to have been long-distance migrants, but on average they had moved a shorter distance than migrants to Paris. Less than 30 percent of migrants to the industrial town of St Etienne, which was smaller than Lyons, were long-distance migrants by this definition (Poussou 1989: 82).

9 The data are taken from the *Statistical Yearbook of German Cities* and relate to urban areas with a population of more than 50,000 people. A person working on an annual contract (for example a domestic servant) would by this method of counting appear as both an in- and an out-migrant, of course.

10 Gross migration rates in Amsterdam exceeded net rates by a factor of eight (De Vries 1984: 234–6).

11 Gross migration for Swedish counties (lan), 1821–59, have been estimated at 5–12 percent in rural areas and 12–15 percent in urban areas. Between 1844 and 1847, Cuenca, a city in Spain with no mechanized industry, had in- and out-migration

rates of 13.7 percent and 16.2 percent per annum, respectively (Bengtsson 1990: 193; Reher 1990: 249–53).

12 The seven systems were centered on the Paris basin, the Po valley, central Italy, East Anglia, Castile, Catalonia and the northern Netherlands.

13 Before the Second World War the data refer to change of residence in German cities with a population of more than 50,000. After the war, the data refer to cities in the Federal Republic with a population of more than 100,000.

14 The most frequently used measure is the net balance of migration – i.e. $M_{1-2} = P_2 - (P_1 + B_{1-2} - D_{1-2})$, where M is net migration (to all destinations), P_1 and P_2 are the enumerated population at the first and second count, and B_{1-2} and D_{1-2} are, respectively, births and deaths in the intervening period. Alternatively, P could measure the population born in a particular area, which would give an estimate of the net balance of migration into or out of that area. It would not be a true estimate, however (Baines 1986: 90–125).

15 Measurement problems may also mean that the idea of a "mobility transition" is problematic. Zelinsky's view of the "mobility transition" is that the main migration flows change from rural–urban to urban–urban. But, as we have said, it is not clear that rural–urban migration rates have ever exceeded urban–urban migration rates. Hence, the reason for the transition is simply that in the twentieth century the possibility of rural–urban migration has been much diminished (Zelinsky 1971).

16 The net migration method may also overstate female internal migration relative to male in the nineteenth century. It is possible that proportionally more females than males were making rural–urban moves because of the large number of female rural–urban moves into domestic service in the urban areas.

17 The direct effect of migration on the growth of European cities was as follows. English cities, including London (1841–1911) c.25 percent; Munich (1820–1900) 28 percent; Paris (1820–90) 36 percent; Copenhagen (1820–90) 43 percent; Swedish cities (1850–1900) c.50 percent; Leipzig (1820–90) 60 percent; Budapest (1850–1910) 80 percent; St Petersburg (1820–90) 100 percent (Cairncross 1949: 82–6; Fridlizius 1979: 128; Weber 1967: 249).

18 This, and similar calculations, assumes that migrant and native age-specific mortality and fertility were identical. There is a view, associated with Alan Sharlin, that migrants had low nuptuality and low fertility. Hence, low urban population growth was caused by migration, not vice versa (Sharlin 1986; see also Reher 1989: 203; Ringrose 1983: 63). It is well known that urban fertility was lower than rural but few authorities believe that it was caused by migration (De Vries 1990: 55–7).

19 The precise number of American immigrants who traveled via Canada is disputed. See McInnis, Chapter 7.

20 A recent paper by Hatton and Williamson (1993) was able to incorporate successfully cross-section data into a model of Irish emigration in the late nineteenth century.

21 Baines (1986: 75–87) also considers the change in the character of British emigration between the early and later nineteenth century. There is also evidence of temporary emigration from England and Scotland in the earlier nineteenth century and there may also have been temporary emigration from Scandinavia in this period.

22 It is also possible that in the early stages, emigration would rise as a consequence of rising income in the origin country even though the income gap with the destination country was falling. (Rising income could be associated with falling transport costs, for example.) See Faini and Venturini, Chapter 4.

23 This raises the question of the relationship between male and female emigration – which is comparatively easy to explain – and the relationship between male emigration and female internal migration – which is very difficult to explain. For obvious reasons this is a very difficult distinction to make.

24 The "emigrants" may have been moving within a single labor market which crossed a national frontier. In this case the appropriate comparators would be the labor market in Europe and the overseas destination.

3

LATECOMERS TO MASS EMIGRATION

The Latin experience*

Timothy J. Hatton and Jeffrey G. Williamson

WERE THE LATINS DIFFERENT?

The Latin countries – Italy, Portugal and Spain – were industrial latecomers, at the European periphery, and only experienced mass emigration late in the nineteenth century. When they did join the European mass migration, they did so in great numbers. The fact that they joined the mass migrations late, that they were poor by west European standards, and that so many went to Latin America, has generated a number of debates on both sides of the Atlantic. The debates imply that the Latins were different. Were they?

Certainly Sir Arthur Lewis thought so. Indeed, he thought that his model of development (Lewis 1954) with immigrant-augmented elastic labor supplies applied to Latin America in the late nineteenth century (Lewis 1978), and many Latin American scholars agree. Carlos Díaz-Alejandro wrote that the labor supply in Argentina before 1930 was "perfectly elastic at the going wage (plus some differential) in the industrial centers of Italy and Spain" (1970: 21–2). Nathaniel Leff believes the same was true of Brazil and that elastic labor supplies can account for stable wages in São Paulo and Santos from the 1880s onwards (Leff 1992: 6). If the elastic labor supply thesis is correct, then late-nineteenth-century Latin emigration should have been far more responsive to wage gaps between home and abroad compared with the early emigrants to the North. Large wage gaps between Latin America and North America, gaps that persist well into the late twentieth century, could then be partially explained by those alleged more elastic Latin labor supplies.

If Latin emigration was really more responsive to wage gaps between home and abroad, why were the wage gaps between southern and northern Europe so big? Urban real-wages for the unskilled in Italy and Spain were far below those in the USA, Argentina and Germany in 1870, but both countries catch up to those destination regions a bit by 1890 (Table 3.1). Between 1890 and 1913, however, these two countries underwent quite different real-wage experience: the wage gap between Italy and destination countries fell (Italian economic success), while it rose for Spain (Spanish economic failure). Italian wages in 1870 were only 22 percent of those in the USA, 41 percent of those in Argentina and 43 percent of those in Germany. By 1913, the Italian figures were 33, 60 and 60 percent, evidence of strong catching up. Spanish wages in 1870 were only 30 percent of those in the USA and 57 percent of those in Argentina. By 1913, the Spanish figures were 30 and 54 percent, revealing no catching up. Table 3.1 shows that Portuguese experience was much like that of Spain. These persistent Iberian wage gaps seem to be inconsistent with elastic emigration responses, and contrast with catching up elsewhere.

Why did so few Latins go North? Did this reflect language affinity and cultural preference, or did it reflect either discrimination in labor markets or the view that emigrants from southern Italy, Spain and Portugal were ill-equipped to meet the demands of European and North American industrial immigrant-absorbing labor markets, or of the coffee plantations in São Paulo and Santos, or of the estates in the Argentine pampas, or of urban service activities in Buenos Aires and Rio de Janeiro?

Given their poverty, why the Latin emigration delay? Since the poorest had the most to gain by a move to higher living standards, why didn't the Latins leave earlier and at higher rates than, say, the Germans or the British? Did poverty breed immobility? Did wage increases at home make it easier to save for the move? Did pioneer migrants play a role by lowering job search costs, by the purchase of pre-paid tickets, and by income-augmenting remittances? If they did, perhaps it might help explain why the Italian migrations were so impressive after the 1890s, and why Latin migrations were so modest prior to the 1890s.

Did early industrialization and rapid development breed emigration? If so,

Table 3.1 Home real wage relative to destination real wage for the Latin countries 1870–1913 (percent)

Home/Destination	1870	1890	1913
Italy relative to:			
USA	22	24	33
Argentina	41	60	60
Germany	43	46	60
Spain relative to:			
USA	30	34	30
Argentina	57	86	54
Portugal relative to:			
USA	27	28	23
Argentina	51	71	42

Note: The figures for Italy, Spain, the USA, Argentina and Germany are from Williamson (1994, Table A2). They refer to purchasing-power-parity deflated urban unskilled wage rates. The figures for Portugal are from Appendix 1, available upon request.

how did this influence work? Did urbanization raise labor mobility as the land lost its grip on the peasant? Was it that peasants were tied to the land, while urban workers were more mobile, so that the Latin agrarian economies recorded lower emigration rates early on?

These questions deal with behavior. But perhaps Latin migration behavior wasn't so different. Perhaps instead it was their economic and demographic environment that was different, and perhaps the different environment was due to the fact that they were latecomers and that they failed in some sense (Molinas and Prados 1989; Federico and Toniolo 1991). What were the forces which drove up Latin emigration after the 1890s? Were they any different than the forces that drove up northern European emigration between the 1870s and the 1890s? Were these forces mostly absent from the Latin economies in the 1870s?

This chapter seeks to answer these questions. In a longer version of this paper, we were able to show that Latin emigrants were pretty much like other European emigrants. In this chapter, therefore, we immediately move on to develop a model of mass emigration and then apply it to panel data which pools the long-run decadal emigration experience of twelve European emigrating countries in the late nineteenth century, including Italy, Portugal and Spain. We then use these econometric results to identify the sources of Latin emigration, and compare them with that of other European countries. We also explore the short-run determinants of emigration from Italy, Portugal and Spain. The chapter concludes by posing two big questions left unanswered: were Latin labor markets and non-Latin labor markets segmented by discrimination or culture? and, if so, how much bigger would Latin emigrations have been without segmentation, and what difference would it have made to the historical evolution of Old World and New World Latin economies?

EXPLAINING EUROPEAN MASS EMIGRATION

In order to gain a comparative perspective on the Latin migrations, we start by examining the emigration experience of twelve countries (including nine non-Latins) over the period 1850 to 1913. These are documented in Table 3.2 as average decadal emigration rates per thousand of the sending country population. The decadal averages are used to smooth out the sharp year-to-year fluctuations since our interest in this and the next section is in the long-run determinants of emigration. An analysis of the short-run timing of these permanent moves is postponed until later (see pp. 66–9). The data include both European intracontinental and New World intercontinental migrations.

What explains late-nineteenth-century emigration rates? The real wage gap between home and abroad plays a key role in all migration models, but such evidence was unavailable to earlier studies (Easterlin 1961; Tomaske 1971;

Table 3.2 Gross (G) and net (N) emigration from Europe, 1850–1913 (emigrants per 1000 population: decade averages)

		1850–9	*1860–9*	*1870–9*	*1880–9*	*1890–9*	*1900–13*
Belgium	G	1.90	2.22	2.03	2.18	1.96	2.32
	N	0.66	0.17	−0.93	−1.06	−1.80	−2.88
Denmark	G	—	—	1.97	3.74	2.60	2.80
	N	—	—	1.95	3.68	2.55	2.58
France	G	—	0.12	0.16	0.29	0.18	0.15
	N	—	0.11	0.09	0.19	0.11	0.01
Germany	G	1.80	1.61	1.35	2.91	1.18	0.43
	N	—	1.61	1.35	2.89	1.12	−2.45
Great Britain	G	4.38	2.47	3.87	5.71	3.92	7.08
	N	—	1.29	1.52	3.23	0.93	3.31
Ireland	G	18.99	15.16	11.28	16.04	9.70	7.93
	N	—	—	—	—	—	—
Italy	G	—	—	4.29	6.09	8.65	17.97
	N	—	—	—	—	6.78	13.01
Netherlands	G	0.50	1.67	2.66	4.06	4.62	5.36
	N	—	—	0.10	0.81	1.16	0.31
Norway	G	—	—	4.33	10.16	4.56	7.15
	N	—	—	—	—	—	—
Portugal	G	—	—	2.91	3.79	5.04	5.67
	N	—	—	—	—	—	—
Spain	G	—	—	—	3.91	4.63	6.70
	N	—	—	—	0.98	0.42	2.50
Sweden	G	0.51	2.52	2.96	8.25	5.32	4.49
	N	—	—	—	7.30	3.77	2.93

Sources: With the exception of Portugal, the data is taken from Hatton and Williamson (1994: Table 1). The Portuguese data is taken from Appendix 1, available upon request.

Williamson 1974b; Gould 1979, 1980; Massey 1988; Baines 1991). Thus, for example, Easterlin had to make do with Mulhall's crude estimates of per capita income. Crippled by lack of adequate data, this important debate has lain dormant for about two decades. The appearance of a recently developed real wage database for internationally comparable urban unskilled male occupations (Williamson 1994) makes it possible to breath new life into the debate. After all, these data offer an income measure far more relevant to the migration decision. Furthermore, since these real wage indices are comparable across time and between countries, the country time-series can be pooled in the emigration analysis, something earlier studies were unable to do.

Real wages were rising strongly everywhere; some – like Denmark, Ireland, Italy, Norway and Sweden – were doing especially well, while others – like Belgium, France, Portugal and Spain – were not. On net, real wages converged in the late nineteenth century (Williamson 1994), and most of that convergence was driven by the gradual erosion in the real wage gap favoring the New World although a weaker convergence was also taking place in

Europe. For example, between the 1870s and the early twentieth century, Danish real wages rose from about 35 percent to about 57 percent of the New World, a significant catch-up over about three decades. Swedish experience was similar, her real wage rising from about 23 percent of the New World in the 1850s to about 56 percent at the end of the period. Ireland and Italy recorded much the same catch-up on the New World. In fact, the only European countries which fail to show some catch up are France, Germany, Portugal and Spain.

In certain cases like Ireland and Norway, an inverse correlation between trends in the emigration rate and the wage ratio (domestic to foreign) is clearly revealed in the raw data. Indeed, the rise in the Irish wage relative to that of destination countries explains much of the secular fall in the Irish emigration rate after the famine (Hatton and Williamson 1993). Italian real wages were rising relative to destination areas and those for Spain were roughly constant (Table 3.1). Yet, in both countries the emigration rate rose, and it rose most in Italy where the home wage rose the most. Clearly, wage gaps by themselves cannot explain the mass emigrations. In addition, if wage gaps had been the sole determinant of European emigration then the mass emigrations would have been led by the poor Latin and east European countries. Instead, they follow, offering further support for the view that we need a richer model to explain these mass emigrations.

This one central stylized fact makes it clear, therefore, that real wage gaps will not suffice to explain emigration by themselves: during the course of modern economic growth, emigration rates rise steeply at first from very low levels, the rise then begins to slow down, emigration rates reach a peak, and subsequently they fall off. This stylized fact has emerged from studies of both the time series of aggregate emigration for a number of countries (Akerman 1976) and of the local emigration rates within individual countries (Gould 1979), and it has been used to make predictions about the future of Mexican immigration into America (Massey 1988). Several explanations have been offered for this stylized fact, but each of them can be characterized by the time path captured by Figure 3.1 where we isolate movements along some downward-sloping home country emigration function (EM) and shifts in that function. In pre-industrial episodes, we observe low emigration rates (e_0) and low wages (w_0). Industrialization and other events then serve both to raise the emigration function to EM' and real wages to w_1. The former dominates in this example since emigration rates have *risen* to e_1; in the absence of the shift in EM, emigration rates would have *fallen* to e'_1. In later stages of development, EM' is taken to be stable so that further improvements in real wages at home, to w_2, cut back emigration rates to e_2. Thus, the stylized emigration facts are reproduced in Figure 3.1. If late-nineteenth-century Latin emigration is to be successfully explained then we need to identify factors that might account for the outward shift in the emigration function as well as the elasticity describing emigrants' response to wage gaps

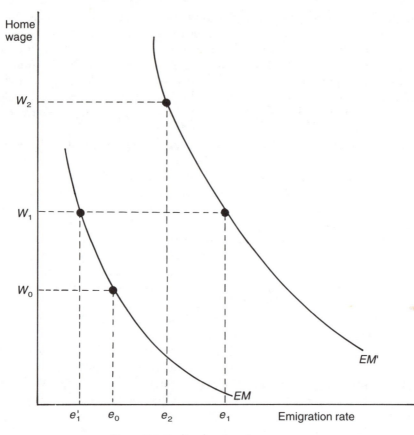

Figure 3.1 Stylized emigration responses

along that function. To the extent that these forces were operating in the same way in Latin and non-Latin countries, the latecomer surge in Latin emigration may simply be a repeat performance of what occurred in northern Europe 30 or 40 years earlier. What, then, accounts for rightward shifts in *EM* during early industrialization and its stability thereafter?

In his pioneering paper published over 30 years ago, Richard Easterlin (1961) argued that European emigration was driven largely by population growth. Comparing average country emigration rates 1861–1910 with rates of natural increase lagged 20 years, Easterlin found a strong positive correlation. Easterlin viewed the rate of natural increase 20 years earlier as a proxy for the current rate of additions to the labor force which would, in turn, lower the real wage and raise emigration (1961: 332). If so, then this would be better captured by an index of current labor market conditions, such as the real wage, which would reflect the net impact of both labor supply and demand. However, there is an alternative interpretation of

Easterlin's correlation. If differences in natural increase were driven chiefly by variations in births and infant mortality then it could act as a proxy for the proportion of the population who, 20 or 30 years later, were in the prime emigration age group. Since this age cohort had a far higher propensity to emigrate, one might observe higher emigration rates associated with faster lagged natural increase even if real wage gaps between home and abroad stayed constant. And since rising fertility rates and falling infant mortality rates are associated with early industrialization, rising emigration rates might possibly be correlated with rising real wages at home if the influence of these demographic transition variables was sufficiently powerful.

A second hypothesis suggests that industrialization and urbanization foster emigration. In many qualitative accounts of European emigration, the key factor is economic development at home, not just rising wages but the whole range of transformations which accompany industrialization and change attitudes towards emigration. The importance of industrialization in raising labor mobility has recently been stressed by Massey (1988). European industrialization involved, above all, reduced attachment to the land and a rise in wage labor. The combination of more commercialized agriculture, more consolidated landholdings, diminished smallholdings, the erosion of common rights, and relatively high and rising wages in the booming cities, all served to produce a rural exodus (Williamson 1990). Thus, rising urban population shares and falling agricultural employment at home might have fostered greater emigration, given the wage gap between home and abroad.[1]

A third hypothesis appeals to the costs of migration. Although there is a strong incentive to flee pre-industrial poverty, the costs may be prohibitive for most workers. After all, the potential migrant cannot get loans for the move, and his income is too close to subsistence to make it possible to accumulate the necessary savings. Thus, enormous wage gaps in the 1870s between a labor-scarce, resource-rich United States and a labor-abundant, resource-poor Spain can be quite consistent with low emigration rates. As industrialization takes place in the home country, real wages rise and the supply constraint on emigration is gradually released: more and more potential emigrants can now finance the move, and, in contrast with conventional theory, the home wage and emigration would be positively correlated. As industrialization continues, the backlog of potential migrants is slowly exhausted as more and more workers find it possible to finance the move. When the migration cost constraint is no longer binding, further increases in the real wage cause the emigration rate to decline from the peak, and, consistent with the downward-sloping *EM* function in Figure 3.1, the home wage and emigration would now be inversely correlated.

One factor which might serve to relax the poverty constraint earlier than otherwise would be the existence of a stock of pioneer migrants already living abroad who could help finance the subsequent emigration of friends and relatives. Historians call these forces "chain migration" or the "friends and relatives" effect. There is abundant evidence that current emigrants' cost of passage was financed by previous emigrants (Kero 1991: 191; Hvidt 1975: 129), and such evidence clearly argues that past emigration encourages present emigration. The idea is that rightward shifts in the *EM* function are driven by the remittances of previous (now rich) emigrants who finance the moves of impecunious latecomers. As the stock of emigrants abroad increases, so too do their remittances home, and thus the current emigration rate rises even though the home wage is increasing. This rising influence continues as long as potential emigrants find their move financially-constrained, but the latter diminishes as the real wage increases at home. At some point, that constraint is no longer binding and further increases in the home wage reduce the emigration rate as the economy moves up the more stable *EM'* function.

How effective are these plausible arguments when confronted with the quantitative record? Where do the Latin latecomers fit into the tale?

WERE THE LATINS DIFFERENT? EMIGRATION PANEL DATA

Here we apply an econometric model to the decade average emigration rates presented in Table 3.2, incorporating where possible the hypotheses just discussed. Table 3.3 presents the results. Not only are they very good in terms of expected signs and conventional significance tests, but they are consistent with our earlier paper on mass migrations (Hatton and Williamson 1994). The core model appears in equation (1) of the table where the gross migration rate (GMIGR) is regressed on: the lagged dependent variable (LGMIGR) – to help guide our distinctions between short- and long-run emigration behavior; the share of the male labor force in agriculture (AGSM) – one minus which is our measure of industrialization; the Easterlin *direct* demographic influence (RNI) – the rate of natural population increase two decades previously; the log of the real wage gap (LRRW) – the log ratio of home to foreign wages, a measure of the gains to emigration where the foreign real wage is, where appropriate, taken as a migration-weighted average of real wages in destination labor markets; the stock of migrants from the country in question which are currently resident abroad (MST) – our measure of "networks;" a dummy for Belgium (BEL) – since we found this to be the only non-Latin country which was "different;" and a Latin dummy (LAT) to test whether the three countries combined were different, at least in their intercept.

Equation (1) reports the following: AGSM has only a weak influence on emigration rates, although the sign is, as predicted, negative. That is, urbanization and industrialization tend to raise the rate of emigration after controlling for other factors. The rate of natural population increase two decades earlier has a powerful and significant positive impact on

Table 3.3 Explaining late-nineteenth-century European emigration

Variable	Equation (1)	Equation (2)	Equation (3)	Equation (4)
Constant	−3.51*	−3.88*	−3.82*	−3.87*
	(1.67)	(1.84)	(1.73)	(1.70)
AGSM	−4.77	−2.17	−5.63*	−5.50
	(1.45)	(0.62)	(1.67)	(1.47)
RNI	+0.26**	+0.29***	+0.26**	+0.27**
	(2.50)	(2.82)	(2.48)	(2.50)
LRRW	−5.92***	−4.71**	−6.77***	−6.62**
	(2.81)	(2.09)	(2.93)	(2.48)
MST	+0.10**	+0.12**	+0.12**	+0.10**
	(2.07)	(2.38)	(2.31)	(2.08)
LGMIGR	+0.47***	+0.39**	+0.43**	+0.47***
	(2.82)	(2.28)	(2.55)	(2.81)
BEL	+3.16*	+2.47	+3.65**	+3.62*
	(1.85)	(1.39)	(2.01)	(1.79)
ITA		+6.63***		
		(4.41)		
POR		+2.86*		
		(1.80)		
SPA		+4.87**		
		(2.36)		
LAT	+4.94***		−68.88	+6.96
	(3.93)		(0.11)	(1.44)
LAT*LRW			+31.98	
			(0.10)	
LAT*LRW²			−3.24	
			(0.08)	
LAT*LRRW				+2.52
				(0.43)
R̄²	0.71	0.73	0.72	0.71
Mean GMIGR	4.97	4.97	4.97	4.97
N	48	48	48	48
RSS	189.77	170.48	178.72	188.86
RESET	0.12	0.71	1.13	0.30

Notes: The dependent variable is measured as emigrants per 1000 population, 't' statistics in parentheses:

      * = significant at 10%;
      ** = significant at 5%;
      *** = significant at 1%.

emigration, just as Easterlin predicted. To repeat, this measures the *direct* effect of population growth, which serves to glut the most mobile cohort two decades after rising fertility rates and declining infant mortality rates have their influence. *Indirect* labor supply effects of RNI through any downward pressure on the home real wage is already captured by our wage gap variable. The ratio of home to destination real wages also tends to have a powerful and significant negative impact on emigration. So too does the stock of migrants abroad, larger migrant stocks abroad serving to raise the current rate of emigration. The lagged dependent variable has a powerful and significant positive impact, a finding common to all migration studies.

Finally, and perhaps most important, the Latin dummy is powerful and significantly positive. Holding everything else constant, the Latins tended to emigrate at greater rates than was true for the rest of Europe. We should remind the reader, however, that the dependent variable in this analysis is the *gross* emigration rate. It may well be that a similar analysis of the *net* emigration rate might weaken the significance of the Latin dummy, just as our earlier paper suggested (Hatton and Williamson 1994). Subject to this qualification, Table 3.3 suggests that the Latins *did* emigrate at greater rates, *ceteris paribus*. Equation (2) explores this issue further by introducing dummies for all three Latin countries. However, a chi-squared test implies that these three countries can indeed be pooled together as "Latin." Thus, for the remainder of this section we focus on the core model in equation (2).

We next ask whether Latin emigration was uniquely constrained by poverty. Recall the argument postulated on p. 61: potential emigrants in poor European countries were so income-constrained by their poverty that they could not afford the move; as real wages rose at home, the constraint was slowly released, but at some point further increases in home wages lost their influence (Faini 1991; Faini and Venturini 1994). When equation (3) introduces the home wage in non-linear form, interacted with the Latin dummy (LAT*LRW and LAT*LRW^2), the hypothesis is rejected as it applied to the Latin countries. It is simply not true that late-nineteenth-century Latin emigration was suppressed by poverty. Although Table 3.3 does not report the results, we were also able to reject the hypotheses that Latin emigration responded differently to AGSM, RNI and MST.

Finally, is it true that Latin migration supplies were more elastic? Equation (4) tests this important hypothesis by adding an interaction term to equation (1), the Latin dummy times the wage gap variable (LAT*LRRW). The hypothesis is soundly rejected: it is simply not true that the Latin economies in the late nineteenth century were characterized by more elastic emigrant labor supplies than the rest of Europe.

If the Latin emigrants seem to have responded to their economic and demographic environment pretty much like the rest of Europe, perhaps it was the environment that they left behind which was different. Table 3.4 explores this proposition by multiplying the estimated coefficients in Table 3.3 (column 1, converted to long-run impact) times the change in the right-hand-side variable of interest. The multiplication yields a figure which tells us just how much of the predicted rise in decadal emigration rates between, say, 1890–1899 and 1900–1913 (the sum of columns 2–5) can be explained by changes in RNI, AGSM, LRRW and MST. The typical northern European patterns are illustrated by Sweden which was on the downside of its emigration cycle after the 1890s, having reached peak emigration rates earlier (Table 3.2). Thus, the decline in the predicted GMIGR in Sweden, −0.845, is explained entirely by two forces: the decline in the rate of natural increase two decades previously (−0.140) and the spectacular catching up of real wages (−1.579), the other two forces tending to have weaker effects serving to increase GMIGR.

Table 3.4 shows that very different economic and demographic forces were at work in the latecomer Latin countries. True, a boom in the natural rate of population increase two decades earlier was a very powerful force serving to push up emigration rates in Italy and Portugal, experience on the upswing of the demographic transition that was replicated in the rest of Europe earlier in the century. These are by far the most powerful forces accounting for the surge in Italian and Portuguese emigration rates after the 1890s. Spain, however, is an exception: two decades earlier rates of natural increase were *falling*, not rising, a fact well appreciated by demographic historians (Moreda 1987).

If emigrant-inducing demographic forces were absent in Spain after the 1890s, why the sharp rise in Spanish emigration rates? The answer seems to lie largely with economic failure at home. The wage gap between Spain and destination countries widened at the end of the century (Table 3.1), and this event explains almost all of the surge in Spanish emigration. The same was true of Portugal, although the failure at home was not nearly as great. In contrast, Italian wages catch up with those in destination countries – the USA, Argentina and Germany – and that wage success at home muted the surge in Italian emigration by partially offsetting those powerful emigrant-inducing demographic forces.

For all three Latin countries there were additional underlying fundamentals that they shared and which served to contribute to the surge in

Table 3.4 Sources of changing emigration rates, 1890s–1900s

Country	(1) Predicted change in emigration rate	(2) $\hat{\beta}_x \Delta RNI$	(3) $\hat{\beta}_x \Delta AGSM$	(4) $\hat{\beta}_x \Delta LRRW$	(5) $\hat{\beta}_x \Delta MST$
Italy	+0.350	+1.305	+0.079	−1.304	+0.270
Spain	+2.803	−0.340	+0.711	+2.102	+0.330
Portugal	+2.526	+1.663	+0.082	+0.512	+0.269
Sweden	−0.845	−0.140	+0.619	−1.579	+0.255
Great Britain	+0.110	−0.500	+0.181	+0.633	−0.204

Notes: The predicted values in col. (1) refer to the change in gross emigration rates between 1890–9 and 1900–13, and they are derived by summing the four entries in cols (2)–(5). The $\hat{\beta}_x$ in cols (2)–(5) refer to the estimated coefficients in Table 3.3, col. 1, evaluated at their long-run values (e.g., each divided by one minus the coefficient on the lagged dependent variable). The ΔX refer to changes in each explanatory variable also between 1890–9 and 1900–13.

emigration: modest rates of industrialization (the fall in AGSM) and rising migrant populations abroad (the rise in MST). None the less, what really made the Latin countries different after the 1890s was the delayed demographic transition and the economic failure in Portugal and Spain.

Latin economic failure helps account for the surge of emigration after the 1890s; oddly enough, the same is true of Britain. British emigration rose to a peak in the 1880s, falling thereafter, thus obeying an emigration life cycle that was repeated by so many countries in nineteenth-century Europe (Hatton and Williamson 1994). We also know that this life cycle was being driven by those economic and demographic forces discussed at length earlier in this section. However, British emigration departed from the long-run pattern after the 1890s, that is, the emigration rate *rose* rather than continuing its fall. What made Britain different after the 1890s? Exactly the same forces that made Spain and Portugal different: economic failure at home.

WERE THE LATINS DIFFERENT? EMIGRATION AS TIME SERIES

The annual fluctuations in emigration rates which characterized most European countries has attracted much discussion, and when Gould (1979) surveyed that literature more than a decade ago, he noted that the Latin countries had largely been neglected. While Baganha (1990) and Sanchez-Alonso (1990) have recently helped fill that gap by their work on Portuguese and Spanish emigration, we still lack econometric studies comparable to those which have been applied to countries in the north and west of Europe.

The standard framework for analyzing emigration is that pioneered by Todaro (1969) and Harris and Todaro (1970) where migration depends on expected wages and the probability of obtaining employment at home and abroad. Hatton (1993) modified the expected income approach in three ways. First, if migrants are risk averse and if access to jobs differs at home and abroad, the expected employment terms should be allowed to take on different coefficients from each other and from the relative wage. Second, migrants consider the whole profile of future earnings at home and abroad, and they use past history to form expectations about the future. Thus, we expect lags to be relevant. Finally, the timing of migration may be influenced by short-run changes in the variables since it may pay to time the move to take advantage of propitious conditions abroad relative to those at home: short-run changes in conditions at home and abroad might be expected to trigger sharp changes in emigration. The general model estimated here can therefore be written as follows:

$$M/P(t) = b_0 + b_1 \Delta \log Ef(t) + b_2 \Delta \log Eh(t) + b_3 \Delta \log[Wf/Wh](t)$$
$$+ b_4 \log Ef(t-1) + b_5 \log Eh(t-1) + b_6 \log[Wf/Wh](t-1)$$
$$+ b_7 M/P(t-1)$$

where M/P is the (gross) emigration rate, W is the (real) wage rate, E is the employment probability and f and h represent the foreign destination and home countries.

The data for gross emigration rates for Portugal are from Baganha (1990), for Spain from Sanchez-Alonso (1990) and for Italy from Ferenczi and Willcox (1929). The relative wage variables were computed from Williamson (1994) using migration-weighted averages for the wage in destination countries. Employment rates are not available and so these were proxied by deviations from trend of the log of industrial production from Mitchell (1978, 1983); for destination countries they are also weighted averages of available series. In preliminary estimation the terms for the change in domestic activity and in the wage ratio were found to be insignificant and so

Table 3.5 Time-series regressions: Portugal, Spain, Italy
(dependent variable: emigrants per thousand population)

	(1) Portugal 1871–1913	(2) To Americas	(3) To Other	(4) To Americas	(5) To Europe
		Spain 1883–1913		Italy 1877–1913	
Constant	−2.68 (1.14)	0.83 (1.14)	0.12 (0.20)	−23.57* (2.02)	1.22 (0.91)
Changes in foreign activity	4.73 (1.28)	9.95*** (2.76)	−0.77 (0.17)	16.06** (2.45)	4.38 (1.14)
Foreign activity $(t-1)$	7.81*** (4.54)	5.89*** (2.93)	12.22*** (3.12)	8.36* (2.00)	−0.23 (0.07)
Domestic activity $(t-1)$	−4.77 (1.70)	−10.37* (1.96)	2.04 (0.47)	−5.17 (1.58)	−1.86** (2.43)
Domestic/foreign wage $(t-1)$	−3.13*** (2.43)	−3.61** (2.39)	−1.28 (0.79)	−5.75** (2.18)	−0.15 (0.07)
Lagged Migration rate	0.36** (2.24)	0.32* (1.96)	0.89** (2.54)	0.36** (2.05)	0.60*** (3.81)
Time	0.16*** (3.43)				
Time from 1895	−0.17* (1.88)			0.19* (1.74)	0.15** (2.28)
1896–8 dummy		1.55 (1.39)			
R^2	0.86	0.85	0.42	0.83	0.95
DW	2.17	2.44	1.54	1.95	1.72
RSS	49.51	35.54	25.40	103.66	9.24
LM(1)	1.31	3.75	0.31	0.14	1.74
RESET	3.61	0.62	16.50	2.42	0.26

Notes: See Table 3.3.

these terms were dropped from the equations in Table 3.5.

Turning first to Portugal in the first column of Table 3.5, we find that the signs of all the variables are exactly as predicted by the model. Both the change in foreign activity and its level yield positive signs, with the latter significant, while the domestic activity variable yields a negative and significant sign. The wage in receiving countries relative to that at home has a strong positive coefficient as does the lagged dependent variable. The long-run or steady state coefficients are derived by taking into account the lagged dependent variable. The long-run effect of a sustained rise of 10 percent in foreign activity raised the annual emigration rate by 1.2 emigrants per thousand population. This foreign activity impact is strong, and since fluctuations in Brazilian GDP take on the overwhelming weight in the activity index, these findings offer powerful support for those who have stressed economic conditions in Brazil as a key determinant of Portuguese emigration. The long-run relative wage coefficient is smaller than that on foreign activity, as the model predicts, suggesting that a sustained fall of 10 percent in the domestic relative to foreign wage raised the annual emigration rate by 0.49 per thousand in the long run.

We experimented with a variety of different trend terms to capture the upward shifts in the Portuguese emigration rate, underlying fundamentals which were not associated with fluctuations in economic activity or with wage rates. The best result was obtained with time and time from 1895 as regressors. The time term indicates a strong upward trend but this is mitigated later in the period by the negative coefficient on the time-from-1895 term. The long-run impact of these time trends can be derived as before by taking into account the lagged dependent variable. The result suggests that there was a strong surge in underlying fundamentals that raised the Portuguese steady state annual emigration rate by as much as 5.0 per thousand between 1871 and 1891. Between 1891 and 1913, these funda-mentals stopped raising trend emigration rates.[2] In addition, economic failure at home mattered: the falling ratio of domestic to foreign wages accounted for an upward shift in the steady state annual emigration rate of 0.95 per thousand.

In contrast with Portugal, Spanish emigration streams to the Americas and other destinations must be treated separately. Unfortunately, we are less able to document conditions in the wider range of destination countries in Latin America to which the Spanish emigrants went, compared with the Portu-guese, and in the case of "other" destinations matters are even worse since we know nothing about economic conditions in North Africa, an important destination for Spanish emigrants. We must be content with a Brazilian economic activity index as our sole proxy for employment conditions in the Americas facing Spanish emigrants, and with the Argentine wage as our sole indicator for wage conditions in the Americas facing Spanish emigrants. In the case of "other" destinations, France is our sole indicator for foreign wage conditions. Given these severe data constraints, it is not surprising that the results for the Spanish emigration to "other" in column 3 of Table 3.5 are so poor, but they are very good in column 2 for the Americas. What follows deals with column 2 alone. The signs are as expected, and the coefficients suggest that, as with Portugal, fluctuations in economic activity at home and abroad had opposing influences on Spanish emigration. The coefficient on the relative wage is similar to that for Portugal: a 10 percent fall in the domestic to foreign wage ratio raised Spain's long-run annual emigration rate to the Americas by about 0.53 per thousand. We also found that time trends were never significant for Spain, a finding which is consistent with the weak Spanish demographic and industrial transition effects noted earlier (see p. 65).

As with Spain, Italian emigration has to be disaggregated into two distinct emigrant streams, one to Europe (column 5) and one to the Americas (column 4). For Europe, the destination activity and wage variables are a weighted average of France and Germany. Like Spain, the results are far better for Italian emigration to the Americas. What follows, therefore, dwells on column 4. The impact of foreign activity and the relative wage on emigration to the Americas are relatively large and significant. The coefficient for the relative wage implies that a 10 percent fall in the domestic to the foreign wage raised Italy's long-run annual emigration rate to the Americas by 0.90 per thousand, a result similar but somewhat bigger than that for total Portuguese emigration and Spanish emigration to the Americas. When we experimented with alternative time trends, we found that the best specification for Italy was obtained with a time-from-1895 trend. This suggests a surge in the underlying fundamentals raising Italian emigration rates after the 1890s, a sharp contrast with both Spain and Portugal, neither of which show any evidence of rising fundamentals after 1890. Its impact was to raise annual emigration rates to the Americas by 5.3 per thousand between 1890 and 1913. The impact of this surge in fundamentals on emigration was muted by the catching up of Italian wages with those destination countries from 1890 to 1913 (Table 3.1). However, the fundamentals dominated, serving to raise emigration rates by 5.3 per thousand, since the surge in Italian wages cut back emigration only by 1.3 per thousand.

Were Latin emigrant supply responses different? The wage gap between home and abroad certainly influenced emigration but the elasticities are relatively small. In all three cases, a 10 percent increase in the wage ratio raised emigration by less than one per thousand in the long run. Compare this with Britain (Hatton 1993) and Ireland (Hatton and Williamson 1993) where long-run responses of 2.2 and 2.3 per thousand are observed. This provides further support for the view that the supply of Latin labor to the New World was *not* relatively elastic as is so often assumed.

Finally, we have tried to capture with time trends some of the fundamentals associated with demographic growth, industrialization and the rising emigrant stock abroad which were also identified earlier in this chapter in the panel data. The results suggest that these fundamentals were strongest in Portugal before the 1890s and weakened subsequently. For Spain, they appear to have been absent altogether, a finding which fits well into the pattern of slow demographic growth identified earlier. For Italy, the surge in fundamentals appears to have begun in the 1890s.

ADDITIONAL QUESTIONS AND A RESEARCH AGENDA

Contrary to conventional wisdom, the Latin emigrants did *not* exhibit a more elastic labor supply response to wages home and abroad. Nor did the Latin emigrations respond any differently to the demographic transition and industrial revolutionary events at home. What distinguished the late-nineteenth-century Latin countries from the rest of Europe to the northwest was their latecomer status and, with the exception of Italy, their weak economic and demographic performance when industrialization arrived late. With the exception of the Irish driven abroad by the famine, mass emigration in Europe had to await the forces of industrialization at home and a glut in the mobile age cohort driven by a demographic transition which industrialization produced. Furthermore, real wages in the early industrializers in the northwest of Europe were catching up with real wages in destination areas, and these forces served to hold, at least partially, the mass emigrations in check. As industrialization and the demographic boom slowed down in northwest Europe, the real wage catch up began to dominate, thus cutting back mass emigration. Italy seems to exhibit the same pattern, but with a lag. The differences lie with the Iberian peninsula. Spain never underwent a powerful demographic transition in the late nineteenth century; its mass emigration was driven instead by economic failure at home, especially after the 1890s. Portugal did undergo a powerful demographic transition in the late nineteenth century, but its mass emigration was also driven, at least in part, by economic failure at home.

Many have argued that Latin labor markets were segmented from those in northwest Europe. This view has it that, in the late nineteenth century at least, Latin labor did not head north in large numbers. Had they done so, wages would have risen at home more due to greater labor scarcity, and wages would have risen in northern Europe less due to greater labor glut. They did not do so, and thus the Latins missed an opportunity – more rapid real wage growth at home even in the absence of dramatic industrialization at home. By not doing so, Latin labor markets remained segmented from the more dynamic parts of Europe. Furthermore, so the argument goes, with the exception of southern Italians, Latin emigrants went overseas to South America, where real wages were lower than they were in North America.

If segmentation was induced by discriminatory immigration policy or cultural preference, then it should be possible to assess its impact. Imagine the following counterfactual: what would Latin emigration rates have been like had they faced the same overseas labor market options that faced the potential British emigrant? We do not have the space here to offer a detailed answer, but we calculate tentatively that Latin emigrations in the 1890s and 1900s would have been higher by 5 per thousand. The more challenging question is to assess the impact of the counterfactually higher emigration on the Latin economies. Would the greater labor scarcity at home have raised Latin living standards considerably, perhaps helping the Latin economies join the convergence process much earlier? This and another question make for an exciting research agenda: why did so few Latins head for the most dynamic high-wage destinations, thereby doing so little to break down international labor market segmentation in the late nineteenth century?

NOTES

* This chapter relies on a data base reported in Hatton and Williamson (1994), but a number of scholars have helped us construct the additional Portuguese data used here. These have our grateful thanks: Maria Baganha, Toni Estevadeordal and Jaime Reis. In addition, we are grateful for the excellent research assistance of Steve Saeger. A longer version of this chapter, with appendix materials, is available upon request from Jeffrey G. Williamson, 216 Littauer Center, Harvard University, Cambridge, Massachusetts 02138 USA.

1 If we rely on urban wage rates to measure wage gaps between countries then the declining agricultural employment share may have an offsetting effect. Agricultural wages are typically lower than those in the cities, so a fall in the agricultural employment share should raise the average wage by more than the urban wage would suggest. Controlling only for the urban wage, a fall in the agricultural employment share might therefore reduce emigration.

2 This contrasts with our cross-section finding that Portuguese fundamentals surged from 1890 to the 1900s.

4

ITALIAN EMIGRATION IN THE PREWAR PERIOD

Riccardo Faini and Alessandra Venturini

INTRODUCTION

For more than a century, and since the country's unification in 1861, Italians have migrated abroad trying to escape poverty and deprivation at home. Migration, therefore, has been an enduring feature in Italian economic life. As in many other aspects of her history, even for migration, however, Italy is somewhat of a latecomer on the international arena. Indeed, until the end of the century, Italian emigration was only for a relatively small share of the country's population and did not provide a substantial contribution to the massive population movements which pervade the New and the Old World. The picture changes quite dramatically at the beginning of the twentieth century. From 1901 until 1913, 8.1 million people emigrated from Italy. On average each year 1.9 percent of the Italian population moved abroad in search of better living conditions. They went both to the Americas and to the rest of Europe and they represented a sizeable part of worldwide migrations.

As emphasized by many historians (Gould 1980b; Hatton and Williamson 1992b), the pattern of Italian emigration is somewhat puzzling. In the wake of unification, Italy was to a large extent a relatively poor and mainly agricultural country. In the second half of the nineteenth century, Italy fell further behind the industrializing world. Relative economic stagnation led to a widening income gap with the traditional destination countries. Yet, the outflow of emigrants, when measured relative to population is below the level achieved in other European countries. At the beginning of the century, the Italian economy took off on the road toward industrial development. Rapid output growth at home meant falling income differentials with the receiving countries. Yet, it is precisely during these years of fast income and employment growth that emigration registered a massive surge, with a steadily increasing share of the Italian population resolving to move abroad.

This chapter tries to uncover the reasons which underlie this behavior. Of course, the presence of a positive link between domestic income and emigration is not entirely new in the literature. In this chapter we argue that the most-cited factors, such as demographic explanations or the fall in transport costs, cannot fully account for the observed pattern. Our results indicate that the steady increase in emigration is explained by the greater well-being in the country which, somewhat paradoxically, prompted an increasing number of people to migrate, and by faster employment growth in the receiving countries which provided wider job opportunities for potential Italian migrants. We depart therefore from existing literature (Gould 1980a) by arguing that the surge in Italian emigration after 1900 cannot be predicated mostly on "diffusion" effects coming from the emulative impact of previous migrants' experience.[1] Undoubtedly, factors such as the spread of better information about working conditions abroad and the desire to emulate other people's success may have been quite important. Our results, however, indicate that changing economic conditions at home and in the main destination countries were instrumental in favoring the surge in migrations after 1900.

The chapter is organized as follows. In the next section, we briefly review the evidence on Italian migrations. We also discuss some of the theoretical explanations which have been put forward in the literature to explain the positive link between income and migrations. We then present our econometric evidence based on pooled migration data from the prewar period. The final section offers some conclusions.

ITALIAN MIGRATIONS, 1861–1913

There is little information about Italian migrations prior to the country's unification. The Italian census of 1861 indicates that at that time there were significant Italian settlements in several foreign countries. Receiving countries' data also show that, starting earlier in the century, Italians had begun moving abroad. However, the numbers involved were quite small. Between 1869 and 1876, intercontinental emigrants from Europe averaged 300,000 each year. Italy however did not provide a significant contribution to this flow. According to Carpi (1972), intercontinental migrations from Italy between 1869 and 1876 averaged about 24,000 per annum. Therefore, only 8 percent of Europe's intercontinental migrants were originating from Italy during this period. Even as a percentage of the sending country's population, Italy was not, at least initially, a large player in the emigration market. In the decade after 1876 only 1.05 percent of the Italian population chose to move to the Americas against, for instance, 5.18 percent in the British Isles (excluding Ireland) (Hatton and Williamson 1992b).

Twenty years later the situation had radically changed. Italians were providing the bulk of European migrations. Between 1901 and 1913 almost 5 million Italians migrated to the Americas, with an average annual flow larger than 360 thousand (Ferenczi and Willcox 1931). For comparison, during the same period intercontinental migrations from Europe reached a yearly average of 1 million. Italy therefore was now providing more than a third of Europe's overseas migrants. Interestingly enough, the growing flow toward the Americas did not come at the expense of migrations to European destinations. As a matter of fact, it is during this very same decade that Italian migrations toward the rest of Europe registered a sizeable increase.

As argued earlier, there are some good reasons to be surprised both by the relatively low migration rate from Italy before 1900 and its surge afterwards. In the wake of unification, Italy was a poor and largely agricultural country. In 1870 the primary sector accounted for 62 percent of total employment against less than 50 percent for France, Germany and the USA. For the UK the figure was only 22.7 percent. Most of the industrial development at that time was concentrated in very few areas, namely Lombardy, Piedmont and a few firms in the region of Naples. The latter survived mainly because of heavy protection and privileged government procurements. Their demise was only a matter of time. Structural change was disappointingly slow. In 1900, the output share of the industrial sector had actually declined from 20 percent in 1870 to 19 percent. Income per capita grew at barely one-third of 1 percent in real terms during the same period. As shown in Figure 4.1, this modest performance led to a widening income gap with Europe and the United States.

Yet, the increasing attractiveness of both European and American destinations did not seem to lead to greater migrations. The long-run trend in emigration remained steady, despite strong annual oscillations, both in absolute (Figures 4.2–4.4) and in relative terms (Figure 4.5). It is difficult to

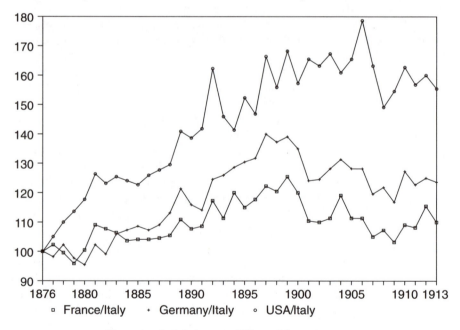

Figure 4.1 Italy's income differentials, 1876–1913

account for this evolution. One could argue perhaps that favorable employment trends in Italy dampened the propensity of risk-averse migrants to migrate, but the evidence is simply not there. Table 4.1 shows that, with the exception of France, Italy's employment growth during the period is never significantly larger than that of the main destination countries. Of course, fast employment growth may simply reflect a more rapid increase in population. If we compare, however, employment and population growth (Table 4.3) we find that Italy is typically characterized by a slower growth of employment relative to population, particularly between 1880 and 1900.

The puzzling behavior of Italian emigration becomes even more intriguing if we extend the analysis into the twentieth century. The Italian economy during the first fifteen years of the century takes its first rapid steps on the way toward industrialization. Structural change accelerates. From 1900 to 1913 the share of primary employment drops from 61 to 58 percent. In 1913 industrial output accounts for 23 percent of total GDP, against 19 in 1900. Per capita income growth finally picks up to average 1.7 percent over the period. The much-improved performance of the Italian economy is reflected in the falling income gap with the main destination countries (Figure 4.1). In turn, rapid output growth leads to a substantially faster increase in employment. The latter grows between 1900 and 1913 at an average annual rate of 0.92 percent, more than double the value in the previous period. Compared to population growth, the employment performance in Italy now approaches that in the receiving countries (Table 4.3). As noticed earlier, there is no sign, however, that this more favorable evolution leads to a decline in the rate of out-migrations. Quite to the contrary, starting just before 1900 all migration indicators register a surge. Italians migrate in increasingly larger

Table 4.1 Employment growth (average annual percentage change)

	France	Germany	Italy	UK	USA	Switzerland
1870–1880	0.10	0.73	0.66	0.55	2.78	0.58
1880–1890	0.25	0.87	0.46	1.30	2.57	0.40
1890–1900	0.23	1.40	0.45	1.10	2.06	1.27
1900–1913	0.22	2.26	0.92	1.20	2.92	1.71

Table 4.2 Population growth (average annual percentage change)

	France	Germany	Italy	UK	USA	Switzerland
1870–1880	−0.26	1.40	0.62	1.03	2.33	0.64
1880–1890	0.25	0.88	0.70	0.80	2.29	0.39
1890–1900	0.14	1.30	0.70	0.94	1.90	1.12
1900–1913	0.21	1.43	0.83	1.04	2.48	1.59

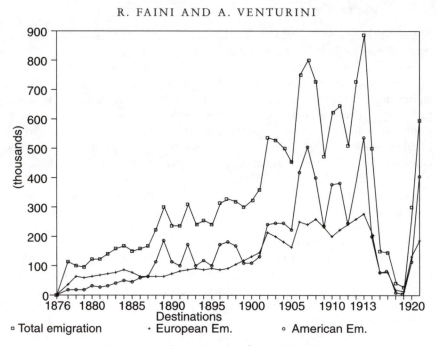

Figure 4.2 Italy: emigration flows, 1876–1920

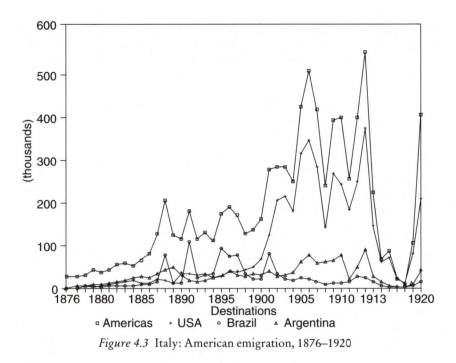

Figure 4.3 Italy: American emigration, 1876–1920

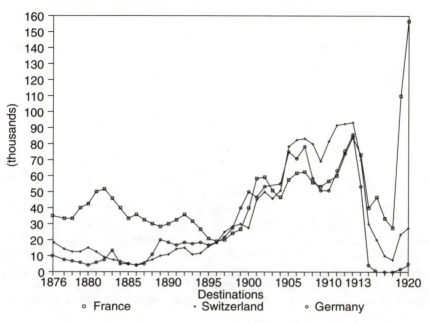

Figure 4.4 Italy: European emigration, 1876–1920

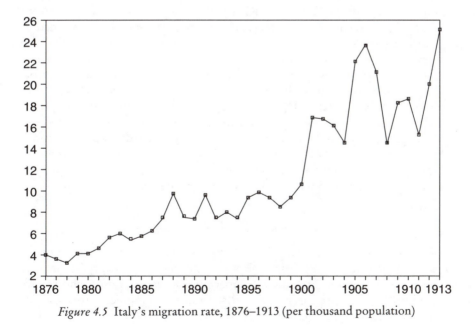

Figure 4.5 Italy's migration rate, 1876–1913 (per thousand population)

Table 4.3 Ratio of employment to population (average annual percentage change)

	France	Germany	Italy	UK	USA	Switzerland
1870–1880	−0.37	0.52	1.06	0.53	1.19	0.90
1880–1890	1.04	0.99	0.66	1.63	1.12	1.02
1890–1900	1.57	1.08	0.65	1.17	1.08	1.13
1900–1913	1.06	1.58	1.12	1.16	1.18	1.08

numbers, irrespective of destinations. A similar evolution is found if we consider the ratio of total migrants to population: from 1.1 percent in 1900 the migration rate jumps to 2.5 percent in 1913.

To sum up, there is little doubt that the behavior of income differentials and relative employment growth cannot fully account for the observed pattern of Italian migrations. This finding is somewhat puzzling. While economic historians tend to agree that income differentials have not played a major role in determining migrations, they also conclude that labor market conditions, in both the sending and the destination countries, have been a crucial determinant of migration decisions. For instance, Gould, in his review of the empirical evidence on migration behavior, argues that "unemployment variables have undoubtedly been more successful than the income ones" (1979: 636). Similarly, in his cross-section study, Easterlin (1961) finds very little role for the income variable. Relying on wages rather than on income does not seem to change the basic conclusion, as shown for instance by Quigley (1972), Pope (1968) and Richardson (1972). The Italian case seems to fit this general pattern. However, there are two new puzzles. First, income growth seems to bear a perverse rather than a negligible relationship with migrations. As Gould remarks, "Italian emigration to the U.S. reached massive proportions in precisely those years when the income differential between the two countries has ceased to widen and was indeed tending to narrow slightly" (1980b: 302). Second, and contrary to other evidence, labor market conditions do not appear to provide a promising avenue to account for the pattern of Italian migrations. Admittedly, more definite conclusions should await the test of more rigorous empirical verification. In the next section, we first discuss some further factors which may have affected the evolution of Italian emigration and then present our econometric results.

AN ECONOMETRIC ANALYSIS

To set the stage for our econometric analysis, we first review some of the factors other than income differentials and employment prospects which are typically cited in the literature as determining the migration choice. We consider two main approaches, one based on demographic factors and the other emphasizing the role of structural change in the economy.

Consider first the role of demography.[2] It is well-known that migrants are typically young adults, while older people are relatively less prone to move abroad. Intuitively, the discounted stream of the benefits from migrating is a negative function of age. This means that aggregate migrations will be a function of the age structure of population. Larger young adult cohorts should be associated with an aggregate greater propensity to migrate. Now demographic transition theory tells us that, when growth takes off, the fall in the infant death rate typically coincides with or precedes the rise in the birth rate, leading therefore to faster population growth and, some twenty years later, increasing the young adult cohort shares. This fact by itself should have a positive impact on migrations. It is not surprising therefore, according to this approach, that in the initial phases of economic growth we should have more rather than less emigration. In what follows, we test for this conjecture by introducing the rate of population growth fifteen (or twenty) years earlier. This variable should capture the effect of changes in the age structure of the population.

Economic growth can have other effects on the propensity to migrate besides its influence on the age composition. First, growth and industrialization are often associated with urbanization. The urban setting is typically more favorable to migrations because of the ease of communications, better transportation links with foreign countries, and better information on working opportunities abroad. Second, the initial phases of economic growth generally bring a deep restructuring in the agricultural sector where the introduction of more modern techniques, the redefinition of property rights and the overall increase in productivity will lead to a break-up in traditional economic links and the uprooting of a vast part of the rural population. Finally, economic growth should relax the financial and educational constraints which, in a relatively poor country, may prevent people from migrating. Paradoxically, this means that the more egalitarian growth is, the more likely it is that it will be accompanied by an increasing propensity to migrate. There is little hope that simple regression analysis can capture the host of social and economic factors which come with growth and impinge on the level of migrations. Furthermore, many of these factors are likely to be highly correlated and it would be extremely difficult to disentangle their effects. In what follows, we simply introduce among the explanatory variables the level of income in the origin country, in addition of course to the income differential between the sending and the receiving countries. The former variable should capture most of the factors (like urbanization, the falling share of agricultural employment, the lessening of financial and educational constraints) which, through the process of economic growth, are likely to increase emigration.

Finally, a further factor should be mentioned as impinging on the pattern of migrations. The second half of the nineteenth century was characterized by a substantial and steady decline in transportation costs. Falling transport costs should in turn lower the monetary costs of moving to foreign destinations and could therefore explain the rising trend in migrations.[3] There are at least two problems with this approach when one tries to account for the pattern of Italian migrations. First, the fall in transport costs was steady throughout the late nineteenth century, whereas the surge in Italian emigration is concentrated at the beginning of the twentieth century. Second, the decline in moving costs should have favored mainly overseas destinations. However, this is not what we observe given that, as mentioned earlier, migrations also increase substantially toward European destinations. In what follows, we try to account for this factor by introducing a time trend in the migration equation from Italy to the US.

The previous considerations suggest the estimation of the following model:

$$\ln(M_{it}/POP) = a_0 + a_1\ln(Y_{it}/Y_t) + a_2\ln Y_t + a_3 EG_{it} + a_4 EG_t + a_5 GPOP_{t-15} + a_6 t + e_t \tag{1}$$

where M_{it} denotes migration at time t to destination i, POP, EG and Y indicate population, employment growth and income in the sending country, Y_i and EG_i represent income and employment growth in the receiving country, while $GPOP$ and t stand for population growth and a time trend. We expect all coefficients to be positive except for a_4 which should be less than zero.

Equation (1) has been applied to emigration data from Italy to France, Germany and the US from 1876 to 1913. The choice of the destination countries is dictated by the availability of comparable data on income. We use initially an income rather than a wage variable, on the grounds that income per capita may be a better proxy of expected earnings for long-term moves. This may not be a palatable approach to Italian migrations, however, given the high rate of return migration, in particular after 1900. Therefore, we also investigate how the use of wage rather than income differentials affect our results. Both income and employment data are taken from Maddison (1982). Employment data however are available only at ten years intervals. We have interpolated the missing years by using domestic output data. Wage data come from Williamson (1994). Finally, migration data are taken from Ferenczi and Willcox (1929).

Estimation results, using income per capita as a proxy for Y, are presented in Table 4.4. We use a fixed-effect approach where the intercept is allowed to differ across destination countries, but slope coefficients are generally assumed to be the same (the only exception, as mentioned earlier, being the time trend which we postulate to be zero for France and Germany).[4] However, rather than stacking the data for the various receiving countries and estimating the equation by OLS, we follow a slightly different procedure. First, we define for each receiving country an equation like

Table 4.4 Determinants of migration (dependent variable: $\log(M_i/POP)$)

	(1)	*(2)*	*(3)*	*(4)*
D_{usa}	0.71	2.84	−3.01	−2.81
	(2.39)	(2.44)	(0.24)	0.22)
D_{fra}	0.12	2.28	2.48	2.50
	(2.64)	(2.00)	(2.05)	(2.07)
D_{ger}	0.36	2.49	2.65	2.67
	(1.96)	(2.19)	(2.23)	(2.25)
$\ln Y_i/Y$	0.60	0.56	0.53	0.53
	(2.32)	(2.24)	(2.03)	(2.03)
$\ln Y$	—	0.35	0.38	0.39
		(1.91)	(1.95)	(1.97)
EG_i	5.89	5.70	5.74	5.72
	(3.37)	(3.28)	(3.31)	(3.30)
EG	−0.95	−0.91	−0.91	−0.92
	(2.43)	(2.42)	(2.43)	(2.46)
$GPOP$	—	—	—	0.0001
				(0.41)
time	—	—	0.003	0.003
			(0.47)	(0.45)
$LDEP$	0.90	0.88	0.87	0.87
	(30.4)	(28.2)	(21.4)	(21.5)
Log. lik.	9.42	11.15	11.25	11.34
$\chi^2(2)$	6.44	6.92	7.08	2.08

Notes: Host country variables. D_i: country's i intercept; Y_i: per capita in country i; EG_i: employment growth in country i. Home country variables. POP: population; Y: income per capita; EG: employment growth; $GPOP$: lagged population growth; M_i: migration to country i; $LDEP$: lagged dep. variable.
T-statistics in parenthesis. χ^2: log. lik. test for equal intercepts. Sample period: 1877–1913.

equation (1). We then estimate the three resulting equations simultaneously by seemingly unrelated methods (SURE) imposing the (cross-equation) restrictions that all slope coefficients are identical across destinations. As noticed by Arellano (1987), this procedure is designed to yield efficiency gains to the extent that it can account for common time shocks to the migration equations in any given year.

In column 1, we report the equation with no time trend and no population growth variable. Here we abstract from the effect of demographic factors and declining transportation costs. We also set the coefficient on the level of domestic income, a_2, equal to zero. All coefficients are statistically different from zero and bear the right sign. Both an increase in the income gap with the destination countries and faster employment growth will boost emigration. Domestic employment growth on the other hand leads to lower emigration. As far as the statistical properties of the equations are concerned, they appear to be satisfactory. We have tested for a (common) pattern of serial correlation, but a standard Breusch–Godfrey test does not provide any reason for concern in this respect. Finally, the hypothesis of equal intercepts is rejected at a 5 percent confidence level.

In column 2, we extend the previous specification to include the level of domestic per capita income in the sending country. As noticed earlier, this variable should capture the (presumably positive) effect of rising domestic income on emigration through the lessening of financial and educational constraints, the disruption of the traditional pattern of production and the greater mobility associated with urbanization. The coefficient on 1n Y is, as expected, positive and (marginally) significantly different from zero, indicating therefore that rising income can account for the greater propensity to migrate in the last part of the period. Again, the standard tests do not provide any indications of misspecification. The hypothesis of common intercepts is rejected.

Next, we try to control for the effect of better transportation and communication facilities. Following a consolidated tradition in the literature (see for instance Hatton and Williamson 1992b), we simply assume that this factor can be captured by a time trend. We further postulate that declining transport costs had a significant impact on intercontinental migrations (i.e. to the US), but did not affect much European destinations. The results are presented in the third column of Table 4.4. The time-trend coefficient has the right sign but is not statistically different from zero. Furthermore, all the other coefficients in column 3 do not differ much from the results in the previous regression. We then investigate whether demographic factors play any role (besides their impact on the level of population) in affecting the pattern of migrations. Following Easterlin (1961), we introduce population growth lagged 15 years.[5] Even this variable does not seem to add much to the estimates. Its coefficient (column 4) is not statistically different from zero, while everything else stays basically unchanged.[6]

We then experiment in several directions to check the robustness of our results. First, we rely on a different specification for the dependent variable. In equation 1, we specified the model as determining the logarithm of the migration rate rather than M_{it}/POP, as most migration studies do. The choice is dictated by our theoretical model (Faini and Venturini, 1994). Yet, it is worth exploring how our results are affected by the use of a more traditional specification of the dependent variable. The new estimates are presented in Table 4.5 (column 2). The sample now covers only the 1882–1913 period (see note 5). For the purpose of comparison, we also report, in column 1, the equation with log (M_{it}/POP) as a dependent variable. There are two main changes: first, the coefficient on the time trend is now significantly different from zero; second, the value of the coefficient on the lagged dependent variables declines substantially (from 0.79 to 0.71) and is now more in line with existing evidence on migration behavior. Also, compared to Table 4.4, the coefficient on per capita income in Italy is much better determined. Everything else is virtually unchanged, including the

Table 4.5 Determinants of migration: alternative specifications

	*(1)**	*(2)*[†]	*(3)*[‡]
ln Y_i/Y	0.80	1.07	1.29
	(2.55)	(3.14)	(3.61)
ln Y	0.66	1.02	0.59
	(3.35)	(3.72)	(3.01)
EG_i	6.04	12.6	2.43
	(3.62)	(4.98)	(1.45)
EG	−0.71	−0.38	−0.83
	(1.97)	(.83)	(2.84)
$GPOP$	−0.001	−0.003	−0.0001
	(1.02)	(1.24)	(1.00)
time	0.004	0.09	0.006
	(0.69)	(3.15)	(0.80)
$LDEP$	0.79	0.71	0.71
	(17.3)	(14.6)	(13.5)
Log. lik.	16.35	−20.8	12.84
$\chi^2(2)$	7.15	10.7	11.9
$\chi^2(9)$	6.78	3.00	10.2

Notes: See Table 4.4.
Sample period: 1882–1913. Country intercepts have been omitted.
*with $\log(M_i/POP)$ as dependent variable.
[†]with M_i/POP as dependent variable.
[‡]with deviations from trend employment.
$\chi^2(2)$: log. lik. test for equal intercepts.
$\chi^2(9)$: Breusch–Godfrey serial correlation test.

insignificant role played by demographic factors.

The result that demographic considerations do not contribute to the explanation of migrations may be ascribed to the fact that we rely on actual rather than natural population growth. Computing the latter requires information on return migration, which is unavailable for the early years. We are indeed left with only 12 observations per destination countries. The results (not reported here) therefore should be taken with some caution. However, they do not indicate any enhanced role for demographic considerations. Finally, we look at whether different specifications of the employment variables affect our results. Following Hatton (1993), we take as a measure of employment conditions the deviation of actual from trend employment. This specification is better suited to capture Gould's (1979) conjecture, according to which labor market conditions have a strong effect on migration fluctuations, while long-run migratory trends depend on income differentials. The results are presented in column 3 of Table 4.5. Compared to column 1, the main change comes from the lower significance of the coefficient associated with foreign employment. Overall, though, even short of a rigorous non-nested test, we would tend to prefer the specification with employment growth. Indeed, the specification using deviations from

Table 4.6 Determinants of migration: wage differential

	(1)*	(2)†	(3)‡
ln Y_i/Y	0.55	0.31	0.62
	(2.14)	(1.51)	(2.22)
ln Y	1.13	1.21	1.21
	(3.90)	(3.51)	(3.97)
EG_i	5.37	12.3	2.88
	(3.27)	(4.18)	(1.76)
EG	−0.84	−0.54	−0.40
	(2.26)	(1.14)	(1.39)
$GPOP$	−0.0001	−0.001	−0.001
	(1.0)	(.84)	(1.13)
time	0.01	0.09	0.02
	(2.36)	(2.96)	(2.67)
$LDEP$	0.72	0.70	0.66
	(12.5)	(10.82)	(10.0)
Log. lik.	15.46	−24.1	9.85
$\chi^2(2)$	8.85	18.5	7.30
$\chi^2(9)$	8.54	3.72	19.01

Notes: See Table 4.4.
Sample period: 1882–1913. Country intercepts have been omitted.
*with $\log(M_i/POP)$ as dependent variable.
†with M_i/POP as dependent variable.
‡with deviations from trend employment.
$\chi^2(2)$: log. lik. test for equal intercepts.
$\chi^2(9)$: Breusch–Godfrey serial correlation test.

trend employment yields less precisely determined coefficients and a lower value of the maximized likelihood function.

We next investigate whether reliance on wage rather than income data affects our results in any significant way. Therefore, in equation (1), we replace the income differential, ln Y_i/Y, with the wage differential. Wages should provide a better indicator of earning opportunities both at home and abroad (Gould 1979). However, we retain income per capita as our indicator of development in the home country. Recall that the introduction of the income level in the sending country, in addition to the income differential between the home and the host countries, was motivated by the need to capture the impact of greater urbanization, diminished educational and financial constraints and better information on migrations. It is arguable that income per capita rather than wages may perform a better duty in this respect.[7] The econometric results are presented in Table 4.6. In column 1, we present our basic specification. In column 2, we use as a dependent variable the migration rate rather than its log, while in column 3 we take the deviation from trend employment as the indicator of labor market conditions both at home and abroad. Several facts stand out from Table 4.6. First, the impact of the level of domestic income on

Table 4.7 Determinants of migration: aggregate equation

	(1)	(2)	(3)
Constant	11.55	4.33	4.69
	(3.22)	(0.16)	(0.18)
ln Y_i/Y	0.94	0.88	0.92
	(2.93)	(2.28)	(2.34)
ln Y	1.88	1.76	1.76
	(3.25)	(2.38)	(2.37)
EG_i	5.60	5.59	5.51
	(2.87)	(2.81)	(2.75)
EG	−0.20	−0.26	−0.27
	(1.15)	(.98)	(1.02)
$GPOP$	—	—	−.001
			(0.74)
time	—	0.003	0.003
		(0.28)	(0.26)
$LDEP$	0.58	0.57	0.56
	(5.28)	(4.36)	(4.31)
R^2	0.96	0.96	0.96
DW	1.64	1.62	1.65
Chow	0.97	0.89	0.89
Hendry	1.27	1.18	1.26
LM	1.63	2.24	1.97

Notes: See Table 4.4.
The Chow, Hendry and LM procedures test for structural stability, predictive power and serial correlation respectively. The Chow test is distributed as $F_{1,30}$, while the LM and Hendry tests are both distributed as χ^2 with one degree of freedom.

migration is quite well determined, suggesting again that the process of economic growth has a distinct impact on migration besides the one working through income and wage differentials. Second, the size of the coefficient on employment abroad highlights the crucial role that labor market conditions in the destination countries play in affecting migration. Finally, the coefficient on the time trend is now consistently positive and quite well determined. As argued earlier, this may indicate that lower transportation costs may have facilitated migrations, but it could also point to the role that better information about life and employment prospects abroad may have had in promoting migrations. The statistical properties of the estimates appear to be satisfactory. There is no indication (with the exception of the equation using the deviation of actual from trend employment) of serial correlation. Also, the hypothesis of equal intercept is systematically rejected.

One shortcoming of our approach is that the decision to migrate to a given destination is a function only of economic conditions there and in the home country. Thus, we have little to say about the choice of destination. One possible way out would be to include among the regressors the relevant variables describing economic conditions in the alternative destinations. Degrees of freedom considerations militate against this approach. Alternatively, one could rely on a multinomial logit or probit model. In what follows, we take a simpler route and concentrate on aggregate migrations from Italy. Income and employment growth in the destination countries are now (weighted) averages across host countries of the relevant variables. The results are presented in Table 4.7. Only the regression with the wage differential is reported. The results, particularly those related to income and employment factors, broadly confirm those of the fixed effect model. Demographic factors once again do not appear to affect migrations. Interestingly enough, the coefficient on the time trend is not significantly different from zero. Recall that, in the fixed effect model, we found the time trend to affect migrations to the US but not to other destinations. Unsurprisingly, with aggregate data, this positive trend effect becomes more difficult to identify.

To sum up, our econometric results indicate that demographic factors and, in the case of European destinations, falling transport and communication costs cannot account for the pattern of Italian migrations. Also, as noticed earlier, the surge in the flow of migrants at the beginning of the twentieth century cannot be predicated on the behavior of either the income gap with the destination countries or domestic employment growth. Both factors would point instead to a reduction rather than an increase in the level of emigration. We are therefore inclined to favor two explanations. The first one stresses the role of employment growth in the host countries. The very large coefficient associated with this variable indicates that even modest increases in labor demand in destination countries would elicit a strong migration response. The second approach emphasizes the role of income growth in the domestic country. As argued more formally by Faini and Venturini (1994), initially higher domestic income will release the constraints on would-be migrants and lead to higher migrations. Changing patterns of production, rising urbanization and the disruption of traditional modes of life will also act in the same direction. All these factors are highly correlated with income growth and it would be hazardous to try to separate their effects.

We are left with the claim that income growth (at least starting from low levels of development) will lead to more migrations. To further quantify this effect, we can use our estimated coefficients to answer the following hypothetical question. Suppose that income per capita in Italy had stayed at its 1900 level until the war, while all other variables, including the income differential with the host countries, had followed their historical pattern. How would the pattern of migrations have changed? Based on our estimates in Table 4.4, we find that a large portion of the emigration surge can indeed be attributed to rising income in the domestic economy. Had Italy's income per capita remained unchanged from its 1900 value, emigration in 1913 would have been almost 10 percent lower than its fitted value. More than 30 percent of the increase in migrations from 1900 to 1913 is therefore accounted for by the increase in income per capita. If we consider the estimates in Table 4.6, which rely on the wage rather than the income differentials, the impact of greater economic welfare at home is even stronger. Indeed, we find that, with income per capita at its 1900 value, migrations in 1913 would have been 27 percent lower than their fitted value. This finding is not surprising in view of the much larger coefficient associated with the level of domestic income that one gets when using the wage rather than the income differential.

THE REGIONAL PATTERN OF ITALIAN MIGRATIONS

By focusing on aggregate Italian migrations, we have so far abstracted from the pattern of migrations within Italy. Yet, the regional differentiation within the Italian economy should probably reflect on the pattern of migrations. Geographical dualism being an increasingly pervasive feature of the Italian economy, it is likely that the motivations to migrate differed significantly among Italian regions. By not distinguishing between northern and southern Italian migrations, we are to some extent guilty, or at least suspect, of an aggregation bias.

The size of interregional income differentials in the wake of Italy's unification has been the object of some controversy. Eckaus (1961) shows convincingly that already in 1861 the Mezzogiorno lagged behind the rest of Italy in terms of income, industrial development and agricultural productivity. Yet, as noticed earlier, economic backwardness was certainly not limited to the South. Therefore, it is not entirely surprising to find that between 1876 and 1900 the pattern of migrations was not biased toward the South. On the contrary, we find that the North, with 62 percent of the country's population, accounts for 71 percent of total migration during this period. Where northern and southern Italy differ is in the geographical pattern of destination countries. Migrants from the Mezzogiorno typically go overseas. Between 1876 and 1900, only 12 percent of southern Italian migrants headed toward Europe. In sharp contrast, more than 65 percent of migrants from the North went to Europe.

After 1900, migrations surge both in northern and southern Italy. The increase, though, is more pronounced in the latter area. On an average annual basis, the absolute number of migrants more than doubled in the North (from 150 thousand in the period 1876–1900 to 339 thousand from 1901–13), but increased more than four times in the South (from 61 thousand to 288 thousand). As a result, the regional pattern of migration became biased toward the Mezzogiorno. With 30 percent of the country's population, this region accounted for 46 percent of total emigration. As in the previous period, overseas destinations accounted for the lion's share of southern Italian migrations.

Clearly enough, there are significant differences in the pattern of migrations among Italian regions, particularly after 1900. Before that time, investigating Italian migrations at an aggregate (national) level is probably not too misleading. Still, as shown by MacDonald (1963), the regional pattern of migrations in Italy is quite complex. Factors such as labor militancy and land tenure in rural areas may have played a crucial role in favoring or discouraging labor emigration.[8] Their effects, however, cannot be easily captured in the context of an econometric study. More crucially, these factors cannot explain the basic puzzle which motivated the writing of this chapter, i.e. why migrations surged at the very same time that economic conditions should have acted to reduce the propensity to move abroad. Overall, we feel that many interesting insights can still come from an aggregate analysis of Italian migrations. Finally, Klein (1983: 315) and Gould (1980a) offer convincing evidence showing a reduction of regional variation in the choice of destination. This provides, we believe, further legitimacy to an aggregate approach.

Moreover, a thorough analysis of the regional pattern of Italian migrations is prevented by the lack of adequate time series on regional migrations and, more crucially, the virtual absence of any information on the historical behavior of regional income. We can only say that, particularly after 1900, Italian migrations become increasingly a southern phenomenon. The process, however, was slow. Reliable information on the interwar period is not available. It is worth noting, however, that even in 1951 there were still more migrants from the richer North (162 thousand) than from the poorer South (131 thousand). Ten years later, however, the situation had changed radically. The flow of migrants from northern Italy had dropped by 40 percent, to 98 thousand. In contrast, migrations from the Mezzogiorno to foreign destinations had more than doubled reaching 268 thousand in 1962. To this figure we should also add the growing number of southern Italians who, during these very same years, migrated in response to a booming economy in northern Italy.

CONCLUSIONS

We have attempted in this chapter to investigate the determinants of Italian emigration in the 1876–1913 period, focusing in particular on the surge after 1900. We have argued that neither the behavior of income differentials, nor the evolution of domestic employment, can by themselves explain the observed pattern. Furthermore, our econometric results suggest that this pattern cannot be predicated either by demographic factors or, to a large extent, by falling transport costs. To account for the massive increase in Italian migrations at the turn of the century, we rely on two complementary explanations: first, the rapid increase in labor demand in destination countries (particularly in the US) which, as indicated by the large coefficient estimate associated with this variable, had a strong pulling effect on Italian migrants; second, the effect of income growth in Italy which, somewhat paradoxically, prompted more people to migrate. Compared to previous literature, we do not attribute the surge in migrations at the beginning of the twentieth century to "diffusion" effects of previous migrations. As in Pope (1981a) and Gould (1979),[9] we stress the role of financial constraints in limiting migrations, but offer a somewhat broader interpretation of the impact of better economic conditions at home. Finally, our simulations suggest that rising domestic income may indeed account for a significant share of the emigration increase.

The inability to distinguish between regional migration flows from Italy is certainly a weakness of our analysis. A thorough investigation of this issue will require, however, a massive research effort to improve our basic knowledge of southern Italian economic history.

NOTES

1   In Gould's words, "the great upsurge in emigration from the South and East Europe was caused, in large part, by the progress of the diffusion of emigration in potentially emigration-prone areas" (1980b: 302).

2   For an analysis of demographic changes in the Italian regions and their potential impact on the migratory flows see Di Comite (1986). For a comparative assessment across all European emigration countries, see Chapter 3 (by Hatton and Williamson) and the classic paper by Easterlin (1961).

3   Historians disagree somewhat on the role of transport costs in affecting migrations. According to MacDonald, "the part played by variations in the ability to pay transportation costs has been exaggerated" (1963: 63). Similarly, Gould (1979) argues that better information rather than cheaper transportation was instrumental in favoring migrations.

4   Throughout the chapter we have tested the validity of the hypothesis of equal slope coefficients. In no case, did this hypothesis come close to being rejected. We therefore feel that pooling across destination countries is, in our case, quite appropriate.

5   By using population growth lagged 20 years, we would lose five observations. To maintain comparability with the previous results, we report in the last column of Table 4.4 the estimates with $GPOP_{t-15}$. We then introduce in Table 4.5 population growth lagged 20 years. In Table 4.5, therefore, the sample starts in 1882 rather than in 1877.

6   The hypothesis of equal intercepts across destination countries, however, is no longer rejected.

7   In Chapter 3, Hatton and Williamson appear to disagree. They use real wages while adding proxies for the correlates of development.

8   MacDonald (1963) does not deny the role of economic factors. He argues, however, that three choices were available to potential poor migrants: labor militancy, acceptance of the *status quo*, or migration. The choice between these

alternatives depended to a significant extent on the pattern of land tenure.

9   In a slightly different context, Gould observes that "while a high rate of unemployment in that country might be expected to strengthen the wish to migrate, it might reduce the ability to do so" (1979: 635).

5

MASS MIGRATION TO DISTANT SOUTHERN SHORES

Argentina and Australia, 1870–1939[*]

Alan M. Taylor

INTRODUCTION

In the course of the century leading up to the First World War about 44 million people left Europe for the New World. This mass migration started small and grew very large as cheaper ocean transport, principally the steamship, opened up the frontiers of the Americas and Australasia to the masses of the Old World. More emigrants came from the British Isles (16 million) than from any other source, and more immigrants chose the United States (32 million) as their destination than any other point. These two labor markets had, of course, been linked since before the turn of the nineteenth century. In time, however, the evolving international labor market developed connections to a multitude of national labor markets. In the years after 1880 a flood of poorer migrants from southern Europe joined the established waves leaving Britain, Ireland, Germany and other northern European countries (Kenwood and Lougheed 1983: Ch. 3).

This unprecedented intercontinental factor reallocation – associated, moreover, with massive exports of capital to the New World – has long attracted the attention of economic historians (Nurkse 1954; Easterlin 1961; Baldwin 1956). Some have focused on the patterns of development in the regions of recent settlement, where a dual scarcity of labor and capital entailed the importation of these mobile factors (McLean 1990; Taylor 1991). One of the best general accounts of international factor movements in the late-nineteenth-century remains the study by Green and Urquhart (1976). In seeking to identify the dynamics of this process of factor transfer, however, authors have generally chosen to analyze the two factors separately (Richardson 1972 is an exception). Studies on the export of British capital are numerous (Davis and Huttenback 1986; Edelstein 1981, 1982; Hall 1968 (1963b on Britain and Australia); Ford 1962, 1971; Williams 1920 on Britain and Argentina), but quantitative treatments of international migration are relatively scarce. Notable exceptions are the United States (Williamson 1974b) and Australia (Kelley 1965; Pope 1976, 1981a, 1981b, 1987; Pope and Withers 1990; Withers 1989), where a long tradition of studying immigration has been established. This chapter seeks to build on that tradition by modeling migration responses in an internationally comparable framework for two important destinations in the Southern Hemisphere: Argentina and Australia. The novelty lies in extending this framework to Argentina – first, to study Argentine immigration dynamics in their own right; and, second, to place those results in comparative perspective.

It should be remembered that, after the United States, Australia and Argentina were the principal New World receiving regions: Argentina taking in 4.7 million over the period 1821–1915, Australia 4.3 million (Kenwood and Lougheed 1983: Ch. 3). However, immigration rates were much higher in Argentina from the late 1800s, and immigration was the dominant source of population growth until 1913. The absorption and assimilation problems posed by this huge influx, and the demographic burden their rapid arrival and procreation soon entailed, characterized the boom years of *belle époque* Argentina, the rapid growth of Buenos Aires into a leading city of the world, and the final push to close the Pampean frontier as Argentina's agricultural export industries reached maturity.

In the following section I discuss the immigration history of Argentina during the period 1870–1939. The natural baseline for comparison is Australia, the other principal receiving region in the Southern Hemisphere. Both countries had similar size and location, and both relied on agricultural exports and factor inflows, so it is no surprise that the comparative tradition runs deep (Korol 1991 provides a good survey of this literature). I then develop what appears to be the first econometric model applied to explain Argentine immigration. A comparison with Australia illustrates the unusual features of the Argentine case: a historically determined cultural linkage with a low-wage migrant pool in southern Europe, as distinct from an exclusionary immigration policy designed to preserve Anglo-Celtic ethnic dominance and shore up wage levels.

The key finding in the chapter is that by a policy choice which excluded migrants (whether for reasons of race, culture or economics) a country such as Australia could inhibit immigration by muting the response of low-wage workers to potential wage-gap gains. In contrast, Argentina, although her migrants were no more responsive to wage gaps than those going to Australia, inevitably faced larger inflows and the threat of greater demographic burdens simply by opening the door to the poor masses of southern Europe. This observation not only illuminates the immigration history of Argentina, but also informs our interpretation of immigration policy debates in Australia and the United States over exactly why they desired to keep such migrants out.

CULTURE, POLICY AND PREJUDICE: A SEGMENTED INTERNATIONAL LABOR MARKET

In this section I discuss the salient features of Argentine and Australian immigration in the late nineteenth and early twentieth centuries. It will be seen that both streams had a tendency to respond to fluctuating business conditions in the sending and receiving countries, and that migration to both countries played an important role in population growth. These similarities aside, the composition of the two migrant streams reveals the very different nature of these labor markets. Australia drew from high-wage, white, northern European labor markets, principally Britain. Argentina drew from low-wage, Latin, southern European labor markets, principally Italy and Spain. These contrasting origins, both unusual in the context of the global pattern of emigration from Europe, explain, in part, the very different impact of immigration on the two countries, and, in particular, the much more rapid population growth and heavier demographic burdens peculiar to Argentina on the eve of the First World War.

Argentine immigration experience

Over the latter half of the nineteenth century, Argentine immigration grew from a small trickle to become one of the principal currents in the international labor market. For a general survey of this expansion the reader may consult Bunge and Garcia Mata (1931) and Díaz-Alejandro (1970), the sources from which the following observations are largely drawn. As is apparent, the literature is rich with assertions concerning the role of immigration, its determinants and responsiveness – a useful starting point as we prepare to formulate a migration model and testable hypotheses.

In the years 1857 to 1880 Argentine immigration increased slowly, albeit with many fluctuations. Migrants were reportedly deterred by occasional outbreaks of hostilities between Buenos Aires and neighboring provinces, and, after 1865, "because of the bloody war against the tyrant Lopez of Paraguay" (Bunge and Garcia Mata 1931: 148). Migration was temporarily depressed by a yellow fever epidemic in the city of Buenos Aires in 1871. A trough in the business cycle is supposed to have placed a firmer brake on immigration during the years 1875–80, as did revolutions in 1874 and 1880, and an episode of money-printing and inflationary crisis in the years 1874–6. In the decade of the 1880s immigration picked up once more, coinciding with the boom years of 1887 to 1889, and the influx grew to previously unseen magnitudes. This was in part a response to a government assistance program whereby money was advanced to immigrants to cover the cost of passage.

In these years Roca's regime expanded the public debt enormously following favorable export growth in the early 1880s, but the economy overextended itself in this respect and, as consumption and imports soared, and export earnings lagged, a series of defaults on loans taken out in London heralded the crash and a period of austere adjustment. The Baring Crisis, as it is known, remains one of the best known crises in the study of international finance, and its impact on the Argentine economy should not be under-estimated. Migration flows plummeted in its wake and the assistance scheme was hastily dismantled.

Despite the continuing depression of the 1890s, immigration again grew large, with annual inflows averaging 67,000 for the years 1891–1903, and net inflows around 30,000. After 1904, however, the flows expanded rapidly as a decade-long wave of migration began that was to exceed all precedents. In those ten years about 2.4 million migrants entered, roughly 240,000 per year. The net inflow was about 1.5 million, indicative of the large return currents which arose during this era. There is ample qualitative evidence suggestive of the integration of the Argentine labor market with those of Europe during the period, and the links with Italy and Spain have received special attention. It was often the case that European workers would cross the ocean just to participate in the Pampean harvests, returning north upon completion of their labors. These were the "birds of passage" whose bi-directional currents provided a remarkable pool of "floating migrants" in the trans-Atlantic labor market, particularly in the period 1907–13.

According to Bunge and Garcia Mata, by the time the First World War broke out, the huge influx of migrants had already caused serious absorption problems in the Argentine labor market, notwithstanding the rapid growth of the economy during the *belle époque* years (Bunge and Garcia Mata 1931: 151). Supposedly, assimilation on this scale proved difficult to sustain, and worsening employment prospects in late 1913 depressed immigration rates considerably, even before the declaration of war.

Immigration remained paralyzed during the war years, with an average yearly net emigration of 19,000 during 1914–19, and it did not revive until the early 1920s, as the after-effects of war dragged on. A depression in Argentina maintained its grip as the terms-of-trade slump persisted. Sluggish activity in international shipping was reflected in the high costs of ocean passage which inhibited the "birds of passage" and left global migration levels far below those of the immediate prewar surge. None the less, by the mid-twenties, migration rates had bounced back to 1890s levels (Figure 5.1), only to fall off again during the Great Depression.

Díaz-Alejandro asserts that Argentina's immigrant supply was extremely elastic during most of the period, both prewar and postwar:

> Before 1930 Argentina could be said to have faced a labor supply schedule made up of two segments: the first one, consisting of most of the labor force already in the country, was probably fairly inelastic with respect to the real wage rate; the second one, applicable for needs slightly below and beyond the labor force already in the country, was

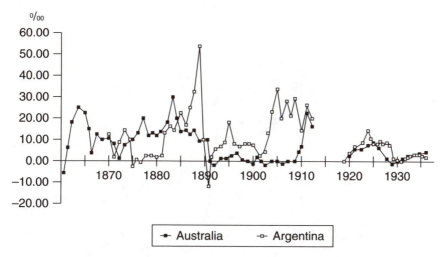

(a) Net immigration rates, Australia and Argentina, 1860–1939

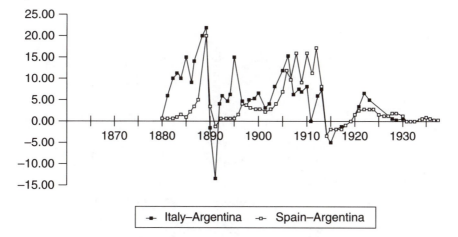

(b) Net immigration rates, Argentina from Italy and Spain, 1860–1939

Figure 5.1 Immigration rates, Australia and Argentina, 1860–1939
Source: See appendix at end of chapter.

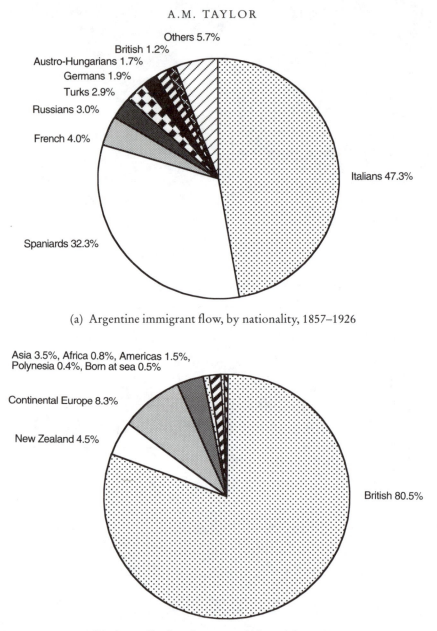

(a) Argentine immigrant flow, by nationality, 1857–1926

(b) Australian immigrant stock, by origin, 1921

Figure 5.2 Immigrant origins, Argentina and Australia
Sources: Bunge and García Mata (1931: 153); McPhee (1931: 173).

more elastic and, as a simplification, could be said to have been perfectly elastic at the going real wage rate (plus some differential) in the industrial centers of Italy and Spain, the main sources of emigration to Argentina.

(Díaz-Alejandro 1970: 21–2)

The basic idea is supported by the rough correlation of the migration flows (Figure 5.1) and the business cycle. However, these crude correlates are best treated with caution as they could support a number of competing hypotheses. For example, were migrants elastic in supply with respect to wage changes? Or were they responsive to changing unemployment conditions, perhaps in the manner of an expected-wage migration model of the Harris–Todaro type? Whatever the appropriate model, it is certain that an effective explanation of the patterns of Argentine immigration over the period would aid our understanding of the growth of the economy.[1]

In the latter half of this chapter I develop and apply a simple model of migration to account for Argentine immigration experience over the pre- and post-First World War periods. The lack of any formal model of Argentine immigration is remarkable given the paramount importance of immigration in the country's population and labor supply growth before 1913. About half of Argentina's population expansion in the period after 1890 can be attributed to immigration, while it was about 30 percent in the case of Australia.[2] In 1914, foreign-born workers comprised over 40 percent of the Argentine labor force, and more than half the population of the Federal District (Díaz-Alejandro 1970). Another striking feature is the cultural differentiation of Argentine immigrant streams from other New World countries. The Argentine inflow was roughly 47 percent Italian and 32 percent Spanish; in Australia, however, the inflow was over 80 percent British (Figure 5.2). More generally, the Argentine share in the migratory flows of non-Latin peoples was small compared with those of Australia, Canada and the United States (Díaz-Alejandro 1970: 24).

The broad picture, then, is one of international labor market segmentation, along a Latin versus non-Latin divide (or, put another way, a southern versus northern European divide). The impression is confirmed when we compare the experience of Argentina and Australia with the global pattern of migration in the late nineteenth century. On the receiving end, the main destination of migrants in the period was the United States, which took in 31.9 million people, or 61.8 percent of total immigration. The next most important destinations were Argentina (4.7 million, 9.1 percent) and Australasia (4.3 million, 8.3 percent), followed by Canada (4.2 million, 8.1 percent). On the sending side, Britain was the prime source of the migrants from the Old World, supplying 16.1 million emigrants over the period 1821–1915, or 36.9 percent of total European emigration. Latin countries were also an important migrant source: Italy accounted for 8 million

97

emigrants (18.3 percent) over these years; Spain and Portugal sent 4.6 million abroad (10.6 percent) (Kenwood and Lougheed 1983: 58–9).

Two points emerge: first, it is worth noting that, aside from the flows to the United States, this study focuses on some of the principal streams in the late-nineteenth-century global labor market; second, these streams are quite atypical in composition and illustrate the segmentation of that labor market.

Australian comparisons

A comparison with Australian experience highlights the distinctive features of the Argentine case. The Australian inflows exhibited comparable fluctuations over the business cycle during the entire sample period (Figure 5.1). It should be noted that in the earlier years, Australian inflows were much more significant than the Argentine inflows. The 1860s were years of buoyant economic performance in Australia following the Victorian gold rush of the previous decade. Migrant labor was drawn in large numbers, and relatively high rates of immigration were observed through the stable period of economic growth up to 1890. Only during the great surge of the late 1880s did Argentine immigration rates exceed those of Australia, as a wave of Latin migrants joined the mounting exodus from southern Europe (Kenwood and Lougheed 1983: 62).

However, as in Argentina, a major depression set in for the 1890s, heralded by the crash in the Melbourne real-estate market in 1890. The downward pressure on wages and the protests of organized labor made the 1890s a watershed in Australian labor history. In terms of the prospects for immigrants, however, the gains made by labor within Australia often entailed tougher entry conditions, as policy-makers struggled to protect the standard of living. Major changes were implemented in the assisted migration program and in the procedures used to exclude undesirable migrants.[3]

The notion of assisted migration schemes runs a long way back in Australian immigration history. Early pioneers of colonization schemes, such as Edward Gibbon Wakefield and his associates, had already helped establish in Britain a number of subsidized emigration ventures – including the notorious South Australian colony which had to be salvaged from bankruptcy by the Crown.[4] Publicly subsidized emigration from Britain, facilitated for many years by the colonization societies and the Poor Law agencies, declined in importance after the 1850s. Increasingly, subsidized immigration came to the fore: between 1861 and 1900 over 388,000 assisted migrants reached Australia, out of a net inflow of 767,000. High unemployment rates in the 1890s made the notion of assisted immigration highly unpopular. Unsurprisingly, this publicly subsidized source of competing labor, thought to undermine the wages and employment opportunities of the indigenous work-force, became a target for elimination. Levels of assisted migration dropped to a trickle: only 17,700 entered in the first decade of the twentieth century, although the schemes were resurrected in New

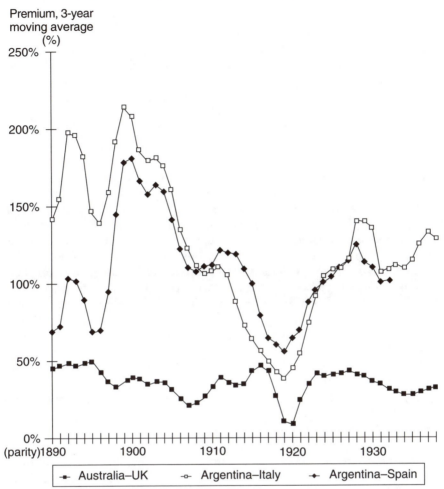

Figure 5.3 Wage gaps between Argentina, Australia and their principal sending
regions
Source: Williamson (1991).
Notes: Based on Williamson's database consisting of national real-wage indices and
international real-wage benchmarks calculated using purchasing-power parities. The pre-1913
benchmarks are used throughout. The wage gap shown is the premium, defined as $(W_R/W_S - 1)$,
where W_R is the wage in the receiving region, and W_S is the wage in the sending region.
Three-year moving averages are displayed.

South Wales and Victoria as recovery advanced in 1906 and 1907. The assisted
migration schemes rose to new importance – both in the decade 1905–14 and
briefly during the interwar period – but a pro-British bias was evident. The
assisted passage scheme once more failed to ride out hard times, however, and
even after joint-British funding was agreed upon under the Empire Settlement
Act of 1922, it was abandoned in 1929 with the onset of depression.[5]

It could be argued that assistance was simply not necessary in Argentina, as compared with Australia. Migrants leaving Italy and Spain for Argentina, faced the prospect of wage levels two to three times higher than in their native countries, whereas the British migrants heading for Australia were opting for a wage typically 20–50 percent above home levels (Figure 5.3). However, absolute wage levels were much lower in southern Europe, say half of British levels, so it might have been the case that some potential migrants to Argentina were trapped close to subsistence, under credit constraints, and with no prospect of saving up the money needed for passage. The question remains open, although Díaz-Alejandro asserts that migration to Argentina needed fewer, if any, subsidies (Díaz-Alejandro 1985: 103).

Aspiring immigrants to Australia unlucky enough to be born outside the British Isles faced significant obstacles to entry on account of their origin. Australia had for most of the century operated a *de facto* "White Australia" policy, actively excluding the Asian migrant pool. Potential entrants from Mediterranean or eastern European regions were also thought undesirable and various devices were employed to prevent them landing – the story that immigration inspectors of the late nineteenth century could offer a "dictation test" to immigrants in any European language of *their* (the inspectors') choosing has achieved almost folklore status. For the most part, the preferred inflow was of northern European origin, predominantly Anglo-Celtic (Offer 1989; Pope 1981a: 37). Shortly after Federation in 1901, the "White Australia" policy was codified in new Commonwealth legislation heavily backed by the unions. By twisting the "prices" this time, further discouragement to the Latin migrant stream was achieved. Landing money requirements for Britons were typically about £3; for poorer southern Europeans, between £50 and £200 (Pope 1981b: 36; Pope 1987: 44).

The "White Australia" exclusion policy effectively robbed the emigrants of poorer southern Europe of a competing destination in the Southern Hemisphere, and maintained the segmentation of the international labor market. As Díaz-Alejandro notes:

The pre-1929 world witnessed massive migrations, but the "international labor market" remained segmented by culture, policy and prejudice ... Argentina and Brazil connected primarily with the labor markets of Southern Europe ... Australia, in contrast, limited its connections to north-western Europe, primarily the British Isles ... Emigrants also had the choice of migrating to the United States or the white dominions, which was a choice made often by Italians but not by Spaniards. On balance, Australia's more restrictive immigration policy placed a higher floor under home wages, and this variety of labor protectionism had probably a greater importance for the welfare of workers within Australia than the celebrated Australian tariff. For excluded migrants, however, the contemplation of advanced Australian social legislation must have proved poor consolation.

(Díaz-Alejandro 1985: 102–3)

In summary, the composition of Australian and Argentine inflows differed markedly from each other, and from the composition of the overall European outflow. Argentine inflows drew primarily from the Latin countries of origin and the Australian inflows concentrated primarily on the British Isles. A combination of cultural conditioning and prejudicial policies, this segmentation of the labor market differentiates the Argentine experience, and a comparative perspective offers insights into the peculiar demographic experience of the country and her unique patterns of economic development.

AN ECONOMETRIC MODEL

The model is essentially an asset-pricing model.[6] Here the competing assets are employment opportunities in the sending and receiving regions. The returns on these assets are the average real wages in the two regions adjusted for cost-of-living differentials. Variability in these asset returns due to uncertainty over employment opportunities introduces a risk-return tradeoff to be weighed up by the potential migrant.[7] The model will be applied here to the immigrant streams of Argentina and Australia between 1870 and 1939. In each case we focus on the principal sending regions for each country – Spain and Italy in the case of Argentina, and Britain for Australia – and we use the characteristics of the labor markets in the sending and receiving regions to explain the pattern of migration over time.[8]

Suppose migration depends on the difference in the expected utility (d) in the sending (s) and receiving (r) regions. Utility will be assumed to depend on income (y). For a given individual, suppressing a time index, and assuming logarithmic utility, this may be written

$$d_i = E \log y_r - E \log y_s + z_i, \tag{1}$$

where z_i is an individual-specific preference term. It is tedious but straightforward to derive the following approximation,

$$d_{it} \sim c_1 + (\log w_{rt} - \log w_{st}) + c_2 \log e_{rt} - c_3 \log e_{st} + z_i, \tag{2}$$

where w represents the commensurate real wage, and e the probability of employment in each of the two regions at time t. Thus migration will depend on the real wage gap between the two regions and the employment prospects in each. It is assumed that the individual preference term z_i does not vary over time.

In a simple expression of the model we may postulate that migration for the individual occurs when d_i is positive. On aggregation, we will assume a

101

linear functional form such that the aggregate migration rate m_t depends on the average value of d_{it} across individuals.[9] Hence, from equation (2) we obtain the "basic model":

$$m_t = \beta_1 + \beta_2(\log w_{rt} - \log w_{st}) + \beta_3 \log e_{rt} - \beta_4 \log e_{st} + \varepsilon_t. \qquad (3)$$

A more sophisticated migration process might entail a decision to migrate based not only on today's value of d_{it} but also on today's expectation of tomorrow's discounted value of d_{it} which we write $d_{it} + d^*{}_{it}$. The term $d^*{}_{it}$ represents today's expectation of the difference in discounted utility between today and tomorrow. Thus, even if d_{it} is positive, it might pay to wait to migrate if tomorrow's prospects are so much better. The value of moving today is $d_{it} + d^*{}_{it}$, but if $d_{it} + d^*{}_{it} < d^*{}_{it}$ then it will pay to wait and move tomorrow. In this case an appropriate model for the richer lag structure is the following first-order error correction (FOEC) model, where Δ denotes the difference operator:[10]

$$\begin{aligned}
m_t = {} & \beta_1 + \beta_2\Delta(\log w_{rt} - \log w_{st}) + \beta_3\Delta\log e_{rt} - \beta_4\Delta\log e_{st} \\
& + \beta_5(\log w_{r,t-1} - \log w_{s,t-1}) + \beta_6\log e_{r,t-1} - \beta_7\log e_{s,t-1} \\
& + \beta_8 m_{t-1} + \varepsilon_t.
\end{aligned} \qquad (4)$$

The FOEC model, equation (4), is now applied to empirically estimate the determinants of migration from Italy and Spain to Argentina and from Britain to Australia in the late nineteenth and early twentieth centuries.

Argentine immigration from Italy and Spain

We first apply the model to Argentine immigration, examining separately the inflows from the two principal sending regions, Italy and Spain, over the entire period of interest from the 1880s to the 1930s. The results are shown in Table 5.1, columns 1–4. The dependent variables are the gross and net immigration rates (MIGR) to Argentina from each country. Explanatory variables include the logarithm of the real wage gap between Argentina and the sending country, LWGAP, and proxies for employment prospects in each country, LEARG, and LESEND (either LEITA or LESPA), defined as the difference between the logarithm of national income and its trend over the sample period.[11] When differenced these variables are denoted DLWGAP, DLEARG, DLEITA and DLESPA respectively. The suffix (–1) indicates a lag of one period.

With ample degrees of freedom the FOEC model works well. The results for Italy appear in columns 1 (gross) and 2 (net), those for Spain in columns 3 (gross) and 4 (net). All coefficients have the correct sign when significant. One has to be disappointed that many coefficients do, however, exhibit low significance levels. None the less, restrictions are inappropriate: in terms of model selection, the test of restrictions usually rejects the null hypothesis that the basic model (with a lagged dependent variable to cope with serial correlation) should be accepted, leading us to prefer the FOEC specification chosen here (although column 3 is a borderline example for this test). Serial correlation is problematic for the Spanish regressions, however. The lagged dependent variable is highly significant, and the lagged independent-variable coefficients must be divided by one minus the coefficient on the lagged dependent variable to derive long-run coefficients (or elasticities) for migration responsiveness. This is done for the case of the wage elasticity of migration.

In the short run, judging from the error-correction (difference) terms, the FOEC model indicates a responsiveness of migration to wage and employment conditions, with the short run employment linkage more sensitive. As intuition would suggest, Argentine employment conditions exercised much more influence over the short run than did employment conditions in Italy or Spain. In the longer run, given the impact of the lagged terms on the right-hand side, relative-wage prospects also affected the migration decision. For both Italian and Spanish inflows, a 10 percent increase in the real-wage gap between home and Argentina would lead to about a 1.0–1.2 per thousand (respectively, 0.8 per thousand) increase in rates of gross (respectively, net) immigration from those countries to Argentina.

I conclude that over the entire period from the 1880s to the 1930s the inflow of Italian and Spanish migrants to Argentina responded to market signals in accord with a rational risk-return tradeoff. Relatively insensitive to short-run changes in employment opportunities at home (where their individual place in the job market was presumably fairly secure), migrants moved to Argentina when employment and long-run real wage opportunities there were relatively good.

Argentine total net immigration

As noted, Argentine immigrant supply was quite similar in its linkages for the Spanish and Italian streams of migrants. It therefore makes sense to integrate the two streams and consider immigration into Argentina from multiple sources. In this next exercise the dependent variable is the net total immigration from all sources, and labor market conditions in the sending countries are proxied by the average of the conditions in Italy and Spain. Thus LWGAP is the average of LWGAP for Italy and Spain, and LESEND the average of LEITA and LESPA. A simple average is used, as it will be recalled that both countries contribute roughly equally to account for four-fifths of Argentine immigration in the period (Figure 5.2).

The advantage of this new approach is that the estimation of total net immigrant supply responses will permit a ready comparison of Argentine and Australian labor supply in the subsequent discussion, and offer insights into the origins of the very different demographic dynamics in the two countries.

Table 5.1 Argentine immigration equations

Dependent variable (definition):	(1) MIGR (gross)	(2) MIGR (net)	(3) MIGR (gross)	(4) MIGR (net)	(5) MIGR (gross)	(6) MIGR (net)
From/to:	ITA/ARG NOTWAR	ITA/ARG NOTWAR	SPA/ARG NOTWAR	SPA/ARG NOTWAR	All/ARG NOTWAR	All/ARG NOTWAR
Sample:	1884–1913 & 1919–39	1884–1913 & 1919–39	1884–1913 & 1919–39	1884–1913 & 1919–39	1884–1913 & 1919–39	1884–1913 & 1919–39
Coefficient (t-statistics)						
CONSTANT	0.111	−0.528	−0.124	−0.695	1.55	1.63
	(0.08)	(0.29)	(0.07)	(0.37)	(0.40)	(0.44)
MIGR(−1)	0.705	0.505	0.443	0.339	0.639	0.538
	(7.73)	(5.03)	(2.99)	(2.23)	(5.49)	(4.53)
DLWGAP	−0.594	2.18	5.98	5.05	4.46	1.73
	(0.16)	(0.49)	(1.51)	(1.27)	(0.51)	(0.20)
DLEARG	44.5	57.6	39.9	37.2	121	127
	(5.13)	(5.52)	(4.24)	(3.94)	(5.99)	(6.50)
DLESEND	−15.6	−27.9	−3.03	−1.82	−28.8	−27.7
	(1.14)	(1.63)	(0.41)	(0.25)	(1.00)	(0.97)
LWGAP(−1)	3.52	3.95	5.55	5.19	8.04	5.39
	(1.57)	(1.67)	(1.79)	(1.67)	(1.40)	(1.02)
Long-run coefficient	12.0	8.0	10.0	7.8	22.3	11.7
LEARG(−1)	0.0977	−3.13	23.4	20.2	25.9	16.1
	(0.02)	(0.49)	(2.84)	(2.74)	(1.61)	(1.11)
LESEND(−1)	12.2	11.9	−13.2	−15.3	−29.8	−28.0
	(1.01)	(0.83)	(1.49)	(1.71)	(0.94)	(0.89)
Degrees of freedom	41	37	35	35	35	35
R^2	0.805	0.695	0.769	0.682	0.785	0.726
SEE	3.26	3.87	3.26	3.28	7.15	6.93

Durbin's h	0.757	1.16	-3.56	-8.81	-1.21	-0.327
[significance level]	[44.9%]	[24.6%]	[0.0%]	[0.0%]	[22.6%]	[74.4%]
Test of restrictions	$F(3,41)=9.93$	$F(3,37)=12.3$	$F(3,35)=1.94$	$F(3,35)=2.75$	$F(3,35)=6.47$	$F(3,35)=10.0$
[significance level]	[0.0%]	[0.0%]	[14.0%]	[5.7%]	[0.1%]	[0.0%]

Sources: See appendix at end of chapter.

Notes: See text. "All" refers to immigration from all sources, with sending region taken as an arithmetic average of Italy and Spain. LWGAP is log of relative real wages between sending region(s) and receiving regions. LESEND is log difference between actual and trend log GDP in the sending region(s). In the test of restrictions in the FOEC model, the null hypothesis is the basic LDV model. Samples are defined in the appendix at end of chapter. Long-run coefficient refers to the regression coefficient divided by one minus the coefficient of the lagged dependent variable.

The results for Argentina are presented in Table 5.1, columns 5 and 6. Again, the FOEC model performs successfully, with all coefficients correctly signed. Employment conditions in Argentina dominate sending-region employment conditions as a determinant of migration, and long-run wage elasticities are of a reasonable magnitude given our earlier findings. Upon a 10 percent real-wage-gap increase, the gross immigrant supply increases by 2.23 per thousand (about equal to the sum of Italian and Spanish effects). The net migration response is slightly smaller at 1.17 per thousand, less than the sum of individual Italian and Spanish responses, perhaps indicative of unusual return flow interactions in the migrant streams.

Australian comparisons

How well integrated was Argentina in the international labor market of the turn of the century? Was migrant supply highly elastic? Such questions are implicitly comparative: was Argentina better integrated into the global labor market than, say, other New World economies? and was her migrant supply more elastic than that of other countries? These questions have not yet, to my knowledge, been addressed by any empirical models or econometric testing, although the ongoing work of Hatton, Williamson and their collaborators is certainly directly aimed at such issues (Hatton and Williamson 1992a, 1993; also Chapter 3, this volume). Here, I present a modest attempt to answer the question by comparing the dynamics of Argentine migrant inflows with those of Australia, since these two Southern Hemisphere regions of new settlement have for so long been compared in all aspects of their economic growth and development.

In order to pursue the comparison it is important that we estimate the same models and test the same hypotheses for both countries, using the same variables and functional form in each as best we can. Accordingly, Table 5.2 presents estimates of the FOEC model for Australia for the full sample and for the pre- and post-First World War periods. Only one modification to the models is made here – the inclusion of a transport cost term (LTCGAP, defined in the appendix at the end of the chapter) to control for the changes in the migrants' cost of passage, including government subsidies via assistance.[12]

The FOEC model performs well once more. The test for restrictions favors the first-order error correction model for all sample choices, and serial correlation is barely detectable. The lagged dependent variable is always significant. The Chow Test indicates that pooling PREWAR and POSTWAR samples (column 1) is only marginally defensible. However, a comparison of the split-sample regressions (columns 2 and 3) indicates that although a good deal of structural change is evident in the coefficients, the long-run wage pseudo-elasticity is more or less stable in the range 20 and 25 for net migration. This compares with the Argentine coefficient estimates of about 22 for gross migration and 11 for net migration, as shown in Table 5.3.[13]

Table 5.2 Australian immigration equations

Dependent variable (definition): From/to: Sample:	(1) MIGR (net) UK/Australia NOTWAR 1871–1913 & 1920–39	(2) MIGR (net) UK/Australia PREWAR 1871–1913	(3) MIGR (net) UK/Australia POSTWAR 1920–1939
Coefficients (t-statistics)			
CONSTANT	−0.212	0.168	−2.86
	(0.12)	(0.91)	(0.97)
MIGR(−1)	0.709	0.486	0.452
	(6.27)	(3.34)	(3.89)
DLWGAP	10.7	13.6	26.6
	(1.15)	(1.34)	(2.67)
DLEAUS	6.70	−2.45	38.7
	(0.57)	(0.18)	(3.04)
DLEUK	22.8	36.8	−39.7
	(1.28)	(1.11)	(3.75)
LWGAP(−1)	5.93	11.0	13.5
	(1.01)	(1.79)	(1.26)
Long-run coefficient	20.4	21.3	24.7
LEAUS(−1)	3.46	13.3	53.0
	(0.51)	(1.48)	(4.29)
LEUK(−1)	7.74	−20.1	−64.9
	(0.83)	(0.81)	(4.68)
LTCGAP	−7.49	−18.3	−0.48
	(2.49)	(3.86)	(0.15)
Degrees of freedom	52	33	10
R^2	0.776	0.812	0.970
SEE	3.50	3.69	0.82
Mean of dependent variable	5.93	7.24	3.13
Durbin's h	2.06	2.01	−1.73
[significance level]	[3.9%]	[4.4%]	[8.3%]
Test of restrictions	$F(3,52)=0.446$	$F(3,33)=1.26$	$F(3,10)=4.77$
[significance level]	[72.1%]	[30.4%]	[2.6%]
Chow test	$F[9,43]=1.89$	–	–
[significance level]	[8.0%]		

Sources: See appendix at end of chapter.
Notes: See text. MIGR is inflow to Australia from all sources. In the test of restrictions the null hypothesis is the basic LDV model. Samples are defined in the appendix at the end of the chapter. Chow Test tests for a 'PREWAR, POSTWAR' sample split. Long-run coefficient refers to the regression coefficient divided by one minus the coefficient of the lagged dependent variable.

A split-sample result is indicative of changing dynamics in the international labor market linkages around the First World War. Wage responsiveness among migrants was little different in Australia in the prewar and postwar periods, but sensitivity to employment conditions increased mark-

Table 5.3 Implied long-run wage elasticities of migration

Migration	Gross migration elasticity	Net migration elasticity
Italy–Argentina, immigration	12.0	8.0
Spain–Argentina, immigration	10.0	7.8
All–Argentina, immigration	22.3	11.7
All–Australia, immigration	—	20.4

Sources: Tables 5.1 and 5.2.

edly after the war (the coefficient on LEAUS(–1) blows up from 13 to 53, that on LEUK(–1) from –20 to –65, and in each case significance rises). In the postwar period transport costs seem unrelated to migration patterns, whereas previously they had entered significantly via LTCGAP. The shifting structures of migration dynamics prompt further research on the determinants of migration and their changing impact over time, and the coincidence of the regime switch in Australia with the war and the reintroduction of assisted migration suggests possible external forces at work. The results are quite possibly consistent with the earlier observation that assisted migration schemes rose to great importance in Australia only after 1906–7; with the help of assistance during the later periods, migrants might have been relatively less influenced by transport-cost fluctuations, and more inclined to base their decision on employment prospects.

Interpretations

These results indicate broad similarities in the mechanics of both the Australian and Argentine immigrant streams over the period as a whole. Wage-elasticities (per thousand migrants) of the order of 10 to 20 seem typical for both countries, indicative of a responsive migrant stream and a measure of integration into the "world labor market." However, a detailed look seems to suggest shifting patterns of integration over time in Australia. All migrant flows were sensitive to employment conditions, but more sensitive to those in the New World than those at home in Europe, as intuition might suggest. However, this sensitivity did show changes over time, particularly in Australia where it increased after the war. Paucity of data and scarce degrees of freedom suggest caution with these interpretations and the imprecise estimates underlying them.

The most striking finding in this chapter is the result that Argentina did not have an unusually elastic supply of migrants. If anything, the results suggest that, with regard to total net inflows, Argentine immigrant supply may have been only half as elastic as Australian immigrant supply. Many authors have raised the demographic burden as a powerful drag on Argentine development during this period, pointing to the unprecedented rates of population growth and high rates of immigration. The origin of this burden, it is often argued, lay not only with the high rates of natural increase amongst a rapidly reproducing population stock in Argentina, but also with the highly elastic supply of labor from overseas, notably Spain and Italy. More often than not, the "birds of passage," the hardy seasonal migrants who ventured from the Mediterranean to the Pampas and back each year, are cited as telling evidence of this highly elastic labor supply response (Gerardi 1985; Díaz-Alejandro 1970: 21–2).

This chapter cautions against such interpretations. Argentine immigrants were not noticeably more responsive to wage signals than immigrants to Australia over this period (if anything, they were slightly less responsive). Why, then, were Argentine rates of population growth and immigration so high? Simply because the average wage gap between Argentina and her sending regions was so much higher than the corresponding wage gap for Australia. The explanatory variable LWGAP used in the econometric estimation takes an average value of 0.32 for Australia over the NOTWAR sample, compared with 0.74 for Argentina (Table 5.4, panel A). Converting to index numbers, with the sending region normalized to 100, these wage gaps translate into indices of 138 for Australia (that is, a 38 percent wage premium over Britain) and a massive 210 for Argentina (a 110 percent premium over Italy and Spain). The pattern is the same over the entire period on a year-to-year basis, although the gaps fluctuate considerably (Figure 5.3).

To see the importance of this, consider the following counterfactual exercises. Suppose that in the PREWAR period, Argentina had Australia's actual wage-gap relative to her (Australia's) sending region (Britain). That is, suppose LWGAP in Argentina had been 0.34, not 0.92. What would this have implied for Argentine rates of immigration before the First World War, the very period when Argentina's population burgeoned so dramatically? Using the Argentine FOEC coefficient estimate of 11.7 (Table 5.1, column 6), we may infer that Argentine immigration would have fallen dramatically in the counterfactual situation (Table 5.4, panel B). The immigration rate would have dropped from its actual level of 17 per thousand per year to a mere 10 per thousand per year. We may recall that the actual Australian rate of immigration over the PREWAR sample was only 7 per thousand per year. Conversely, had Australia been given a counterfactual Argentine log wage-gap of 0.92 – say, by opening its doors wider to the huddled masses of southern Europe – Australian immigration rates would have risen from the actual 7 per thousand to as much as 19 per thousand, exceeding actual Argentine levels of 17 per thousand (here we use the Australian FOEC coefficient estimate of 20.4 from Table 5.2, column 1). Hence, by this reckoning, the much larger wage gap in the Argentine case accounts for much – if not all – of the excess of Argentine immigration over Australian levels.

Table 5.4 Immigration rates and wage gaps, Argentina and Australia

Country	Sample	Sample Mean LWGAP	MIGR (net, ‰)
A. Sample Statistics			
Argentina	NOTWAR	0.74	12
Argentina	PREWAR	0.92	17
Argentina	POSTWAR	0.49	4
Australia	NOTWAR	0.32	6
Australia	PREWAR	0.34	7
Australia	POSTWAR	0.28	3
B. PREWAR counterfactual comparisons (Australia and Argentina with each other's LWGAP)			
Argentina	PREWAR actual	0.92	17
Argentina	PREWAR counterfactual	0.34	10
Australia	PREWAR actual	0.34	7
Australia	PREWAR counterfactual	0.92	19

Sources: See appendix at end of chapter.
Notes: See text. MIGR is net immigration rate.

CONCLUSIONS

We cannot truly speak of "the international labor market" of the late nineteenth century. In reality, global migration dynamics were characterized by a multiplicity of different streams, from a range of Old World countries to the various frontiers in the New World. There were, in effect, multiple international labor markets, as these migrant streams divided on racial, national and cultural lines, and this market segmentation had significant implications for the sending and receiving regions. Cultural norms and political choices shaped the destiny of the millions who left Europe for better prospects in the distant lands. Some, like the British, faced a wealth of opportunity, and, potentially, had a wider choice of destination than almost any other group. Dominant in Australia, they also formed significant cohorts in all the New World countries, save Argentina, where low real wage levels made that particular destination least attractive. The poorer migrants from southern Europe faced a much tougher challenge in securing entry to several New World regions: Australia stands out, but the policy debates of the late-nineteenth-century United States also reflect concern at the growing tide of immigrants arriving from the least-developed regions of Europe. Given these competing destinations, and the cultural proximity of Argentina, the inevitability of a large flux of Latin migrants to the River Plate seems obvious.

The implications of a segmented international labor market now become more apparent. The migrant inflow to Argentina, contrary to the prevailing wisdom, was not highly elastic. Rather, the inflow was so large relative to competing destinations simply because the sending–receiving region wage gaps were so huge. This was just an artifact of the segmented international labor market of the day. The Latin migrants would have jumped at the opportunity to enter a job market like Australia where real-wage levels were even higher – but they were excluded as a matter of policy choice. Those countries, like Australia, which effectively blocked out low-wage immigrant sources could preserve lower rates of immigration, even when their migrant supply was just as elastic as that of any other country. By dint of her "White Australia" policy stance – which, in practice, amounted almost to a British-only immigration policy – Australia allowed entrance only to a group of potential migrants with real-wage levels only just below her own. Arguably, this policy kept labor relatively scarce in Australia and placed a floor under real wages. Argentina, conversely, opened her doors to a wave of low-wage migrants from southern Europe who came from countries offering wage levels less than half those available in Buenos Aires. As a counterfactual exercise has shown, much of the difference between Argentine and Australian migration rates is accounted for by the larger wage gaps in the Latin segment of the global labor market.

We can only begin to speculate at the dramatic implications of the open-door immigration policy for development in Argentina, both at the time, and in the decades that followed. Undeniably, the large migrant stream contributed to the rapid population growth of the country, and the ensuing demographic burden. Elsewhere, I argue that such a demographic burden hindered Argentine development on two counts: it directly retarded capital deepening and it indirectly depressed investment in the interwar period when Argentina was unable to borrow overseas and was constrained by demographically-induced low domestic savings rates (Taylor 1992b).

Further research will be needed to estimate the impact of the migrant inflow on real wages in Australia and Argentina – the next stage in the analysis, and a crucial step which would link the migration-policy debate to the debate over standards of living. The challenge remains to figure out the true impact of the "White Australia" policy on propping up Australian wages and to fully understand the problems posed by the absorption of the huge influx of labor to Argentina immediately before the First World War.

It would be enlightening to construct equilibrium models of the Argentine and Australian economies and examine the implications of the different migration policies. We could then address the question of whether Australia's restrictive immigration policy did effectively place a floor under home wages, and whether similar policies could have augmented real wage growth in Argentina. If intuition is any guide, the influence of the segmented international labor market could have been far more pervasive than has previously been acknowledged.

APPENDIX: STATISTICAL SOURCES

A full listing of the time series used are available from the author upon request.

Argentina

MIGR: (i) Rates of gross and net immigration from Italy per thousand of population. Argentine population in thousands (POP) from Vázquez-Presedo (1971–6, vol. 1: 15–16, column 1; vol. 2: 19). Italian migration from 1880–1924: Dirección General de Inmigración (1925); 1925–7 (gross only): Vázquez-Presedo (1971–6, vol. 2: 35); 1928–39: Dirección General de la Estadística de la Nación (1938–40). (ii) Rates of gross and net immigration from Spain per thousand of population. Argentine population as above. Spanish gross immigration from 1880–1924 and 1928–39: as Italy above; 1925–7: Sanchez Alonso (1988). (iii) Rates of gross and net immigration per thousand of population. Argentine population as above. Immigration (IMG) and emigration (EMG) from 1857–1924: Willcox (1929–31, vol. 1: 546) using averages as necessary; 1924–39: Mitchell (1983: 142–3).

LWGAP: Difference in the natural logarithm of the real wage in Argentina (RW) and the real wage in either Italy (RWITA) or Spain (RWSPA) or an average of the two (see text). Internationally commensurate real wages from Williamson (1994: Appendix 2).

LEARG: Difference in the natural logarithm of real national income in Argentina (RY) and its linear trend over the sample period. Real national income from 1884–1913: Della Paolera (1988: 186). Real output 1913–39: IEERAL (1986: 114–15). Real GDP at market prices.

LEITA: Difference in the natural logarithm of real national income in Italy (RYITA) and its linear trend over the sample period. Real national income from Maddison (1982: 173, 175).

LESPA: Difference in the natural logarithm of real national income in Spain (RYSPA) and its linear trend over the sample period. Real national income from Barciela *et al.* (1989: 173, 175).

LECOM: Simple arithmetic average of LEITA and LESPA.

The following samples are defined for Argentina: NOTWAR, 1884–1913 and 1919–39; PREWAR, 1884–1913; POSTWAR, 1919–39.

Australia

MIGR: Rate of net immigration per thousand of population. Population in thousands (POP) from Mitchell (1983: 53) using linear interpolation. Net migration in thousands (NET) from Price (1987: 6–7).

LWGAP: Difference in the natural logarithm of the real wage in Australia (RW) and the real wage in Britain (RWUK). Internationally commensurate real wages from Williamson (1994: Appendix 2).

LEAUS: Difference in the natural logarithm of real national income in Australia (RY) and its linear trend over the sample period. Real national income from Maddison (1982: 172, 174).

LEUK: Difference in the natural logarithm of real national income in Britain (RYUK) and its linear trend over the sample period. Real national income from Maddison (1982: 173, 175).

LTCGAP: Difference in the natural logarithm of TC and its linear trend over the sample period, where TC equals the ratio of UK–Australia transport costs to UK wage levels, adjusted for financial assistance in the form of passage subsidies by governments. For accurate definition and sources see Pope (1976). The log-trend differencing is used to ensure stationarity in keeping with the other variables included in the regression.

The following samples are defined for Australia: NOTWAR, 1870–1913 and 1920–39; PREWAR, 1870–1913; POSTWAR, 1920–39. The year 1919 is omitted from the POSTWAR sample because of the unusually large return troop movements contained in the migration data.

NOTES

* An earlier version of this paper formed part of a dissertation completed in 1992 at the Department of Economics, Harvard University under the supervision of Jeffrey G. Williamson (Alan M. Taylor, "Argentine Economic Growth in Comparative Perspective," Ph. D. dissertation, Harvard University, July 1992). The author benefited from the comments of his thesis committee – Brad De Long, Peter Timmer and Jeff Williamson – and from the help, encouragement and criticism of Roberto Cortés Conde, Gerardo Della Paolera, Ezéquiel Gallo, Tulio Halperín, Marcela Harriague, Tim Hatton, Barry Howarth, Juan Carlos Korol, Mary MacKinnon, Andrew Mason, Ian McLean, David Pope, Graeme Snooks, Mark Thomas, Malcolm Urquhart, Claire Waters, John Womack, Jr. and seminar participants at Harvard University, Stanford University, the University of California at Berkeley, the East–West Center of the University of Hawaii, the Australian National University, the University of Adelaide, the University of Melbourne and the Instituto Torcuato Di Tella. Research was supported in part by the Harvard Academy for International & Area Studies, the Tinker Foundation, the Fundación del Hemisferio, the Center for Latin American and Iberian Studies, Harvard University, the Center for International Affairs, Harvard University, the Instituto Torcuato Di Tella, Buenos Aires and the Research School of Social Sciences, Australian National University.

1 In the Harris–Todaro model, migrants use the expected wage in the destination as the opportunity cost of staying put. The model was originally devised to account for continuing trends of rural–urban migration in the developing world, even in the face of substantial urban unemployment (Harris and Todaro 1970; Todaro 1969).

2 For a comparison over the period 1890–1913 with other New World countries, I am grateful to Jeffrey Williamson for the following figures from his (unpublished) migration database:

113

	(1) Net immigration rate (%)	(2) Population growth rate (%)	(3) Share of (1) in (2) (%)
Argentina	1.32	1.81	73
Australia	0.31	0.96	32
Canada	1.49	1.05	142
United States	0.41	0.98	42

3 Withers (1987) identifies the 1890s as a watershed in the Australian labor market, and discusses the rise of unions and the institutional changes characteristic of the period.

4 Wakefield's (1849) tract was one of the seminal works on the subject of colonization.

5 For detailed accounts of the patterns of Australia immigration over the period consult Boehm (1979); Kenwood and Lougheed (1983); Pope (1976, 1981b, 1987); Sinclair (1976).

6 A detailed exposition of the model, featured in an earlier draft, is available from the author upon request.

7 It is well known that in asset-pricing models mean-variance analysis is only rigorously appropriate in an expected-utility framework when the utility function is quadratic in form, entailing a bliss level of consumption or income. Here we derive a model using a logarithmic expected utility function and, with judicious approximations, derive a tractable model for empirical estimation.

8 The model is based on the ongoing work of Timothy Hatton and Jeffrey Williamson. They have successfully applied a similar analysis to explain the net rate of emigration from Britain and Ireland to a group of competing international destinations for the period 1870–1913 (Hatton 1993, where a detailed account of the model appears; Hatton and Williamson 1993).

9 In a study of emigration from the Old World it would be natural to consider emigration rates, as in the original implementation by Hatton and Williamson. Here, however, the focus is on the elasticity of immigrant supply in the receiving regions of the New World; hence, it is natural to consider immigration rates. For a given pair of countries, however, the analysis only differs in the denominator – sending- versus receiving-region population. The analysis and econometrics performed here go through all the same when the emigration processes are modeled, albeit with modified coefficients.

10 In the regression equation, we expect $\beta_i > 0$ for all i. Some words on parameter restrictions are in order. The basic model, equation (3), obtains when the following coefficient restrictions apply: (a) $\beta_2 = \beta_5$, $\beta_3 = \beta_6$, $\beta_4 = \beta_7$; and (b) $\beta_8 = 0$. This yields a simple test of restrictions to discriminate between the basic and FOEC models. Note also that the FOEC form incorporates the classic lagged-dependent-variable (LDV) model as a special case: when just (a) holds, the model reverts to a simple LDV model such as has been commonly estimated in previous studies (Williamson 1974a). The LDV specification is useful since it incorporates the long-run relationships, even in FOEC form. It is important, however, that such a specification is applied carefully, since it is well known that a serial-correlation model can easily be mistaken for an LDV model (Maddala 1977: 146–8; Griliches 1967). Accordingly, autoregressive versions of the basic model may be used as an alternate specification when serial-correlation difficulties arise with an ordinary least-squares (OLS) implementation of the LDV model. An

alternative route is to use decadal averaging to weed out serial correlation (Hatton and Williamson 1992a), though such an approach is ill-suited to individual-country time-series and few observations.

11 If an Okun's Law relationship applies then a "GDP gap" measure such as this is directly related to the rate of unemployment (or the rate of employment).

12 As noted earlier, assisted migration schemes were much more important in the Australian case. Early studies on Australian immigration focused on income-differentials and unemployment conditions, but, in the most thorough work, David Pope has convincingly demonstrated that transport-cost effects, including passage assistance, in addition to wage and employment conditions, were significant determinants of Australian immigration over the period 1900–30, and I follow his lead in controlling for such effects (Kelley 1965; Pope 1976, 1981a).

13 It is difficult to offer comparisons of these elasticities with earlier Australian immigration elasticity estimates. Kelley and Pope both regressed migrant flows (not rates) on income levels (not log-levels), and sample statistics are not readily available to make the conversion (Pope 1981a; Kelley 1965).

Part III

HOW WERE THEY ABSORBED?

6

FOREIGN IMMIGRATION AND THE FRENCH LABOR FORCE, 1896–1926

*Pierre Sicsic**

INTRODUCTION

In the general debates about whether a labor shortage impeded French industrialization, immigration has been seen as a major source of incremental supply satisfying labor requirements in modernizing industries. According to this view, foreign labor was necessary for these industries because it was difficult and costly to lure French peasants into these new jobs. Thus, labor market flexibility was provided by immigrants. Even if the view that French natives were unwilling to move into these new jobs were correct, this reluctance to move would still not have impeded French industrialization to the extent that foreign labor was easy to tap. This point has been made by Kindleberger (1964: 367) who wrote: "There was no labor scarcity up to 1895. Thereafter local labor scarcities in the north and east were met by immigration, at the same time that the rural exodus in the south and west provided France with functionaries, both civil and military."

The literature on French labor scarcity and industrialization has focused on the nineteenth century. The literature on French immigration has focused on the twentieth century, partly because, in compensation for drastic French losses during the Great War, foreign labor flooded the country, doubling the proportion of the alien population from 3 percent in 1911 to 6 percent in 1926. The literature dealing with this influx has dwelt on employment distribution, showing that immigrants were disproportionately represented in the heavy industries. There is general agreement that a new pattern of controlled immigration emerged after 1914, with foreigners more heavily concentrated in primary production.

Commenting on pre-1914 immigration, Prost (1966: 534) viewed it as a rural out-migration that happened to cross a border, while Cross (1983: 11) wrote that "the rudiments of a dual labor market appeared in France as early as the 1880s." Cross argued that "economic growth became possible in a society in which the native workforce was unwilling to participate fully in its costs" since "immigration provided a relief for modernizing firms, enabling them to expand rapidly with adequate supplies of labor." Evidence on this point rests on the shares of French nationals and foreigners in different industries. The contribution of foreign migrants to the build-up of the labor force in France in particular industries is relevant to the debate about labor scarcity impeding French industrialization. If this contribution was large, then we might conclude that French industrialization did not suffer from inelastic and relative immobile local labor supplies because international labor supplies were more elastic and relatively mobile. If correct, we would reject Prost's thesis that immigration was merely a rural out-migration which crossed a border, in favor of the thesis supported by Cross and Kindleberger.

This chapter aims to show that immigration before the First World War was little different from internal migration, and that the build-up of the industrial labor force between 1896 and 1913, characterized by a sharp increase in the French growth rate, cannot be seen as the outcome of a major immigration flow. Both these characteristics were reversed after 1918. The size of immigration flows after the war could have been the result of war losses, but the skewed distribution of the immigrants by occupation shows that something else was going on. The organized procedures used to bring in foreign workers were effective in isolating migrants from certain segments of the labor market.

The underlying concern of this chapter is to compare international and internal labor flows. When looking at the outcome of these flows, whether it is the wages paid to immigrants or their occupational distribution, one should bear in mind that the foreign-born have one obvious distinctive feature: they have moved away from their place of birth. Thus, the relevant population with which to compare foreign immigrants job outcomes is not the total native-born population, but rather those native-born who have moved – native-born internal migrants. Therefore, instead of comparing the occupation distributions of immigrants and native-born – as is so typical of migration research, we should compare the occupation distributions of movers, both within the country and crossing a border, and of stayers.

The first section links the literature on internal labor markets with the literature on immigration and discrimination. In particular, it asks how the interpretation of the wage-gap evidence relevant for the reluctant-French-rural-emigrant hypothesis could be changed, once immigration is considered. In a second section the immigrant contribution to labor force increases are presented. It turns out that the flow of immigrants did not account for more than 20 percent of the labor force increase between 1896 and 1911, while after the First World War immigration's contribution to the labor force was overwhelming. The occupational distributions of immigrants, French "stayers" and French "movers" are described in a third section. Before the First World War, the occupational distributions of international migrants and internal migrants were closer than were those of French movers – the internal migrants – and French stayers. After 1918, as the foreigners became much more likely to work in mining, iron and steel, and in the building trades, the occupation distribution of immigrants drifted apart from those of French citizens. A conclusion explains this drift by appealing to institutional changes in the organization of immigration.

INTERNAL AND INTERNATIONAL LABOR MARKETS

The vast literature on ethnic discrimination in the United States is framed in terms of a reduced form wage equation from a recursive model that relates earnings to skill, occupation and nativity and then occupation to skill and nativity (Hannon 1982b: 831). Occupational segregation appears to have been more important than the strict wage discrimination, the latter consisting of lower pay for immigrants doing the same job as native-born (Eichengreen and Gemery 1986: 453). The population benchmark used in this literature is based on the native-born. If one thinks that migration is a self-selection process, then for the same demographic characteristics – age, schooling – immigrants should have more innate ability or motivation which labor markets value than native-born. In the absence of discrimination and controlling for demographic variables, immigrants should therefore have *higher* earnings than native-born (Chiswick 1978: 919). That is, such tests bias foreign immigrant performance upwards and thus bias downwards estimates of discrimination. Using native-born internal migrants as a benchmark would alleviate this bias, since they should have unobservable characteristics of motivation more like foreign migrants.

Any study of discrimination in mining and manufacturing in the United States at the end of the nineteenth century is likely to deal with a sample in which native-born workers were themselves predominantly internal migrants. This fact plus the fact that foreign immigrants to the US then were of low "quality" – e.g. that selectivity was less prevalent during the period of mass migration (Eichengreen and Gemery 1986: 451), suggest that studies of ethnic discrimination in the late-nineteenth-century US (based upon the state surveys on immigrants' earnings carried out in the 1890s), are not biased although they too make no distinction between native-born movers and stayers. Neither of these two facts were present in France in the period 1896–1926. Studies of discrimination should not lean on occupational comparisons between immigrants and native-born. Such comparisons would only tell us that a French stayer was much more likely to work in agriculture than any migrant, foreign or native-born. Comparisons between the occupational distributions of immigrants and internal migrants carried out in the third section of this chapter suggest that there is evidence of discrimination before the First World War, but that the organized migration following the war fostered an occupational segregation.

Issues of segregation aside, French immigration is worth studying to help inform the general debate about French labor immobility. Using the wage-gap methodology to assess whether industrialization was choked off by labor scarcity induced by "reluctant" rural emigrants, I found that increased peasant reluctance to move cannot be a major explanation for the industrial slowdown occurring at the beginning of the Third Republic, because peasants' reluctance to move was not reflected in large wage gaps between city and countryside (Sicsic 1992: 693). However, this evidence is not conclusive about the mobility of French workers. With an immobile internal labor force and a mobile international labor force, a shift in city-based industrial labor demand could have been met by an inflow of immigrants without any opening in the rural–urban wage-gap. If there were two sources of labor supply, one French and one foreign, the wage-gap measure alone cannot shed conclusive light on the way the internal labor market worked: with inelastic domestic labor supply and elastic international labor supply there would be no wage gap. The corresponding analysis for capital markets is that with domestic saving inelastic to the interest rate, a shift in the investment demand cannot influence the interest rate when the supply of international capital is very elastic. Thus a test of the reluctant-French-rural-emigrant hypothesis cannot be carried out by looking only at wage gaps. A direct measure of sensitivity of sector migration to wages would be necessary.[1] However, a consequence of this hypothesis can be checked by looking at the immigrants' contribution to the labor force increase in expanding sectors: a large contribution would indeed be consistent with immigration substituting for sluggish urban–rural internal migration.[2] This is the topic addressed in the next section.

THE CONTRIBUTION OF IMMIGRATION TO THE INCREASE IN LABOR FORCE

Immigration in France can only be assessed through figures about foreigners from census data. There was no administrative constraint to immigration during the nineteenth century, and therefore no count of the immigrant flows at the borders. One has to compute immigration flows from stocks of enumerated foreigners in the census.[3] Thus, in order to measure immigration by using the enumerated increase in foreigners between censuses, one has to check that some immigrants did not change legal status: some reported as aliens in the censuses might have not been immigrants since they were born in France, and some of the foreign-born, therefore immigrants, could have become French by naturalization and therefore not have been enumerated as foreigners. It will be shown below that these issues can be ignored for the study of immigration between 1896 and 1926. But there is another reason why net immigration might not be equal to the difference in the number of enumerated foreigners between censuses: foreigners enumerated in the first census might have left the labor force before the second census. A constant number of enumerated foreigners in each census would imply that some new immigrants replaced older immigrants who left the labor force between censuses. This "loss" is estimated by applying a disappearance rate to the initial foreign population.

With regard to the foreigners born in France, it is known that there were few French-born adult foreigners in France after 1896. According to the June 1889 law, people born in France with parents themselves not French citizens automatically became French at 21. In 1901 only 10 percent of foreign males over 30 were born in France, this share declining to 7 percent in 1911; for 1926 the share of foreign male labor force made up by foreigners born in France was only 5 percent, while the share of enumerated foreigners (inside and outside the labor force, any age) born in France was 10 percent (Depoid 1942: 81-2).

Available data on naturalization show that this issue is unimportant between 1896 and 1926: the number of enumerated naturalized people in the total population increased before and after these dates but was stable between them. There were only 15,000 naturalized in the 1872 population census. This number increased to 203,000 in 1896, 253,000 in 1911, and 249,000 in 1926 (Depoid 1942: 69). The law regarding French citizenship changed in 1927, making naturalization easier. It is therefore no surprise to find a surge to 517,000 naturalized people in the 1936 census. The size of the naturalized population in the labor force is unavailable before 1901 because naturalized people were aggregated with other French citizens in the labor force census. In 1901, there were 125,000 naturalized people engaged in the work-force (army excluded). This number increased to 144,000 in 1911, then declined to 116,000 in 1926.

The only major discrepancy between the net flow of new immigrants and the change in the enumerated foreign labor force is therefore the number of active foreigners who died or retired between censuses. The increase in labor force due to immigration has therefore been computed in this chapter as the difference between the numbers of enumerated foreigners in two successive censuses, plus the share of the initial foreign population who should have disappeared from the labor force because of ageing. This is the method used by Tugault (1971: 696) to estimate the overall foreign immigration, rather than the "residual" method, where immigration equals the change in the enumerated population plus deaths minus births during the inter-census period. The two methods yield very different results: from 1896 to 1911 the residual method offers a net immigration estimate of 277,000, instead of 499,000 when a survival rate is applied to the initial stock. I judge the "residual" method to be less accurate.

Mortality rates in 1891 in France were 8.6 per thousand between the ages 20 and 39, and 15.9 per thousand between the ages 40 and 59 (Bideau *et al.* 1988: 296). Thus an approximate mortality and retirement rate for foreigners in the labor force of 1.5 percent per year has been assumed to compute the immigrants' contribution to the labor force increase.

The aim of the accounting exercise is to evaluate what the labor force in France would have been without any immigration. The difference between the observed labor force and this counterfactual labor force, divided by the absolute change in the labor force, is that part of the labor force increase due to immigration. A contribution of 100 percent means that all of the increase in the labor force was due to immigration, or that without any immigration the labor force would have remained constant.

The total increase in the labor force at the end of the nineteenth century is not as well known, in spite of the availability of published census tables. The 1896 census, the first one adopting a new methodology, is known to have missed about a million people (including 450,000 draftees). Furthermore, the female labor force in agriculture was poorly observed as is shown by the wide fluctuations of the ratio of male to female labor force across the censuses.[4] The immigrants' contribution to the labor force increase has been computed between different benchmark years to avoid the underestimation of the 1896 census, and computations have been redone on a labor force without agriculture to avoid the issue of the female labor force in agriculture. As the industry breakdown in 1911 was different from the other censuses, this census cannot be used to assess the evolution of sectoral employment distribution, so only the 1901 and 1906 censuses are strictly comparable.[5] However instead of using two censuses only five years apart, I have chosen to rely on the 1896 and 1906 censuses to look at the immigrant contribution to different industries before the war.

The striking result reported in Table 6.1 is that before the First World War the immigrant contribution was smaller than 20 percent, while between 1911 and 1926 it was close to 100 percent. In other words, without the immigrants, the labor force would have remained constant after 1911, even though Alsace and Lorraine were added to the French totals. When agriculture is excluded, the contribution is lower, since many foreign workers went into agriculture after the war. The exclusion of agriculture is designed to avoid the issue of female participation. When one looks only at the male labor force (including agriculture, and excluding the army), the immigrant contribution was 39 percent from 1896 to 1911, and 104 percent from 1911 to 1926.

The relatively minor immigrant contribution before the war seems at odds with two well-known facts: first, the major contribution of immigrants to the total population living in France (the last column of Table 6.1), and second, a labor participation rate which was larger for foreigners than for French citizens (58.5 percent and 51.4 percent in 1911). Given these participation rates and the large immigrant contribution to the total population, one would have expected a large immigrant contribution to the labor force, but we don't find it. Why? The French case is made more complex by the fact that the participation rate for nationals increased at the beginning of the twentieth century; thus, even with a constant population of French nationals, the labor

Table 6.1 France: contributions of immigration to the increase in the labor force
(first lines, army excluded; second lines, army and agriculture excluded)

	Growth in labor force	Contribution to labor force increase from				Contribution of immigrants to overall population increase
		French females	Foreign females	French males	Foreign males	
1896–1911	9.6	69.1	6.4	13.5	11.0	57.7
	18.1	42.8	5.9	41.6	9.7	
1901–1911	5.7	78.9	4.5	5.7	10.9	52.5
	7.7	35.5	5.3	46.1	13.1	
1911–1926	4.1	−0.9	15.6	1.1	84.2	138.5
	9.8	−10.0	7.3	50.8	51.9	

Notes: Let LF_i be the labor force of gender i, and LF^*_i the labor force made up by foreigners, army excluded, the contribution of foreigners of gender i from census $t-d$ to census t is

$$100\,\frac{LF^*_{it} - (1 - \partial d)LF^*_{it-d}}{LF_{ft} + LF_{mt} - LF_{ft-d} - LF_{mt-d}}.$$

where ∂ is the disappearing yearly rate; contribution of French nationals is the other part, that is,

$$100\,\frac{LF_{it} - LF_{it-d} - LF^*_{it} + (1 - \partial d)LF^*_{it-d}}{LF_{ft} + LF_{mt} - LF_{ft-d} - LF_{mt-d}}.$$

The contribution of immigrants to overall population increase has been computed with the net immigration figures taken in Tugault (1971: 698) except for 1911 to 1921, because estimates are not provided for this period. Net immigration has been computed with Tugault's formula: $E_t - s^d E_{t-d}$, where s is the survival rate and E_t is the number of enumerated people born abroad in the t census, from numbers of enumerated people born abroad in the 1911 and 1921 census. The number of net immigrants from 1911 to 1921 is found to be 440,000, close to Bunle (1943: 80) who found 500,000. Contributions of immigration to population increase given in Tugault (1974: 116) have been duplicated: his figures were 54.5 percent, and 69.6 percent from 1921 to 1936.

force would have increased.[6] Imagine a population in France increasing from 38 to 38.5 million people over 15 years, with a French citizen component stable at 37 million. All of the increase would be due to immigration: therefore the immigrant contribution to population increase would be 100 percent. Assume, however, that the labor participation rate increased from 48 to 51 percent for French citizens while remaining at 55 percent for foreigners. This 3 percentage point increase in the participation rate of French citizens would lead to an increase in the French labor force of 1.1 million, while the labor force increase due to immigration would be 400,000, the contribution of immigration would be 400/1,500 or 27 percent.[7] This example is not very different from the facts: the labor force (excluding army) increased by 1.8 million from 1896 to 1911, the immigration flow was 300,000, and thus the immigrant contribution was about 17 percent of the labor force increase. The increase in the labor force around the turn of the century is likely to have been more the result of the entry of French women into the labor force rather than simply the result of an international inflow. The increase in the female participation rate was obviously related to the decrease in the fecundity rate, although the causal chain itself is far from obvious (Garden 1988: 258).

The contribution of French women to the labor force increase has been noted by Tilly and Scott (1978: 150) who also reported a shift in female employment from industry to services. This shift was not much larger than the shift among the overall labor force, since the contribution of French women to the labor force increase when agriculture and white-collar jobs are excluded was 38.4 percent from 1896 to 1911, instead of the 42.8 percent reported in Table 6.1 when only agriculture is excluded.

The immigrant contribution to the French labor force from 1896 to 1911 might be compared with the impact of the Irish on the British labor force in the 1840s. The context was of course quite different: famine-induced Irish immigration could be interpreted as an exogenous shift in unskilled labor supply, perhaps glutting the British labor market, while the working hypothesis for the French case is that Belgian and Italian immigration was an endogenous move, induced by an industrial labor demand shift combined with a rigid internal labor market. However, since these are two oft-cited examples of immigration in the Old World during the nineteenth century, a comparison of their magnitudes makes some sense.

Williamson (1986: 707) found that the increase in the numbers of Irish laborers in Great Britain peaked from 1841 to 1850 and was then equal to 23.5 percent of the total increase in the British labor force.[8] With this comparison in mind, immigration into France before 1911 might appear quite substantial, given the attention given to the Irish "shock troops" during the British industrialization. Before drawing any conclusion about the relative elasticity of the French labor supply from the comparison, one has to remember that the overall growth of the French population was quite low. Thus, even with an intersectoral wage elasticity among the living French population equal to the elasticity among potential foreign migrants, contribution from this pool could be about a fifth of the total increase in the face of a shifting labor demand. With the casualties of the First World War domestic sources became even drier.

War casualties are estimated to be 1.4 million, 11 percent of the 1911 male active population or 7 percent of the total active population. Losses were larger for agriculture than for other industries: 49.4 percent of the casualties had agricultural origins, while the share of agriculture in the 1911 male labor force was 42.3 percent (Mauco 1932: 77). The immigrant inflow into the labor force of 702,000 men and 130,000 women from 1911 to 1926 was clearly a response, at least in part, to these war losses. This response was organized by the immigration offices and it yielded a skewed occupational distribution.

Although I have shown that immigration played a minor role in the total

Table 6.2 France: contribution of foreigners to the labor force by industry/status

		Share in 1926 labor force	Increase in the cell size	Contribution of foreigners	Increase in the cell size	Contribution of foreigners
			1906 to 1926		1896 to 1906	
Agriculture	EO	15.97	−3.48	−15	−7.57	−0
Agriculture	Pa	23.00	0.22	116	9.26	0
Mining	EO	2.04	0.77	85	0.28	16
Mining	Pa	0.03	−0.01	−9	0.00	7
Food processing	EO	1.87	0.22	50	0.15	15
Food processing	Pa	0.61	−0.05	−22	0.06	7
Chemicals	EO	2.34	0.96	23	0.48	7
Chemicals	Pa	0.11	0.02	16	0.02	5
Textiles	EO	4.22	0.23	69	−0.04	3
Textiles	Pa	0.22	−0.13	−2	0.11	2
Garments	EO	4.40	−2.15	−4	1.13	6
Garments	Pa	0.67	−0.26	−6	0.21	8
Leather	EO	1.43	−0.08	−83	−0.01	−273
Leather	Pa	0.20	−0.08	−9	0.05	12
Wood	EO	2.87	0.13	118	0.08	37
Wood	Pa	0.55	−0.05	−22	0.06	5
Iron and steel	EO	1.69	0.69	42	0.16	18
Iron and steel	Pa	0.16	0.00	13	0.02	3
Metal working	EO	5.23	2.76	17	0.65	6
Metal working	Pa	0.41	0.09	17	0.07	7
Building	EO	3.08	0.88	60	−0.05	−118
Building	Pa	0.46	0.09	38	0.04	13
Bricks and tiles	EO	1.16	0.24	69	0.07	32
Bricks and tiles	Pa	0.07	−0.01	−21	−0.00	−33
Goods handling	EO	1.17	−0.73	−9	0.56	15
Goods handling	Pa	0.00	0.00	50	0.00	28
Transports	EO	3.59	1.46	5	0.33	2
Transports	Pa	0.13	−0.01	−37	0.05	20
Trade	EO	7.45	1.26	23	1.28	8
Trade	Pa	2.70	0.09	87	0.73	6
Banking and entertainment	EO	1.31	0.80	6	0.11	11
Banking and entertainment	Pa	0.19	0.07	11	0.05	11
Professionals	EO	2.56	0.55	20	0.69	6
Professionals	Pa	0.23	−0.03	−12	0.10	2
Personal service	EO	3.93	−0.83	−10	0.28	108
Personal service	Pa	0.10	0.00	50	0.03	7
Civil servants	EO	3.87	0.93	3	−0.34	2
		100.00	4.55	101	9.13	12

Notes: Inside each industry there are two statuses: EO for hired people or isolated workers, and Pa for owners.

Denoting N_{it} and N^{*}_{it} as the numbers of enumerated people and foreign people in the cell i during the t census, the contribution of foreigners is $100(N^{*}_{it} - (1 - d\partial)N^{*}_{it-d}) / (N_{it} - N_{it-d})$, while the increase in the cell relative to the initial labor force is $100(N_{it} - N_{it-d}) / (\sum_i N_{it-d})$, and the last line of these columns is therefore the labor force growth rate between two censuses.

labor force increase before the war, could the contribution have been large for some industries? Contributions of foreign workers reported in Table 6.2 have been computed as the ratio of the difference of the number of foreign workers, corrected by a disappearance rate applied to the initial stock, to the change in the labor force in a given industry/status cell. To give a sense of the movement in a given cell, the difference between two censuses in the number of people enumerated in that cell has been divided by the overall labor force in France (army excluded, as usual).

Large (that is larger than 25 percent) contributions of foreign workers from 1896 to 1906 show up only in industries with a stagnant labor force.[9] For instance, the 1906 census enumerated 1,900 less wage-earners in the leather industry than the 1896 census, but 3,100 more alien wage-earners. The overall decline in building wage-earners was 9,300, but there were 4,800 more foreigners enumerated in 1906 than in 1896. In mining and iron and steel the contribution of foreigners between 1896 and 1906 was hardly larger than in the total labor force. The numbers of servants and miners increased by the same amount but the contribution of immigrants was more than 100 percent for servants: without immigration, there would have been a decline in the number of servants between 1896 and 1906 instead of the observed increase by 52,000. These figures show that immigrants were not disproportionately moving into heavy modernizing industries before the First World War.

Between 1906 and 1926, the influx of foreigners showed up where it might be expected had occupational discrimination been present: in mining. While there were 155,000 more workers in mining in 1926 than in 1906, the increase in the number of foreigners was 127,000. If one looks at the industries in which the 740,000 net foreigners (not corrected by a disappearance rate) were employed, after mining came building (91,300) and agriculture (89,300 wage-earners and 45,700 self-employed), which is not surprising when one recalls the large war losses. Net foreign immigration accounted for all of the increase in the self-employed, and dampened the decrease of 700,000 wage-earners in agriculture. In iron and steel, out of an increase of 139,300 workers, there was an increase of 53,400 enumerated foreigners. The picture drawn by Noiriel (1984: 214) of an industrial labor force around Longwy in iron and steel and mining increasing after the First World War only through immigration does not hold for the country as a whole: the immigrant contribution to the labor force increase in iron and steel from 1906 to 1926 was 42 percent. There were some shifts inside the French labor force away from agriculture toward manufacturing, immigrants taking up the slack in agriculture.

THE OCCUPATIONAL DISTRIBUTION OF IMMIGRANTS AND FRENCH INTERNAL MIGRANTS

The claim that immigrants were essential to French industrialization, and that foreigners suffered from occupational discrimination, is primarily based upon sectoral breakdown of the French and foreign work-force. Foreigners appear to have been more heavily engaged in manufacturing, particularly in heavy manufacturing, than the French. However, to assess whether immigrants were engaged in occupations where French people were unwilling to work, the relevant population is the one made up by French internal migrants rather than by the total French population. If the foreign migrants and the internal French migrants had closer sectoral breakdown than French migrants and French non-migrants, then Prost's view, which has seen foreign immigration only as a rural exodus crossing the borders, would be confirmed.

The most remarkable feature of foreign workers during the 1920s, according to Mauco (1932: 268), was their low skill. In coal-mining in the *départements* of Nord and Pas-de-Calais, foreigners accounted for 40 percent of the overall work-force, with 46 percent of miners (under the ground), and only 17 percent of workers employed above the ground. This feature cannot be directly quantified with census data since all workers are aggregated, whatever their skill. However, it is likely that skill requirements were different across industries, and therefore the concentration of foreigners in low skill occupations should show up in the concentration of foreigners in some industries.

The French labor force census distinguished between French citizens born in the *département* where they were enumerated, French citizens born elsewhere, those who were naturalized, and foreigners. In 1906 out of a labor force of 20.127 million, there were 617,000 foreigners, 132,000 naturalized, and 4.269 million French citizens living in a *département* different from the one where they were born. By dividing the shares of foreigners engaged in different industries by the respective shares among French migrants one gets the likelihood of a foreigner to be working in a given industry, relative to the French migrants. These ratios are reported in Table 6.3, along with the French stayer/mover relative shares. In short, the benchmark population is made up by French citizens who were not working in the *département* where they were born.

The main difference between French movers and French stayers regarding their occupation lies in the share engaged in agriculture: in 1896 French stayers were more than three times more likely to work in agriculture than French movers; a foreigner was almost as likely to work in agriculture as a French migrant (the relative share among foreigners for agriculture is 0.9, see Table 6.3). Foreigners were twice as likely to work in iron and steel or mining

Table 6.3 France: relative occupational distributions

1896	Shares among French internal migrants	Relative shares among non-migrant French	Relative shares among foreigners	Shares among French internal migrants	Relative shares among non-migrant French	Relative shares among foreigners	Shares among French internal migrants	Relative shares among non-migrant French	Relative shares among foreigners
	Males and females			Males			Females		
Agriculture	16.1	3.2	0.9	16.9	3.2	0.9	14.2	3.4	0.9
Mining	1.2	1.1	2.1	1.8	1.1	2.0	0.0	1.2	1.8
Food processing	3.5	0.7	1.0	4.2	0.7	0.9	1.8	0.7	1.0
Chemicals	2.4	0.5	1.3	2.8	0.4	1.2	1.4	0.6	1.4
Textiles	4.3	1.4	2.7	3.0	1.3	3.1	7.1	1.4	2.5
Garments	10.3	0.7	0.7	2.3	0.5	1.4	28.0	0.7	0.7
Leather	2.8	0.7	1.2	3.4	0.7	1.2	1.5	0.7	1.0
Wood	4.0	1.0	1.0	5.5	1.0	0.9	0.8	0.9	1.2
Iron and steel	1.4	0.9	2.2	1.9	0.9	2.0	0.2	0.6	1.6
Metalworking	4.3	0.6	1.2	5.9	0.6	1.1	0.9	0.7	1.4
Building	4.4	0.6	2.1	6.4	0.6	1.9	0.0	0.5	1.7
Bricks and tiles	1.5	0.7	2.3	2.0	0.7	2.1	0.4	0.9	2.8
Goods handling	3.0	0.4	1.4	2.1	0.5	1.8	5.0	0.4	1.2
Transports	6.5	0.2	0.4	9.0	0.2	0.4	1.0	0.3	0.5
Trade	16.2	0.4	0.8	15.6	0.4	0.7	17.4	0.5	0.9
Bank. and entert.	1.5	0.3	1.0	1.8	0.3	0.9	0.8	0.2	1.1
Professionals	4.6	0.3	0.8	3.8	0.3	0.7	6.4	0.2	1.1
Personal service	4.5	0.3	0.7	2.2	0.3	0.6	9.6	0.3	0.9
Civil servants	7.4	0.5	0.1	9.2	0.4	0.0	3.4	0.5	0.3

1906	Males and Females			Males			Females		
Agriculture	19.2	2.7	0.7	19.2	2.8	0.7	19.1	2.7	0.5
Mining	1.4	1.0	2.3	2.2	0.9	2.0	0.0	1.8	1.6
Food processing	3.2	0.7	1.0	4.1	0.7	0.9	1.7	0.7	0.9
Chemicals	2.4	0.5	1.3	3.2	0.5	1.3	1.2	0.7	1.1
Textiles	3.2	1.5	2.4	2.3	1.5	2.7	4.7	1.5	2.2
Garments	9.2	0.8	0.8	2.0	0.6	1.9	20.8	0.8	0.8
Leather	2.1	0.8	1.5	2.8	0.8	1.5	1.1	0.8	1.1
Wood	3.3	1.1	1.1	5.1	1.1	1.0	0.6	1.0	1.6
Iron and steel	1.3	0.9	2.3	2.0	0.9	2.1	0.0	1.4	2.2
Metalworking	4.2	0.6	1.2	6.4	0.6	1.1	0.7	0.7	1.0
Building	3.3	0.7	2.4	5.4	0.7	2.2	0.0	0.5	1.3
Bricks and tiles	1.2	0.8	2.5	1.8	0.8	2.3	0.3	1.0	2.4
Goods handling	2.8	0.6	1.9	2.1	0.6	2.3	4.0	0.5	1.7
Transports	5.8	0.3	0.4	8.8	0.3	0.3	1.0	0.3	0.9
Trade	15.3	0.5	0.8	15.8	0.4	0.8	14.6	0.6	0.9
Bank. and entert.	1.4	0.3	1.1	1.9	0.3	1.0	0.6	0.2	1.0
Professionals	5.0	0.3	0.7	4.4	0.4	0.6	5.9	0.2	1.0
Personal service	10.5	0.3	1.1	3.8	0.3	0.7	21.3	0.3	1.4
Civil servants	5.1	0.5	0.0	6.8	0.5	0.0	2.2	0.6	0.2

1926	Males and females			Males			Females		
	Shares among French internal migrants	Relative shares among non-migrant French	Relative shares among foreigners	Shares among French internal migrants	Relative shares among non-migrant French	Relative shares among foreigners	Shares among French internal migrants	Relative shares among non-migrant French	Relative shares among foreigners
Agriculture	17.5	2.8	0.9	15.7	3.0	0.9	20.6	2.5	1.0
Mining	1.2	1.3	9.2	1.8	1.3	7.4	0.0	1.6	13.5
Food processing	3.1	0.7	0.9	3.7	0.7	0.8	2.3	0.7	1.1
Chemicals	3.4	0.6	1.3	3.9	0.6	1.2	2.6	0.6	1.2
Textiles	3.1	1.6	1.5	2.0	1.6	1.4	4.8	1.6	2.4
Garments	5.6	0.9	0.7	1.5	0.6	1.4	12.5	0.9	0.8
Leather	1.7	0.9	1.3	1.9	0.9	1.2	1.3	0.9	1.3
Wood	3.2	1.1	1.1	4.6	1.1	0.9	0.8	0.9	1.4
Iron and steel	1.5	1.1	3.4	2.3	1.1	2.8	0.2	1.0	3.4
Metal working	8.1	0.6	1.1	11.3	0.6	0.9	2.7	0.5	1.1
Building	3.7	0.8	2.9	5.8	0.8	2.4	0.2	0.6	1.0
Bricks and tiles	1.2	0.8	2.8	1.6	0.9	2.4	0.5	0.8	3.0
Goods handling	1.3	0.8	2.1	1.1	0.8	2.4	1.5	0.7	1.7
Transports	7.6	0.3	0.2	11.1	0.4	0.2	1.6	0.3	0.3
Trade	15.4	0.5	0.6	14.8	0.5	0.6	16.6	0.6	0.8
Bank. and entert.	2.7	0.4	0.5	3.1	0.4	0.4	2.1	0.4	0.5
Professionals	5.4	0.4	0.5	4.1	0.4	0.4	7.5	0.3	0.9
Personal service	8.1	0.3	0.6	2.3	0.4	0.5	17.8	0.3	1.0
Civil servants	6.2	0.5	0.0	7.3	0.6	0.0	4.4	0.5	0.1

Notes: Denote N_i^m, N_i^{nm}, and N_i^*, the numbers of French internal migrants, non-migrant French, and foreigners engaged in the industry i. The first, fourth and seventh columns display the share of the industry for the French internal migrants ($p_i^m = 100 N_i^m / (\sum_j N_j^m)$). The other columns report the shares among non-migrant French and foreigners divided by the share among French internal migrants, that is

$$\frac{p_i^{nm}}{p_i^m} = \frac{N_i^{nm} / \sum_j N_j^{nm}}{N_i^m / (\sum_j N_j^m)}, \text{ and } \frac{p_i^*}{p_i^m}.$$

as French people in 1896, and the foreigner share engaged in textiles was 2.7 the French migrant share. There is no clear-cut movement from 1896 to 1906, but by 1926 the concentration of foreigners in mining and heavy industries had become obvious: among foreigners, the share working in mining was almost ten times the share among French, either movers or stayers, and the ratio of these shares was about three for iron and steel and the building trades.

The distance between the occupational distribution of foreigners and that of internal French migrants seems to increase between 1906 and 1926. To give more quantitative bite to this observation, one needs a measure of distance between populations. The standard procedure to test whether two populations are drawn from the same theoretical distribution is the χ^2 (chi squared) test: χ^2 statistics based upon the industry/status distribution of Table 6.2, without the sample size, are reported in Table 6.4. The meaning of these statistics is as follows. For the first panel of Table 6.4 the population is broken down into 37 occupation/status categories, a χ^2 statistic computed from a sample of size n should be compared to a χ^2 with 36 degrees of freedom, with a critical value for a significance level at 5 percent equal to 51. Therefore for a sample of size smaller than 134 (51/0.38) drawn from the foreigner population, the null hypothesis that the foreigners' distribution was the same as the French migrants' distribution would not be rejected. For a sample of the same size drawn from the French non-migrant population, the χ^2 statistic would be 145 (134 times 1.08), larger than the critical value, and the null hypothesis of identical distribution with the French migrants would be rejected.

According to the χ^2 statistics reported in Table 6.4, French migrants' distribution was closer to immigrants' distribution than to French non-migrants' distribution before 1911. There is no movement in the first statistics between 1896 and 1911, and a slight decrease in the statistics measuring distance between the two French population distributions. The distribution of foreigners became really different after the First World War, when the χ^2 statistic between foreign migrants and French migrants becomes larger than the statistic for French movers and French stayers. These results come from the male rather than the female distribution, since the distance between the two distributions of French women remained larger, even in 1926, than the distance between the distributions of foreign women and French migrant women.

The observation of the shares of work-force in agriculture, mining, and iron and steel suggested that the difference between the distributions lies in these industries. To investigate the origin of the evolution in the χ^2 statistics, they have been computed again on distributions restricted to work-forces with particular industries excluded. When agriculture is excluded (panel 3 of Table 6.4), French migrants are no longer closer to foreigners than to French stayers before 1911. When mining, iron and steel, and building are excluded

Table 6.4 χ^2 statistics between populations (reference distribution: French internal migrants)

	Both genders		Male		Female	
	Foreigners	Non-migrant French	Foreigners	Non-migrant French	Foreigners	Non-migrant French
1. Army excluded (m=37)						
1896	0.38	1.08	0.44	1.11	0.26	1.04
1901	0.35	0.91	0.44	0.88	0.20	0.96
1906	0.37	0.82	0.46	0.89	0.24	0.77
1911	0.40	0.82	0.50	0.89	0.26	0.76
1926	1.34	0.75	1.25	0.83	0.42	0.70
2. Army and civil servants excluded (m=36)						
1896	0.30	1.05	0.33	1.06	0.24	1.03
1901	0.29	0.89	0.35	0.87	0.19	0.95
1906	0.31	0.81	0.37	0.88	0.22	0.77
1911	0.35	0.80	0.41	0.87	0.26	0.74
1926	1.22	0.74	1.11	0.82	0.37	0.70
3. Army, civil servants and agriculture excluded (m=34)						
1896	0.33	0.24	0.37	0.24	0.26	0.24
1901	0.29	0.25	0.35	0.24	0.16	0.29
1906	0.28	0.24	0.36	0.23	0.16	0.29
1911	0.32	0.26	0.40	0.26	0.18	0.30
1926	1.35	0.24	1.23	0.21	0.38	0.32
4. Army, civil servants, mining, iron and steel, and building excluded (m=30)						
1896	0.28	1.08	0.34	1.10	0.24	1.03
1901	0.27	0.92	0.39	0.90	0.19	0.95
1906	0.25	0.84	0.35	0.92	0.22	0.77
1911	0.30	0.82	0.43	0.91	0.26	0.75
1926	0.34	0.78	0.37	0.90	0.24	0.70
5. Manufacturing (m=18)						
1896	0.29	0.10	0.26	0.12	0.39	0.08
1901	0.23	0.09	0.19	0.11	0.33	0.07
1906	0.22	0.10	0.19	0.12	0.30	0.08
1911	0.18	0.12	0.20	0.16	0.36	0.08
1926	0.31	0.14	0.26	0.14	0.28	0.12

Notes: The χ^2 statistic of a population sample of size n with observed share p_i following a distribution p_i^0 is: $n \sum_{i=1}^{m} \frac{(p_i - p_i^0)^2}{p_i^0}$.

The figures reported in the table are $\sum_{i=1}^{m} \frac{(p_i^* - p_i^m)^2}{p_i^m}$ for foreigners and $\sum_{i=1}^{m} \frac{(p_i^{nm} - p_i^m)^2}{p_i^m}$ for non-migrant French.

the increase in the distance of the distribution of foreigners and French migrants over the war disappear (panel 4: 0.30 to 0.34, instead of 0.35 to 1.22 in panel 2). When only mining is excluded most of the increase disappears: the statistic between foreigners and French migrants rises from 0.33 in 1911 to 0.57 in 1926. When one looks at the distributions within manufacturing, foreigners appear to have always been further away from French migrants than French non-migrants were (panel 5 of Table 6.4).

In summary, foreign immigrants and French migrants were much less engaged in agriculture than French non-migrants, and the distributions of the three populations were close before the First World War once agriculture is excluded. In the 1920s foreigners became, relative to French citizens, much more likely to work in mining, iron and steel and in the building trades than before the Great War: the foreigner and native-born occupational distributions drifted apart.

CONCLUSION

During the nineteenth century French immigration was free and unregulated: the only regulation after 1888 was that foreigners had to register at the town hall within two weeks of their arrival. Parliament did not vote proposals aiming at regulating immigration (Mauco 1932: 12). This is not to say that there were no legal distinctions between French and foreign workers. The 1889 citizenship law clarified a previously blurred distinction between French citizens and aliens (Noiriel 1992: 84), and when the first attempts to create the welfare state were initiated, the programs excluded immigrant workers for some time (Noiriel 1992: 112). However, there was no serious regulation of immigrant labor in France before 1914.

Immigration began to be organized in 1911: the Comité des Forges (Iron and Steel Association) setting up a recruitment service which negotiated with the Italian administration. By 1913, 25–30,000 Polish and Italian people had been recruited through this channel. During the First World War the French administration organized immigration, and afterward international treaties regarding immigration were negotiated which authorized French business associations to recruit and select workers abroad and to organize their journeys to France (Mauco 1932: 116).

As a consequence of this organized immigration, aliens in France came from places further away than before 1913 (Table 6.5). The international context of immigration in the 1920s is characterized by the closing off of the United States. It would be interesting to check whether the origin of Italian immigrants into France shifted between 1910 and 1920, because places which used to send people across the Atlantic Ocean began to send people to France instead. This hypothesis is not supported by the evidence from Longwy, since Noiriel (1984: 221) reported that the place of birth of Italian migrants (north of the Marches) was remarkably constant.

Table 6.5 Shares of alien residents in France, by country of origin

	Total	Germans	Belgians	Spaniards	Italians	Polish	Swiss
1881	1,001,090	8	43	7	24	–	7
1901	1,033,871	9	31	8	32	–	7
1911	1,159,935	9	25	9	36	–	6
1926	2,409,335	3	14	13	32	13	5

Source: Rabut (1974: 148, 150).

The 1920s saw the decline of liberal immigration, a pattern which before the war produced a mobile immigrant work-force. The state (and business) actively discriminated against alien labor, denying it full occupational mobility (Cross 1983: 162). French firms had to apply to hire foreigners, stating wage, occupation, work length and general working conditions in a standardized labor contract. This request had then to be cleared by the French ministries to check that there was no excess French labor supply for that kind of work. Finally, the request was sent either to the recruiting centers of Central Europe, or to the border centers where immigrants were waiting for such offers. Administrative controls were further increased in 1926 to limit work movements among immigrants. A firm hiring an immigrant worker who had not yet completed the spell stated in the hiring contract which brought him into France, had to pay damages to the injured party. Immigrants who entered the country to work in agriculture were forbidden to work in other industries (Mauco 1932: 278).

State interventions, illustrated by these regulatory procedures, rather than simply war casualties, explain why immigration into France after the war differed significantly from the prewar influx, as shown by the occupation distributions analyzed in this chapter. At the turn of the century, occupational distributions of international immigrants and of French migrants were close enough. This observation buttresses Prost's view which described immigration before 1913 as a rural out-migration which happened to cross a border. The labor force increase, either for the whole economy or for specific industries, did not appear to be strongly dependent on immigrant inflows during this period. These findings are not consistent with the hypothesis that native-born labor supply was particularly inelastic in France.

Future work could look at "international" regional labor markets. The region comprising the North of France and part of Belgium might well be a very relevant unit to analyze labor flows, and wage correlations might be larger within this region than within France. It would be interesting to discriminate between places of birth, within the origin country, of immigrants living in different French *départements*. Given the influence of distance on migration, it should not be surprising to find out that labor demand in the North of France was more easily met by labor supply from

Belgium than from the southwest of France. These, however, are issues for future research.

NOTES

*   The author is grateful to Hank Gemery, Elizabeth Kremp, Gilles Postel-Vinay, and the editors for comments and advice. The views expressed in this chapter are his own and do not necessarily reflect official positions of the Banque de France.

1   A direct measure of internal migration in response to wages in France has shown that this elasticity was not that low (Sicsic 1991: 72), but international migration probably exhibited an even higher elasticity.

2   A first step in that direction was taken by Sicsic (1992: 691) by checking that foreign immigration was always much smaller than rural migration as a source of urban population growth.

3   Censuses were carried out in March to avoid enumerating seasonal migrants, either French or foreigners. Mauco (1932: 40) estimated the number of foreign seasonal migrants into France around the beginning of the twentieth century at 100,000.

4   See Carré, Dubois, and Malinvaud (1972: 124), and Marchand and Thélot (1991: 48). Recent estimates of labor force participation (including the army) by Marchand and Thélot (1991: 69), are 50.5 percent in 1896, 51.3 percent in 1911, and 51.6 percent in 1926.

5   In the 1911 census individual occupation was recorded, while in the other census it was the sector in which the firm was engaged. For example, a handler in an iron and steel factory was enumerated under the heading "Iron and steel" in 1901 (or 1906), and under the heading "Goods handling" in 1911. For example, there were 544,000 more people engaged in handling in 1911 than in 1906, while the labor force (army excluded) increased by only 83,000.

6   The labour force participation rates (excluding army) from the published censuses were in 1896, 1901, 1911, and 1926: 45.5 percent, 58.0 percent, 58.5 percent, and 56.3 percent for the foreigners, and 48.3 percent, 49.5 percent, 51.4 percent, and 52.1 percent for the French citizens.

7   The initial foreign labor force would be 550,000 (55 percent of 1 million), the final foreign labor force would be 825,000 (55 percent of 1.5 million), and the immigration flow would equal $825 - 550 + 0.015 \times 15 \times 550$, or 398,750.

8   The computations of the increase in the labor force due to immigration are somewhat different: immediate descendants of the Irish-born are included in Williamson's accounting.

9   With a small denominator (the increase in the industry/status cell) the contribution may appear large, although the absolute immigrant inflow within this industry/status was also very small.

7

IMMIGRATION AND EMIGRATION
Canada in the late nineteenth century
Marvin McInnis

CANADA AS A COUNTRY OF BOTH IMMIGRATION AND EMIGRATION

From what has been written about international migration to and from Canada in the late nineteenth century, this country would appear to be a peculiar and intriguing case. The commonly accepted record shows that Canada received immigrants in very large numbers yet at the same time sent emigrants to the United States, also on a very large scale. For most other participants in the "great migration" circumstances were much simpler. The United States received vast numbers of immigrants and, while some of them undoubtedly returned home, the great preponderance of the flow was inward. Some of the other destination countries, such as Argentina, may have experienced a relatively greater return flow but, for most of the destination countries, the great flow of migration was in one direction. Canada stands alone in receiving, or at least appearing to receive, large numbers of immigrants from Europe while at the same time experiencing a large outflow of migration to the United States. This is an intriguing phenomenon in itself but it also has important implications for the interpretation and analysis of migration to the United States. Models of immigration to the United States should take into account the role of Canada as a complicating intermediary. Analyses based on measured responses of migration to income or wage differentials should be consistent in their implications for flows to both North American nations.

The widely reproduced, conventional accounting for the migration element in Canadian population change is shown here as panel A of Table 7.1. These are the figures presented in *Historical Statistics of Canada* (1965: series 244–8) and, although they are originally attributable to Keyfitz (1950: 62), they have taken on the air of "official" estimates. They portray immigration to Canada as rising from an aggregate of 353,000 over the 1871–81 intercensal decade to a remarkable 903,000 during 1881–91. The emigration from Canada implied as a residual calculation from those numbers was 438,000 and

Table 7.1 Accounting for Canadian population change (1871–1901)

| | Intercensal years | | |
| | 1871–1881 | 1881–1891 | 1891–1901 |
		(thousands of people)	
A.	Conventional (HSC) figures		
Initial population	3,689	4,325	4,833
Estimated natural increase	723	714	718
Recorded immigration	353	903	326
Calculated net migration	−85	−205	−181
Implied emigration	438	1,108	507
B.	Revised figures		
1. Canadian-born:			
Initial population	3,105	3,715	4,186
Estimated natural increase	921	988	1,097
Terminal population	3,715	4,186	4,955
Implied emigration	311	517	328
2. Foreign-born:			
Initial population	584	609	647
Estimated survivors	505	529	564
Net change	+104	+118	+120
Immigration	154	296	292
Out-migration of foreign-born	50	178	172
3. Total emigration from Canada	361	695	500

Sources: Urquhart and Buckley (1965: 22). Population totals: Decennial censuses of Canada (various years). Immigration: Canada, Commissioner of Immigration (1882).

1.108 million, respectively. For a country with about 4 million people, these are massive movements. These are the immigration numbers used by Hatton and Williamson (1992b: Table 2) to calculate ratios of immigration to mean decadal populations that in the three late-nineteenth-century decades are about the same for Canada as for the United States. The rate for Canada in the 1870s (54.8) is almost identical to that for the United States, and for the decade of the 1880s it is only slightly lower (78.4 compared with 85.8).

Attention is focused here on the last three decades of the nineteenth century because that is the period in which the Canadian situation appears to be unique. Circumstances changed in the early twentieth century. Immigration to Canada increased greatly in volume and Canada became more directly a country of large-scale immigration. Prior to 1861 it seems also to be the case that Canada was essentially a country of immigration. It was in the last four decades of the nineteenth century that the unusual situation of simultaneous immigration and emigration on a large scale emerged. The decade beginning in 1871 is the first that is covered by national censuses in the period after the formation of Canada as it is now constituted by the Confederation arrangements of 1867.

In their consideration of emigration rates Hatton and Williamson (1992b: Table 1) limit their presentation to European countries. If the figures for Canada were included they would top the list. In the decade 1871–80, the Canadian emigration rate of 109.3 is almost double that shown for Ireland, the European country with the highest rate. In the following decade the Canadian rate soared to 243.1 – far higher than experienced by any European country. Outstandingly high rates of emigration were long thought to have been typified by Ireland and Norway where half or more of young people reaching adulthood left the country. The rate for Canada in the 1880s would be much higher even than that. If we are to believe the conventionally used figures the emigration from Canada in that decade would have been equal to one-quarter of the whole population, at a time when about half of the population was under fifteen years of age. That is little short of astonishing and compels one seriously to question the validity of the data. Even scaled down considerably, however, these rates of emigration would be as high as those found in the highest emigration countries of Europe, but coming from a country that at the same time was receiving immigrants in about the same proportion as the United States. It is a situation that cries out for re-examination. The first step, as suggested above, may be to reassess the quantitative record, and that will indeed be one of the principal matters dealt with in this chapter. There remains an issue of how to reconcile the Canadian migration pattern with the performance of the economy, especially in relation to what was happening to the economy of the United States.

Suppose for the moment that, after reassessment, the Canadian migration figures hold up at even half the levels indicated above. Even with such a drastic downward revision of the numbers we would be looking at a situation that poses challenges for the explanation of trans-Atlantic migration worked out strictly in the context of the United States. If the sort of economic inducements estimated to draw migration from Europe to the United States were applied to Canada, where migrants were purported to be arriving in about the same relative numbers, how then would the high rates of emigration from Canada to the United States be generated? Some element of consistency has to be found in the relationships, or else we are left to rely on non-economic, cultural stories. A further complication is that the commonly used statistics on immigration to the United States do not include immigration from, or by way of, Canada. At the very least they do not count migration across the land boundary. If the latter flow were truly as high as implied by the Canadian figures, analyses of immigration to the United States may be misconstrued. Even if the temporal pattern were in phase, statistical estimates of response elasticities would be distorted. Furthermore, the flow through Canada relates mostly to migration from one European source (Britain) and not others.

To add to the complications of placing in context the Canadian component of the great Atlantic migration, there has been considerable dispute over the assessment of the performance of the Canadian economy in the last three decades of the nineteenth century. In the United States this was a period of both rapid economic growth and dramatic geographic expansion of settlement. Within these three decades there was rapid industrialization and urbanization, especially in the northeastern region of the United States, and the completion of the settlement of the trans-Mississippi West. Both developments together provided the basis for a strong attraction to millions of migrants from Europe. The situation in Canada, however, was quite different.

The Canadian nation that was formed in 1867 comprised three British colonies – Canada (divided into the provinces of Ontario and Quebec), New Brunswick and Nova Scotia – shortly augmented by the small colony of Prince Edward Island, all of which were by that time fully settled. A Canadian West – the counterpart of the trans-Mississippi West of the United States – was immediately added. Two British colonies on the Pacific coast were consolidated into the province of British Columbia, and a large territory that belonged to the Hudson's Bay Company was acquired. The latter was, in turn, divided into the province of Manitoba and the Northwest Territories. Over the last three decades of the nineteenth century settlement began in this vast new part of the nation but it was quite limited. In the early years of the twentieth century that situation was to change dramatically and western settlement came to play a major role in the attraction of immigrants and in the dynamic of the nation's economy generally. For the purposes of this chapter, however, that is set aside as another story. For Canada in the 1870–1900 period, the western settlement that played so important a role in the population history of the United States was scarcely a part of the picture.

The vigor of Canadian industrialization and economic development in this same period has also been called into question. Indeed, the traditional interpretation of the performance of the Canadian economy in the 1870–1900 period has been a pessimistic one. It is most likely that the Canadian economy was growing quite rapidly and industrializing successfully around the time of Confederation in 1867. A lengthy period of depression is thought to have ensued over the period from 1874 until 1897 and the economy has frequently been described by historians of those years as in a condition of stagnation (Skelton 1913; Mackintosh 1939). More recently a revisionist view has emerged that depicts the late-nineteenth-century decades in a more favorable light and, in particular, identifies the decade of the 1880s as one of relatively rapid economic development in Canada (Bertram 1963; Firestone 1960; McDougall 1961). The 1880s is precisely the decade when emigration is supposed to have been at such a high level. The more optimistic, revisionist interpretation of late-nineteenth-century Canadian economic development may help to explain why Canada would have been attractive to the large numbers of European emigrants it is purported to have received but that interpretation adds to the puzzle of why, at the same time, so many people should have been leaving the country.

Several possible explanations have been offered to account for the apparent coincidence of large-scale immigration and emigration in Canada, especially in the 1880s when the magnitudes of the flows were so great. The one that may have received the most attention in previous writing on the topic emphasizes transiency. By that account much of the emigration consisted of immigrants to the United States who were merely passing through Canada or spent only a short time there. The point was raised by Coats (1931) and received more detailed attention by McDougall (1961). That many migrants to the United States traveled through Canada has been long and widely appreciated. The issue is the magnitude of the problem and the extent to which the statistical record has not already netted out those movements. Trans-Atlantic passages to Quebec were low in comparison to New York, and migrants going further west could get relatively cheaper fares on the Grand Trunk Railway of Canada. Many used that route to Chicago and on to the western plains. We should not suppose that the Canadian authorities were unaware of the problem and made no attempt to do anything about it. Indeed, the Canadian immigration authorities kept a separate account of "passengers" bound for the United States and the numbers were large. Those numbers, though, have not conventionally been incorporated into the statistics of immigration into the United States. In addition to those passing directly to the United States, however, there may have been many others who remained in Canada for somewhat longer periods before moving on. Others may have actually intended to settle in Canada but were disappointed with what they found there. If the problem is largely one of transiency it would be helpful to have that confirmed, to establish the magnitude of the problem if possible, and to make appropriate adjustments to the immigration statistics of the United States.

We might suspect that transiency is not the only factor at work because it is known that significant numbers of persons born in Canada moved to the United States in the period under examination. The flow of these emigrants was not regularly recorded, either by the Canadian or the American authorities, although some count was made of Canadians arriving by sea, and in a few years figures were reported for Canadians moving into the United States by rail – figures that the Canadian government asserted were falsely constructed (Canada, *Sessional Papers*, 1882). The censuses of the United States give evidence of a large and growing stock of Canadian-born. Boston and its environs was home to many persons from the Maritime provinces and many of the mill towns of southern New England were heavily populated by French Canadians. In Minnesota and the Dakota Territory the northernmost row of counties was largely settled by Canadians who appeared just to have spilled over the border. Similarly, eastern Michigan had a large concentration of persons born in Canada. The 1880 census of the United States recorded 717,000 residents of British North American birth, almost 20 percent of the number living in Canada. Quite apart, then, from whatever number of

European emigrants made their way to the United States via Canada, a large number of Canadians themselves moved to the neighboring republic.

If large numbers of Canadians were emigrating to the United States while large numbers of Europeans (British) were emigrating to Canada we are still posed with a problem of explanation. Was this a straightforward matter of displacement? Earlier Canadian historical writers (Coats 1931; Lower 1930) saw it that way. But did the immigrants have similar or contrasting characteristics to the native-born emigrants? Were immigrants drawn to Canada by the unsatisfied labor demand left in the wake of large-scale emigration of Canadians? Or were British emigrants drawn to the generally prosperous conditions of North America and, in competing for jobs available in Canada, drove native-born workers southward? This was an issue raised by earlier writers but never conclusively resolved. Was the Canadian labor market of the 1880s strongly segmented, with immigrants filling positions in some sectors of the economy while native-born workers departed mainly from others? The southward flow of French Canadians has received a lot of attention, such that one might almost suppose that emigration from Canada was largely a French phenomenon, while the English-speaking segment of the labor force was being greatly augmented by immigrants. It is not difficult to dispose of that notion but there remains the possibility that English-speaking emigrants from Canada were evacuating different segments of the labor market than the immigrants were flowing into. A rural–urban distinction is a real possibility. Were immigrants moving into the growing Canadian cities while Canadians were abandoning the countryside for better economic prospects in the United States?

The international flows of population to and from Canada raise a number of issues of explanation. For those interested in the development of the Canadian economy and Canadian society it would be desirable to get the record straight – or at least to get a clearer picture of what was happening than we have at present. For those whose interest is in international migration *per se* it would be helpful to have the Canadian situation cleared up and to determine whether it indeed has to be looked upon as a special case. For those interested in the role of immigrants in the labor market of the United States it would be helpful to know whether a major alteration to the statistical record has to be made adequately to incorporate the Canadian element. These issues will not be resolved in this chapter but a few steps will be taken at least to clarify them. A starting point is the empirical record of immigration to Canada and emigration from Canada to the United States.

RECONSIDERATION OF THE STATISTICAL EVIDENCE

The statistical evidence for immigration to Canada has not gone without question. Indeed, the notes provided by Kenneth Buckley for the "official" series in *Historical Statistics of Canada* warn that the series is "grossly exaggerated from 1873 to 1891" (1965: 11). Most commonly that warning has gone without much heed, although many writers give nodding recognition to the problem of transiency. The most severe criticism of the Canadian immigration statistics was by McDougall (1961) although most of his attention was directed to the early years of the twentieth century. In passing, he notes (p. 174) that there appears to be a particular problem in the years 1881 through 1885, but he leaves the matter at that, merely expressing his doubt that in those years immigration to Canada could have been so high in the absence of a really strong export boom. For the most part, though, writers have continued to reproduce the "official" (Keyfitz 1950) series.

It has already been pointed out that the Canadian immigration authorities were quite aware of the problem of transiency and made an effort separately to record arriving persons who were ticketed directly to the United States, designated as "passengers." That series is shown as column 2 in Table 7.2. Column 1 of that table reproduces the "official" series of "immigrant arrivals with intention of settling in Canada." The series for "passengers" continued only to 1891. After that year responsibility for the recording of immigrants was passed from the Department of Agriculture to the Department of the Interior. With that change there was a shift in the recording of numbers of immigrants, evidently in a more conservative direction. At the same time less detail was given in the reports so that it becomes no longer possible regularly to track sub-components of the immigrant total. Over the two decades for which the series of transient arrivals can be obtained, though, the number of "passengers" to the United States was as often as not greater than the number of arrivals indicating an intention to settle in Canada. In the decade of the 1870s 285,000 immigrants went directly to the United States from Canadian ports of entry. Over the following decade the number rose to 730,000. About 85 percent of these would have been British. It cannot be claimed, then, that the "official" Canadian immigration series glibly and thoughtlessly included transients headed to the United States. Nevertheless, as Urquhart and Buckley (1965: 11) warned, the series almost certainly is "grossly over-stated."

A careful examination of the published records of the immigration agents, and the detailed components of the aggregate series, discloses several sources of overstatement. First we might begin with the determination of who were immigrants with the intention of settling in Canada and who were simply passengers en route to the United States. This was reported at the ports of entry. Trans-Atlantic arrivals to Canada were recorded at the ports of Quebec, Halifax, Saint John and Portland, Maine. By far the largest number usually landed at Quebec. The separation of arrivals into immigrants and passengers was regularly reported only for Quebec. Separate numbers can be obtained for Halifax and Saint John only for some years, mostly early in the

Table 7.2 Canada: comparative migration statistics, 1870–1900
(thousands of persons)

Year	(1) Immigrant arrivals	(2) Transient "passengers"	(3) Arrivals less customs entries	(4) Inter-continental immigration
1870	25	44	25	15
1871	28	38	28	19
1872	37	53	37	22
1873	50	49	41	28
1874	39	41	25	21
1875	27	9	19	13
1876	26	11	14	8
1877	27	6	15	5
1878	30	11	18	8
1879	40	21	31	14
1880	39	47	28	17
1881	48	69	33	19
1882	112	81	82	44
1883	134	72	99	49
1884	104	63	69	36
1885	79	26	47	25
1886	69	53	44	23
1887	84	91	55	34
1888	89	86	57	25
1889	92	85	53	23
1890	75	104	42	18
1891	82	105	45	35
1892	31	–	31	31
1893	30	–	30	30
1894	21	–	21	21
1895	19	–	19	19
1896	17	–	17	17
1897	20	–	20	20
1898	31	–	31	31
1899	45	–	45	45
1900	45	–	45	45

Sources: Immigrants arrivals: Urquhart and Buckley (1965: 23, series A-254). Other columns extracted from annual reports of the Commissioner of Immigration in Canada (various years).

period when relatively few arrivals were recorded at those ports. In later years, when the numbers landing at Halifax grew quite large, the record becomes fuzzy and in several of the peak years it is almost certain that all arrivals, with destinations undistinguished, were included in the immigrant total. In only a few years did any significant number of immigrants land at Portland, the Atlantic terminus of the Grand Trunk Railway of Canada. In most years, however, the Portland figure gets grouped with train passengers of all sorts going to Montreal from New York and Boston. What it boils down to is that the determined separation-out of passengers to the United

States is a series for Quebec landings only. There, the distinction was based on railway ticketing. Arrivals with "intention of settling in Canada" were taken to be those ticketed to Canadian destinations. Only adult tickets were determined and a routine grossing up by one-third was made to account for children. That this procedure undercounts the numbers actually proceeding to the United States is indicated by the disposition of non-British arrivals. In several years relatively large numbers of persons arrived from Germany and Scandinavia. At a time when there was very little German and almost no Scandinavian settlement in Canada many of these people were counted in the number of immigrants intending to settle in Canada. The Grand Trunk Railway offered cheap passage as far west as Chicago. Many immigrants would have found that to be an economical route to the American midwest and beyond.

Arrivals at Pacific coast ports of Canada are reported after 1880. The numbers of orientals, shown separately, are the only certain immigrants. In some years the number includes all arrivals of whites, in others it is an arbitrary guess by the immigration agent of the proportion likely to be actual settlers. Reports from the immigration agents at Winnipeg and other western border stations are an almost undecipherable jumble. The agents generally acknowledge that their figures miss many people who moved over the border from the United States. On the other hand, the reported numbers frequently include Canadians from Ontario and other eastern provinces and commonly recount European immigrants who have already been included in the record of Quebec. In short, the numbers for the western inland ports are unusable. They are partly responsible, though, for inflating the official series to very high levels in the early 1880s.

The immigration reported for eastern inland ports of entry is almost entirely overstatement. By far the greatest part occurred at the Niagara suspension bridge and consisted of all passengers not directly ticketed to destinations in the United States. Few of that number would have been actual immigrants. Many would have been Canadian residents of the United States making visits home. In a revised series of immigration it would be best not to include any persons entering Canada in this way. Any oversights there would be more than offset by an unavoidable overcounting of probable immigrants at the sea ports.

One of the most serious sources of overstatement can be dealt with quite straightforwardly. From 1873 until the Department of Agriculture relinquished responsibility for immigration to the Department of the Interior, the immigration figures were augmented by numbers of persons recorded by the customs houses as entering with goods to declare. Whether these were actual immigrants or not is impossible to determine but the composition of the numbers argues against it. Some were Europeans who would already have been included in the count of arrivals at the sea ports. There is some quite obvious double counting in that regard. A few were Americans, whether actual immigrants or just visitors. A large number were Canadians. Many of these might have been previous emigrants from Canada actually returning to take up residence in their native country but there is no clear indication of that. The count is simply of Canadians returning with goods to declare at customs. It is quite plausible that few, if any, of these should be counted as immigrants. At least the number of persons counted at the customs houses is an explicit figure. Column 3 of Table 7.2 shows the numbers of immigrant arrivals with intention of settling in Canada net of the count made at the customs houses. That series is still beset by all of the other reasons for overstatement but would represent at least a first step towards a more reliable and realistic immigration series for Canada.

More preferable still as a usable series of statistics of immigration to Canada may be the numbers of intercontinental arrivals shown in column 4 of Table 7.2. This is constructed from the internal components of the immigration reports and counts only arrivals at ocean ports. It excludes all attempts at measuring immigration from the United States. Essentially it consists of European and oriental immigrants to Canada, net of obvious double counting. It is a lean and trim measure of Canadian immigration, yet, to some extent, it is still probably an overstatement. It includes arrivals at Canadian ports who were ticketed to Canadian destinations but who, in one way or another, ended up in the United States. This includes two significant elements. First, there were those who were using Canada as a route to destinations in the United States but who gave no such indication. In some years at least, it was not a small number. Then there were those who genuinely planned to settle in Canada but who were soon disappointed and moved on to more southern locations. This latter group would be more prominently represented in the surge of immigration in the early 1880s that reflected a settlement boom in Manitoba that quickly soured. At present, however, this intercontinental immigrant series (column 4, Table 7.2) is arguably the most accurate representation of Canadian immigration available. It is the basis for the further reconstruction offered in this chapter. It makes a substantial downward revision of the flow of immigration to Canada. Over the 1871–80 decade, this new series would show that immigration to Canada amounted to only 155,000 persons – a little less than half of that indicated by the conventionally used series. In the following decade immigration would total 296,000 – much less than the more than 900,000 usually cited. It is the 1880s where the biggest revision occurs. Only the first year of the final decade of the century is affected by the revision, although that by a large amount, since the official series, as recorded by the Department of the Interior, is incorporated from that date forward. It, too, may be somewhat upwardly biased but there is no basis for trimming out obvious excess.

With a revised and more realistic immigration series in hand we can reconsider the accounting for Canadian population change in the last three decades of the nineteenth century. Instead of working with the aggregate Canadian population, though, as Keyfitz (1950) and McDougall (1961) had done, it is revealing to make separate calculations for the Canadian and foreign-born populations. At the same time we can bring into account the Canadian-born population residing in the United States. The results of these calculations are shown in panel B of Table 7.1.

The intercensal change of the Canadian-born population living in Canada can be compared with the change that would be estimated to occur at assumed rates of natural increase. Birth rates and rates of infant mortality are drawn from my own ongoing research.[1] The overall death rate is derived by fusing a rate of infant mortality onto the mortality rates for ages above one year that are inherent in the historical life tables for Canada of Bourbeau and Legare (1982).[2] With these assumed rates of natural increase the expected survivors of the Canadian-born population of Canada can be calculated and compared with the numbers enumerated at the succeeding census. The difference is an estimate of the emigration of the Canadian-born, virtually all residing in the United States.[3] These estimates confirm that the outflow of Canadians was large throughout this period. In the 1871–80 decade it amounted to 311,000. That would make an emigration rate of 91 per thousand mid-decade population. In the 1880s the estimated number of emigrants rose to 517,000 and a rate of 131 per thousand population. That is higher than found in any European country in this period. In the last decade of the century the emigration of Canadians to the United States remained large but dropped back to 328,000.

There is a check that can be made on at least the general magnitudes of these estimates. Persons born in Canada but residing in the United States and Canada together comprise a closed population. The number of Canadian-born residing in the United States was also enumerated in decennial censuses. These were one year earlier than the Canadian censuses but the numbers in the United States can be adjusted to account for the change of one year and the same survival rates applied. A comparison with the actual number of Canadian-born enumerated in the United States provides an estimate from the American side of the intercensal immigration of Canadians. For two of the three decades the resulting figure is quite close to the estimates described above of the emigration of Canadian-born from Canada. For the decade 1871–80 immigration of Canadians into the United States works out to be 290,000, less than 10 percent below the estimate of Canadians emigrating. In the 1891–1900 decade the estimates come out to virtually identical numbers. There is quite a large difference, however, for the middle decade of the period. Immigration of Canadians into the United States is estimated at 339,000 while the estimate of emigration from Canada is 517,000 – a difference of almost 50 percent. Of course these are residual estimates and are subject to fairly wide margins of error. A coincidence of numbers, as in 1891–1900, should not be taken too seriously but a difference as large as that found in the 1881–90 decade is worrisome. For the immigration estimate made with data from the United States to be pushed as high as the Canadian-based estimate, the assumed survival rate would have to be reduced to an unbelievably low level. There is no ready resolution of this problem.[4] If the problem were thought to lie with the completeness of enumeration in 1880, it would imply greater errors of estimation in the other two decades as well. About the most that can be concluded at present about the decade of the 1880s is that the emigration of Canadians to the United States was large and probably greater than in the other two decades.

The main point of interest that emerges from these fairly rough calculations is that large numbers of Canadians were moving to the United States. Second, the Canadian emigration did not fall off greatly after 1891 as earlier studies have implied. Throughout the late nineteenth century rates of emigration of Canadians to the United States were high in comparison with the experience of European countries.

A similar sort of calculation can be made with the foreign-born population of Canada. The change in the enumerated stock of foreign-born in Canada can be compared with estimates of the numbers surviving from the initial census date. These figures are also shown in panel B of Table 7.1. The increase in the number of foreign-born at each census date over the estimated survivors from the preceding census is in each case less than the number of immigrants to Canada over the decade. The difference is least for the first decade, 1871–80. Immigration amounted to 155,000 while the stock of foreign-born was only 104,000 greater than the estimated survivors of the stock enumerated ten years earlier. The out-migration of foreign-born could have been made up both of immigrants over the course of the decade and immigrants of previous periods. It is not possible to distinguish between the two categories. The point is simply that the number of foreign-born remaining in Canada at the end of the decade was 50,000 less than the number immigrating over the course of the decade. The outflow was even greater in the two following decades: 178,000 and 172,000 respectively. More immigrants were passing through than were staying in Canada.

The estimates of emigration of Canadian- and foreign-born from Canada can be combined, as in the last line of panel B, Table 7.1. What they show is that, over the last three decades of the nineteenth century, Canada was essentially a country of emigration. Immigration was considerably less than it has commonly been thought to be, and it was offset to a considerable extent by the emigration of recent or earlier immigrants to Canada. The actual contribution of immigration to the Canadian population was only a little more than 100,000 in each of the three decades. In relation to population size and to the outflow to the United States, this immigration could almost be described as incidental. By contrast, emigration was large. True, it consisted in part of immigrants to Canada who moved on to the United States, but the greater part of the outflow was of native-born Canadians. The emigration was not just an illusory flow-through of Europeans en route to the United States. The small contribution of immigrants to the growth of Canadian population hardly justifies characterizing Canada in this period as a country of immigration. This may simplify the interpretation of Canada's role in the trans-Atlantic movement of labor. Canada was essentially a source country, not a destination country. It remains to be seen how this fits with our understanding of the way the Canadian economy was developing over the last three decades of the nineteenth century.

THE PERFORMANCE OF THE CANADIAN ECONOMY IN THE LATE NINETEENTH CENTURY

The revised view of Canada as essentially just a country of emigration in the late nineteenth century, with a greatly scaled-down record of immigration, would be consistent with an older, traditional portrayal of the Canadian economy in this period as one in a prolonged condition of stagnation. The difficulty is that this "pessimistic" depiction of the late-nineteenth-century economy has come largely to be set aside. In its place has been put a more "optimistic" interpretation that emphasizes the relatively high rates of industrial growth that Canada achieved, especially in the decade of the 1880s.

The traditional view was an impressionistic one, not based on hard statistical evidence. It reflected the expressed dissatisfaction with their economic situation of contemporary Canadian political and business leaders, and it reflected the slower growth of traditional exports and the failure of new "staple" exports to emerge to take their place and invigorate the economy. Settlement in the newly acquired region of the western plains of Canada was an important element of the plan of nation building; but it was not working out as planned. To a large extent, though, it also reflected the perception that large numbers of people were leaving the country for more prosperous conditions in the United States. That is, the very phenomenon we are trying to appraise was an important element of the traditional, "pessimistic" assessment of the performance of the economy.

The more "optimistic," revisionist portrayal of the Canadian economy in this period is based on statistical evidence of real income growth and industrial expansion. This newer interpretation was ushered in by Firestone (1958, 1960) with his pioneering estimates of historical national income. Firestone's data covered only decennial census benchmark dates in the period before 1926 but they indicated that over the 1870–1900 period the annual average rate of growth of real per capita income was not markedly less than over the span of the twentieth century (1900–1953) that could be observed at the time of writing. Of course, over the subsequent thirty-five years the Canadian economy has continued to grow at a relatively rapid rate so that the comparison no longer looks quite so favorable.

The real income growth shown in Firestone's estimates was decidedly slower in the last decade of the nineteenth century, but in the 1870–80 and 1880–90 intercensal periods, especially the latter, it appeared to be about the average found for early developing countries. The limitation of the data to individual census years, however, makes the Firestone analysis subject to cyclical as well as longer-term change. There was also some suspicion that the Firestone data overstated growth in the 1870–80 decade. The pioneering national income estimates were hardly conclusive but they at least raised a serious question about whether the economy should be thought of as stagnating over the last three decades of the century. Evidence put forward by Bertram (1963) and McDougall (1971) had a more convincing impact. They looked at industrial growth and showed that Canada was experiencing fairly rapid rates of growth of manufacturing output at that time. Indeed, by the late nineteenth century Canada had become an advanced manufacturing nation. In 1900 only three other nations (the United States, the United Kingdom and Belgium) surpassed Canada in manufacturing output per capita. Again, the industrial data pointed to a slowing down in the 1890s but quite rapid growth of manufacturing output and employment in the preceding decade. The industrial data, like the income data, are subject to the interpretative limitation of being restricted to census dates. Nevertheless, the indications of successful industrialization in late-nineteenth-century Canada have brought most recent writers into the "optimist" camp (e.g. Marr and Paterson 1980; Norrie and Owram 1991). The notion that the Canadian economy was not stagnating but growing and industrializing satisfactorily gave succor to the perception that Canada could have been attracting large numbers of immigrants through those years.

Important new evidence has recently been made available in the form of a much more satisfactory set of historical national income estimates (Urquhart 1993). These are more soundly established than the old Firestone figures and they are available on an annual basis so the problem of having to compare different points on the business cycle can be averted. In addition, it is widely believed that the Canadian economy underwent a fundamental change at the end of the nineteenth century and grew much more rapidly after 1897 than previously. Carrying comparisons through to the 1900 census year adds some of that more rapid growth back into the late-nineteenth-century period. From 1897 to 1926 real output in Canada grew much more rapidly than in the years from 1870 to 1897, and the growth of real output per capita was almost twice as rapid in the later period than in the earlier. That said, the late-nineteenth-century rate of real per capita income growth in Canada (1.39 percent per annum) was not drastically low by international standards. The average rate of growth in the United States over this same period, though, was 2.08 percent.

What was most striking about the growth of the Canadian economy during the late years of the nineteenth century was its sporadic nature. About three-quarters of all the real income growth in Canada occurred in just eight (or a little less than 30 percent) of the twenty-seven years between 1870 and 1897. The growth came mainly in two relatively short spurts in a period that was otherwise rather flat. As indicated by real national output, the growth that had evidently been fairly rapid in the 1860s was tapering off by the early 1870s and by 1878 per capita output was no greater than it had been at the opening of the decade. There then ensued the biggest growth spurt of the whole period and by 1884 output was 50 percent greater than it had been in 1878. Some part of that was recovery from the depression of the late 1870s but by 1879 output was above the previously attained peak. The economy paused noticeably between 1884 and 1887 and then grew once again. This second surge of growth was shorter and less pronounced. It was all over by 1891 and the economy remained quite stagnant from then until 1897.

In the United States growth was steadier as well as being at a higher overall rate. The growth pattern, however, is only part of the story. To understand migration patterns it would be more pertinent to know about the comparative levels of real income and wages in the two countries. In that regard we are not well served by the available statistical evidence. We are limited to comparisons of real income per capita in prices that may not be strictly comparable. Real wages would be a better indicator but the available evidence is just too shaky.[5] For Canada there is only a scattering of nominal wage data and the available price deflators are weak and questionable as well.

At the very end of the nineteenth century it is probably not far off to assume that prices in Canadian and US dollars were equivalent.[6] Canadian per capita income in 1900 was just two-thirds of that in the United States. The ratio was slightly higher in 1890 and slightly lower in 1880. Earlier than that the comparison is more problematic. We can have much less confidence in the price comparisons in the greenback era in the United States. Moreover, in 1870 the American economy, in all likelihood, had still not recovered from the losses of the Civil War. Hence the high ratio (0.77) of Canadian to US per capita income in that year should be looked upon with considerable skepticism. A contemporary investigation reported by Snell (1979) indicates that wages in Ontario were in the range of 70 to 85 percent of wages in New York. Quebec City wages were considerably lower. Average incomes in Canada, overall, were almost certainly lower than in the United States and by a margin that would have made it understandably attractive for Canadians to emigrate to the United States.

Under the circumstances one might also question why Europeans would choose to emigrate to Canada if they had the opportunity to move to the United States. A principal theme of this chapter is that, contrary to the impression given by the long and widely used Canadian statistical series on immigration, they were not really emigrating to Canada. The picture is complicated by variations in economic circumstances within Canada. Two aspects of that might be dealt with briefly. These are interrelated to a considerable extent. Canadian industrial growth was concentrated especially in the province of Ontario and the city of Montreal in Quebec. The best-documented emigration from Canada was the heavy outflow from Quebec and the Maritime provinces. For persons in those regions economic opportunities were more appealing and more abundant in districts of the United States that were also closer than the industrial cities of Ontario or the plains of Manitoba. Furthermore, there was an important urban–rural differential in Canada. Much of the migration of the period was from farm to city. The nearest and most attractive cities, for many Canadians, were in the United States. Central Ontario and Montreal, where the urban, industrial opportunities for employment were expanding, had their own nearby rural hinterlands with an abundance of surplus population.

Two features of Canada's rural sector stand out in the period from 1870 until the end of the century. One is that past rates of natural growth of population had been very high. As late as 1870 the birth rates of much of rural Canada – a still quite newly settled area – were exceptionally high. For Canada to have absorbed all of that growth of population in its industrial sector would have required that Canada experience more rapid rates of industrialization than found in any country before the end of the Second World War. Second, Canada's rural sector was itself weak in generating economic opportunities. Total farm output grew very little in absolute terms after 1874. The surges of growth in the Canadian economy were very largely in the industrial sector. They were not matched by increased output in the farm sector. There were some bright spots, as in dairying to produce cheese for export, but they were not extensive enough to give vitality to the whole of the agricultural sector. Canada's principal hope for expanding its economy in general and the agricultural sector in particular was to foster the settlement of the western plains. That really did not happen until after 1897, when it attracted a great influx of immigrants. A modest foretaste of that was experienced with the opening of Manitoba by railway connections in 1879 and 1883. The ensuing settlement boom was sharp but short lived. The area of Manitoba suitable to settlement was quickly filled and both immigrants and westward-moving Canadians passed on to farms in the western United States. The Manitoba settlement boom coincides both with the sharpest surge of economic growth experienced by the Canadian economy over the entire three decades and with a prominent upswing in immigration. It would have taken no more than 40,000 immigrants (the arrivals of just one year) to provide for the increase in foreign-born population in Manitoba and the Northwest Territories up to 1891.

Much research needs to be done to fill in the quantitative record so that a thorough explanation of Canadian economic development and population change in the period between Confederation and 1897 can be given. The indications are, however, that the revised view of migration presented here by which Canada received far fewer immigrants than has commonly been thought, and retained only a fraction of those, and at the same time lost large numbers of native-born Canadians to the United States, is consistent with the relative economic circumstances and performance of the two economies. It should be clearer than ever that, by and large, immigrants just passed Canada by for destinations in the United States. Canada in the late nineteenth century was purely and simply a country of emigration.

NOTES

1 The birth rates and infant mortality rates used here are those presented in summary form in Kerr and Holdsworth (1990: plate 29). More detail on the estimates of infant mortality is given in McInnis (1992).

2 Bourbeau and Legare (1982) present life tables for Quebec and Canada as a whole that seem to be reasonable representations of the likely levels of mortality except in the first year of life. Their estimates do not take into account the unusually high rates of infant mortality in Quebec. See the discussion in McInnis (1992).

3 By comparison the numbers of Canadians residing in Britain and other countries were trivial. The movement of Canadians to destinations other than the United States can safely be ignored.

4 If anything, the actual survival rate might be higher than assumed here. The Canadian population of the United States in 1880 contained a large number of recent immigrants. Most likely they were also very young. That would tend to raise the average survival rate. A drastic, Third World, assumption about survival would raise the estimate of immigration by only about 30,000.

5 Williamson (1994) provides a Canadian real wage series. It rather anomalously puts Canadian wages above those in the United States most of the time from 1878 to 1900. Although it is based on standard sources, there are several reasons for believing this series to be unreliable. Canadian economic historians ought therefore to place a revision of such series near the top of their research priorities.

6 At the beginning of the twentieth century there were numerous investigations made by the United States government of the wage situation in Canada. These were for highly specific occupations in specific locations.

8

INTERNATIONAL MIGRATION AND THE EVOLUTION OF PRAIRIE LABOR MARKETS IN CANADA, 1900–1930

*Alan G. Green**

INTRODUCTION

Despite the central importance of immigration to the development of the Canadian economy, detailed work on the impact of large flows of foreign labor on the domestic economy has received very little attention by Canadian historians. Canada is a unique country with regard to the flow of international migrants across its borders. For the last three decades of the nineteenth century the country experienced net emigration. Beginning at the turn of the century this condition was reversed, and from 1900 to 1930 Canada witnessed thirty years of net immigration. Canada has been referred to as an "intermediate country," that is neither a net sender of people such as Britain nor a net receiver like the United States, but an advanced country with a large two-way flow of migrants (Thomas 1972: 201–5).

These large two-way population flows provide a unique setting for the study of the relationship between economic opportunity and labor market adjustment. In addition to market forces, these flows were influenced by an increasing array of government regulations beginning in 1910, especially over the selection of immigrants. Therefore any study of the impact of immigration on the domestic labor markets must include both the influence of market forces and the effect of government intervention on the observed level and composition of population inflow.

This chapter explores only one small aspect of this problem – the impact of immigration on prairie wages. The western economy was the key factor in Canadian development between 1900 and 1930.[1] At the turn of the century it was largely unsettled and was only weakly integrated into the Canadian economy as a whole. By 1930 this situation was completely reversed. The West, which in 1900 consisted of only one province, Manitoba, plus a vast area known as the Northwest Territories was now three provinces, Manitoba plus

Saskatchewan and Alberta (British Columbia existed as a separate province before 1900). By the end of the third decade the region was settled and was producing, with great success, the country's chief export, wheat.

At the center of this transformation was a large movement of people. The immigrants came not only from eastern regions in Canada but from Europe, especially Britain, and a significant number came from the United States. This northward movement was largely composed of American farmers seeking cheap land in the newly opened regions of western Canada. The rapidity of this transformation from uninhabited lands to a settled viable economy remains one of the central dynamic features of Canadian development during this three-decade period.

Immigration to Canada during this period was not confined solely to the West. In fact, as will be shown, immigrants settled in all regions and flowed to all sectors, especially during the years before the First World War. The flow became much more focused on western farming during the 1920s and the impact of this switch in the geographical and sectoral distribution of immigration between the prewar and postwar period is closely examined. In addition, since the economy as a whole became more integrated between 1900 and 1930, the study includes the relative relationship between urban and rural wages.

IMMIGRATION AND CANADIAN DEVELOPMENTS, 1900–1930

Population movements both internal and external have played an important role in Canadian development. This is certainly the case from 1900 to 1930. In fact in the decade and a half before 1914 immigration accounted for nearly 46 percent of Canada's average population during this period (Green and Green 1993: 31). The dramatic shift between these large net inflows after 1930 and the equally large net outflows in the preceding decade is central to any understanding of Canadian developments during these years.

What, then, might explain this dramatic switch in the direction of net immigration between the late-nineteenth- and early-twentieth-centuries? Although a number of factors were apparently at work, the first among them appears to be the developments that made the production of wheat on the prairies economically viable (Green and Urquhart 1987: 191). A key factor was the drop in transportation costs which came with the completion of the Canadian Pacific Railroad and improvements in Great Lakes shipping. In addition, new strains of wheat were produced that reduced the time for the grain to mature and hence reduced the probability of a killing frost wiping out the crop. Finally, dry farming techniques developed in the American midwest were adopted thus increasing the yield of wheat per acre. In addition, the terms of trade moved in Canada's favor after 1900. These changes provided the prospect of a profitable return to wheat farming in this region. The result was not only large-scale immigration but these prospects led to an enormous investment expenditure on new railways, on housing, on industrial plants and in agriculture.

The hallmark of the period from 1896 to 1914 was the enormous investment expenditure. This became the real driving force behind the acceleration of income growth which subsequently transformed the country's performance from one of desultory growth in the last decades of the nineteenth century to a level of expansion that exceeded that of the American economy during the opening years of this century. For example, the ratio of gross fixed capital formation per dollar of GNP rose to over 30 percent by 1911 and held this until 1913. By 1914, however, the investment boom had come to an end. This ratio fell to 24 percent in that year and never rose above 20 percent from then until 1930.

Canada was saved from a major recession beginning in 1914 by the outbreak of hostilities in Europe. Wheat exports soared and wheat prices increased sharply with the expansion of wartime demand. In addition capital imports virtually ceased and indeed for much of the next decade Canada was a small net exporter of capital – exactly the outcome the foreign investors hoped for when they poured capital into Canada during the years leading up to the war. Demand for Canadian wheat on international markets, with the exception of the three or four years immediately following the end of the war, remained high. The main reasons for this were the end of large wheat exports from Russia following the 1917 revolution and the retreat from large-scale international sales by the United States as domestic consumption gradually came to absorb most of domestic production. By the mid-1920s net exports of wheat and flour were running at close to 300 million bushels a year. This is in sharp contrast to the years before the war when net exports averaged less than 25 million bushels a year. With strong terms of trade continuing from 1914 until the late 1920s western agricultural prosperity was assured (Green and Urquhart 1987: 194).

What effect did these events have on the level and composition of immigration to Canada? Figure 8.1 sets out the annual flow of gross immigration to Canada over our study period. As the figure shows, the level of immigration started at less than 50,000 in 1900 and by 1913 had reached over 400,000. The war sharply curtailed total immigration but it picked up again in the 1920s, averaging over 100,000 a year. It is interesting to note the sources of this inflow. For the years before the war Britain, the United States and Europe contributed about equal shares to the total. During the war virtually the whole inflow was accounted for by Americans moving northward, presumably to take advantage of the strong demand for Canadian wheat and the rising price of farm land. After the war the sources changed. The share from the United States dropped, while the inflow from Europe, especially central and eastern Europe steadily increased until its share was greater than that coming from Britain (Green 1993).

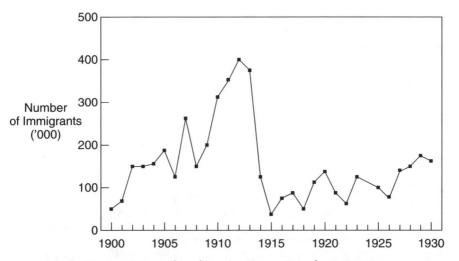

Figure 8.1 Annual total immigration to Canada, 1900–30
Source: Canada, Department of Colonization, *Annual Report*, 1930, Table 5.

Table 8.1 Percentage distribution of immigration to Canada by intended province of destination, selected years 1901–29

Province	(1) 1901	(2) 1906	(3) 1911	(4) 1921	(5) 1927	(6) 1929
Maritimes*	7.1	4.8	4.8	4.3	0.7	2.4
Quebec	33.7	18.9	15.7	14.2	9.3	10.3
Ontario	18.0	38.9	34.5	42.1	17.8	25.7
Prairies†	36.7	32.4	31.0	29.6	68.5	57.3
British Columbia	4.5	5.0	14.0	9.8	3.7	4.4
Total	100.0	100.0	100.0	100.0	100.0	100.0

Sources: Cols (1) and (2), Green and Green (1993: 36); cols (3), (4), (5) and (6) Canada Department of Immigration and Colonization (1922, 1928).
Notes: *Maritimes includes Prince Edward Island, Nova Scotia and New Brunswick; †Prairies includes Manitoba, Saskatchewan, and Alberta.

The geographical distribution of immigration across regions in Canada changed over the course of these three decades as did the countries of origin of immigrants. Table 8.1 sets out the regional and provincial distribution of immigration for selected years from 1900 to 1930. One should note at the start how uneven the distribution was at given points of time and within this uneven distribution how the regional shares changed. For example, the Maritime provinces, the most easterly region in Canada, received a diminishing share of arrivals, falling from slightly over 7 percent in 1901 to a low of less than 1 percent by 1927. The share of the population in this region to total

159

Canadian population was roughly 10 percent during this period. For the central provinces the pattern was sharply divergent. Quebec's share declined while Ontario's rose sharply during the investment boom years before the First World War and then declined during the interwar period. It is the prairies where the changes are the most dramatic. During the settlement years, that is before 1914, the share held steadily at about 30 percent. By the mid-1920s, however, this share had increased to close to 70 percent. Manitoba, the most easterly of the prairies provinces, and the one settled the first, was receiving almost half of all arrivals by 1925 while its share of total population was only 7 percent.

THE DETERMINANTS OF THE GEOGRAPHIC DISTRIBUTION OF IMMIGRATION

The standard textbook interpretation of the role of immigration during the period of western settlement is that immigrants entering Canada during this period were largely destined to settle in the West. It is not hard to understand the origins of such a view. Immigration policy during this period was focused on securing individuals who would work on Canadian farms and particularly on western farms. Indeed the central purpose of the Department of the Interior, established in 1894, was to foster western settlement, and the central means was through the encouragement of immigration. An interesting aspect of this land settlement policy was that the government was not concerned so much with the source of these immigrants as in securing as many potential farmers as it could in the shortest possible time. A recent study has shown that if this was the goal of immigration policy before the war, it was a failure (Green and Green 1993). As it turns out immigrants entering Canada during these years went to every province (see Table 8.1), and entered all sectors of the economy (Green and Green 1993: Table 4, p. 40).

How does one account for such a divergence in the interpretation of the role played by immigration during this period? Green and Green suggest that the traditional interpretation originates in the use of the staple model interpretation of Canadian economic history. Among other things this model focuses all attention on the export region. Recent evidence on long-term growth suggests that Canadian development was balanced rather than unbalanced (Green and Urquhart 1987: 196–7). In essence the agricultural and manufacturing sectors grew at about the same rate from 1870 to 1930. Since the manufacturing was located in the East, the movement of labor to all regions is understandable.

The main implication of this finding is that immigrants were being matched to the demand for their labor across all regions and sectors. To examine this match more precisely a simple multinomial logit (MNL) model was tested. The problem was to relate individual choices of immigrants across a fixed set of alternatives – that is locations within Canada – to the characteristics of these locations and to the characteristics of the individual making these choices. To the underlying two explanatory variables in a standard gravity model – that is, size of the receiving region and distance – several additional variables were introduced to augment the picture of the attractiveness of the location. These were output per person, the percentage of the labor force in the construction sector, the proportion of land taken up in 1921 that had already been taken up in 1911, and, finally, a variable was used to estimate the size of the immigrant stock (Green and Green 1993: 44). These variables it was felt would capture the main dimensions of the attractiveness of the various locations across Canada.

In addition to the location-specific variables, several relating to immigrant-specific characteristics were included. These were the immigrant's sex, the immigrant's marital status and the area of origin. The latter took a value of one if the immigrant was born in any part of the world except the British Isles, and zero otherwise.

To test this model Green and Green (1993) used a sample of immigrants drawn from the manifests of ships landing at Halifax and Quebec city during 1912. These manifests recorded information on age, sex, marital status, intended destination, country of origin and, for migrants destined to the labor force, intended occupation. The original sample size was 4,714 but this was reduced to 2,723 since the test was targeted at only those immigrants destined for the labor force. This unique data set, then, permitted cross tabulation of immigrants by intended province of destination and by intended occupation.

The results using the full sample were most encouraging (Green and Green 1993: Table 6, p. 47). With the exception of the distance variable and a weak showing of the stock variables all the remaining variables registered their expected signs and were statistically significant. This same pattern of a strong showing for demand variables was repeated when we divided the sample into three sectors – manufacturing, service and agriculture. These results suggest a matching of the immigrant flow to demand across sectors and regions in Canada. In essence expanding sectors regardless of where they were located could expect to receive a flow of immigrant labor. Market forces were clearly the dominant factor determining the geographic distribution of immigrants landing in Canada during the decade and a half before the beginning of the First World War.

How, then, do we explain this strong showing of market forces when, as outlined above the government was attempting to steer immigrants towards the West? There is no doubt about the goal of Canadian immigration policy before 1914 but, as has been argued elsewhere, the government lacked the administrative and legal ability to put such a plan into effect (Green 1993). Up to 1910 immigration policy, in theory at least, could be characterized as *laissez-faire*. The only proscribed classes of immigrants were the poor, the sick and the criminal. Even after the passage of the 1910 Immigration Act in which the government was given broad powers of exclusion, these were not used. The desire to fill the West as quickly as possible meant that the immigration door was kept open until 1914. Market forces, then, determined the composition of prewar immigration. Hence those arriving sought employment in areas and in sectors that were expanding and that complemented their personal skills.

This situation changed dramatically after the First World War. By the early 1920s the bureaucracy in the immigration department was effective in implementing policy. The main thrust of immigration policy was the same – secure immigrants willing to settle on western farms. Pressure to implement such a policy intensified from 1924 onwards as demand for Canadian wheat expanded and as wheat prices remained strong. This was partly revealed in Table 8.1 which showed that by the late 1920s almost 70 percent of immigrants were heading to the prairie provinces. What is not shown is that over 70 percent of the new arrivals listed agriculture as their intended occupation (Green 1993). Market forces in the first decade after the end of hostilities were still operating but now government intervention was playing a more important role in the geographic distribution of immigration.

The central question, then, is how did these events shape the observed pattern of urban wages in general and prairie wages in particular between 1900 and 1930? A start at answering this question occupies the balance of this chapter.

RURAL–URBAN LABOR MARKETS

There has been an explosion of work on analyzing the magnitude and causes of the persistence of wage gaps between rural and urban workers (Hatton and Williamson 1991b, 1992a; Alston and Hatton 1991). It is not my intention to review this literature here. However, extensive use will be made of the Hatton and Williamson (1992a) piece in drawing comparisons between the Canadian and American experience in the trend in relative rural/urban earnings, and hopefully gain thereby some useful insights into the operation of the prairie labor market. One of the central themes of this chapter is that a great deal can be learned from a close study of national labor markets, especially in cases where market forces are influenced by direct government intervention.

Since very little work has been done on the topic of nominal or real wage trends in Canada, it might be useful to explain the source of the evidence used in what follows. The non-farm wage series is drawn from work undertaken by Mary MacKinnon (1993).[2] The primary source of this series is a sample drawn from the Canadian Pacific Railway histories of about 9,000 employees of that company. These individual work histories have been drawn together into a unique database that provides a new set of evidence on wages paid across a wide spectrum of skills and across various regions in Canada. All work on wages for this period prior to the MacKinnon sample used the official record, *Wages and Hours of Labour in Canada*. This was first published in 1920 but collected wage data back to 1900. MacKinnon claims that the official series is upward biased since it covers mainly unionized workers. Its main purpose was to show "prevailing" wage rates across a range of cities and occupations. MacKinnon claims that the series for laborers, used here to represent non-farm workers, is largely free from such bias – hence it was used in place of the official wage series. The wages for laborers are in nominal dollars.

The farm labor wage series was drawn from the *Historical Statistics of Canada* first edition (1965) series L349 and the second edition (1983) series M78–M88. This series, as in the case of non-farm laborers, is in nominal terms. The farm wage levels, by province, were cross-checked with estimates recorded in the 1911 *Census of Canada*, vol. IV. Farm wages exclude board. However, neither farm nor non-farm wages have been adjusted for differences in the cost of living, worker characteristics, perquisites, or urban unemployment. What follows then is a first cut at examining long-term trends in rural–urban wage differentials for the period 1900 to 1930 across three Canadian regions. Although further modification of these series along the lines undertaken by Alston and Hatton (1991) might help us define more precisely the level of the ratios, it is doubtful that trends in these series would be substantially different from what we show in the following figures.

Figure 8.2 shows the ratio of rural to urban wages annually from 1900 to 1930 for Ontario, Quebec, the Prairies and Canada. The latter is a simple average of provincial ratios. Immigration exerted a different influence on these three regional labor markets, especially when we compare the years before and after the First World War. In the prewar period, immigrants entered all regions, although the shares were reversed between Ontario and Quebec between 1901 and 1911. After the war the pattern was different. Ontario's share in arrivals gradually declined to what it had been at the turn of the century while Quebec's share plummeted to less than 10 percent of the total. By way of contrast the share of immigrants indicating the Prairies as their destination doubled between the prewar and postwar years.

Trends in the ratio of rural to urban wages reveal three distinct periods – the prewar years, the war period and the postwar period. For the prewar period the ratio is relatively flat. An absence of any distinct trend can be seen as well for the decade of the 1920s. However, during the war years there is a spike in the ratio – that is, rural wages move sharply ahead of urban wages – a consequence of the heavy demand for farm labor and a cessation of European immigration. It is interesting that the trends in the ratio are reversed for Ontario and Quebec before the war but are trendless for the 1920s. The Prairies reveal a pattern which parallels the Canadian case – that is, trendless before and after the First World War with a huge spike during the war.

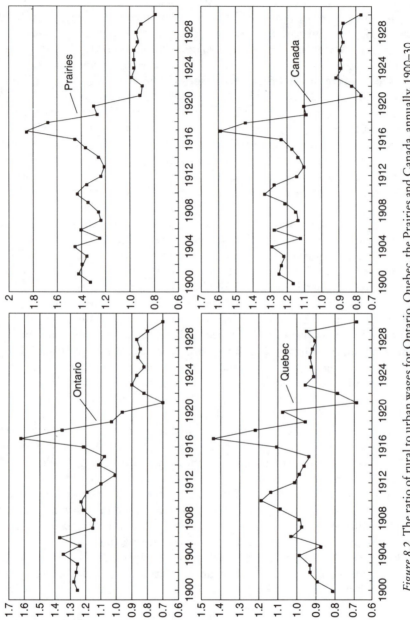

Figure 8.2 The ratio of rural to urban wages for Ontario, Quebec, the Prairies and Canada, annually, 1900–30

Source: See Appendix A at end of chapter.

The levels of the ratio of rural–urban wages shown in Figure 8.2, at least for the prewar period, are surprising. Throughout this period they are universally greater than one. This is in sharp contrast to the experience in the United States and a number of other countries. The usual perception is that rural wages are about half of urban wages. Hatton and Williamson (1992a: 269) show that the ratio of farm to urban nominal wages is 60 percent or less over their entire study period from 1890 to 1941. For an adjusted ratio of this type, Alston and Hatton (1991: 93) find that the gap is about 20 to 25 percent in favor of urban workers during the 1920s. In the Canadian case the gap is reversed. Agricultural workers' wages average about 20 to 25 percent above urban workers' wages in the prewar period and spike to close to 60 percent above during the First World War. For the Prairies the ratio averages between 20 and 40 percent before the war. This changes sharply in the 1920s. The rural–urban wage ratio falls about 10 percent to parity in Ontario, Quebec and for Canada as a whole. In the case of the Prairies, we observe a ratio that is close to parity for the decade.

How do these trends and levels compare with the American experience over this three-decade period? The United States farm-to-city nominal wage ratio for the decades from 1890 to 1941 exhibits a very different time pattern (Hatton and Williamson 1992a: 269). During the prewar years rural wages rose sharply against urban wages, reaching a peak during the war years. After the war, and for the next two decades, the ratio falls monotonically. Recall in the Canadian case the ratio fell immediately after the end of hostilities but is flat during the 1920s. It appears, then, that the labor market response in the two countries is quite different during these three decades. The only exception to this is during the war period when both show a sharp rise in rural relative to urban wages. Finally the levels are very different. In the American case the rural wage never gets above 65 percent and falls by the 1930s to below 40 percent.

How might we explain this anomaly? It could simply be a measurement problem. The MacKinnon series on railway labor wages might be too low. However, given the regional breadth of the evidence this does not seem likely. It could be the case that the farmworker's wages before the First World War do not fully capture all the room and board costs as suggested in the *Historical Statistics of Canada*. At this stage, I do not have an answer. However, using extensions of the same series into the 1920s gives similar results to Alston and Hatton (1991), but still well above those shown by Hatton and Williamson (1992a).

Except for a few suggestive comments it is beyond the scope of this chapter to explain these substantial differences between Canada and the United States in labor market behavior. Instead the intention is to concentrate on trying to bring some understanding to the Canadian experience.[3] During the three-decade period covered here Canada went through a change in immigration policy regimes as it moved from a country driven largely by high levels of investment to one where wheat exports defined the pace of economic change. Recall that in the years before the First World War immigration policy was largely *laissez-faire*. Even with the passage of the Immigration Act of 1910, and the powers of exclusion given to the government under the terms of the Act, little direct control over the composition of immigration was exerted. This changed after the war. The export sector (mainly wheat) came into its own. In addition, by this time the government had the legislative authority and the bureaucracy to influence immigration directly. In essence, the government had the potential to steer immigration to specific regions and specific occupations – that is, towards western farming.

The existence of two very different determinants of the composition of immigrant flows to Canada over the period 1900 to 1930 leads to the possibility that regional labor markets performed differently between the prewar and postwar periods. In the case of the pre-1914 period, as discussed above, demand factors apparently influenced the composition and geographical distribution of immigration. Every sector and most regions could expect a steady flow of foreign labor to help meet their expanding needs. We see this reflected in the relative flatness of the rural–urban wage ratio between 1900 and 1914.

It is the contention here that these conditions changed after the First World War. Immigration was directed explicitly towards the rural sector in general and to western wheat farming in particular. We get a sense that this streaming did have some influence on relative wages in the time trend for the Prairies during the 1920s (Figure 8.2). Rural wages move slightly below urban wages (less than is the case in Ontario or Quebec) even during a period of rapidly growing foreign demand for Canadian wheat. If, then, the policy was to have any effect it would be on the prairie farm wages. We turn now to examining the determinants of western rural wages during the period 1900 to 1930.

SEARCHING FOR THE DETERMINANTS OF WESTERN FARM WAGES

This section sets out and tests an explicit model of the determinants of prairie wages between 1900 and 1930. We have not modeled, at this stage, either urban wages or the rural–urban wage ratio for two reasons. First labor supply to urban labor markets comes from internal as well as external migration and, although we have information on the latter, we know very little about the timing and size of the former. Second, in a small open economy we would expect wages to be set in the export sector. In this case wheat farming. Hence the decision was made to concentrate on prairie farm wage determination, especially for the period under review here where a large share of international migration was targeted to this sector.[4]

To assess the determinants of prairie farm wages, equation (1) was estimated:

$$PWAGE_t = \alpha + \beta_1 \cdot TOT1_t + \beta_2 \cdot IRAT_t + u_t \qquad (1)$$

This model suggests that wages in the prairie farm sector were influenced by two factors – the terms of trade (the demand factor) and the flow of immigrants to the region (the supply factor). This is a very simple representation of the forces setting the nominal wage levels in the Prairies but, as is shown, it gives some interesting results. The dependent variable, *PWAGE*, measures the level of prairie farm wages and is specified in nominal terms. The independent variables are *TOT*1 and *IRAT*. *TOT*1 represents the terms of trade for Canada, that is, the ratio of export to import prices and is set in index terms. *IRAT* is the ratio of annual immigration to the Prairies divided by the population in that region. The denominator is calculated by means of straight-line interpolation between census estimates of the size of the prairie population. Fortunately for this exercise the government took a special census of this region between the regular decennial census. The first such special census was in 1906 and this continued until 1926.

The model works as follows. A rise in the terms of trade signals increased demand for farm products (here wheat). In the short-run this puts upward pressure on demand for farm workers as landowners seek to expand production – that is, at the prevailing wage, excess demand emerges. The government seeks to fill this demand by opening immigration flows to the region, thus encouraging more immigrants to come to Canada, especially those stating their willingness to settle in the West. In the very short-run nominal wages rise.[5] The increased inflow of immigrants, therefore, puts downward pressure on nominal wages.

To study the time trend of our dependent variable, Figure 8.3 was constructed. Not surprisingly it follows closely the pattern of rural–urban wages shown in Figure 8.2. Prairie nominal wages were relatively trendless during the first decade of the century. The major change came with the outbreak of war when, by the end of the war, wages had doubled. With the end of hostilities international commodity markets went into a period of turmoil, wheat prices dropped sharply and so did farm wages. During the 1920s nominal wages in the West were again relatively trendless.[6]

The regression results are presented in Table 8.2. Two test runs were undertaken. One covers the period 1901 to 1921 – basically the years where market forces dominated – and one for the whole period, 1901 to 1930, where more intervention in the process occurs, especially after 1921. Both runs provide reasonably encouraging results. The independent variables exhibit the expected sign – that is, positive for the terms of trade and negative for labor supply.[7] Unfortunately they are not as significant as one would like but again given the preliminary nature of the test they are respectable. The *R*-squared indicates that these two variables account for over half of the observed variation in *PWAGE*. Of the two runs the longer period (1901 to 1930) yields slightly better results, especially for the supply variable. Finally,

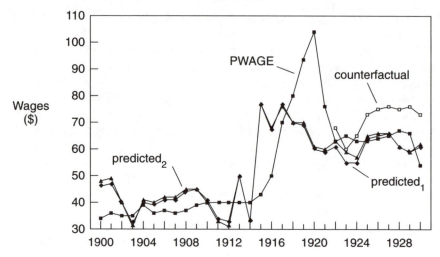

Figure 8.3 The determination of actual agricultural wages, actual versus predicted
values for the Canadian Prairies, 1900–30

Notes: 1 Predicted₁ uses coefficients generated over 1900–21 (see equation 1, Table 8.2) to
create a predicted series for agricultural wages through to 1930.
2 Predicted₂ uses coefficients generated over 1900–30 (see equation 2, Table 8.2) to
create a predicted series for agricultural wages through to 1930.
3 Counterfactual uses coefficients from equation 1, Table 8.2, but sets the immigration
ratio, *IRAT*, to zero from 1922 to 1930.

Table 8.2 Determining prairie farm wages in Canada, 1901–30
(Dependent variable: *PWAGE*, the level of prairie farm wage)

	Equation 1 *1901–21*	*Equation 2* *1901–30*
Constant	1.887	15.895
	(58.60)	(37.89)
*TOT*1	0.5798	0.4768
	(0.458)	(0.302)
IRAT	−353.89	−392.61
	(175.08)	(113.40)
R-squared	0.4332	0.5094
D–W	0.822	0.92
SE	21.42	19.07

Sources: Appendix B, Figure 8.A2; see end of chapter.
Note: Standard errors are in parentheses.

as Figure 8.3 shows, the predicted values track the actual values of *PWAGE*
fairly closely, both for the shorter and for the full test period. The latter is
the "Predicted₂" value in Figure 8.3. The major deviation between the actual
and predicted series occurs during the war period.

In outlining events during this three-decade period it was suggested that the First World War separated the period into two parts. After the war immigration policy steered immigrants to farming in the West, and this region – at least after 1924 – experienced a period of prosperity as wheat prices rose and exports expanded. To explore the implications of this change values of the 1920s were applied to the estimated coefficients derived in column 1 of Table 8.2. The predicted values for *PWAGE* were derived for the period from 1922 to 1930. These are shown in Figure 8.3. The predicted values (Predicted$_1$) are below the actual values until 1924 when they converge towards the latter quickly and follow the actual values closely until the end of the decade. This deviation between predicted and actual follows closely the trend in the terms of trade which are down until 1923 and then rise sharply and stay at the higher level until 1929. (See Appendix B, Figure 8.A2, at end of chapter.)

The other factor affecting *PWAGE* is labor supply. In order to test the effect of this variable the counterfactual proposition that the Canadian authorities followed the American experience by restricting immigration after 1921 was invoked. Recall that the United States passed the Immigration Quota Act in 1921. This severely limited the number of immigrants who could be admitted to that country. We took this one step further and assumed Canada had closed its borders to all immigrants in 1921 – that is, *IRAT* was given a zero weight. Using the remaining coefficients in equation (1) new values of the *PWAGE* were calculated. As shown in Figure 8.3 the counterfactual values rise above the actual *PWAGE* values and remain above for the balance of the decade. The suggestion is that the policy of streaming immigrants to the West did have some impact on the course of nominal wages in this region. Those promoting this policy seem to have benefited in the sense of controlling the cost of farm labor.[8]

SUMMARY AND CONCLUSIONS

Between 1900 and 1930 Canadian immigration policy was focused on the rapid settlement of the Canadian West. Despite this focus the application of this policy was split between the pre-First World War years and the decade following the end of hostilities. Before the war immigration was largely *laissez-faire*. After the war it became more selective and focused. Focused in the sense that immigration policy attempted to steer immigrants directly towards farming in the West. In light of these large inflows of foreign labor we examined the potential impact these may have exerted on prairie farm wages. To gain perspective on the latter we established a rural–urban farm wage index and examined its trend and level, comparing these results with those for a similar period in the United States.

First, Canadian rural–urban wages moved very differently than did their counterparts in the United States. The latter formed an inverted "U," whereas the Canadian ratio exhibited a spike during the war preceded and followed by relatively trendless values. In Canada, again unlike the United States, the ratio of farm to urban wages was greater than one in the prewar years, rose sharply above one during the war, and then fell below parity during the 1920s. On the basis of this evidence it was apparently the case that wage performance was very different in the two countries during the period.

Second, a simple wage equation was estimated in an attempt to identify the main determinant of prairie farm wages between 1900 and 1930. The results were encouraging in the sense that the coefficients exhibited their expected signs and they accounted for about half of the variation in the level of prairie farm wages. To see whether immigration played a role in setting the level of farm wages in this region a counterfactual proposition was tested. Immigration was set at zero and wages for the 1920s were recalculated. The predicted values moved above the actual values, suggesting that immigration may indeed have had the desired effect of directing low wage labor to the West.

What, then, might we learn from this examination of Canadian prairie wage movements? The most surprising discovery was how differently the rural–urban wage series in the two countries moved during the first three decades of the twentieth century. Apparently, at least for farm wages, much of the difference was due to divergence in the terms of trade for the two countries during the 1920s – that is, Canada saw an improvement while the ratio fell in the United States after 1920. In addition, Canadian government immigration policy steered immigrants towards the Prairies, whereas there was no such policy in the US. Certainly, wages in the farm sector of the two countries do not appear to have been converging, at least during our study period. These results suggest that close attention to the operation of national labor markets is essential to any understanding of trends in global labor markets, especially where government intervention is important.

APPENDIX A

Table 8.A1 Monthly farm and non-farm wage series for Ontario, Quebec, the Prairies and Canada, annually, 1900–30

Year	Farm wages				Non-farm wages			
	Quebec ($)	Ontario ($)	Prairies ($)	Canada ($)	Prairies ($)	Ontario ($)	Quebec ($)	Canada ($)
1900	25.18	25.73	33.97	29.89	31.20	20.24	31.20	27.55
1901	26.58	27.05	36.04	31.57	32.40	21.12	29.76	27.76
1902	26.58	27.51	35.00	31.07	32.40	21.65	28.80	27.62
1903	27.49	28.04	35.52	31.63	34.56	22.18	29.76	28.83
1904	30.77	31.02	39.05	34.92	36.48	23.06	31.20	30.25
1905	28.10	31.32	36.11	32.62	38.16	25.17	32.64	31.99
1906	30.06	31.90	36.89	33.52	39.60	23.41	29.38	30.79
1907	29.95	31.50	36.16	32.99	41.76	27.28	30.46	33.17
1908	30.75	31.07	36.57	33.49	43.20	26.93	31.10	33.74
1909	33.00	32.00	38.00	34.89	43.20	26.40	30.46	33.35
1910	36.00	31.00	40.00	37.67	44.40	25.34	30.46	33.40
1911	35.50	32.00	40.00	37.28	44.16	26.75	31.32	34.08
1912	35.00	32.00	40.00	36.78	51.60	29.39	34.78	38.59
1913	34.50	31.00	40.00	36.17	51.12	30.98	34.78	38.96
1914	34.00	32.00	40.00	35.78	52.08	28.69	34.99	38.59
1915	33.00	31.00	43.67	37.56	50.88	28.86	35.21	38.32
1916	41.00	39.00	49.67	42.78	51.12	32.03	37.37	40.17
1917	59.00	59.00	72.33	62.67	55.20	36.61	42.34	44.71
1918	65.00	62.00	83.33	71.22	59.28	45.41	53.78	52.82
1919	76.00	70.00	92.67	79.89	91.68	67.76	78.62	79.35
1920	86.00	75.00	102.33	86.11	105.60	77.09	79.40	87.36
1921	58.00	60.00	79.00	65.44	114.00	85.89	89.80	96.56
1922	53.00	57.00	63.67	57.67	95.04	69.17	73.40	79.20
1923	59.00	59.00	65.67	61.00	87.84	66.00	68.60	74.15
1924	56.00	57.00	63.67	58.89	87.84	65.30	68.40	73.85
1925	56.00	54.00	64.67	59.22	88.56	66.00	68.00	74.19
1926	57.00	58.00	65.33	60.56	88.32	66.88	68.60	74.60
1927	58.00	59.00	65.67	61.11	90.72	69.70	70.40	76.94
1928	58.00	58.00	67.33	61.78	88.80	66.53	72.20	75.84
1929	61.00	57.00	66.00	62.33	90.24	70.93	71.23	77.47
1930	52.00	51.00	57.67	56.22	96.00	72.69	72.38	80.36

Source: The basic CPR wages series is from MacKinnon (1993: 26–7).

Notes: (1) The non-farm wage data are based on the CPR workers wages, quoted as cents per hour. This was transformed into monthly wages by multiplying these hourly series by the number of hours worked per week in Winnipeg, Toronto, and Montreal, then multiplying the latter by 4.0. Hours worked per week were derived from "Wages and Hours of Labor in Canada."

(2) Farm wage data, see text.

APPENDIX B

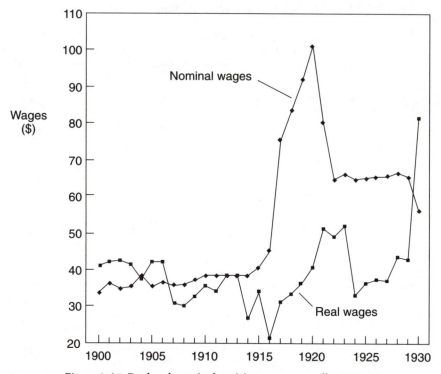

Figure 8.A1 Real and nominal prairie wages, annually, 1900–30
Sources: For nominal prairie wages see Appendix A. For wheat prices, see *Historical Statistics of Canada*, (2nd edn), Series M228-238.
Notes: Real wages = nominal / [the price of wheat].

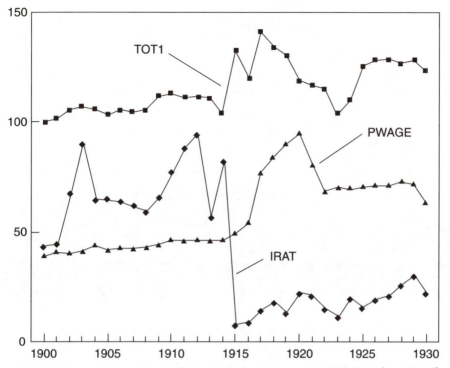

Figure 8.A2 Annual estimates of the nominal prairie wages (*PWAGE*), the terms of trade (*TOT1*) and the ratio of western immigration to regional population (*IRAT*), annually, 1900–30

Notes: 1 For *TOT1*, 1912 = 100.
2 *PWAGE* is expressed in nominal dollars.
3 *IRAT* is presented as IRAT*1000.

Sources: *PWAGE*: see Appendix A. *TOT1*: Green and Sparks (1991). *IRAT* (= prairie immigration/prairie population): *Historical Statistics of Canada* (1st edn) Series A1 and Series A2-A14, Toronto, Macmillan.

NOTES

* The author wishes to thank Mark Smith for his heroic efforts in drawing the material together. The chapter could not have been written without his help. Also I would like to thank David Green for the advice he gave on the direction of this chapter. This continues collaboration with David that began several years ago and, hopefully, will continue as we explore the whole role of immigration in Canadian development.

1 For a discussion of the general patterns of growth during the opening decades of this century see Green and Urquhart (1987).

2 I am indebted to Mary MacKinnon for allowing me to use her new data-set prior to its publication.

3 This diversity in long run trends in rural–urban wage ratios between Canada and

the United States is extended when other countries are added to the list. See Hatton and Williamson (1991b: 416–17).

4   For an opposite view where wages are set in the import competing sector, see Chambers and Gordon (1987).

5   The whole question on the relationship between nominal wages and the level of immigration has been raised by Dales (1966). Dales sees immigration as inversely related to Canadian unemployment levels with the level of flow adjusted to maintain a constant nominal wage over time. This model was tested by Easton, Gibson and Reed (1988). Although they rejected the constant money wage thesis, nevertheless they did agree with Dales that Canadian immigration authorities ran a flexible immigration policy.

6   For the trend pattern in real prairie wages (nominal wages deflated by the price of wheat) see Appendix B, Figure 8.A1. Note the steep rise in real farm wages during the 1920s.

7   Hatton and Williamson (1992b: 274) found in the American case a strong positive association between the terms of trade and changes in nominal farm wages. In this case, however, the terms of trade fell during the 1920s, as did farm wages. We need to know why such a deviation in the trend in terms of trade occurred in the two countries during the 1920s.

The performance of the immigration ratio (see Figure 8.A2, Appendix B) appears at variance with our regression results. However, the sharp decrease in *IRAT* occurs only during the First World War when European immigration drops to zero. For the balance of the study period the ratio has the desired positive slope.

8   It would be interesting to apply a similar model to the Australian economy. During this period, farm wages increased steadily against urban wages. Australian immigration policy was also resolutely committed to encourage immigration from Britain. From 1900 until 1930, 75 percent of all immigrants landing in Australia came from the United Kingdom. Did this pattern of immigration affect the observed trend in Australian farm wages? For relative farm wages see Hatton and Williamson (1991b: 417). For immigration to Australia, see Withers (1987: 262–3).

9

IMMIGRANTS AND EMIGRANTS

International migration and the US labor market in the Great Depression

Henry A. Gemery

The great unknown of the prewar [World War II] era is the supply side of the labor market.

(Weir 1992: 325)

Labor force variability from year to year in those decades [1900–30] was generated largely by immigrants and women.

(Lebergott 1992: 380)

The dramatic decline in US immigration in the 1920s and 1930s is well known. Less well known are its causes and its labor market effects. To the extent that US and other labor markets were integrated internationally, there are questions as to the degree of international migration, its causes, its alterations, and its effects on both observed wage gaps and unemployment. Studies of wage gaps (Alston and Hatton 1991; Hatton and Williamson 1992a) and of interwar unemployment (Eichengreen and Hatton 1988; Margo 1993) give scant attention to the impact of international labor mobility on wage differentials and employment levels. An impact is not unrecognized, but few data are available that readily link domestic labor markets with international migration and even fewer studies have attempted to define such a link empirically. The wide disparity in available estimates suggests that the choice of a measure of labor market integration is also a question.

There are further questions: was the restrictionist legislation of the 1920s the cause of the drop in immigration in both the 1920s and the 1930s? How did net international migration compare in level with internal migration? If much of the job loss or job formation occurred in the urban sector, how did immigration or emigration bear on the sectoral labor markets? We know that rural to urban migration was sizable in the interwar decades. Hatton and Williamson, in examining US wage gaps between farm and city, point to real flows of "impressive" magnitude between those sectors, i.e. net farm emigration that averaged 549,000 per year between 1921 and 1941 (Hatton and Williamson 1992a: 276). However, those flows reversed in the depths of the Depression as net farm immigration appeared in both 1931 and 1932. They reversed again as a recovery developed. "Following the trough of the Great Depression, farm emigration surged to World War II, and in 1941 it was higher than at any time during the interwar period" (ibid.). How much did immigration to city and farm add to those numbers? Were international migration flows synchronous over the same time period? From all countries?

In examining the international integration of the US labor market, this chapter addresses questions of the causes of declining immigration, the robustness of Todaro-like models of migration when a switching from immigrant to emigrant flows occurs, and the relative significance of internal sectoral migration and international migration.

INTERNATIONAL MIGRATION TO THE US: THE QUANTITATIVE RECORD

The migration literature has long identified the international migrations of 1881–1910 as the peak decades of labor market integration for the historical period extending to the mid-twentieth century. Those three decades saw a net international migration from Europe of 5.89 million persons per decade, a volume two and one half times greater than that of the decade averages for the prior three decades (Kuznets and Rubin 1954: 52). Seventy percent of that European emigrant flow, decade averages of 4.1 million, was immigration into the US. In the following three decades, 1911–40, European emigration dropped nearly half, to 3.2 million per decade with the US receiving 64 percent of that total. Table 9.1 details the net migration from all sources to the US for the decades from 1850–60 to 1970–80. Beginning with the decade preceding the Civil War and continuing to that preceding the First World War, the rate of net migration accounted for a quarter to a third of the total population increase in every decade. With the the First World War decade, a pronounced decline begins. The migration rate approximately halves in that decade, nearly halves again in the 1920–30 decade, and then turns negative in the 1930s. Not until 1970–80 does migration return to its nineteenth-century size as a contributor to population change.

The precipitous decline in the rate of net migration in the decade 1910–20 and in the interwar decades, is a clear indication of the decreasing factor mobility characteristic of that era. The First World War itself was an obvious impediment to civilian mobility; however, the continuous fall in migration over the next two decades suggests the appearance of further disincentives and/or direct barriers to labor movement. Table 9.2 focuses on those three decades with detail on the origin country sources of US immigration, in

Table 9.1 United States: components of population growth, 1850–1980
(rates per 1,000 population per year)*

Period	Average population (000s)	RTI	CBR	CDR	RNI†	RNM†	RNM as % of RTI
1850–1860	26,721	30.44	—	—	20.35	10.09	33.1
1860–1870	35,156	23.62	—	—	17.64	5.98	25.3
1870–1880	44,414	23.08	41.16	23.66	17.50	5.58	24.2
1880–1890	55,853	22.72	37.03	21.34	15.69	7.03	30.9
1890–1900	68,876	18.83	32.22	19.44	12.78	6.06	32.2
1900–1910	83,245	19.08	30.10	17.27	12.83	6.25	32.8
1910–1920	98,807	14.86	27.15	15.70	11.45	3.41	23.0
1920–1930	114,184	14.01	23.40	11.08	12.32	1.68	12.0
1930–1940	127,058	7.01	18.39	11.18	7.21	−0.20	−2.9
1940–1950	140,555	13.50	22.48	10.39	12.09	1.41	10.4
1950–1960	164,011	17.67	24.81	9.47	15.34	2.33	13.2
1960–1970	190,857	12.27	20.26	9.55	10.71	1.56	12.7
1970–1980	214,306	10.83	15.49	9.00	6.49	4.34	40.1

Source: Haines (forthcoming).
Notes: *RTI = rate of total increase. CBR = crude birth rate (live births per 1,000 population per year). CDR = crude death rate (deaths per 1,000 population per year). RNI = rate of natural increase (=CBR−CDR). RNM = rate of net migration.
†Rate of net migration calculated directly from net migrants 1790–1860. Gross migrants used for 1860–1870. For 1870–1980, RNM = RTI−RNI and thus is a residual. Prior to 1870, RNI is calculated as a residual (= RTI−RNM).

particular the numbers of "old" and "new" immigrants. Those figures indicate the dramatic shift of immigration away from sources in eastern and southern Europe (the "new" immigrants) in the post-First World War decade. Their numbers drop by 79 percent from their earlier decade total while the numbers from "old" European sources (northern and western Europe) expand by 9 percent in the 1920s. Immigration from Mexico and Canada/Newfoundland boomed in the 1920s as the number of immigrants from those Western Hemisphere nations increased by 148 percent.

In the 1930s decade, immigration from all sources fell drastically, though the drop in "old" European immigration was now far greater than that for the "new", the "old" slumping to 8 percent of its decade-earlier level, while the comparable figure for the "new" immigrants is 21 percent. Immigration from Canada and Newfoundland fell to 16 percent of the decade-earlier level, and that for Mexico and "other countries" (in the net) turned negative, i.e. emigration from the US occurred. For the decade, the rate of net migration was negative.

Table 9.3 shows that the sex composition of immigrant flow changed significantly from the prewar to the Depression decade. Heavily male at 64.9 percent in 1911–15, the sex ratio changes to one heavily female with the female proportion rising progressively to peak at 59.2 percent in 1931–5.

Table 9.2 Net immigration into the United States by country of origin, by decade, 1910–39

	1910–19	1920–9	1930–9
All countries	4,286,265	3,008,780	210,437
All Europe	3,458,762	1,533,186	190,855
"Old"	910,309	991,128	77,839
"New"	2,548,453	542,058	113,016
Mexico	135,678	455,502	−75,240
Canada/Newfoundland	417,016	912,651	144,325
Other countries	274,809	107,441	−49,503

Sources: Calculated from United States Department of Commerce (1912, 1915, 1918, 1921, 1924, 1928, 1931, 1934, 1936, 1939, and 1941).
Notes: "Old" refers to the countries of northern and western Europe, namely: Belgium, Denmark, France, Germany, the Netherlands, Norway, Sweden, Switzerland, and the United Kingdom. "New" refers to the countries of eastern and southern Europe: Austria, Bulgaria, Czechoslovakia, Finland, Greece, Hungary, Italy, Poland, Portugal, Romania, Russia, Spain, Turkey in Europe, Yugoslavia, and certain other small countries.

Table 9.3 Percentage distribution of United States immigrants by sex and occupation for five-year periods, fiscal years ended June 30, 1911–40

	1911–16	1916–20	1921–5	1926–30	1931–5	1936–40
Male	64.9	58.7	56.6	53.8	40.8	45.2
Female	35.1	41.3	43.4	46.2	59.2	54.8
Total	100.0	100.0	100.0	100.0	100.0	100.0
Professional	1.4	3.2	2.9	3.6	6.1	8.5
Commercial	1.6	2.7	2.2	1.8	3.2	9.9
Skilled	14.9	16.7	18.6	18.7	11.7	12.2
Farmers	1.2	2.6	2.9	3.1	2.0	1.6
Servants	12.3	8.8	10.5	10.3	6.2	6.1
Laborers	39.9	23.1	20.2	18.7	6.1	3.5
Miscellaneous	1.5	4.8	4.0	3.5	3.3	2.5
No occupation (women & children)	27.2	38.1	38.7	40.3	61.4	55.7
Total	100.0	100.0	100.0	100.0	100.0	100.0

Sources: Calculated from United States Department of Labor, Bureau of Immigration (1911–32); United States Department of Labor (1933–40); and United States Department of Commerce, Bureau of the Census (1922–41).

Accompanying the shift in sex ratios and country origins was a shift in the skill composition of the immigration. Unskilled labor, servants and laborers, made up 52 percent of the immigrant numbers in 1911–15; however that proportion dropped progressively – to 32 percent in 1916–20, then to 12 percent with the beginning of the Depression, 1931–5. Though the proportion of unskilled fell, the proportion of skilled did not rise significantly;

rather, the immigrant stream changed toward a higher share of women and children with no listed occupations. This dependent portion rose from 27 percent pre-First World War to 38 percent after the war, remained around that level to 1926–30, then rose to 61 percent at the beginning of the Depression.

THE CAUSES OF DECLINING INTERNATIONAL MIGRATION TO THE US

The patterns described for the war and interwar decades were shaped by war, the increasingly restrictionist immigration policies adopted in the US, and the deteriorating economic circumstances of the Depression. The First World War closed off European migration during the war years and had a longer-term impact via (1) the "echo effect" of demographic loss stemming from direct casualties and a birth deficit, and (2) a diminished "family and friends effect" resulting from fewer wartime migrants. An echo effect from the decline in rates of natural increase is indeed apparent but, given a twenty-year lag, its trough appears in 1938.

The family and friends effect, the notion that "migration begets migration" since prior migrants provide information, passage aid, and accommodation to later migrants, is found to be significant in nearly all migration studies (Greenwood 1975: 405–6; Hatton and Williamson, Chapter 3). A weakening of the family–friends effect can be inferred from the drop in the rate of net migration during the wartime decade, i.e., the rate in 1900–10 was 6.25, but it drops to 3.41 in the 1910–20 decade (see Table 9.1). If a family–friends effect were operative, migration in the subsequent decade, 1920–9, should reflect that earlier drop. The migration rate for that decade does indeed fall, to 1.69, but when the migrant flows are disaggregated, it is apparent that the fall occurred only with the "new" immigrants and those from "other countries." "Old" immigrant numbers expanded. Could the "old" immigrants have been immune to the weakened family–friends effects? Dunlevy and Gemery found that both "old" and "new" migrants responded to family–friends effects in making migration decisions at the turn of the century and it seems implausible to argue that, two decades later, "old" immigrants were unresponsive to those effects (Dunlevy and Gemery 1978). The econometric work undertaken in a later section (see pp. 183–5) confirms that, for the UK and Germany, the role of a family–friends variable is strong. The family–friends effect then should have equally affected "old" and "new" migrants. That it did not makes clear the fact that an explanation for the declining 1920s migration lies elsewhere. An explanation specific to the "new" immigrants is needed and that need points directly to the restrictionist legislation in the US.

Three pieces of legislation whose intent was broadly restrictive were enacted in the 1910s and 1920s. The Immigration Act of 1917 began the process. It imposed a literacy test that proved to have little effect on the number of admissions, so it was followed in turn by the Quota Act of 1921 that set numerical limits on immigration from countries outside the Western Hemisphere. That Act was then succeeded by The Immigration Act of 1924 (Hutchinson 1981; Bernard 1982; Briggs 1984; Goldin 1993). The quotas in the 1921 and 1924 Acts were addressed primarily to the control of immigration from southern and eastern Europe and in that they succeeded as Table 9.2 indicates. In the decade prior to quotas, "new" immigrants made up 59 percent of the net immigrant total, but only 18 percent in the 1920s as quotas came into place. Figure 9.1 illustrates the constraint placed on "new" immigrants once quotas were fully operational in the latter half of the decade of the 1920s; quota fulfillments were 100 percent for that category in 1926–8 and only slightly below that level in 1929–30. Though the quota for northern and western Europe was seven times larger than that for southern and eastern Europe – 140,995 as opposed to 20,247 – Figure 9.1 demonstrates that the quotas were nearly, though not fully, met by the "old" immigrants as well. In those same five years, quota fulfillments for "old" immigrants averaged over 90 percent. No constraints appeared on immigrants from countries of the Western Hemisphere since quota restrictions did not apply; thus immigration from Mexico and Canada/Newfoundland expanded by 148 percent as noted earlier.

The limiting effect of the quotas is most evident in the annual detail of Table 9.4 that focuses on the target nationalities of the restrictionist legislation, the "new" immigrants. As the decade of the 1920s began, gross migration of the "new" migrants surged from 159,000 to 580,000 despite the constraint of the literacy test. As the quota legislation of 1921 took effect in fiscal 1922, the ceilings set by the quotas of 157,000 and 158,000 through 1924 effectively determined gross migration. With the sizable quota decrease to 20,247 in fiscal 1925, the number of admitted immigrants decreased sharply to at or below that annual level. The totals shown for gross migration are generally greater than the admitted and quota totals since the 1924 Act excluded wives and dependent children of US citizens as well as other selected categories from the quota limits (Bernard 1982: 95; Briggs 1984: 45). Because return migration occurred, net migration from southern and eastern Europe was actually negative in four years of the decade, 1920, 1922, 1925, and 1926. Thus quotas, set for gross admissions rather than net migration, were actually more constraining than the raw quota numbers would indicate.

In the decade of the 1930s, the quotas became non-binding as Figure 9.1 illustrates. From 1930 to 1931, quota immigration dropped by 62 percent. In 1933 only 8,220 quota immigrants out of a permissible total of 153,879 were admitted. No immigrant category fulfilled its quota for any year in the decade. Southern and eastern European nations did reach nearly 90 percent of their quota, but only in one year, 1939, as refugee emigrants fled Europe. No other sources reached more than 41 percent of their quotas.

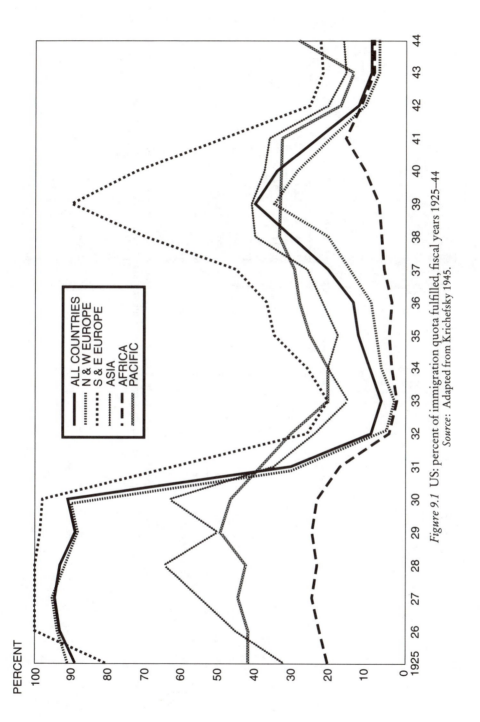

Figure 9.1 US: percent of immigration quota fulfilled, fiscal years 1925–44
Source: Adapted from Krichefsky 1945.

Table 9.4 Quota restrictions and migration from southern and eastern Europe to the United States, fiscal years ended 30 June, 1920–9

	1920	1921	1922	1923	1924	1925	1926	1927	1928	1929
Quota totals	—	—	157,416*	158,597	158,632	20,247†	20,247	20,247	20,247	20,247
Number admitted under quota			149,789	155,905	158,503	16,777	20,375	20,147	20,195	19,586
Gross migration	159,297	513,813	136,948	151,491	160,993	23,268	29,252	41,758	42,352	61,913
Net migration	−61,976	327,388	−5,870	104,819	114,509	−32,001	−13,206	32,408	31,380	34,570

Sources: United States Department of Commerce, Bureau of the Census (1922–30) [e.g. "Table No. 79 – Immigration Under the Per Centum Limit: By Country or Region of Birth, Years Ended June 30," (1924)].
Notes: *Quota Act, 19 May, 1921.
†Immigration Act of 1924, 26 May, 1924.
The quota totals were calculated as the sum of the individual quotas for each country. Gross migration is less than the number admitted under the quotas in 1922 and 1923. That may be due to both immigrant and non-immigrant aliens being intermixed in quota statistics, as noted in the example above.

This tremendous drop in quota immigration ... was due primarily to the depression in the United States, financial inability of United States residents to bring their relatives, and a strict interpretation by United States consuls abroad of the clause "likely to become a public charge" in the Immigration Act of 1917.

(Krichefsky 1945: 159)

Economic circumstance not only severely limited immigration in the 1930s, it also fostered emigration from the US. Emigrants appeared in sufficient numbers to turn the rate of net migration negative for the decade. For that decade, net emigration from the US occurred despite real wages rising more rapidly in the US than in any of the other fourteen countries appearing in the Williamson data on international real wage comparisons (Williamson 1994: Table A3). The United Kingdom, a prime immigrant source, is illustrative. It experienced net out-migration to the US from 1920 to 1931, but then immigration from the US for eight years of the 1930s decade.

DO TODARO-TYPE MODELS APPLY IN DISINTEGRATING LABOR MARKETS?

Are standard migration models applicable to the interwar period? Given the quota constraints of the 1920s and the switching from immigration to emigration occurring in the 1930s, will the real wage differentials and destination employment prospects emphasized in Todaro-type migration models perform well in explaining the migration patterns? (Todaro 1969; Greenwood 1975: 403–4; Hatton and Williamson 1992a). Such models have been applied to internal migration in the US in the interwar decades, but their application to international migration in those same decades has only recently been possible with the development of data on real wage differentials adjusted on a purchasing-power-parity basis (Williamson 1992).

Several alternative specifications of Todaro-form migration models did yield significant results for the UK migration patterns in the interwar period. Table 9.5 summarizes the results. Of the variables in the equations, employment in the US performed as expected, having a positive and statistically significant effect on migration, whether the variable was expressed as a US rate or as a ratio of employment rates. The role of wage differentials was more problematical. When expressed as a simple ratio, US divided by UK wages, the variable had an unexpected negative coefficient. When expressed as the change in a lagged ratio, the coefficient was positive but only statistically significant in two of the four equations, (3) and (5). When a variable for the family-and-friends effect, the net migration rate from the UK to the US lagged one year, was added to the model, its effect was positive and significant at the 5 percent level.

Similar results, summarized in panel B of Table 9.5, occur with the German

Table 9.5 Explaining net international migration, UK–US and Germany–US, 1920–39: a simple structural model

(A): UK–US	Equation (1)	Equation (2)	Equation (3)	Equation (4)	Equation (5)
Constant	−1.749	−2.644*	−1.409**	−3.513*	−1.955**
	(1.21)	(0.65)	(0.73)	(0.79)	(0.93)
Wage ratio	−0.430	—	—	—	—
(US/UK)	(0.53)				
Change in lagged	—	0.616	1.697‡	1.112	1.894‡
wage ratio†		(1.04)	(0.97)	(1.011)	(0.93)
US employment rate	3.252*	3.605*	1.803**	—	—
	(0.85)	(0.78)	(0.95)		
Ratio of employment					
rates	—	—	—	4.008*	2.137**
(US/UK)				(0.81)	(1.04)
Net migration rate	—	—	513.985*	—	481.651*
(UK to US) lagged			(195.80)		(197.47)
1 year					
R^2 adjusted	0.54	0.53	0.66	0.57	0.68
D-W	1.12	1.04	2.20	1.10	2.20
SE	0.375	0.379	0.321	0.364	0.315
N	20	18	18	18	18

(B): Germany–US	Equation (1)	Equation (2)	Equation (3)	Equation (4)	Equation (5)
Constant	−1.078*	−1.231*	−1.475*	0.153**	0.980
	(0.38)	(0.25)	(0.34)	(0.71)	(0.63)
Wage ratio	−0.144	—	—	—	—
(US/Germany)	(0.12)				
Change in lagged	—	−0.433**	−0.467**	−0.989	−1.041**
wage ratio†		(0.24)	(0.24)	(0.62)	(0.49)
US employment rate	1.991*	1.887*	2.265*	—	—
	(0.30)	(0.30)	(0.46)		
Ratio of employment					
rates	—	—	—	0.168	−0.873
(US/Germany)				(0.70)	(0.66)
Net migration rate	—	—	−0.192	—	0.659*
(Germany to US)					
lagged 1 year			(0.18)		(0.23)
R^2 adjusted	0.79	0.82	0.82	0.21	0.51
D-W	1.30	1.81	1.60	0.80	2.18
SE	0.135	0.126	0.125	0.264	0.208
N	15	15	15	15	15

Notes: † The change in lagged wage ratio is calculated as the wage ratio lagged one year minus the wage ratio lagged two years.
‡ This is significant at the 0.05 level for a one-tailed t-test. That test is permissible since theory predicts that the sign on the coefficient will be positive.
*Significant at 0.05 level for a two-tailed t-test.
**Significant at 0.10 level for a two-tailed t-test.
Standard errors are in parentheses.

case, though the real wage gap became even more problematical with negative coefficients for that variable appearing in all versions of the migration equation. In these models, the widening real wage gap between the US and European origin countries had a lesser impact than either the employment rate or the family–friends effect. Why should a rise in US real wages relative to these origin country wages not have been a prime inducement to emigration to the US? For the interwar period, a host of answers appear in the literature:

(1) *The increased probability of encountering unemployment in the US.* Prospective migrants increasingly assessed the probability of obtaining high US wages as minimal given their perception of the unemployment rates in the US and the "last in line" status they were likely to face in the labor market. The communication role of family and friends may well have been significant in producing that assessment. Did, in fact, immigrants experience higher unemployment rates than was true of the aggregate US labor market? Only anecdotal evidence is available for the 1920s and the beginning years of the Depression, but for 1935–40 a *Special Report of the Sixteenth Census* allows for the calculation of unemployment rates by migration status. Table 9.6 contrasts immigrant unemployment rates with rates for several categories of internal migrants and non-migrants. Immigrants did experience higher unemployment rates – 22 percent higher than the overall labor force, 11.7 percent compared to 9.6 percent. Immigrant males encountered a 28 percent higher rate, 12.3 percent rather than the 9.6 percent of the male labor force. Women immigrants encountered a far lesser disadvantage of 4.1 percent – 10.1 percent in comparison to the 9.7 percent for all females in the labor force. Only in the rural non-farm category for both sexes did immigrants fare better than the labor force aggregate – a 6.7 percent unemployment rate compared to 10.6 percent overall. However, few immigrants, only 12.8 percent, were in that category. Thus, in general, the immigrant experience was one of higher unemployment. If that was demonstrably the case for the immigrants of 1935–40, a period when total US employment was rising by 14 percent, it was undoubtedly true for the contracting employment years, 1930–4, when total employment fell by 9 percent.[1] Return migrants were, in many cases, a visible affirmation of these unemployment prospects.

(2) *Forgoing social insurance – formal and informal – in origin countries.* Real wage comparisons alone fail to capture the risks of forgoing support from either government or family-and-friends sources that existed in origin countries, but were problematical or nonexistent in destination countries. Dudley Kirk, in surveying the decline of migration in the interwar years, noted: "The introduction of social insurance also probably acted as a deterrent in the more industrialized countries. People who have the security of unemployment insurance, old age pensions, and other forms of advanced social legislation are naturally loath to jettison them for a speculative advantage in a foreign land" (Kirk 1946: 88). When coupled with the prospect

Table 9.6 United States unemployment rates by migration status, 1940

| | Total population 14+ in labor force | Non-migrants | All migrants | Migrants 1935–40 | | | |
				Within State	Between contiguous states	Between non-contiguous states	Immigrant
Total unemployment rate*	9.6	9.8	8.8	7.8	8.8	11.2	11.7
Male	9.6	9.7	8.9	7.9	8.8	11.4	12.3
Female	9.7	10.0	8.3	7.3	8.8	10.5	10.1
Urban, both sexes	11.0	11.3	9.2	8.2	9.1	10.9	12.6†
Rural, non-farm, both sexes	10.6	11.0	9.2	8.5	9.0	11.9	6.7†
Rural, farm, both sexes	4.4	4.1	6.7	5.7	6.9	12.1	7.5†

Source: Calculated from United States Department of Commerce, Bureau of the Census (1946: 5, Table 1).
Notes: *The unemployment rate is the percentage of those "seeking work" to total "in labor force" for each category. Those on "public emergency work" are considered employed, i.e. the Darby definition of unemployment is being followed (Darby 1976: 487–93).
†"Urban, both sexes" comprised 82.6 percent of all immigrants, 1935–40; 12.8 percent were "Rural, non–farm," and 4.6 percent "Rural, farm."

of higher probabilities of unemployment that might well accompany an international move, this factor may have been determining in migrant decision-making.

(3) *Rising legislative and other barriers to movement, in both origin and destination countries.* Though the quota limitations put in place in the American context were severe constraints on Southern and Eastern Europe in the 1920s, they were non-binding in the 1930s. None the less they spoke for an attitude that deterred potential migrants. In origin countries as well, restrictions on movement appeared in the interwar years. Italy made emigration more difficult and costly when, in 1927, it terminated the railway fare subsidy for emigrants and, in 1928, required Italians leaving the country "to promise not to have their families follow them abroad" (Kirk 1946: 88).

(4) *Reduction in available capital for a migration move.* Since an international move was more costly than an internal one, the slack labor markets of the interwar years reduced the savings potential of both prior migrants, a prime source of assistance for later migrants, and as well, the prospects for saving prior to a move. Widening real wage differentials by themselves do not recognize the impact of declining savings.

(5) *The appearance of alternative, and closer, destinations for European migrants.* France, Belgium, and even England itself began to receive in-migration from other European countries in the interwar period. That in-migration was at least in part a substitute for movement overseas (Kirk 1946: 88).

All of these factors served to weaken or even negate the impact of widening real wage differentials on migration decisions. However, such factors carried far less or no weight in the rural/urban migration decisions within the US. The first, the probability of experiencing unemployment, was actually lower for internal migrants than for non-migrants as Table 9.6 shows. Thus there were employment gains to be made from internal migration for all migrants except for those who moved between non-contiguous states. The latter group of internal migrants were the only ones who experienced unemployment rates similar to immigrants.

The prospect of forgoing public aid or the aid of family-and-friends was also far less for internal migrants. If they became unemployed, US citizens had better access to what existed in the way of public relief and, by 1935, when WPA programs were in place, to public emergency work employment. In many states, relief was available only to those meeting residency requirements – residencies as long as five years in some cases – and several states had laws that required aliens to be deported when they became public charges (Howard 1943: 304). Though alien status did not automatically disbar immigrants from public emergency work, progressively stringent regulations on alien employment were enacted from 1937, with the result shown in Table 9.7 (Howard 1943: 269–350). The immigrants of 1935–40 were far less likely to receive public emergency work: 1.4 percent of

Table 9.7 United States: employment status of population and immigrants of
1935–40, by sex, 14 years old and over, 1940

	Total	Percent	Immigrants	Percent
Population, 14+	101,102,924	100.0	323,397	100.0
In labor force	52,789,499	52.2	188,346	58.2
Employed	45,166,083	85.6*	163,770	87.0*
On pub. emerg. wk.	2,529,606	4.8*	2,593	1.4*
Seeking work	5,093,810	9.6*	21,985	11.7*
Male				
Population, 14+	50,553,748	100.0	172,435	100.0
In labor force	39,944,240	79.0	136,230	79.0
Employed	34,027,905	85.2*	117,207	86.0*
On pub. emerg. wk.	2,072,094	5.2*	2,307	1.7*
Seeking work	3,844,241	9.6*	16,716	12.3*
Female				
Population, 14+	50,549,176	100.0	150,962	100.0
In labor force	12,845,259	25.4	52,116	34.5
Employed	11,138,178	86.7*	46,563	89.3*
On pub. emerg. wk.	457,512	3.6*	286	0.5*
Seeking work	1,249,569	9.7*	5,267	10.1*

Source: United States Department of Commerce, Bureau of the Census (1946).
Notes:*Percent of those in labor force.

immigrants were on public emergency work whereas 4.8 percent of the
overall labor force were employed there.

Thus, internal migrants were – relatively – advantaged when compared
with immigrants. The combination of high prospects of unemployment and
fewer recourses from the costs of unemployment made prospective immigrants less responsive to the high real wages in the US. Given anticipations
of employment, those wages may well have appeared a chimera from a
vantage point abroad.

THE EFFECTS OF INTERNATIONAL MIGRATION
ON THE US LABOR MARKET: DISAGGREGATING
THE INTERWAR DECADES

Three questions are at issue in this section: (1) How large an effect did
international migration have on the US labor market in the interwar years?
(2) Did international migration flows serve to offset or reinforce the internal
migration patterns in the US? (3) Who were the emigrants of the 1930s?

An answer to the first question is not readily available in the existing
literature. For the United States, the number of such studies that span the
interwar period (and are known to this author) is two: Kuznets and Rubin's
NBER Occasional Paper, *Immigration and the Foreign Born* (1954) and

Easterlin's NBER volume *Population, Labor Force, and Long Swings in Economic Growth* (1968). The paucity of work derives in part from the difficulty of assembling annual data on the composition of immigrant and emigrant flows in the decade of the 1930s and in part from the presumption that international migration to the US had dwindled to insignificance by that decade, given the restrictionist immigration legislation passed in 1921 and 1924. Nor is analysis aided by the fact that the two studies, both using decadal data only, give radically different results for the aggregate impact of international migration on the US labor market in the 1930s. Kuznets and Rubin conclude that the foreign-born were responsible for a negative 40.7 percent share of the decade's labor force change, while Easterlin's figure is a negative 2.4 percent for net migration's role.

As the wide disparity between the Kuznets/Rubin and Easterlin estimates might suggest, there are measurement issues implicit in the first question: immigration's labor market effects may be measured in either a broadly inclusive fashion or in a narrower form. Kuznets and Rubin, in adopting a "foreign-born" measure, chose the most inclusive. The methodology they followed counted not only net migrants of labor force age as augmenting/ decreasing the labor force, but also the immigrant children – those born abroad – who reached labor force entry age within a given decade. Withdrawals from the labor force occurred as a result of the mortality experience of the already-resident foreign-born as well as the decade's migrants. Conceptually, the Easterlin measure is a far narrower one that counts only the direct labor market effects of net immigration. "The migration contribution was obtained as the product of the end-of-decade participation rate and the population change due to net immigration during the decade" (Easterlin 1968: 198). Lagged labor force entrants play no part in this measure, despite their foreign birth, nor is mortality of the foreign-born directly considered. Aging and mortality are accounted for as another component in Easterlin's decomposition process.

The measure adopted in this chapter is akin to Easterlin's in that it is a lower-bound estimate of the direct effects of annual net migration on the labor market. Thus it defines the contribution or loss of labor force entrants at the margin. Since it is an annual measure, no direct account of migrant mortality is taken. The error introduced by that omission is small. Summed over five years, there would be an overstatement of migrant numbers of from 1 percent to 4.25 percent; thus annual figures are overstated by less than 1 percent, i.e., 0.2 percent to 0.85 percent.[2] The labor force series used is that of Lebergott, a series that gives a substantially larger labor force growth figure for the 1930s than either the Kuznets and Rubin or the Easterlin studies.[3]

Table 9.8 provides the detail for answering the first question posed: how large an effect did international migration have on US labor markets? Net immigration diminished from highs of 557,000 and 630,000 in the first half

Table 9.8 Immigration components of United States population and labor force change, 1920–1 to 1940–1 (absolute figures in thousands)

Year	Total population change (1)	Net immigration (2)	Labor force change (3)	Net immigrant accessions to labor force (4)	Percent immigrant share of labor force change (5)	Percent immigrant share of population change (6)	Immigrant marginal participation rate (percent) (7)
1920–1	2,077	141.7	621	4.7	0.8	6.8	3.3
1921–2	1,511	557.5	431	243.0	56.4	36.9	43.6
1922–3	1,898	110.8	927	4.5	0.5	5.8	4.1
1923–4	2,162	441.5	803	233.7	29.1	20.4	52.9
1924–5	1,720	630.1	929	334.3	36.0	36.6	53.1
1925–6	1,568	201.6	454	88.7	19.5	12.9	44.0
1926–7	1,638	227.5	749	112.0	15.0	13.9	49.2
1927–8	1,474	261.8	733	135.8	18.5	17.8	51.9
1928–9	1,258	225.8	650	108.7	16.7	17.9	48.1
1929–30	1,310	210.5	766	94.7	12.4	16.1	45.0
1930–1	963	191.0	802	86.0	10.7	8.9	45.0
1931–2	800	35.3	763	3.1	0.4	4.4	8.8
1932–3	739	−67.7	784	−51.2	−6.5	−9.2	75.6
1933–4	795	−57.0	778	−41.3	−5.3	−7.2	72.5
1934–5	876	−10.3	643	−11.9	−1.8	−1.2	115.6
1935–6	803	−3.9	766	−9.6	−1.3	−0.5	246.2
1936–7	772	0.5	769	−6.1	−0.8	0.0	−12.2
1937–8	1,000	23.5	784	6.6	0.8	2.4	28.1
1938–9	1,055	42.7	716	17.0	2.4	4.0	39.8
1939–40	1,242	56.3	592	24.6	4.2	4.5	43.7
1940–1	1,280	49.3	1,350	21.8	1.6	3.9	44.2

Sources and Notes:
    Column (1): *Historical Statistics of the United States, Colonial Times to 1970, Part I*, United States Department of Commerce, Bureau of the Census (1975, Series A 23–28: 9).
    Column (2): "Immigrant Aliens Admitted and Emigrant Aliens Departed: By Country of Last or Future Permanent Residence," *United States Statistical Abstract*. United States Department of Commerce (Years: 1921: Table 74; 1923: Table 80; 1924: Table 73; 1928: Table 102; 1930: Table 106; 1931: Table 99; 1933: Table 91; 1935: Table 99; 1936: Table 99; 1937: Table 99; 1938: Table 100; 1941: Table 112; 1942: Table 114).
    Column (3): *Historical Statistics of the United States, Colonial Times to 1970*, Part I, United States Department of Commerce, Bureau of the Census (1975, Series D 1–10: 126).
    Column (4): The measurement of net immigrant accessions to the labor force is a two-step process. The net immigration figures from column (2) are converted into a working age net immigrant series by subtracting the net immigrants aged 16 years and under. The age group data was obtained from the following sources:
    United States Department of Labor, Bureau of Immigration, *Annual Report of the Commissioner General of Immigration to the Secretary of Labor* (1920–4: Table VII-B, Table VII-C; 1925–7: Table 8, Table 14; 1928–32: Table 8, Table 16).
    "Immigrant Aliens Admitted and Emigrant Aliens Departed, By Sex and Age; and Illiteracy of Immigrants," *United States Statistical Abstract*. United States Department of Commerce (1934).
    "Immigrant aliens admitted and emigrant aliens departed, fiscal years 1934 to 1937, by principal occupations, sex, and age groups," United States Department of Labor, Bureau of Immigration (1937). Sex ratios are assumed to hold for all age groups in order to estimate actual

Sources and Notes (contd)

figures. For 1933 we assumed that 1934 sex ratios hold across all age groups and the percentage distribution of age groups is the same as in 1934.

US Department of Labor, Bureau of Immigration. *Annual Report of the Secretary of Labor,* 1939, Table III. (Note: Sex ratios assumed to hold for all age groups in order to estimate actual figures.)

"Immigrant Aliens Admitted, By Sex, Age, Occupation, Illiteracy, and Amount of Money Brought; Emigrant Aliens Departed, By Sex, Age, and Occupation," *United States Statistical Abstract,* 1941.

This working age net immigrant series was then adjusted by sex-specific participation rates. A male participation rate of 91 percent was assumed for the working age net immigrants. A female participation rate of 30 percent was assumed. Those rates were rounded from the mid-decade participation rates characterizing the 16–44 age group as calculated from Lee *et al.* (1957: Table L-3). The mid-decade participation rates for that age group, those most applicable to an immigrant age structure, were:

	Male %	Female %
1920s	90.4	28.8
1930s	87.6	31.1

The only participation rates specific to immigrants are those shown for the immigrants of 1935–40 in Table 9.7. For that half decade, the male immigrants' participation rate was lower, the female higher than those found in the Lee, Miller, Brainerd and Easterlin (1957) data.

Column (5): Column (4) divided by Column (3).
Column (6): Column (2) divided by Column (1).
Column (7): Column (4) divided by Column (2).

of the 1920s to figures in the 200,000 range in the latter half. By 1931–2, immigration had dropped to 35,300, turned to net emigration for the four middle years of the decade, then returned to net immigration figures of 42,000 and 56,000 in the last two years of the 1930s.

What were the direct labor force effects of those changing flows? Net immigrant accessions to the labor force and the immigrant share of labor force changes are given in columns 4 and 5 of Table 9.8. The annual addition of some 200,000 to 300,000 immigrants to the labor force in the early and mid-1920s accounted for 29–36 percent of the labor force change, 56 percent of that in 1921–2. In the later 1920s, immigrant accessions to the labor force dropped to annual levels around 100,000, still some 16–19 percent of labor force change. With the advent of the Depression and the appearance of negative net immigration, immigrant withdrawals from the labor force subtract 5–6 percent from labor force change numbers. It is possible that the negative impact may have been larger than that since some uncertainty attaches to how deportees were counted. For 1930–40, Kuznets and Rubin conclude:

> The annual emigration statistics do not include the number of aliens deported or those who left the United States voluntarily in lieu of deportation. Between 1930 and 1940 there were approximately 200 thousand aliens in this special category, 90 percent of whom were males.

(Kuznets and Rubin 1954: 78)

191

However, from 1928 to 1932, the *Annual Reports of the Commissioner General of Immigration* include the following note associated with the column giving number of deportees: "These deportees included among aliens departed ..." (*Annual Report of the Commissioner General of Immigration* 1930: Table 1). Given that note, this chapter assumes, conservatively, that that procedure remained in place throughout the decade, though the abbreviated *Reports* from 1933 on are too incomplete to provide an answer. Thus the net out-migration of 138,900 shown for four years and the 120,100 withdrawals from the labor force over five years are assumed to include deportees. This results in a low-bound estimate of immigration's effect on the labor force.

For the five middle years of the 1930s, net immigration clearly served to reduce labor force growth. Such negative proportions are not large in themselves, but when compared with the positive 20–30 percent of labor force change that immigration accounted for in the 1920s, the shift in immigration's role is sizable. In 1937 and later years, refugee immigrants from Europe turned the flows back to positive net migration figures once again. A positive 2 to 4 percent of labor force change is then attributable to immigration.

Did the immigration and emigration of the 1920s and 1930s reinforce or offset internal US migration? Immigrant destinations by state can be used to proxy the flow of immigrants into rural and urban sectors. In Table 9.9, immigrants destined for a given state were allocated to rural and urban sectors based on the state's mid-decade rural–urban population ratio. That procedure undoubtedly underallocates immigrants to urban areas since the composition and trend of occupations for admitted aliens indicates a movement away from rural occupations (farmers, laborers) to urban (professional, commercial, skilled) for the period 1911–40 (see Table 9.3). Even if the immigrant urban flows are understated, the data of Table 9.9 provide a clear indication of the relative sizes of the two migrations and their changes. International migration is approximately two-thirds the size of internal migration in the 1920–4 period, 38 percent in 1925–9, 39 percent in 1930–4, and a mere 4 percent in 1935–9. Both types of migration fall precipitously with the onset of the Depression, immigration drops to 2–7 percent of its 1920–4 annual rate and internal migration to 8 percent. By 1935–9, internal migration more than recovers to 118 percent of its 1920–4 rate; however, immigration remains at only 7 percent of its 1920–4 rate and contributes only 2.8 percent of all flows into the urban sector. That share had been 30.2 percent in 1920–4. The conclusion is unambiguous: domestic internal migration substituted fully for the population – and undoubtedly the labor – withdrawn from the urban sector by the falling international migration.

Who were the emigrants of the 1930s? The beginnings of a switch to emigration from the US appear in 1930 and 1931. Of the twenty-eight European origin countries listed in the Immigration Commission data, only one, Spain, showed a reversal of migrant flows as early as 1930. In the

Table 9.9 Average annual migration flows to United States urban areas due to net international migration and internal migration, semi-decadal, 1920–39

	1920–4	1925–9	1930–4	1935–9
Net International Migration				
To US (1)	375,715	226,259	18,975	25,536
Index	100	60	5	7
To rural areas (2)	129,500	81,771	2,952	5,986
Index	100	63	2	5
To urban areas (3)	246,215	144,488	16,023	19,550
Index	100	59	7	8
Net migration, rural to urban				
Areas within US (4)	568,800	595,000	47,600	673,200
Index	100	105	8	118
Total flows to urban areas (5)	815,015	739,488	63,623	692,750
Index	100	91	8	85
Net international migration to urban areas as a percent of total flows to urban areas (6)	30.2%	19.5%	25.2%	2.8%
Net international migration as a percent of net migration rural to urban areas (7)	66.0%	38.0%	39.9%	3.8%

Sources and Notes:

Row (1): Calculated from data underlying column (2), Table 9.8.

Row (2): United States Department of Labor, Bureau of Immigration (Years: 1920–31: Table V; 1932: Table 41).

United States Department of Labor, Bureau of Immigration (1934–6).

Department of Justice, Immigration and Naturalization Service, Philadelphia.

Additional data was also provided by United States Department of Justice, Immigration and Naturalization Service, Washington, DC.

Each state's immigration total is calculated from the above sources. That figure is multiplied by the percent rural for the state in either 1920 or 1930. The summation of individual state figures makes up the national total. Percent rural from United States Department of Commerce, Bureau of the Census (1975: 24–37, Total Column 195 and Rural Resident Column 203; Series A 195–209).

Row (3): Following the same assumption as for rural areas, this figure is the difference between rows (1) and (2).

Row (4): United States Department of Commerce, Bureau of the Census (1975: 96, Series C 76–80. (Rural-to-urban migration totals are inflated to the extent that immigrants destined for rural states re-migrated to urban states within the 5-year period.)

Row (5): The sum of rows (3) and (4).

Row (6): Row (3) divided by Row (5).

Row (7): Row (1) divided by Row (4).

following year, seven countries appear in that category, twenty-four in 1932, and twenty-five in 1933. The turn-around in migration is thus broadly characteristic of all of European sending countries. Among non-European sources, Mexico was prime in the shift from sending to receiving migrants. Displaced from Mexico by revolution and by the disintegration of the hacienda system, large numbers of Mexicans immigrated – legally and illegally – to the US in the decades of the 1910s and 1920s; however, they found little prospect of agricultural employment in the depths of the Depression as both wages and employment fell. Wage rates for hired farm labor dropped from an index of 162 in 1930 (base: 1910–14) to 87 in 1933; employment of farm labor fell from an index of 100 to 85 (USDA 1943: 175). Mexicans, largely unskilled farm workers and their dependants, returned to Mexico from the agricultural areas of Arizona, Texas and California. The departures were frequently actively "promoted" by state and local relief agencies who saw lesser costs involved in subsidizing return migration than in continuing relief payments for an apparently indefinite period.[4]

Thus in 1932, Mexicans comprised more than a third of the emigrant departures. Table 9.10 summarizes the characteristics of the major emigrant nationalities of 1931 and 1932. Northern Europe, the source of the "old emigrants" of the 1890s, accounted for a further quarter of emigration as English, German, Scandinavian, and Scottish departed – in the main – for their origin countries. Unlike the Mexicans, these emigrants were skilled and professional workers withdrawing from the urban and industrial regions of the US – New York, Michigan, Illinois, and New Jersey.

In the aggregate then, direct withdrawals from the US labor force run across a broad range of nationalities and across an occupational range that extends from farm laborers to professionals. Both urban industrial and rural farm laborers moved back to their origin country sources as labor market conditions worsened in the early 1930s.

SUMMARY AND CONCLUSIONS

In the decade of the 1930s the US became – for the first time in its history – an emigrant nation. The prelude to the negative net migration of that decade was a precipitous fall in the rate of net migration that began with the the First World War decade. The rate of net migration fell from an annual rate of 6.25 per thousand in 1900–10 to 3.41 in the wartime decade and then to 1.68 and –0.20 in the 1920s and 1930s respectively. With the decline in immigrant numbers, the composition of immigrant flows changed as well from one heavily male to one predominantly female and with a high proportion of dependants.

The causes of the immigration decline and its compositional shift lay in legislative actions in the US and in economic circumstances in the US and abroad. In the 1920s, US quota restrictions, placed primarily on immigrants from southern and eastern Europe, effectively capped immigration from that source. From a 1921 pre-quota total of a half million gross migrants, the so-called "new" immigrants were squeezed to gross migration levels of 30–40,000 in the last half of the decade. Their net migration was smaller still and negative in three of the years after the quotas came into effect – 1922, 1925, and 1926. Immigration from northern and western Europe, subject to quotas as well but quotas seven times larger, actually expanded in the 1920s decade over its decade-earlier level but still did not fully exhaust its quotas. Immigration from Mexico and Canada/Newfoundland, countries not subject to quotas, expanded in a major fashion.

The deteriorating labor markets of the Depression decade made quotas a non-issue in the 1930s. At no point in that decade were quotas a constraint on immigrant numbers. Net immigration dropped from a level near 200,000 at the start of the decade to negative levels of 50–60,000 in the depths of the Depression, then returned to positive levels of 40–50,000 with the rise of refugee immigration in 1939–40. Quota fulfillments were at only 10 percent in the worst of the Depression years and did not exceed 41 percent from any sources except for southern and eastern Europe's refugee flows in 1939.

The labor markets of the interwar years, combining as they did the effects of quota restrictions and depression, pose problems for standard migration models that include real wage differentials as one of the prime variables. The expectation that migrants moved in response to relatively higher real wages elsewhere was only partially borne out for the interwar period when a straightforward Todaro-type model was tested with annual data from the UK, Germany, and the US. For the UK, that variable, expressed in lagged change form, did have the expected positive sign; however, in the German case the sign was negative for all variants of the model. In eight of the ten equations the employment and family–friends variables were more significant than was the real wage ratio. The weakened effect of wage gaps on migrant decision-making appears due to the increasing risk of encountering unemployment in a distant land with little or no recourse to aid from family and friends or from public authorities. That risk was real and correctly forecast by prospective immigrants. The immigrants of 1935–40 did experience a 22 percent higher unemployment rate than the US labor force as a whole.

The labor force effects of declining and negative net migration are assessed in this chapter by estimating the immigrant share of annual labor force changes. Previous studies that included the interwar period, Kuznets/Rubin and Easterlin, covered decade intervals, employed labor force series that showed less growth in the 1930s than does the Lebergott series used here, and, in the case of Kuznets/Rubin, adopted a more inclusive foreign-born basis for measurement rather than the narrower net migration measure. Because the estimates of the present study are made at the margin, annually, they are conceptually quite different from the Kuznets/Rubin estimates of the effect of the foreign-born; however, they are approximately comparable with East-erlin's calculations when decade comparisons are made. For the decade of the 1920s, Easterlin found net immigration accounting for a positive 18 percent share of labor force growth. For the 1930s, the figure is a negative 2.4 percent. Summing across the years in Table 9.8, the comparable figures in this study are a positive 19.2 percent and a positive 0.23 percent, i.e. only 17,200 net immigrants in a labor force growth of 7.4 million in the 1930s. The Kuznets/Rubin estimates of negative 5.3 percent and negative 40.7 percent for the respective

Table 9.10 United States: characteristics of five major emigrant nationalities, 1931 and 1932

Emigrant aliens (major 5 nationalities for 1931–2)	Number 1931 (% of total emigrants)	Number 1932 (% of total emigrants)	Destination, % returning to origin country, 1931	Destination, % returning to origin country, 1932	Major 2 states departed from, 1931 (% of all emigrants from state shown)	Major 2 states departed from, 1932 (% of all emigrants from state shown)	Occupation, 1931 (% of emigrants for nationality shown)	Occupation, 1932 (% of emigrants for nationality shown)
Mexican	14,406 (23.3)	36,992 (35.8)	99.51	99.89	Texas (52.99) California (27.12)	California (40.37) Texas (30.79)	Professional (0.62) Skilled (4.16) Miscellaneous (50.32) No occupation (44.90)	Professional (0.34) Skilled (2.25) Miscellaneous (51.34) No occupation (46.07)
English	6,582 (10.6)	8,478 (8.2)	62.32	73.01	New York (42.71) Michigan (17.08)	New York (38.90) Michigan (15.11)	Professional (7.23) Skilled (24.45) Miscellaneous (27.26) No occupation (41.06)	Professional (6.51) Skilled (25.28) Miscellaneous (24.91) No occupation (43.30)
German	4,379 (7.1)	6,953 (6.7)	74.58	77.95	New York (55.93) New Jersey (7.60)	New York (55.73) Illinois (8.39)	Professional (7.08) Skilled (21.72) Miscellaneous (35.74) No occupation (35.46)	Professional (5.69) Skilled (21.62) Miscellaneous (37.47) No occupation (35.22)

Scandinavian	3,761 (6.1)	5,403 (5.2)	92.58	96.67	New York (47.83) Illinois (12.04)	New York (44.48) Illinois (15.39)	Professional (4.79) Skilled (30.15) Miscellaneous (42.28) No occupation (22.78)	Professional (2.83) Skilled (29.47) Miscellaneous (44.49) No occupation (23.21)
Scottish	3,435 (5.6)	4,724 (4.6)	77.96	85.79	Michigan (31.27) New York (25.94)	New York (28.64) Michigan (21.68)	Professional (4.54) Skilled (30.07) Miscellaneous (26.78) No occupation (38.61)	Professional (3.05) Skilled (29.83) Miscellaneous (27.37) No occupation (39.75)

Source: Calculated from Department of Labor, Bureau of Immigration (fiscal years ending 30 June, 1931 and 30 June, 1932: Tables 25, 29, and 34).
Note: The miscellaneous occupation category includes farm laborers.

decades are of interest in assessing the native and immigrant sources of longer-term labor force growth but are less relevant in addressing the market questions of unemployment and wage gaps.

During the decade of the 1920s, the US labor market drew an annual average of 20.5 percent of its labor force accessions from immigration. In the 1930s, that figure was negative – withdrawals of from 1 to 6.5 percent of the labor force – for the five years 1932–6. For the remaining five years, net immigration's contribution was positive but small – 10.7 percent in 1930–1 but no more than 4.2 percent in any of the years 1937–40.

The annual net immigration figures have the additional virtue of permitting a calculation of the relative size of immigration flows and internal migration to the urban sector in the US. The bulk of immigrant flows went to urban areas in both the 1920s and 1930s. In 1920–4, immigration accounted for 30 percent of the total flows into urban areas, and 20 percent in 1925–9. With the onset of the Depression, both immigration and internal migration to urban areas fell dramatically to 7–8 percent of their 1920–4 levels. At those low levels, immigration continued to account for a quarter of the total urban flow. The economic recovery that began in 1934 gave no apparent stimulus to immigrant flows to the urban sector. Those flows remained at 8 percent of their 1920–4 level throughout the period 1935–9; conversely, internal migration rebounded to 118 percent of its 1920–4 level. Internal migration to urban areas thus fully substituted for the earlier immigrant movement to the cities. In the five years 1935–9, only 2.8 percent of the flows into the urban sector were attributable to immigration.

Depression emigration from the US appeared from 1932 to 1936 and ran broadly across nationalities, occupations, and geographic regions. In large measure it was a return migration with from 75 to 99 percent of emigrants returning to their origin country. Working ages dominated; only 3 to 6 percent of the emigrants were 16 or under in contrast with immigrants where from 16 to 20 percent were in that age category. Mexicans and northern Europeans dominated the emigrant flow, accounting for more than half of all emigrants in 1931 and 1932. Mexican farm laborers left from the Southwest and West while English, German, Scandinavian, and Scottish left the urban and industrial regions of New York, Michigan, Illinois, and New Jersey. These latter emigrants were largely skilled and professional workers. For the only time in its history, the US experienced a negative net migration that withdrew labor from its markets.

The wage gaps observed in the 1930s between the US and other countries and the extent of unemployment in the US were significantly shaped by the effective absence of immigration in that decade. The former widened more than if immigration had continued and the latter did not rise to levels as high as an immigration-augmented labor force would imply. More than an absence of immigration, an actual withdrawal of labor occurred from 1932 to

1936. For the Depression decade, economic circumstance proved more restrictive to international migration than any restrictionist legislation enacted in the US in the 1920s.

NOTES

*   This chapter is a revised version of an earlier paper presented at the Conference on Real Wages, Migration and Labor Market Integration, Bellagio, Italy, 14–18 June, 1993. The author is indebted to the participants at that conference for their comments, in particular Timothy J. Hatton and Jeffrey G. Williamson for their written critique. Stanley Lebergott and my colleague, Clifford E. Reid, provided invaluable comments as well. The volume of research required for the paper was done in a most able fashion by Louann E. Pope. Additional research assistance was provided by Wang S. Lee and Michelle Rowell. Regrettably the remaining shortcomings of the paper remain the author's responsibility.

1   See Lebergott (1964: 512, Table A-3).

2   For the decades covered in this paper, 74.7 percent of the immigrants were in the age range 16–44 in the 1920s, and 66.5 to 70.5 percent in that same age range in the 1930s (Davie 1947: 39). Kuznets and Rubin's estimates of the five-year survival ratios for the foreign-born white population ranged from 0.977870 (15–19 to 20–4) to 0.95750 (35–9 to 40–4) in the 1920s, to 0.991006 and 0.970473 for the same age groups in the 1930s (Kuznets and Rubin 1954: Table B-2).

3   See Easterlin (1968) Appendix F, for a discussion of alternative labor force series and a comparison of average growth rates for each. See also Weir (1992) for a review and revision of the Lebergott labor force estimates.

4   For a discussion of the Mexican repatriation movement, see Briggs (1984: 52–6).

Part IV

WHAT WAS THEIR IMPACT?

10

MASS MIGRATION, COMMODITY MARKET INTEGRATION AND REAL WAGE CONVERGENCE
The late-nineteenth-century Atlantic economy

*Kevin O'Rourke, Jeffrey G. Williamson
and Timothy J. Hatton*

INTRODUCTION

Most economists know about the post Second World War economic convergence among members of the OECD industrialized club. They are less likely to know that convergence has been a fact of economic life since the 1850s (Baumol *et al.* 1989; de Long 1988; Williamson 1992). The experience has been manifested by three regimes: the late-nineteenth-century convergence up to 1913; a cessation of convergence between the start of the First World War and the conclusion of the Second World War; and the resumption of convergence since. The late-nineteenth-century convergence among members of the current OECD club is especially interesting for three reasons: it was as dramatic as the more recent experience since 1950; it was manifested primarily by the erosion of gaps between the New World and the Old, rather than by an erosion of gaps within either region; and it took place in an environment of relatively free factor and commodity flows.

This chapter tries to identify the sources of the late-nineteenth-century economic convergence by assessing the relative performance of the two most important economies in the Old World and the New World – Britain and the USA. We approach the problem by identifying that portion of the factor price convergence which was set in motion by commodity trade and factor flows, thus emerging with a residual which might be assigned to those forces stressed by Alexander Gerschenkron (1952), Moses Abramovitz (1986) and the new growth theory. We find that the latter did not contribute to factor price convergence. The convergence forces that mattered were commodity market integration, stressed by Eli Heckscher and Bertil Ohlin, and mass migration, stressed by Knut Wicksell. It turns out that *offsetting* forces were contributing to late-nineteenth-century *divergence*, a finding consistent with economic history's traditional attention to Britain's alleged industrial failure (McCloskey 1970) and America's spectacular rise to industrial supremacy (Wright 1990; Nelson and Wright 1992).

THE IMPACT OF MIGRATION: MAINTAINING WICKSELL'S CLASSICAL ASSUMPTIONS

International migration certainly improves the living standards of those who move. But what do such migrations do for those who stay behind in the emigrating country, and what do they do for those who compete with the immigrants abroad? Debate on these questions is at least as old as the Industrial Revolution in Europe, which sent so many emigrants to the New World in the nineteenth century. The debate also has a long history in the United States, the New World country which absorbed the majority of the emigrants leaving Europe. It reached a crescendo in 1911 after the Immigration Commission had pondered the problem for five years. The Commission concluded that immigration was a bad thing, contributing to poor working conditions, and those findings helped create the quota legislation implemented in the 1920s. Since the Immigration Commission had no model which could be used to assess a counterfactual world without immigrants, it is hard to imagine how it reached its conclusion.

There is no doubt about the fact that population and labor shifted its center of gravity away from Europe in the nineteenth century. After all, scarce labor in the New World encouraged exactly that kind of supply response. Part of that supply response took the form of high fertility and low mortality, and part of it took the form of migration. Up to 1913, immigration accounted for 50 percent of Argentina's, and 30 percent of Australia's population increase (Taylor 1992a: Table 1.1). Between 1870 and 1910, immigration accounted for 28 percent of population increase in the United States (Easterlin 1968: 189). Between 1871 and 1890, emigration reduced Swedish population increase by 44 percent (Karlstrom 1985: 155, 181); between 1870 and 1910 it reduced British population increase by 21 percent (Mitchell and Deane 1962: 9–10); while, based on emigration rates, even bigger shares must have characterized Ireland, Italy, and Norway. Furthermore, since the migrations were selective of young adult males with high labor participation rates, the impact was even larger on the sending and receiving labor force.

So, by how much did these mass migrations cause real wages and living standards in the labor-abundant Old World to catch up with the labor-scarce New World? While the US Immigration Commission was dealing with the New World side of the process, what about the Old World side? In the early 1880s, Sweden was in the midst of lively protection and emigration debates, generated by two decades of massive out-migration to the New World and an "invasion of grains" from the same source. Knut Wicksell, then a relatively young economic theorist and a neo-Malthusian, wrote a tract stating that emigration would solve the pauper problem which blighted labor-abundant and land-scarce Swedish agriculture (Wicksell 1882; cited in Karlstrom 1985: 1). Indeed, he concluded that Swedish emigration should have been encouraged. In spite of the intensity of the debate on the impact of late-nineteenth-century mass migrations that has ensued since Wicksell and the US Immigration Commission wrote, their assertions had, until very recently, never been tested either for emigrating or for immigrating countries.

Furthermore, what literature there is typically asks what the impact on the receiving (or less frequently, the sending) region was alone, rather than asking questions about convergence between them. The difference matters. After all, if real wages were growing at 2 percent per annum in the labor-scarce country and 3 percent in the labor-abundant country, and if the 1 percent difference were attributable entirely to external migration, we might correctly conclude that migration accounted for only one-quarter of real wage growth in the labor scarce immigrating country (say, half of the 1 percent, 0.5 percent, divided by 2 percent) and for only one-sixth in the labor abundant emigrating country (0.5 percent divided by 3 percent), while incorrectly concluding that migration didn't contribute much to the (significant) convergence when in fact it accounted for *all* of it. The moral of the story is that we must explore the two regions simultaneously.

The standard way of presenting the problem on the blackboard is illustrated in Figure 10.1. New World wages and labor's marginal product are on the left-hand side and Old World wages and labor's marginal product are on the right-hand side. The world labor supply is measured along the horizontal axis. An equilibrium distribution of labor, of course, occurs at the intersection of the two derived labor demand schedules (O and N). Instead, we start at l^1 where labor is scarce in the New World, and thus where the wage gap between the two regions is very large, $w_n^1 - w_o^1$. If "mass" migrations redistribute labor towards the New World, say to l^2, the wage gap collapses to $w_n^2 - w_o^2$, and all the observed convergence would be attributable to migration. However, the same kind of convergence could have been achieved by a relative shift in O to O', an event driven perhaps by relative price shocks favoring labor in the Old World or by faster accumulation and technological "catching up" there, events which would close the wage gap to $w_n^1 - w_o^3$. Figure 10.1 is certainly an elegant statement of the question, but how do we implement the answer empirically?

The way to proceed, of course, is to develop a model in which the long-run impact of the mass migrations can be assessed. We favor the application of computable general equilibrium (CGE) models, but we are well aware of the debatable assumptions which may drive the results. That the models focus on long-run supply-side forces seems appropriate, but, following Wicksell, we also assume the absence of scale economies, accumulation responses, and

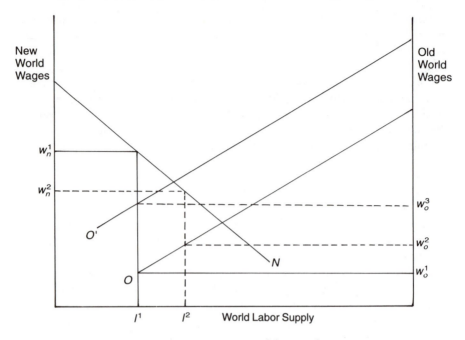

Figure 10.1 A two sector labor market

influences on the rate of technological change. It seems to us sensible to ask first whether those migrations would have mattered to the evolution of international wage gaps if standard classical, comparative static assumptions were approximated by reality. With first order impacts estimated, we can then explore whether the relaxation of Wicksell's classical assumptions are likely to overturn our interpretation of history. While Wicksell had his eye on the impact of Swedish emigration, this chapter will focus instead on Anglo-American performance.

We start with the Anglo-American wage gaps themselves. As Chapter 1 pointed out, one of the present authors (Williamson 1994) has constructed a purchasing-power-parity adjusted urban unskilled real wage database for 15 countries over the very long run. The 1870–1913 evidence is summarized in Figure 10.2 by a coefficient of variation, C(15), and it documents considerable convergence. Furthermore, the late-nineteenth-century real wage convergence is similar in magnitude to the better-known convergence after the Second World War. Perhaps most interesting, however, is the finding that most of the late-nineteenth-century real wage convergence can be attributed to an erosion in the real wage gap between the Old and New World (Dno in Figure 10.2), and not to any significant convergence within the Old World (Do) or within the New (Dn). Around 1870, real wages in the labor-scarce New World (Argentina, Australia, Canada and the USA) were much higher

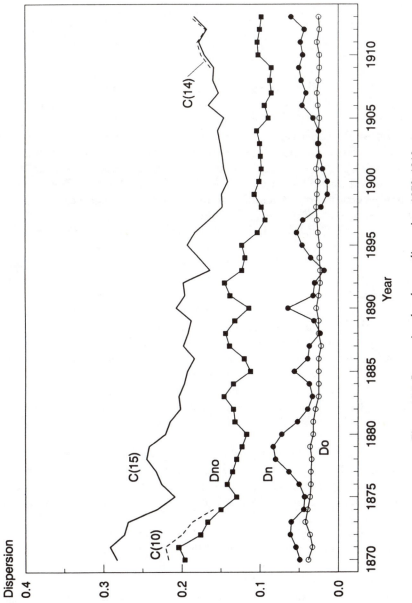

Figure 10.2 International real wage dispersion, 1870–1913
Source Williamson (1994).

than in the labor-abundant Old World (Ireland, Great Britain, Denmark, Norway, Sweden, Germany, Belgium, Netherlands, France, Italy and Spain) – 136 percent higher. By 1895, real wages in the New World were "only" 100 percent higher, and in 1913 they were "only" about 87 percent higher. In short, the real wage gap between Old World and New fell 36 percentage points over the twenty-five years up to 1895, and by 49 percentage points over the forty-three years up to 1913. The Old World caught up quite a bit with the New. While the magnitudes were less dramatic, what was true of the Old and New Worlds was also true of two of the most important members in each: in 1870, real wages in the USA were 66.7 percent higher than in Britain while in 1890 they were "only" 49.5 percent higher, in 1895 44 percent higher, in 1910 61.9 percent higher, and in 1913 54 percent higher. Thus, the Anglo-American real wage gap fell by 17.2 percentage points over the twenty years up to 1890, by 4.8 percentage points over the forty years up to 1910, and by 12.7 percentage points over the forty-three years up to 1913. Britain caught up a bit with the United States, a surprising finding given all that has been said about Britain losing her leadership to America. It must be said, however, that *all* of the British catch-up took place prior to 1895, not afterwards, when American industrial ascendancy was most dramatic (e.g., Wright 1990). We shall have more to say about these two regimes below.

We now ask how much of the Anglo-American real wage convergence after 1870 can be explained by total British net emigration and total American net immigration? The open, multi-sector British and American CGEs are in the classical, comparative static tradition: in the counterfactual experiment, land, capital and technologies are, at least initially, kept fixed; only labor is allowed to vary in the no-American-immigration and no-British-emigration counterfactuals. The US labor force would have been about 13 percent smaller in 1890 without the net immigrations 1870–90, and about 27 percent smaller in 1910 without the net immigrations 1870–1910. The British labor force would have been about 11 percent larger in 1891 without the net emigrations 1871–91, and about 16 percent larger in 1911 without the net emigrations 1871–1911. (All of these calculations include the influence of migrant children born after the move. If the children of the migrants are ignored, the 1910 US labor force would have been about 18 percent smaller in the absence of immigration, not 27 percent; and the 1911 British labor force would have been 10 percent larger in the absence of emigrants, not 11 percent.)

What would have been the impact on these two economies had these migrations not taken place? The results are presented in panel A of Table 10.1, and the impacts are very big. In 1910, real wages would have been 34 percent higher in the US and 12.2 percent lower in Britain. American real wage rates were actually about 61.9 percent higher than British in 1910; without the late-nineteenth-century migrations they would have been about 147 percent higher. The Anglo-American real wage gap fell between 1870 and

Table 10.1 Counterfactual: what would have been the impact on Britain and the United States without international migrations? (in percent)

Variable	United States		Great Britain		United States less Great Britain	
	1870–90 flows on 1890 economy	*1870–1910 flows on 1910 economy*	*1870–90 flows on 1890 economy*	*1870–1910 flows on 1910 economy*	*1870–90 flows on 1890 economy*	*1870–1910 flows on 1910 economy*
Panel A: Labor migration only, with no capital flow response: capital does *not* chase after labor						
Urban real wage	+14.4	+34.0	−8.8	−12.2	+23.2	+46.2
Return to capital	−14.5	−23.8	+8.4	+12.7	−22.9	−36.5
Panel B: Labor migration with elastic capital flow response: capital chases after labor						
Urban real wage	+3.7	+9.2	−4.7	−6.6	+8.4	+15.8
Return to capital	0	0	0	0	0	0

Source: Entries refer to percentage change in variables' levels. See text. The estimated CGEs underlying the experiments can be found in O'Rourke and Williamson (1992). The counterfactual migrations include the impact of migrant children.

1910; without the late-nineteenth-century migrations it would have more than doubled!

There would have been no Anglo-American convergence without international migration.

RELAXING WICKSELL'S CLASSICAL ASSUMPTIONS

It could be argued that the classical assumptions made thus far overstate the impact of the late-nineteenth-century mass migrations.

First, we have assumed that labor is homogeneous: natives and migrants are taken to be unskilled, and they compete for the same jobs. In contrast, economists assessing postwar American experience with immigration tend to view migrants and natives more as complements (see the summaries in Simon 1989, and Borjas 1990). While two of us have offered argument elsewhere as to why the modern complementarity position should be viewed with skepticism (Hatton and Williamson 1992b), and while more recent research on post-Second World War American experience confirms that skepticism (Borjas and Freeman 1992), there is reason in any case to think that conditions were quite different a century ago. After all, skilled labor was a much smaller share of the labor force in both sending and receiving regions in the late nineteenth century than it is now; skills (post-literacy formal education in particular) were much less important to 1890 technologies than they are to 1990 technologies. Furthermore, human capital gaps between migrants and native-born were much smaller than they are today (especially in the 1980s: Borjas 1991), and there is very little evidence to suggest that foreign labor entered segmented occupations or lacked mobility. Substitutability is far more likely to have characterized labor markets in the late nineteenth century than complementarity: new emigrants competed directly with the native-born and old emigrants at the bottom end of the labor market. Claudia Goldin (1993: 20) has recently offered some American evidence from the turn of the century which is consistent with our view.

Second, we have stressed the supply-side and ignored aggregate demand. The latter view was certainly dominant in the historical literature of the 1950s and 1960s when Keynesian thinking was in vogue (Thomas 1954; Easterlin 1968; Abramovitz 1961, 1968), and a modern version has recently been offered to account for the view that immigrants never robbed jobs from Australians in the past (Pope and Withers 1990). While this argument might be credible for the short run, it is very unlikely, in our view, to be credible for periods spanning as much as forty years.

Third, we have ignored the possibility of increasing returns, even though it is now firmly embedded in the new growth theory (Romer 1986). The reason is simple: no persuasive evidence has been offered to confirm it for the nineteenth century.

Finally, there are the more conventional accumulation and comparative advantage responses to consider. Might there have been immigrant-induced long-run supply-side responses which simultaneously shifted the labor demand curve to the right just when immigrant-induced rightward shifts in labor supply were taking place? We find these arguments more compelling, and we shall now explore them at length.

DID CAPITAL CHASE AFTER LABOR AND DID IT MATTER?

In the simple two-factor model, labor should migrate from the low-wage to the high-wage country, and capital should migrate from the high-wage (low returns) to the low-wage (high returns) country. The better integrated are world capital markets, the faster the real wage convergence. And if world capital markets become better integrated over time, the rate of convergence should accelerate, and if world capital markets break down, convergence should slow down.

Crude correlations would appear to be consistent with these predictions. After all, there was dramatic real wage convergence during the second half of the nineteenth century, trends which appear to track evolving world capital market integration. The size of the international capital flows was very large, with Britain at the center (Edelstein 1982). Furthermore, there is evidence that world capital markets were at least as well integrated around 1890 as they were around 1980 (Zevin 1992). In addition, real wage convergence ceased from the start of the First World War to the end of the Second World War, three decades during which global capital markets collapsed.

Crude correlations may be misleading, however, since the two-factor model is an inadequate characterization of late-nineteenth-century history. What really distinguished the Old World from the New was natural resource endowment, and that fact motivates the concept of New World "dual scarcity" (Temin 1966). Resources were abundant there, while both capital and labor were scarce. And there is plenty of evidence that capital and labor moved together as a consequence: that is, labor emigrated from capital-exporting Old World countries (like Britain, Germany and France) and labor immigrated into capital-importing New World countries (like Argentina, Australia, Canada and the USA).

If capital and labor moved together, can it still be said that the overseas mass migrations really contributed to Anglo-America real wage convergence? We need to know whether the international flow of labor dominated the flow of capital. If it did, then it served to lower the capital–labor ratio in America compared with Britain, thus contributing to wage convergence. Capital-deepening over time can be written as $\Delta(K/L) = (K/L)*\{[\Delta Kd/K - \Delta Ld/L] + [NFI/K - MIG/L]\}$. The first term on the right-hand side of this expression refers to domestic and the second to foreign sources of capital-deepening (*NFI* is equal to the current account balance and *MIG* is equal to net migration). It is the second term which interests us, and the background paper to this chapter offers some evidence for the labor and capital importing United States and labor and capital exporting Britain.

Labor migration clearly dominated capital migration in the United States between 1870 and 1910: while foreign capital imports served on average to raise the rate of accumulation by a trivial amount over the four decades as a whole – 0.03 percent per annum – foreign immigration tended to raise the rate of labor force growth by a lot – 0.82 percent per annum. In combination, international factor flows served to lower the rate of capital-deepening in the US by 0.79 percentage points per annum: external factor flows into the United States cut the rate of capital-deepening by more than a quarter.

Britain, however, appears to offer a different story. British capital moved with labor in such massive amounts that international factor migration must have inhibited convergence: emigration served to lower the rate of labor force growth in Britain by about 0.4 percent per annum between 1870 and 1910, but capital exports served to lower the rate of accumulation by far more, 2.15 percent per annum. External factor flows did not raise the rate of capital-deepening in Britain, but rather lowered it by about 1.8 percent per annum: according to this calculation, British export of capital and labor served to cut the rate of capital-deepening by almost three-quarters. Thus, it appears that British factor exports could not have contributed to Anglo-American real wage convergence in the late nineteenth century.

Yet, while capital was exiting Britain faster than was labor, how much of it was actually *chasing after labor*? The answer is elusive, but we can take a crude cut at the problem by identifying the direction of the flows. Almost all British emigrants went to North America, Australia and New Zealand, but only 45 percent of her capital exports went to the same regions (Simon 1967). Thus, the "chasing" component of British capital exports cannot have reduced the rate of capital accumulation by more than about 1 percentage point per annum, thus reducing the measured impact on capital-deepening to about 0.6 percent per annum. Even then, we do not know how much of the British capital exports to North America, Australia and New Zealand were actually chasing after that labor, and how much were responding to third factors.

To estimate the impact of labor migration on real wage convergence, we need to identify that share of British capital flowing to the New World which was chasing after labor. We cannot. But we can place an upper bound on the estimate by exploring a second question: what happens in the no-migration counterfactual reported in Table 10.1 when capital is allowed to chase after labor – that is, when world capital markets are treated as perfectly integrated? Panel B supplies the answer. But before we look at panel B, note in panel A the impact on the return to capital in the no-migration counterfactual when international capital is assumed immobile. The capital–labor ratio rises in the US and falls in Britain so the return to capital falls in the US and rises in Britain. Thus, if capital is now allowed to be perfectly mobile, some of it will retreat from America and stay home in Britain, muting the impact of migration's effects. Now look at panel B: in this no-migration counterfactual 1910 real wages would have been 9.2 percent higher in the US and 6.6 percent lower in Britain. American real wages were 61.9 percent higher than in Britain in 1910; without the late-nineteenth-century migrations, *and* without that part of the capital flows that chased after the migrants, the American real wage advantage would have been even higher, 89.3 percent; furthermore, there would have been no Anglo-American real wage convergence at all, since the 1870 American real wage advantage of 66.7 percent would have risen to 89.3 percent by the end of the period.

The moral of the story is that international migration contributed to Anglo-American real wage convergence even if we allow for perfect capital market integration and thus for an elastic accumulation response. The central reason why these results are so robust is, of course, the presence of an important third factor in the late nineteenth century: natural resources.

WHAT ABOUT COMMODITY MARKETS AND THE FACTOR-PRICE-EQUALIZATION THEOREM?

Ever since Eli Heckscher and Bertil Ohlin made their pioneering contributions shortly after the First World War, trade theorists have understood that real wage convergence can take place in the absence of international migrations: commodity trade can serve as a substitute for labor migration. What role did the integration of international commodity markets play in forging a global labor market and contributing to real wage convergence? In spite of the importance this issue has played in the trade literature, until recently (O'Rourke and Williamson 1992; O'Rourke, Taylor and Williamson 1993) no one has explored its empirical relevance for the late nineteenth century, the period that motivated Heckscher and Ohlin in the first place.

The factor-price-equalization (FPE) theorem has been a durable tool in trade theory for seventy years. The Heckscher–Ohlin paradigm has it that countries tend to export commodities which use intensively the factors in which they are well endowed while they tend to import commodities which use intensively the factors in which they are poorly endowed. Furthermore, it can be shown under (very) restrictive assumptions that a move from no trade to free trade can in fact equalize factor prices where wide differences existed before. For example, let falling transport costs tend to equalize prices of traded commodities. Countries will now export more of the goods which exploit their favorable factor endowment. The demand for the abundant and cheap factor booms while that for the scarce and expensive factor slumps. Thus, commodity price convergence tends to produce factor price

213

convergence, although theory is ambiguous about how much.

When Heckscher was writing in 1919 and Ohlin in 1924, they were motivated by the commodity price convergence which they thought had taken place between the Old World and the New in the late nineteenth century (Flam and Flanders 1991). Their economic metaphor was driven by primary foodstuffs: what economic historians now call the invasion of grains from the New World, driven by the sharp decline in transport costs, served to lower the relative price of grains in the Old World (like Britain) and raise it in the New World (like America). Britain and the smaller economies on the Continent did not respond to the challenge with tariffs, although the bigger economies on the Continent did (like France, Germany and Italy). What occurred in the late nineteenth century was exactly the kind of exogenous relative price shock which is supposed to set factor-price convergence in motion. According to the FPE theorem, the invasion of grains should have tended to raise real wages in America while lowering them in Britain. Did it?

Actually, there are three questions here, not just one. First, were factor endowments really the key determinants of trade patterns in the late nineteenth century? Second, was there pronounced commodity price convergence in the late nineteenth century? Third, if the first two propositions hold, did commodity price convergence also make a significant contribution to the observed real wage convergence?

Consider the first question. Two recent and influential papers by economic historians have analyzed the determinants of comparative advantage in British and American manufacturing in the late nineteenth century. Nick Crafts and Mark Thomas (1986) find support for the Heckscher–Ohlin hypothesis, since endowments explain the pattern of trade in British manufacturing between 1910 and 1935, as well as the United States in 1909. Gavin Wright (1990) finds the same in accounting for the evolution of US trade patterns between 1879 and 1940. More recently, Antoni Estevadeordal (1992) has found more support based on a large sample of 18 countries around 1913. Indeed, the 1913 evidence is far more supportive of the Heckscher–Ohlin hypothesis (Estevadeordal 1992: 9) than Edward Leamer (1984) was able to report on post-Second World War data. Finally, it seems relevant to note that William Whitney (1968) found no evidence of a Leontief Paradox in the US 1899 data.

Consider the second question. Economic historians have long been aware of the revolutionary decline in transport costs underlying overseas trade in the late nineteenth century. Douglass North (1958: 537) called the decline "radical" both for railroads and ocean shipping. When deflated by a general price index, North's freight rate index along American North Atlantic export routes dropped by more than 41 percent between 1870 and 1910. His wheat-specific American east coast real freight rate index fell by even more: about 53 percent. Similar evidence has been offered more recently by Knick Harley (1988), based on British overseas coal freight rates. Meanwhile, rail rates to the American interior fell, perhaps by even more (Williamson 1974a: 282).

In assessing the radical decline in overseas freight rates and the cost reductions along the rails between Chicago and New York, what mattered, of course, was its impact on the price convergence of tradables. Almost without exception, the literature has explored the question by looking at the international grain market. It turns out, however, that Anglo-American price convergence was far more comprehensive. A recent paper by two of the present authors has shown that while Liverpool grain prices exceeded Chicago prices by 60.2 percent in 1870, the spread was only 14.2 percent in 1912 (O'Rourke and Williamson 1992). The price gap for meat and animal fats declined from 93 percent to 18 percent over the same period. The price gap for iron products fell from 80 to 20 percent, cotton textiles from 14 to 1 percent, and so on. Quite clearly, there was dramatic convergence of tradable prices in the Atlantic economy between 1870 and the First World War.

Consider now the third question. In an effort to assess the FPE theorem, the same computable general equilibrium (CGE) models that were used above to assess Anglo-American migrations were also used to assess the impact of price convergence (O'Rourke and Williamson 1992: O'Rourke, Taylor and Williamson 1993). The first results, which do not allow for any external capital flow response, are summarized in panel A of Table 10.2. The table offers estimates of the impact of commodity price convergence on Anglo-American real wages and other factor prices for both the earlier 1870-90 period as well as the full 1870–1910 period. Our interest here is in the real wage gap. The Anglo-American real wage gap declined in fact by 17.2 percentage points up to 1890. Table 10.2 (panel A) implies that about two-thirds of that convergence can be assigned to commodity price equalization forces, about 12.2 percentage points. Over the full period 1870–1910, it served to reduce the wage gap by about 26.6 percentage points, a figure which exceeds the actual measured convergence over the four decades as a whole suggesting that the effects of the superior American industrial performance was dominant after 1890 (consistent with Wright 1990). In short, commodity price convergence played a significant role in contributing to convergence up to 1890, and in muting the divergence effects of superior American industrialization thereafter.

Note, in addition, that commodity price convergence served to erode relative capital scarcity in America. Compared with the rest of the economy, agriculture was less capital intensive in both America and Britain. Thus, the price shocks by themselves served to lower the return to capital and increase the relative size of agriculture in America (partially offsetting America's dramatic industrialization trends) and to raise the return to capital and reduce the relative size of agriculture in Britain (reinforcing Britain's industrialization trends). On net, commodity price convergence served to erode the rate of return gap (which favored capital-scarce America). These results suggest that if world capital markets had been perfectly integrated, commodity price

Table 10.2 Counterfactual: did Anglo-American commodity price equalization contribute to factor price convergence?

Variable	United States	Great Britain	Great Britain minus United States
	Percentage difference between counterfactual and actual at end year		
Panel A: Without international capital flows			
Early period: 1870–90			
Urban real wage	+0.1	+8.0	+7.9
Land real rent	+3.5	−26.0	−29.5
Return to capital	−2.4	+7.5	+9.9
Wage rental ratio	−3.3	+45.9	+49.2
Full period: 1870–1910			
Urban real wage	+0.3	+19.3	+19.0
Land real rent	+11.5	−50.7	−62.2
Return to capital	−7.9	+18.4	+26.3
Wage rental ratio	−10.1	+142.1	+152.2
Panel B: With perfectly elastic international capital flows			
Early period: 1870–90			
Urban real wage	+1.0	+11.1	+10.1
Land real rent	+3.7	−26.0	−29.7
Wage rental ratio	−2.6	+50.1	+52.7
Full period: 1870–1910			
Urban real wage	+1.7	+25.4	+23.7
Land real rent	+11.8	−50.7	−62.5
Wage rental ratio	−9.1	+154.5	+163.6
Panel C: With endogenous international migration responses			
Early period: 1870–90			
Urban real wage	+0.1	+6.2	+6.1
Land real rent	+3.5	−25.7	−29.2
Return to capital	−2.4	+10.8	+13.2
Wage rental ratio	−3.3	+43.0	+46.3
Full Period: 1870–1910			
Urban real wage	+0.2	+13.7	+13.5
Land real rent	+11.6	−50.1	−61.7
Return to capital	−7.8	+28.8	+36.6
Wage rental ratio	−10.2	+128.0	+138.2

Sources: Panels A and B are revisions of O'Rourke and Williamson (1992), Tables 2 and 3. Panel C is calculated by endogenizing migration.

convergence would have served by itself to accelerate accumulation in Britain relative to America, to increase the capital–labor ratio in Britain relative to America, thus to reinforce real wage convergence. Panel B of Table 10.2 suggests, however, that such supportive accumulation responses would have had only a modest impact: an (extreme) assumption of perfectly elastic world capital flows in response to the price shocks implies that induced real wage convergence up to 1910 would have been 31.5 percentage points (perfectly elastic capital flows) rather than 26.6 percentage points (no capital flows). Thus, our results are robust to assumptions about world capital markets, at least in terms of the FPE theorem.

ENDOGENIZING MIGRATION

The previous section shows that Heckscher and Ohlin were right: commodity price convergence served to erase some of the Anglo-American wage gap in the late nineteenth century. But we should remember that international trade and labor migrations are partial substitutes: if commodity price convergence served to erase part of the Anglo-American wage gap, then it should also have diminished the size of the mass migrations. In short, by failing to allow migration to respond to Anglo-American wage gaps, we have overstated the net impact of commodity price convergence. The interesting question, of course, is "how much?" This section offers an answer by endogenizing United States immigration and British emigration.

We rely on two studies which have estimated US immigrant (Williamson 1974b: 236) and British emigrant (Hatton 1993) elasticities in response to changes in home wages, and when embedded in the model they convert migrant elasticities to migrant-induced labor force elasticities.

A comparison of panel C with panel A of Table 10.2 shows how little endogenous migration responses diminish the net impact of commodity price convergence. This, of course, does not imply that migration had a weak impact on real wage convergence since, indeed, Table 10.1 has already shown the contrary. Rather, it simply suggests that the endogenous migrant-induced labor force responses to these price shocks were modest.

WHAT EXPLAINS THE LATE NINETEENTH ANGLO-AMERICAN CONVERGENCE?

Factor prices converged among the currently industrialized OECD countries between 1870 and the First World War. It was manifested in relatives – the wage/rental ratio (O'Rourke, Taylor and Williamson 1993) – and in absolutes – the real wage (Williamson 1992). The convergence was as dramatic as it has been in the more familiar post-Second World War decades. Furthermore, the convergence was driven primarily by the erosion of the average wage gap between the New World and the Old, rather than by convergence within either of the two regions. While the real wage convergence between the resource-rich and labor-scarce United States and resource-poor and labor-abundant Britain was far less spectacular than was true for the rest of the OECD sample, and while it was far greater in the first half than in the second half of the period, some Anglo-American convergence did take place.

How much of the Anglo-American convergence in the late nineteenth century was due to the mass migrations? How much of it was due to commodity price convergence? And how much of it to the residual forces of resource accumulation and productivity advance? Table 10.3 offers our tentative answers. The first row reports the observed real wage convergence, the US losing some of its real wage advantage between 1870 and 1890, while recovering most of that lost ground between 1890 and 1910. The second row reports the independent impact of US immigrations and British emigrations on the Anglo-American wage gap, netting out the possible endogenous response of external capital flows – that is, including the possibility that capital chased after labor (from Table 10.1, panel B). Row 2 offers a lower bound of the impact of the mass migrations since it makes the extreme assumption of perfectly elastic capital flow responses to rate of return differentials in the two economies. The third row reports the impact of Anglo-American commodity price convergence, the forces made famous by Heckscher and Ohlin (from Table 10.2, panel C). It subtracts out the likely endogenous migrant responses to the price shocks, so there is no double counting with row 2.[1] Row 4 reports the combined impact of the labor migration and commodity price convergence forces. Finally, Row 5 offers a residual: it estimates what would have happened to the Anglo-American wage gap in the absence of the convergence forces associated with mass migration and commodity price convergence. It is an upper bound, and it includes the impact of resource-deepening and productivity advance favoring the US, all of which have been stressed by Gerschenkron (1952), Abramovitz (1986) and Wright (1990).

What do we find? The story is written in two parts, and we start with the first part, the 1870s and 1880s.

Between 1870 and 1890, what might be called "open economy" forces were working hard to erase America's real wage advantage over Britain. In the absence of any other influences, these combined open economy forces – commodity price convergence and mass migration – by themselves would have cut the Anglo-American wage gap by about a third, from 66.7 percent to 44.4 percent. Furthermore, international migration and commodity price convergence had roughly equal influence, so Wicksell and Heckscher and Ohlin were about equally right. None the less, these open economy forces of convergence were partially offset by the combined influence of more rapid productivity advance and resource accumulation in America. We have no way of knowing which of these residual forces was most important, although a recent paper involving two of the present authors suggests that it was productivity advance (O'Rourke, Taylor and Williamson 1993). The open economy convergence forces dominated the residual divergence forces in the 1870s and 1880s, however, so the observed Anglo-American wage gap declined from 66.7 to 49.5 percent. Had those open economy convergence

Table 10.3 The sources of late-nineteenth-century Anglo-American real wage convergence: wage gap (in percent)

	Source	1870	1890	1910
1.	Wage gap trend observed	66.7%	49.5%	61.9%
	Due to:			
2.	Post-1870 labor migration, with capital flow response	66.7	53.2	42.6
3.	Post-1870 commodity price convergence, with capital flow and migration response	66.7	57.2	46.9
4.	Both (2) and (3)	66.7	44.4	25.6
5.	Residual: due to post-1870 productivity advance and resource accumulation favoring the US	66.7	72.5	114.9

Notes: Row (1) reports the percent by which real wage rates in the USA exceeded Britain in 1870, 1890 and 1910.

Row (2) can be illustrated by the 1890 calculation: Table 10.1, panel B, reports that the US wage would have increased 3.7 percent in the absence of immigration (to $172.9 = 1.037 \times 166.7$), so it follows that immigration by itself served to reduce the US wage 3.6 percent ($[166.7-172.9]/172.9 = -0.036$), that is from 166.7 (Britain = 100) in 1870 to 160.7 in 1890 (= 0.964×166.7); Table 10.1, panel B, reports that the British wage would have decreased 4.7 percent in the absence of emigration (to $95.3 = 0.953 \times 100$), so it follows that emigration by itself served to raise the British wage 4.9 percent ($[100-95.3]/95.3 = +0.049$) – that is, from 100 in 1870 to 104.9 in 1890; thus, migration by itself served to reduce the wage gap from 66.7 percent in 1870 to 53.2 percent in 1890 ($[160.7-104.9]/104.9 = 0.532$).

Row (3) can also be illustrated by the 1890 calculation: Table 10.2, panel C, reports that the US wage was increased 0.1 percent by price convergence to 166.9 in 1890 ($166.7 \times 1.001 = 166.9$); Table 10.2, panel C, reports that the British wage was increased by 6.2 percent to 106.2 in 1890; thus, price convergence by itself served to reduce the wage gap from 66.7 percent in 1870 to 57.2 percent in 1890 ($[166.9-106.2]/106.2 = 0.572$).

Row (4) multiplies the two effects in Rows 2 and 3: due to these two forces, the US wage in 1890 would have been 160.9 (= $0.964 \times 1.001 \times 166.7$), the British wage would have been 111.4 (= $1.049 \times 1.062 \times 100$), and the wage gap would have been 44.4 percent ($[160.9-111.4]/111.4 = 0.444$).

Row (5) calculates the residual: price and migration shocks alone imply an 1890 wage ratio of 1.444 (Row 4). These same shocks, together with all other shocks, produced the actual 1890 wage ratio of 1.495 (Row 1). Thus the other shocks raised the wage ratio by $[1.495-1.444]/1.444 = 3.5$ percent. Other shocks on their own would have implied a 1890 wage ratio of $[1.035 \times 1.667] = 1.725$ or a gap of 72.5 percent. Price and migration shocks alone imply a 1910 wage ratio of 1.256 (Row 4). All shocks produced the 1910 actual wage ratio of 1.619 (Row 1). Other shocks thus raised the wage ratio by $[1.619-1.256]/1.256 = 28.9$ percent. Other shocks on their own would have implied a 1910 wage ratio of $[1.289 \times 1.667] = 214.9$ or a gap of 114.9 percent.

forces not been at work, the Anglo-American wage gap would have *increased* from 66.7 percent in 1870 to 72.5 percent in 1890.

Between 1890 and 1910, the story seems to be quite different. Looks, however, can often be deceiving. Open economy convergence forces were working just as hard to erase the wage gap. In the absence of other influences, the combined open economy forces by themselves would have cut the Anglo-American wage gap still further, down to 25.6 percent by 1910. And, once again, international migrations and commodity price convergence made about equal contributions to the further erosion in the wage gap. What is different after 1890 is the residual: rapid productivity advance and resource accumulation favoring America were so spectacular that the open economy forces fostering convergence were swamped by these residual divergence forces, thus allowing the USA to regain most of real wage advantage lost in the 1870s and 1880s. Indeed, in the absence of the combined open economy forces, the Anglo-American wage gap would have *risen* over these four decades from 66.7 percent to 114.9 percent, and the vast majority of the rise would have taken place after 1890. To put it another way, a rapidly industrializing US bucked the convergence tide after 1890 (and up to 1940: Wright 1990), but the tide was still running strong, and it still was being pushed by the open economy forces of migration and commodity price convergence.

These Anglo-American findings are directly relevant to debates about convergence, but can they be generalized for the late-nineteenth-century "world" economy? In some ways yes, in some ways no. "No" in the sense that these commodity price convergence factors were weaker for many other European trading partners (due, of course, to protection: O'Rourke, Taylor and Williamson 1993). "Yes" in the sense that Old World mass emigrations were even bigger in Ireland, Italy and Norway than in Britain, and in the sense that New World mass immigrations were even bigger in Argentina and Canada than in the USA. "Maybe" in the sense that those residual factors were likely to have favored convergence for other pairs of countries, poor countries catching up technologically with the rich. What we need, of course, are more studies like this one to find out whether the late-nineteenth-century Anglo-American convergence forces were replicated at the global level.

NOTES

* The research assistance of Kimiko Cautero and Boris Simkovich is acknowledged with pleasure. A longer version of this chapter, with appendix materials, is available upon request from Jeffrey Williamson, 216 Littauer, Harvard University, Cambridge, MA 02138.
1 Row 3 does *not* net out external capital flow responses since the results in panel B are so similar to panel A in Table 10.2 even though the former makes the extreme assumption of perfect external capital mobility.

11

THE IMPACT OF EMIGRATION ON REAL WAGES IN IRELAND, 1850–1914

George R. Boyer, Timothy J. Hatton and Kevin O'Rourke

INTRODUCTION

Ireland's post-famine economic history presents an unusual picture. Largely as a result of mass emigration the Irish population fell to little over half its prefamine level by 1914. Though the proportion of the labor force in agriculture fell, Ireland failed to industrialize as rapidly as other western European countries. Total national income grew slowly although there was a substantial rise in national income per capita.

The effects of mass emigration and falling population on the Irish economy have been debated. Some have seen the mass emigration as depriving Ireland of its brightest and best citizens, reducing Ireland's economic vitality and condemning it to retarded economic development. Others have argued that the emigration itself acted as a vent for surplus population and permitted a growth in per capita incomes and wages which would not have been possible otherwise. In this chapter we argue for the latter view. In terms of the growth rates of real wages, Ireland's performance in the late nineteenth century looks reasonably good by international standards. We maintain that this impressive performance in the absence of rapid industrialization owes much to the decline in the labor force caused by emigration. The key link was the mobility of the Irish population. Integration into the Atlantic labor market meant that the Irish were responsive to relative wage signals. Consequently the large relative wage gap between Ireland and the countries which received Irish immigrants led to mass emigration. The emigration itself tended to relieve pressure on the land and raise Irish wages relative to these receiving countries.

The chapter is organized as follows. First, we examine the growth of Irish wages and living standards in comparison with other countries. Second, we examine the hypothesis that the Irish agricultural wage was responsive to movements in the male population. Third, we attempt to estimate the effect of emigration on the population and labor force of Ireland from 1851–1911. In order to estimate the impact of faster labor force growth, we specify a computable general equilibrium model of the Irish economy. Then the effects of emigration are evaluated in a general equilibrium framework. Finally, we summarize the main findings of the chapter in a short conclusion.

IRISH WAGES AND LIVING STANDARDS, 1850–1914

There have been both optimistic and pessimistic views of Ireland's economic progress after the famine. In both cases Ireland's performance is seen as having been closely linked with mass emigration and the fall in population. On the pessimistic side, Joseph Lee has pointed to the slow growth of Irish national income which at about 0.5 percent per annum was the slowest in Europe. He associates this with the failure of industrial development to spread as widely as in other countries (1973: 35). In addition: "Although the average standard of living increased sharply between 1848 and 1877, the actual standard of living rose only slowly. The increase in per capita income reflects the artificial impact of the disappearance of the poorest quarter of the population whose presence had depressed the pre-famine averages without resulting in a remotely comparable increase in the income of the survivors" (1973: 12).

Similarly, Fitzpatrick (1984: 37) has argued that: "Emigration from the poorest districts was seldom sufficient to eliminate underemployment; and wage levels for those actually employed rose only slowly and unevenly during the second half of the century."

On the optimistic side Arnold Schrier concluded that:

> there can be little doubt that the over-all impact of emigration on the Irish economy was generally favorable. To some extent it relieved the pressure of unemployment and improved the condition of the laborers and tenantry by raising wages and leading to better living accommodations for a larger proportion of the population. It also facilitated the consolidation of small holdings and helped place agriculture on a more economic basis. In addition it made possible a transition in Irish agriculture which can justly be described as revolutionary. Whether in itself it appreciably retarded the development of Irish industry is doubtful since the fiscal and commercial policy of Great Britain operated as a far greater deterrent.
>
> (Schrier 1958: 82)

To some extent differing views of Irish economic performance and the link with emigration can be reconciled. The pessimists would argue that backward agriculture and stunted industrial development drove many Irish men and women abroad and the effects of their emigration was simply to mitigate conditions in Ireland. The optimists would no doubt stress that in the absence of emigration things would have been very much worse. In both cases two key issues are raised. First, how good or bad was the growth in Irish real wages and living standards? Here we suggest that international comparisons can shed additional light on the issue. Second, what would wages and living standards have looked like in the absence of mass emigration? We investigate this issue in later sections of the chapter.

Let us turn to the growth of Irish living standards. Though estimates of Irish national income for the late nineteenth century are somewhat sketchy, Cormac Ó Gráda (forthcoming: Ch. 8) has recently suggested that Irish national income per capita rose threefold between 1845 and 1913. While total national income grew at about 0.7 percent per annum, per capita income grew by 1.6 percent. Thus Irish income per capita rose over the period from about two-fifths that of Britain to about three-fifths. He also notes substantial improvements in a number of other measures of well-being. The proportion of the population in poverty declined and the proportion of families living in lower-quality housing (third and fourth class) fell from 63 percent in 1861 to 29 percent 50 years later. Furthermore, increasing prosperity is reflected in the growing commercialization and the increasing variety of consumer goods sold in the shops. The volume of bank deposits increased sharply and small savings, as reflected in post office and trustee savings accounts, grew by a factor of four between 1881 and 1912.

Though the indicators of GNP per capita and other measures of well-being suggest significant improvement over the period, we can examine labor market conditions more closely through real wage indices, which are more relevant to the labor market situation. Furthermore, they afford direct comparison with other countries, specifically the United States and Britain (the countries to which most Irish emigrants went).[1] We have constructed wage indices for four occupations, two skilled and two unskilled. The skilled occupations are fitters and carpenters and the unskilled are bricklayers' laborers and agricultural laborers. The construction of these series is discussed in detail in Boyer, Hatton and O'Rourke (1993: Appendix 1).

Using an index for the cost of living we can measure the growth of real wage rates from 1860 on. The striking result is that real agricultural wage rates doubled between 1860 and 1913 with most of the increase occurring before 1895. From 1860 to 1895 the average annual growth rate was 1.9 percent and for the whole period to 1913 it was 1.6 percent. But it was not only agricultural wages which grew rapidly. Unskilled building wages doubled between 1860 and the early 1890s, exhibiting an annual growth rate of 2.2 percent. Again, wage growth was slower after 1895 and the average growth rate up to 1913 was 1.5 percent. Taking the comparison back to 1850, the data for unskilled building workers reported by Williamson (1994) indicate that between 1850 and 1913 real wage rates increased by a factor

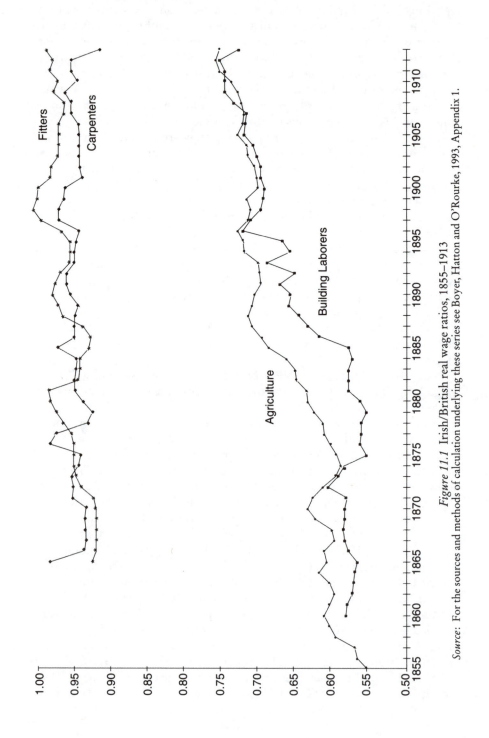

Figure 11.1 Irish/British real wage ratios, 1855–1913

Source: For the sources and methods of calculation underlying these series see Boyer, Hatton and O'Rourke, 1993, Appendix 1.

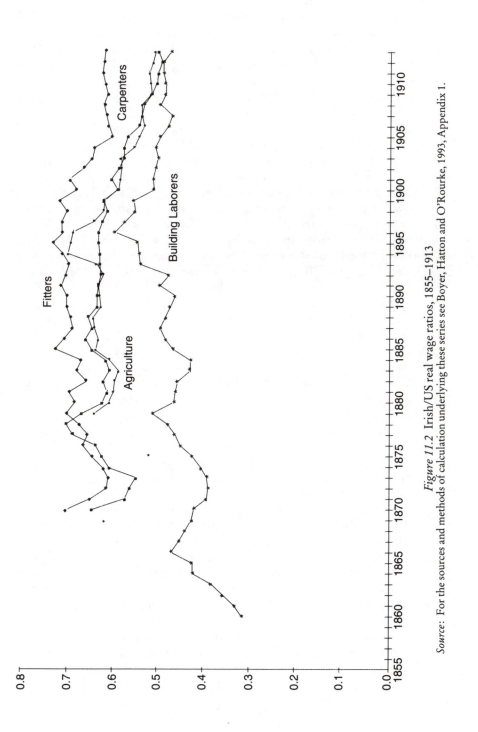

Figure 11.2 Irish/US real wage ratios, 1855–1913

Source: For the sources and methods of calculation underlying these series see Boyer, Hatton and O'Rourke, 1993, Appendix 1.

of 2.4, an average growth rate of 1.4 percent per annum.

Our wage series for the skilled trades, carpenters and fitters, begin only in 1866 and exhibit somewhat slower growth than the unskilled wage rates. For carpenters the real wage increased by 56 percent between 1866 and 1895 and, for fitters, 58 percent. The real wage for both groups declined slightly from the mid-1890s to 1913 so that, although both real wages grew by a healthy 1.5 percent annually up to 1895, they grew by only 0.9 percent per annum over the whole period from 1866 to 1913. Despite the slow growth of all real wages after 1895 and somewhat slower growth of skilled wages, the wage growth for the bulk of workers, the unskilled, was dramatic over the whole period and especially up to the turn of the century. This contrasts sharply with some of the more pessimistic statements about Irish living standards.

In order to compare Irish real wages with those for Britain and the United States, weekly wage rates for each country were adjusted for the absolute difference in price levels between them. The real wage ratios were constructed using methods similar to those used by Williamson (1994) though the individual series used here are different.

Figure 11.1 plots Irish real wages relative to British for the four occupations. For both carpenters and fitters the Irish real wage hovered around 90 percent of the British between 1870 and 1913. The fact that the ratio was so high and the fact that there was so little trend in it suggests that the Irish skilled labor market was closely integrated with the British. What difference remained in real wages might be explained as a compensating differential for the greater attraction to Irish skilled workers of remaining in Ireland rather than moving to Britain. As has often been noted skilled workers in Ireland can be viewed as circulating in the wider labor market for skilled labor in the United Kingdom as a whole. By contrast, both unskilled building and agricultural real wages were much lower in Ireland than in Britain, although they showed a steady advance over time on the British wage. Between 1860 and 1913 the unskilled building wage rose from 58 percent to 72 percent of the British and the agricultural wage rose from 61 to 75 percent of the British.

Because it has not been viewed in international perspective this dramatic growth in unskilled wages has often been neglected in discussions of progress in living standards. The gradual convergence of unskilled wage rates on the British suggests that unskilled labor markets were not as well integrated within the United Kingdom as skilled. But the fact that the Irish/British wage ratios for unskilled building and agriculture were at similar levels during most of the period, and that they advanced at a similar rate in the long run, is suggestive of a closer degree of integration within the unskilled labor market. Relative to Britain at least, these data are consistent with the idea of a gradually declining unskilled labor "surplus" both in rural and urban areas.

Figure 11.2 shows real wage ratios for the four occupations between Ireland and the United States. These present a somewhat mixed picture. In the 1860s they are dominated by the sharp rise in American real wages after the Civil War. Between the early 1870s and the late 1890s, Irish real wages rose relative to American wages for each of the four occupations. But the extent of this increase varied across occupations. It was largest for urban unskilled labor where the Irish/American real wage ratio increased from 0.39 in 1870–3 to 0.54 in 1896–9, and lowest for carpenters, where the ratio increased from 0.59 in 1870–3 to 0.64 in 1893–7. However, from the late 1890s until the outbreak of the First World War the Irish/American wage ratio declined for each occupation. Again, the extent of the decline varied across occupations, being largest for agricultural laborers, where the ratio declined from 0.70 in 1894–6 to 0.50 in 1910–13, and smallest for urban unskilled laborers. Thus it was not until a significant gap in productivity trends opened up between the United States and the United Kingdom in the 1890s that Irish real wages began to grow more slowly than American wages.

In sum, Irish real wages grew faster than British wages between the 1860s and 1913, and faster than American wages between the early 1870s and the late 1890s. This convergence was part of the general trend identified by Williamson (1994) though it was attenuated towards the end of the period. Over the whole period from 1850 to 1913 he finds that Irish unskilled urban real wages rose from 61 to 83 percent of British and from 44 to 54 percent of American (1994: Table A2.1). Given that Ireland did not industrialize rapidly during this period and that its population declined, it is tempting to conclude that the fall in the labor force, by raising the marginal product of labor, particularly in agriculture, underpinned much of the observed real wage growth. This would also be consistent with the rapid growth of unskilled wage rates and a declining rural labor surplus. However, further evidence is needed to support such a conclusion.

GROWTH IN THE AGRICULTURAL REAL WAGE OVER TIME

Most of the decline in the population and labor force from the famine up to 1913 came in rural areas and in the agricultural sector of the economy. Between 1851 and 1913 the population living in towns of 5,000 or more rose by about 0.5 million; as a proportion of total population it grew from 12 percent in 1851 to 29 percent in 1911. Even more striking is the fact that only two of the 32 Irish counties experienced an increase in population over the period. These were Co. Dublin and Co. Antrim which included the two major Irish cities of Dublin and Belfast; indeed about half of the growth in urban population can be accounted for by Belfast alone.

The consequence of these trends was that the rural population fell by over 2.6 million, almost halving its 1851 level by 1911. However, due to the decline in population and labor force as a whole, the proportion of occupied males engaged in farming fell only gradually, from 66.3 percent to 54.7 percent between 1851 and 1911 (Fitzpatrick 1980: 87). The most severe decline occurred among agricultural laborers. The ratio of farm workers to farmers declined over the period from 2.3 to 1.3. Hence, farm laborers were becoming an increasingly small minority of the work-force. However, as Fitzpatrick emphasizes, the line between farm laborer and farmer was extremely blurred. Many farm families, particularly on smallholdings, combined work on their own farm with some wage labor. The agricultural wage should therefore accurately reflect the opportunity cost of labor, even where no wage labor was employed directly.

Figure 11.3 plots the weekly agricultural wage divided by an index of the price of farm output.[2] In relation to the output price, farm wages rose considerably over the period. The rise in the agricultural product wage could be due either to a sustained upward shift in the marginal product of labor due to improved techniques or more capital or because of a movement along the marginal productivity schedule due to the declining labor force. We cannot compare this with the trend in the agricultural labor force or with the labor force as a whole because we lack annual data for these. Instead the graph shows an index of the total male population which declined gradually from 2.9 million to 2.2 million over the period.

One might conclude from the opposite trends in the real wage and male population that this inverse relation reflects a movement along the marginal productivity schedule. However, Irish agriculture underwent substantial change over this period. Most impressive was the shift in the composition of output away from relatively labor-intensive arable production towards relatively land-intensive livestock.[3] Using a multi-sector computable general equilibrium model of Irish agriculture O'Rourke (1991) has shown that almost all of the decline in the tillage sector between 1856 and 1876 was due to the increasing scarcity of labor. These trends continued later in the century but this was not the only source of rising agricultural productivity. As a number of agricultural historians have shown, there was also steady progress in agricultural techniques.[4]

To what extent can the rise in the product wage be attributed to declining rural population and labor force? As a first step we estimate a dynamic model of the relation between the real wage and male population. In order to account for the short-run fluctuations in labor demand in agriculture we include a variable for the deviation of agricultural output from its logarithmic trend. We include this variable and population lagged one period as well as the lagged dependent variable in order to avoid simultaneous equations bias. The result for the period 1867 to 1913 appears as the first column of Table 11.1.

This equation supports the finding of an inverse relation between the real agricultural wage and population, with a long-run elasticity of −3.2, which is surprisingly large. Two other points should be noted. First, the negative coefficient for the time trend indicates that in the absence of population

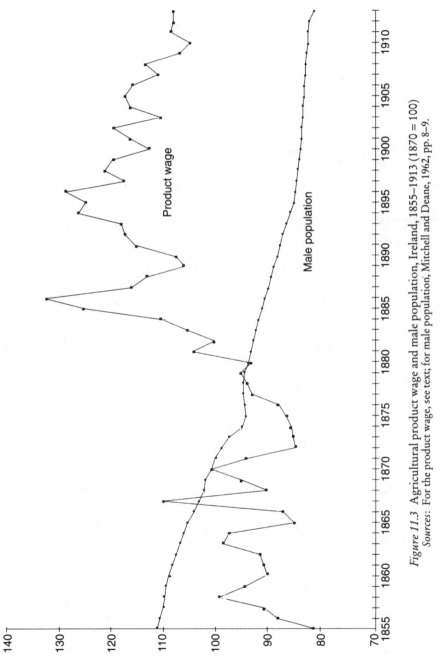

Figure 11.3 Agricultural product wage and male population, Ireland, 1855–1913 (1870 = 100)
Sources: For the product wage, see text; for male population, Mitchell and Deane, 1962, pp. 8–9.

Table 11.1 Ireland: time-series equations for the agricultural product wage, 1867–1913

	(OLS)	(IV)
Constant	11.35	14.58
	(2.23)	(2.38)
Time	−0.006	−0.006
	(1.85)	(1.83)
Log male population (t−1)	−1.43	−1.86
	(2.25)	(2.39)
Log product wage (t−1)	0.55	0.51
	(4.27)	(3.41)
Deviation from trend of log	−0.30	
agricultural production (t−1)	(1.84)	
Male emigration rate (t)		6.21
		(1.70)
R^2	0.80	0.71
DW	1.79	0.14
RSS	0.12	0.14

decline the real wage would have fallen. On the face of it, this would suggest an absence of technical progress and capital accumulation which would normally be expected to raise the real wage. However, population fell more slowly than the labor force in agriculture, hence the time trend may be compensating for the understated decline in the agricultural labor force. Second, the agricultural output term takes a negative sign rather than the positive sign that might have been associated with demand shocks.

The first equation excludes any variable representing the current change in the labor force so the second equation includes the current male emigration rate in place of the agricultural production variable. When this equation was estimated by ordinary least squares the male emigration variable gave a negative and insignificant coefficient. This is not surprising since emigration is found to be inversely related to the Irish wage in the emigration function (see Hatton and Williamson 1993). When instrumental variables are used, the emigration variable gives a positive sign though it is only significant at the 10 percent level. Consistent with its importance in the emigration function, the lagged output variable is used as an instrument for the migration variable.

The point estimate for the emigration rate suggests a large short-run effect of emigration on labor supply which acted to drive up the real wage in agriculture. But this just reflects the current outflow of labor. In the long run the cumulative effect of emigration is still reflected in the declining population. It is worth noting therefore that the lagged population variable remains negative and significant even in the presence of the emigration term. The long-run elasticity is even higher than before at −3.8. These results are certainly very suggestive of a powerful impact of emigration-driven population decline on the real wage in Irish agriculture. However, we cannot be very certain of the magnitudes both because the trend in population was different from the trend in the agricultural labor force and because we have not yet studied the long-run impact of emigration on either the population or the labor force.

DEMOGRAPHIC TRENDS AND EMIGRATION

An appropriate way to examine the effects of emigration on the real wage and other variables over a long period of time is to use a computable general equilibrium model of the economy to consider the counterfactual outcome if there had been no emigration. In order to do this we therefore need an estimate of how the Irish population and labor force would have grown if there had been no emigration from 1851 to 1911. Such estimates can be little more than controlled conjectures since it is likely that a series of demo-graphic adjustments would have been set in train had there been no emigration. Our objective then is to suggest a range of plausible values rather than to arrive at a definitive estimate.

In 1911 the total stock of Irish-born living abroad was 1.878 million or 30 percent of the total population of Irish-born. Had all the emigrants been living in Ireland the population would have been 6.259 million, a little below the actual population 60 years earlier. A few of these would have been pre-1851 emigrants but this number would have been dwarfed by the number of second-generation Irish living abroad. In the United States alone there were 2.141 million of Irish parentage and over a million with one Irish parent though some of these would have been the children of pre-1851 emigrants.

It is likely that the birth rate of the Irish population would have been lower in the absence of emigration. Cormac Ó Gráda (1988: 164) found that in 1911, county level marital fertility rates in Ireland were strongly and positively correlated with previous emigration. This suggests that previous emigrants were partially "replaced" or compensated for. Ó Gráda suggests that the rate of replacement was somewhat less than half.

In order to produce a more concrete estimate of the counterfactual Irish population in 1911 we consider a simple demographic model.[5] Population change from one year to the next depends on the birth rate (B), the death rate (D), and the emigration rate (E). Hence we have:

$$P_t = P_{t-1}(1 + B_{t-1} - D_{t-1} - E_{t-1} + Z_{t-1}) \qquad (1)$$

where Z is the residual error. Such errors might be considerable. It has been shown that from the beginning of civil registration in 1864 recorded birth and death rates substantially underestimate the true rates (see Walsh 1970; Coward 1982; Ó Gráda 1991). The degree of under-registration appears to have decreased over time but was still about 3 percent for births and 5 percent for deaths in 1911. Ó Gráda (1975) has shown that emigration to Britain was also underenumerated although to a decreasing degree over time.

We can use the relationship above to simulate the Irish population from 1851 eliminating emigration (but leaving in Z).[6] The result of this exercise indicates that the Irish population would have been more than double its actual level in 1911 at 9.773 million and exactly 1.5 times the 1851 level. However, this takes no account of the demographic response to lower emigration. As we have seen there is some evidence that as many as half of the Irish emigrants were "replaced" by increased fertility. An alternative simulation therefore reduces births by half of the emigration rate. The result gives a 1911 population of 6.527 million, close to the actual population level in 1851. These conjectures, though crude, suggest a counterfactual population in 1911 either the same as the 1851 population (low estimate) or one and a half times the 1851 population (high estimate). In terms of growth rates these would be 0.675 percent per year on the high estimate and zero on the low estimate, compared with the actual of –0.661 percent per year. Though these estimates are for the total population growth, it is likely that, over a period as long as 60 years, the labor force effects would be of a similar magnitude.[7]

A GENERAL EQUILIBRIUM MODEL OF THE IRISH ECONOMY, 1907–8

An appropriate way to assess such large-scale effects is through a general equilibrium approach which allows for the full set of interrelationships within the economy. Such methods have been used successfully to estimate the effects of Irish immigration to Britain, 1821–61 (Williamson 1990: Ch. 6), to assess the effects of emigration on Irish agriculture, 1856–76 (O'Rourke 1991), and to evaluate the effects of immigration to the US and emigration from Britain, 1870–1910 (O'Rourke, Williamson and Hatton, Chapter 10). What follows is a summary description of a simple model of the Irish economy in 1907–8, designed to address the issue of the effects of post-famine emigration on Irish living standards. A more detailed description of the model is available in Boyer, Hatton and O'Rourke (1993: Appendix 2).

There are three production sectors in the model: agriculture (A), manufacturing (M), and services (S). The agriculture sector produces food (A), using agricultural labor (L_A), capital (K), land (R), and imported manufactures (M_F, representing imported fertilizers). The manufacturing sector produces manufactured goods (M), using non-agricultural labor (L_{NA}), capital, agricultural goods (food-processing was an important sector in Ireland at the time), imported manufactured goods (M_F, for example, yarns), and "exotic imports" (F), goods for which no domestically produced substitutes are available (for example, raw cotton). Services (S) are produced with non-agricultural labor, capital, and agricultural goods (horses and horse-feed sold to the sector). The production functions can be written:

$$A = A(L_A, K_A, R, M_{FA}) \tag{2}$$

$$M = M(L_{NAM}, K_M, A_M, M_{FM}, F_M) \tag{3}$$

$$S = S(L_{NAS}, K_S, A_S) \tag{4}$$

All production functions are CES. Elasticities of substitution in manufacturing and services are 0.5, and in agriculture 1.0 (the Cobb–Douglas case). To each production function there corresponds a cost function, which depends only on factor prices due to the assumption of constant returns; competition assures that price equals cost in each sector.

Food and manufactures are internationally traded: Ireland exports domestic manufactures and food, and imports foreign manufactures and exotic imports. Prices of these goods are taken as exogenous, with the exception of domestic manufactured goods prices. As is standard in the literature, Irish manufactured exports face a constant elasticity demand function abroad. Services, by contrast, are non-traded, and their price is endogenously determined.

Agricultural exports are treated as a process whereby a unit of food is transformed into a quantity of "foreign exchange" via a fictitious production function, at a fixed ratio reflecting the exogenous export price. Manufactured exports convert domestic manufactures into foreign exchange via a Cobb-Douglas production function. Imports convert foreign exchange into import goods through further artificial production functions, again at a constant exogenous ratio reflecting exogenous import prices.

Irish and foreign manufactures are treated as distinct goods. However, they substitute closely with each other in consumption. The representative consumer has a nested utility function: an upper-level Cobb–Douglas utility function defined over food, aggregate manufactures, services and exotic imports (for example tea); and a lower level CES utility function in which Irish and foreign manufactures substitute with each other in the "production" of the aggregate manufactured good, with an elasticity of substitution of 10.

The consumer is endowed with enough of the *numéraire* good to allow him to run the (tiny) trade deficit that was observed in 1908. The consumer is also endowed with capital, land, and raw labor (L_R). Land is only used in agriculture. Capital is freely mobile between sectors. The raw labor is transformed into agricultural and non-agricultural labor via a further pseudo-production function:

$$(L_A, L_{NA}) = L(L_R) \tag{5}$$

This function is of the constant elasticity of transformation form. The elasticity of transformation reflects the sensitivity of the distribution of labor between town and country to rural–urban wage gaps. This formulation allows labor to be mobile between town and country, while at the same time allowing for the existence of persistent (and endogenous) rural–urban wage gaps.

To each sector there corresponds an activity level to be determined; for each sector, price equals cost. (This also holds for the artificial sectors reflecting trade and rural–urban migration. The price–cost equations for the trade sectors tie down the exogenous goods prices.) For each commodity, there is a price to be determined, as well as a demand equals supply equation. The consumer's income (and hence utility) have to be determined; income and expenditure are constrained to be equal. There are thus as many equations in the model as there are unknowns; as usual, Walras's Law implies that one can only solve for relative prices. The "foreign exchange" good, whose only purpose in the model is to facilitate international trade, is taken to be the *numéraire*. This is analogous to fixing the nominal trade deficit (at its actual insignificant level).

GENERAL EQUILIBRIUM RESULTS

In order to evaluate the effects of emigration from Ireland in the post-famine era we take our model for 1907–8 and examine the effects of increasing the population and labor force by an amount which reflects the no-emigration counterfactual. We then compare the magnitudes of the model's endogenous variables with the actual values for 1907–8. In the light of our discussion of the demographic impact of emigration we evaluate two alternatives: the low estimate in which population and labor force in 1907–8 are set at their 1851 levels and the high estimate where these are set at one and a half times the 1851 values. We also examine two alternative assumptions about international capital mobility: in the first, capital is completely immobile so that the capital stock in the counterfactual is held at its actual level in 1907–8; in the second, capital is completely mobile at the ruling world interest rate.[8]

The counterfactual values of some of the key variables in the model as a proportion of the actual values in 1907–8 are reported in Table 11.2. Turning first to the results with immobile capital, the two real wage rates (nominal wages divided by the cost of living index) not surprisingly would have been lower in the absence of emigration. The agricultural wage would have been 16 (29) percent lower had the labor force been 49 (123) percent higher. The non-agricultural wage would have been 19–34 percent lower with no emigration. The elasticity of the real agricultural wage with respect to the labor force is between minus a quarter and minus a third. Though these effects are large, they are not nearly as large as the effects of population on the product wage estimated earlier.

The overall change in national income is quite substantial, rising by two-thirds in the upper estimate, but per capita income would have fallen by up to 25 percent. Would this have involved a massive shift in the labor force into manufacturing and services? Given our assumption about relatively high

Table 11.2 Computable general equilibrium analysis, Ireland, 1907–8

	Capital immobile		Capital mobile	
	Lower (1)	Upper (2)	Lower (3)	Upper (4)
Counterfactual labor force increase	1.49	2.23	1.49	2.23
Agricultural real wage	0.84	0.71	0.94	0.89
Non-agricultural real wage	0.81	0.66	0.94	0.89
Gross National Product	1.29	1.66	1.42	2.02
GNP per capita	0.87	0.75	0.95	0.91
Labor force in:				
Agriculture	1.77	3.08	1.48	2.20
Manufacturing	1.18	1.30	1.51	2.30
Services	1.37	1.88	1.47	2.17
Real rental rates:				
Land	1.50	2.20	1.39	1.96
Capital	1.38	1.83	1.02	1.03

internal labor mobility, the results suggest that a greater proportion of the labor force would have been in agriculture, and the manufacturing labor force would have increased by much less.

The bottom two rows indicate that more labor would have dramatically increased marginal productivity and therefore the real rental rates on both land and capital. However, with internationally mobile capital as in columns 3 and 4 of Table 11.2, the return on capital rises only slightly (because of the fall in consumer prices) but that on land still nearly doubles on the upper estimate. With a substantial capital inflow, the marginal productivity of labor in services and especially manufacturing is higher than otherwise and more labor is shifted into the manufacturing and service sectors. The results suggest that with mobile capital, the share of the labor force in the manufacturing sector would have been slightly higher than the actual share in 1907–8.

The fall in real wages is much attenuated under international capital mobility. Both the agricultural and non-agricultural wage would have declined by a modest 11 percent under the upper estimate, and by only 6 percent under the lower estimate. Gross national product would also have been substantially higher, more than doubling on the upper estimate, and accordingly the decline in per capita income would have been smaller. These results indicate the importance of the capital mobility assumption. Changing other important assumptions appears to have less quantitative impact on the results.[9]

To give a perspective on the results in growth terms, in Table 11.3 we compare actual with counterfactual growth rates of wages and income from 1858 to 1908. To do this we use the real wage index discussed earlier, using

Table 11.3 Counterfactual growth rates of wages and income, Ireland, 1858–1908

| | Actual | Counterfactual | | | |
| | | Capital immobile | | Capital mobile | |
		Lower	Upper	Lower	Upper
Labor force	−0.59	0.20	1.01	0.20	1.01
Agricultural real wage	1.07	0.73	0.39	0.96	0.84
Non-agricultural real wage	1.60	1.19	0.78	1.49	1.37
GNP	0.70	1.21	1.71	1.40	2.11
GNP per capita	1.29	1.01	0.70	1.20	1.10

Table 11.4 Counterfactual changes in real wage ratios, Ireland, 1858–1908

| | Actual | Counterfactual | | | |
| | | Capital immobile | | Capital mobile | |
		Lower	Upper	Lower	Upper
Ireland/GB					
Agricultural real wage	0.14	0.02	−0.07	0.10	0.06
Non-agricultural real wage	0.15	0.01	−0.10	0.11	0.07
Ireland/US					
Agricultural real wage	−0.10	−0.23	−0.34	−0.13	−0.17
Non-agricultural real wage	0.15	0.01	−0.10	0.11	0.07

the unskilled building wage to represent the non-agricultural wage.[10] Not surprisingly, in the case where capital is immobile there are sharp declines in the rates of real wage growth, in the upper estimate reducing agricultural wage growth from 1.1 percent per annum to only 0.4 percent. However, with mobile capital the rate of growth of agricultural wages only would have declined by about a quarter and the non-agricultural wage by less than a fifth.

For the growth of GNP, we assume a benchmark of 0.7 percent per annum based on Ó Gráda's estimate for the period from 1845. The counterfactual estimates suggest that the growth rate would have been a little less than double the actual on the lowest estimate and about three times the actual on the highest estimate. GNP per capita growth would have fallen by a little less than a quarter on the lowest estimate and by only 7 percent in the case with the lower emigration effect and mobile capital.

Finally, in Table 11.4 we examine the effects of the alternative growth rates of real wages on the real wage ratios between Ireland and Great Britain and Ireland and the United States respectively. With immobile capital, the Irish/British real wage ratio would have remained constant or declined from 1858 to 1908. With capital mobile, there was still room for some gains in relative real wages, although the higher emigration estimate suggests that the gain over the whole 50-year period would have been cut by more than half. Each counterfactual estimate suggests that the Irish/US real agricultural wage ratio would have fallen by more than the actual 10 point decline.[11] The Irish/US non-agricultural wage ratio would have still increased slightly except in the case of the high estimate with immobile capital.

The results can be compared with those obtained by O'Rourke, Williamson and Hatton in Chapter 10, using general equilibrium models for both the USA and Britain. These suggest that if there had been no emigration from Britain from 1871 to 1911 the unskilled urban wage would have been 12.2 percent lower if capital was immobile and 6.6 percent lower with capital mobile. Applying the same approach to the United States (no immigration from 1870 to 1910) indicates that American wages would have been higher by 34.0 and 9.2 percent respectively. Thus, allowing for the impact of migrations on these two countries would strengthen the Irish real wage convergence on the United States as a result of migration but weaken it against Britain.

CONCLUSION

During the period 1850–1913 Irish real wages and per capita income increased at a rate that was quite respectable compared to wage and income growth in Great Britain and the United States. The Irish/British unskilled real wage ratio increased sharply, while the skilled real wage ratio remained roughly constant at 0.90 throughout the period. Irish/United States skilled and unskilled wage ratios increased from the early 1870s to the mid 1890s, then declined somewhat to 1913. The increase in Irish living standards took place despite very slow industrialization.

This chapter has attempted to determine the extent to which Ireland's strong wage performance was a result of its unparalleled emigration rates. From 1851 to 1911 the Irish population declined by 25 percent. We estimate that, in the absence of emigration, the Irish population and labor force in 1911 would have been in a range between the 1851 level and 50 percent greater than the 1851 level.

We construct a computable general equilibrium model of the Irish economy in 1908, and use it to examine the effects of increasing the population and labor force by an amount which reflects the no-emigration counterfactual. Our results indicate that real wages and per capita income would have been lower in 1908 in the absence of emigration. The magnitude of the decline is strongly affected by our assumptions about international capital mobility. If capital was completely immobile, we estimate that the real unskilled urban wage would have been 66–81 percent of its actual 1908 level, and per capita income 75–87 percent of its actual level. If capital was internationally mobile, the unskilled urban wage would have been 89–94 percent of its actual 1908 level, and per capita income 91–5 percent of its actual level. The estimates imply that emigration could have accounted for a significant amount of Ireland's real wage gain relative to Britain and for all of the gain relative to the United States.

NOTES

* We have benefited from many useful comments from participants at the conference on Real Wages, Migration and International Labor Market Integration in the Nineteenth and Twentieth Centuries, Bellagio, Italy, 14–18 June, and especially from Jeff Williamson. Cormac Ó Gráda and Andy Bielenberg provided valuable help with the data for the CGE model. In addition we are grateful to Theo Charitidis and Owen Darbishire for research assistance. Financial support from the National Science Foundation (Grant no. SES-9021951) and from the Royal Irish Academy for Economics and Social Sciences is gratefully acknowledged.

1 For comparison with a larger set of countries and over a longer period of time see Williamson (1994).

2 The agricultural price index is taken from Turner (1987: 135–6).

3 For discussions of agricultural output and its composition, see Staehle (1950–1), Crotty (1966), and Ó Gráda (1988).

4 Ó Gráda (1988: Ch. 4) points to the diffusion of a number of innovations including the use of new potato varieties, crop spraying, the diffusion of the milk separator, and towards the end of the period, the introduction of mechanization in the form of threshers and tractors. He estimates that between 1854 and 1908 total factor productivity in agriculture grew by 34 percent, or about half of 1 percent per annum.

5 An alternative method of estimating the counterfactual population and labor force would be to work from the stock of emigrants reported above. Such methods have been used by Williamson (1990: Ch. 6) to measure the labor force impact of Irish emigration to Britain, and in Chapter 10 by O'Rourke, Williamson and Hatton to estimate the impact of immigration to the United States and emigration from the United Kingdom.

6 The vital rates used for this simulation were taken from Mitchell and Deane (1962: 32–3, 36–7). Prior to the beginning of civil registration in 1864, the birth rate was assumed to be 26.7 per thousand and the death rate 16.9 per thousand.

7 Using different methods to calculate the impact of the Irish on the labor force in Britain, Williamson (1990: 143) estimates that between 1821 and 1871 the Irish-born population grew at 2.9 percent per annum, the total Irish population grew at 2.8 percent per annum, and the Irish labor force by 3 percent per annum. Similarly, Ó Gráda and Walsh (1993: 27) report that simulations of different rates of emigration for present-day Ireland have little effect on the age structure of the population in the long run.

8 This assumption would evidently have been preferred by the Irish Commission on Population who observed: "Irish capital formed part of the world market and Irish industrial projects had to compete for capital with the opportunities for

investment, not only in Great Britain but throughout the world that were freely offered to the investor" (1954: 26).

9   Two assumptions in particular were examined. First, the elasticity of substitution between Irish and foreign manufactured goods was reduced from 10 to 2. With capital mobile, this gave a fall of 12 percent in the agricultural real wage on the upper estimate compared with the 11 percent in Table 11.2. Second, we tried an alternative estimate of industrial output in 1907 which is 25 percent lower (see Boyer, Hatton and O'Rourke, 1993, Appendix 3). With mobile capital, this gave a fall in the agricultural wage of 6 percent compared to the 11 percent estimate in Table 11.2.

10 For the building laborers' wage growth we take the 1860 real wage as representing 1858.

11 We only have an estimate of the agricultural wage for the United States back to 1870. The figure for the growth rate of the agricultural wage was obtained by extrapolating the real agricultural wage back to 1858 using the non-agricultural unskilled wage.

12

WAGE EFFECTS OF IMMIGRATION IN LATE-NINETEENTH-CENTURY AUSTRALIA

David Pope and Glenn Withers

INTRODUCTION

An important question has recently been posed by Hatton and Williamson (1992a) and O'Rourke, Taylor and Williamson (1993). There is evidence that European emigration rates followed a bell-shaped curve; emigration rates from Europe rose, but as industrialization in due course delivered benefits to European workers the rate peaked, then fell. Were real wages in sending and receiving economies converging in the years before the First World War as part of this process?

So what does our chapter set out to do? First, we investigate whether British migration to Australia (specifically, Australia's net migration rate) drove down Australian real wages as the net migration rose. Our methodology involves a simultaneous equations set, with real wages on center stage. Second, there is a further question that needs to be addressed. Given that emigrants to different New World economies carried within them human capital in skills, how might this have affected *relative* wage rewards in labor markets?

These issues are addressed below. The first section of this chapter provides some historical background. The second section examines migrants' impact on Australian real wages rates, and the third the influence of migrant flows on Australian relative wages for skill. Our conclusions occupy the final section of the chapter. We find no evidence of migrants depressing Australian real wages over this period, but evidence for their negative effect on relative wages in Australia.

BACKGROUND

The long-run contribution of the rate of net migration to Australia's total increase in population is shown as the shaded area of Figure 12.1. In the boom years of last century and just prior to the First World War, migrants

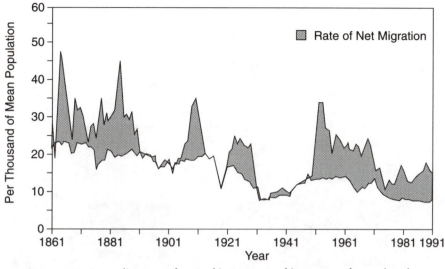

Figure 12.1 Australia: rates of natural increase, total increase and net migration, 1861–1991
Sources: Pope and Withers (1990: 3); ABS update.

accounted for around one-half of Australia's population increase and an even greater proportion indirectly when Australian-born children of migrants are taken into account. A similar conclusion is warranted for the peaks since the Second World War. That migrants until recently have had higher work-force participation rates than native-born residents has meant that they have contributed even more to Australia's work-force than to population growth. This suggests a role that should be discernible in the aggregate behavior of the economy. For Australia, migration was at the center of the development process in the nineteenth century.

The single most important change between earlier episodes and migration after 1945 is in the composition of the arrivals. The Australian Prime Minister, Stanley Bruce, recorded in 1924 that it was his government's policy to keep Australia white and 98 percent British, a policy implemented via a "color bar," steep landing-money requirements and quotas on visas issued. After 1945, Arthur Calwell, the Minister of Immigration, was to extend a welcome and bestow the title "New Australians" on non-British from Europe. By the 1971 Census 12 percent of Australia's population was non-British-born. The preponderance of British in the years before the First World War is, however, clearly shown in Figure 12.2, and our subsequent analyses focus on these.

Most British migrants to Australia came from England. For instance, among United Kingdom emigrants in 1912 the British Board of Trade recorded 82 percent from England, 11.5 percent from Scotland, 3.0 percent from Ireland and the balance from Wales. Arrivals to Australia were mainly

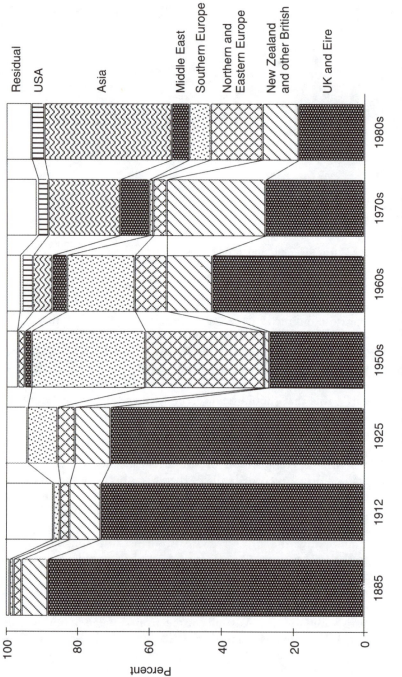

Figure 12.2 Origins of Australia's immigrants, 1885–1980s
Sources: Pope and Withers (1990: 3); ABS update.

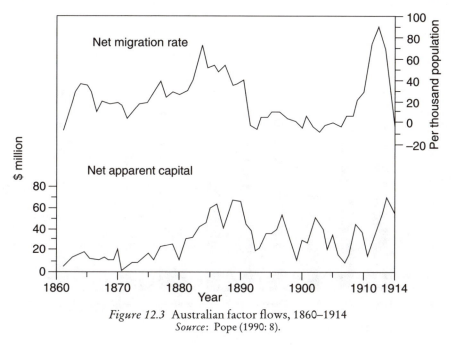

Figure 12.3 Australian factor flows, 1860–1914
Source: Pope (1990: 8).

families – youthfulness was a key feature – and they mainly came from urban areas. The immigrants landed mostly in the populated urbanized states on the southeastern seaboard, New South Wales and Victoria. Only a minority were bound for agricultural or pastoral work in the "bush;" the majority sought new lives in town- and city-based skilled and semi-skilled jobs (Pope 1976: 190).

Governments also actively promoted immigration from the United Kingdom, the most direct way of doing this being by reducing the cost of transport (Pope 1981a). It seems unlikely that those assisted with their passage costs were reaping "windfall gains" in the sense of simply taking advantage of Australian government benefits when they would have emigrated anyway. In the early twentieth century a United Kingdom household head of the average family size, facing average UK–Australian fares to be paid from average UK savings, could take as long as two years to accumulate the necessary funds (Pope 1981a: 260), and such a calculation abstracts from the forgone earnings during the long voyage.

Governments also took more roundabout means of intervening in labor markets to promote international mobility, including tariff increases, in part to explicitly increase the local demand for labor. With this went public works, which boosted the demand for local labor. Moreover, as more labor arrived, capital was consequentially drawn towards Australia's shores.

There was a strong correspondence between Australia's net migration rate

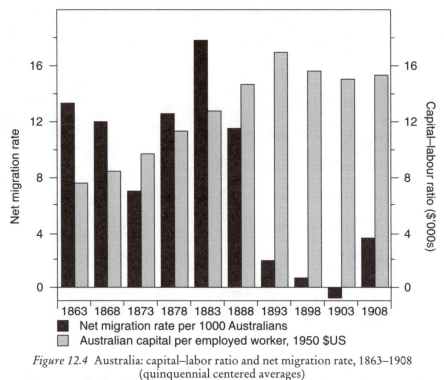

Figure 12.4 Australia: capital–labor ratio and net migration rate, 1863–1908
(quinquennial centered averages)
Source: Pope (1990).

and her international capital movements, illustrated in Figure 12.3. These patterns reflected both private and public decisions. In the case of the latter, Australian colonial governments raised capital in London for their railways and allied development programs.

The influx of capital helps to explain why Australia's capital–labor ratio did not fall in the face of increasing net migration in the 1880s, nor rise with the decline in the net migration rate in the 1890s (see Figure 12.4).

Factor flows influenced, and were influenced by, the Australian real economy (as well as, of course, by other variables). With respect to the Australian economy, deviations of actual output from potential output were major; certainly major enough to be canvassed in any analysis of the Australian labor market in relation to migration, as Figure 12.5 shows.

There is evidence from the numerous studies of the determinants of migration that "pull" forces played a significant role in influencing migrant inflow into Australia over the period. "Push" forces from the source country (Britain) are much harder to discern. So a focus on the gyrations of the Australian real economy before 1914 is useful as a background to examining how migration may relate to real (and relative) wages.

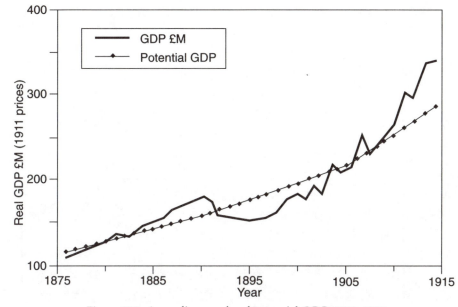

Figure 12.5 Australia: actual and potential GDP, 1875–1915
Source: Pope (1988: 16).

In Figure 12.5 the cycle is seen as deviations from long-run trend, or potential output meaning sustainable full employment GDP. The Great Depression of the 1890s and the booms of the 1880s and pre-First World War are clearly delineated. Our period embraces substantial cyclical experience.

What of the course of Australian real wages? These are shown in Figure 12.6 along with their UK equivalents. Strict comparison is difficult because, among other things, the comparability of labor, hours worked, consumption baskets, price weights, and so on. None the less, the figure is suggestive of the following: no researcher has argued that Australian workers' wages in 1860 (or real per capita incomes) were below UK levels – indeed the opposite (Maddison 1992: 4). Thus indexed to 1.00 in 1860, the UK real wage should thereafter rise above the Australian index if convergence of workers' incomes in these two labor markets was occurring. Figure 12.6 raises some doubt about this result.

Figure 12.7 makes the point more clearly: it shows the mean difference between UK and Australian real wages using two UK wage series, Feinstein (1972) and Thomas (forthcoming). Neither series suggests long-term convergence down to 1914. Here, one qualification might be noted: Australian wages could have behaved differently to Australian *national income* (rural incomes slumped heavily, for instance, in the 1890s).

We note too that our result is somewhat different than that reported for Australia and Great Britain in Jeffrey Williamson's work (1994). His series

245

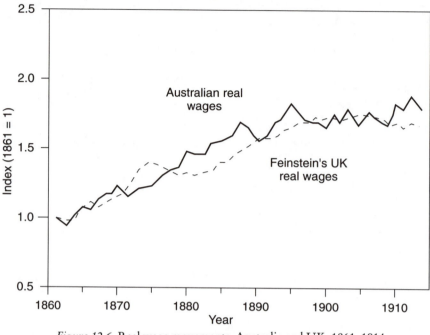

Figure 12.6 Real wage movements, Australia and UK, 1861–1914
Source: See appendix at end of chapter.

suggests some convergence. However, our Australian wage series is more comprehensive and thus is, we believe, an improvement over the Williamson series. Let us briefly explain. The Williamson series uses a single occupation component of Fahour's (1987) wage series to 1900 and splices this onto a single occupation series from Allen (1990). This provides a wage series for unskilled urban laborers in three Australian colonies (but not New South Wales), linked to unskilled laborers in the principal city of New South Wales, Sydney. Our broader-based series embraces wages for five different representative occupations, weighted by employment for the groups represented, for all colonies except the small colony of Western Australia. This applies to 1900. For 1900 to 1906, average wages per manufacturing employee, taken from Factory Inspector returns for New South Wales and Victoria are used and spliced to Australia-wide series for average wages per manufacturing employee from the annual Manufacturing Census. The Allen and Williamson series generate a more volatile and less representative Australian wage series, especially in the presence of distinctive immigration compositional effects to be discussed below and in the light of the fortunes of a particular industry such as construction. However, the Allen and Williamson series may offer the advantage of comparing comparable labor between countries.

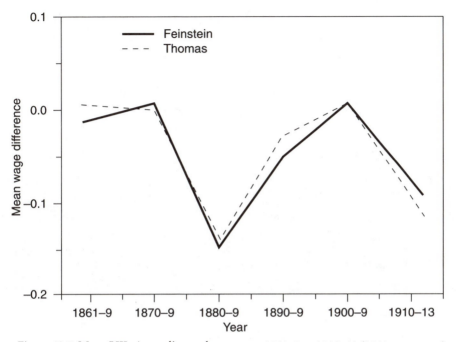

Figure 12.7 Mean UK–Australian real wage gap, 1861–9 to 1910–13 (1861 set at zero)

Our immediate purpose is to address these questions: What forces determined the movements in Australian real wages? Specifically, what long-run effect did migrants have on Australian real wages? Then, subsequently, we enquire into their relative wage effects.

MIGRANTS' IMPACT ON AUSTRALIAN REAL WAGES

Elementary theorizing provides a simple story. If real wages are flexible downwards, then the arrival of more migrants depresses the local real wage via reduced marginal product of labor (though, as an aside, migrants themselves might still be better off relative to their real wage in the country of origin). Figure 12.8 indicates the local fall and implicitly how this could work to compress wages between UK and Australian labor markets. The rightward shift in the aggregate labor supply curve from S^N to $S^N + M$ causes the real wage to drop from $(W/P)_0$ to $(W/P)_1$.

The labor movement in Australia (Labor Party and unionists) certainly viewed the effects of international labor migration on real wages as detrimental. The capitalists, it was said, wanted six men competing for one job to drive down wages (Commonwealth Parliamentary Debates 1912:

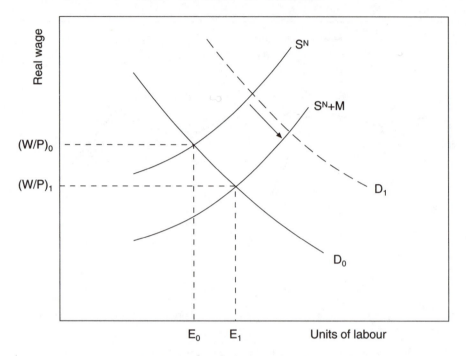

Figure 12.8 Real wages with supply and demand shifts
Note: S^N is native labor supply: $(S^N + M)$ is native supply augmented by migration (M).

1487). Not only would immigrants reduce nominal wages, but increase house rents and food prices received by renters and farmers respectively.

But there is another side to be considered, migrant-generated demand for output, and hence the derived demand for labor. Economic historians have not ignored such effects. For example, Simon Kuznets (1958) developed his case for American long swings in real output from an analysis of "population sensitive" investment; A.R. Hall (1963a) examined the effects of changes in the age distribution of population on Australian housing demand, and Allen Kelley (1968) the effects of Australian population structure on housing demand, savings and other dimensions of economic growth.

Some shift of the demand curve for labor can be expected for a number of reasons. Basically, (positive) net migration shifts the demand curve for goods and services outward and this in turn increases the aggregate derived demand for labor. Immigrants increase the demand for consumer goods, government services and public investment goods, as well as increasing private investment via their demand for housing and their effects on aggregate output (via the accelerator mechanism) and on business expectations (which affects the marginal rate of return on investment). These demands translate back into an increased demand for labor. A rightward shift in labor demand (e.g. from D_0

to D_1) could therefore offset the effect on the wage of the increase in labor supply shown in Figure 12.8.

It may be thought that such agnosticism based on balancing of supply and demand effects is premature. Would not, in the long run, the addition of labor to the factors of capital and land inevitably ensure that real wages fell under the influence of the law of diminishing marginal product? Yes, but five quite important counter-balancing points must be made. First, new territories were being opened to development (for instance, the western third of Australia was little exploited until the end of the century), so land was not yet a fixed factor economically. Second, the application of technology to Australian agriculture at this time greatly raised its productivity. As Davidson points out:

> The agricultural and pastoral frontier was expanded by the linkage of farming land to the ports by the railways, by the discovery of artesian water in 1871 and by inventions such as the stump-jump plough in 1876. Similarly, the widespread adoption of refrigeration in the 1890s made it possible for Australia to export fresh meat and dairy products ... The invention of labor saving devices also raised agricultural productivity. In Victoria in 1884 H.V. McKay invented a harvester which reaped and winnowed wheat in one operation ... Former Cambridge mathematician William Farrer began to develop important new strains of wheat in the late 1890s in New South Wales. Artificial fertilizers boosted crop yields.
>
> (Davidson 1987: 70–1)

Adherents of the Habakkuk thesis might well explain some of this as endogenous technological change responding to the world's highest-paid labor, though it was in fact not only labor-saving. Third, recall that the New World was a set of countries of abundant natural resources and small populations for which scale economies might, for some time, form an effective counterweight to the law of (eventually) diminishing returns. The Australian economy was small, protected by distance and tariffs. Larger or more open economies such as the United States might reap less from immigration by way of scale economies at this time. If so, this might imply a negative rather than independent relationship running from immigration to real wages for economies like Australia's. Indeed, just such a relationship has been hypothesized for an earlier era in the United States by Williamson (1974a) and confirmed empirically by Geary and Ó Gráda (1985) using causality analysis. Fourth, as we have seen above, the capital–labor ratio held up under increasing numbers of workers. This is even consistent with labor migration itself attracting capital inflow in various ways, including money demand (Pope 1990).

What all this adds up to is that even in the longer run, the sequence of demand and supply impact effects of migration might not track a declining real wage equilibrium down the demand curve for Australia for this period.

249

Economies of scale for a small but rapidly growing population, the irrelevance of fixed factor effects due to an expanding frontier and large-scale capital inflow (possibly induced), the emergence of substantial sustained technological change (possibly induced), plus even favorable movements in the commodity terms of trade (except for the 1890s) could together fend off for quite some time the law of diminishing marginal product of labor that would otherwise be emphasized by neoclassical economic theory as determining real wages.

In our view this analysis gives some cause for a priori agnosticism over the effects of migration on real wages during this formative period of Australia's economic development. The best way forward to resolve the issue seems that of direct empirical testing of the real wage–migration linkage.

One approach is to deploy "causality" analysis to examine the link between immigration and real wages. This has been done by some researchers. Using such methods, Geary and Ó Gráda (1985) found a negative relationship running from immigration to real wages in the United States for this period. In contrast, Pope and Withers (1990) found an independent relationship for Australia. But this causality analysis relies only upon purely statistical decomposition techniques for these two variables. We now seek to augment the Australian evidence by invoking a more detailed structural analysis.

Our test is based on the following methodology. To begin, we need to model the key relationships between macroeconomic and labor market variables in a way which permits interaction between these. Our model has four equations: the real wage rate, net migration rate, unemployment rate, and the capacity utilization rate (the percentage gap between actual and potential output as measured by the former's trend). Separate equations for nominal wages and prices are not offered. Instead these variables are combined into the real wage variable of direct interest, so implying that Australian nominal wages and prices are taken as homogeneous of degree one. To control for problems relating to simultaneity – i.e. the two-way interaction between our designated endogenous terms – the real wage equation is estimated by Two Stage Least Squares, the instruments being the exogenous variables of the full model. This procedure is a special case of the instrumental variable technique. A good instrument is highly correlated with the regressor for which it is acting, so taking an endogenous variable on the right-hand side, regressing it on all the exogenous variables in the full system of equations and using these estimated values as instruments for it provides the best instrumental variable.

Formally, our simultaneous equations set is

$$\left(\frac{W^A}{P^A}\right)_t = f\left(\left(\frac{W^A}{P^A}\right)_L, MR^A_{tL}, U^A_{tL}, UZ^A_{tL}, \left(\frac{RGDP}{EMP}\right)_{tL}, NR^A_L\right) \quad (1)$$

$$\qquad\qquad +\,or- \quad +\,or- \quad\;\; - \qquad + \qquad\qquad + \qquad\qquad +\,or-$$

$$MR^A_t = f(MR^A_L, U^A_{tL}, U^F_{tL}, \left(\frac{W^A}{P^A}\right)_{tL}, \left(\frac{W^F}{P^A}\right)_{tL}, TC^A_{tL}) \qquad (2)$$

$$\text{+ or −}\quad\text{+ or −}\quad\text{+}\qquad\text{+}\qquad\qquad\text{−}\qquad\qquad\text{−}$$

$$U^A_t = f(U^A_L, MR^A_{tL}, MQ^A_{tL}, \left(\frac{W^A}{P^A}\right)_{tL}, CAP^A_{tL}, \left(\frac{BR^A}{P^A}\right)_{tL}, STO^A_{tL}) \qquad (3)$$

$$\text{+}\qquad\text{+ or −}\qquad\text{−}\qquad\quad\text{+}\qquad\quad\text{−}\qquad\qquad\text{−}\qquad\quad\text{+}$$

$$CAP^A_t = f(CAP^A_L, RGNE^A_{tL}, UMS^A_{tL}, AMG^A_{tL}, \left(\frac{W^A}{P^A}\right)_{tL}, MR^A_{tL}) \qquad (4)$$

$$\text{+ or −}\qquad\text{+}\qquad\qquad\text{+}\qquad\qquad\text{+}\qquad\qquad\text{−}\qquad\quad\text{+ or −}$$

where U is unemployment rate,
        MR is net migration per 1,000 Australia's population,
        NR is natural rate of increase,
        MQ is migrant quality (human capital, savings and spending potential),
        W is nominal wage rate,
        P is price deflator,
        $RGDP$ is real gross domestic product,
        EMP is total employment,
        BR is unemployment benefits per unemployed,
        STO is change in industrial structure of employment measured by the Stoikov index,
        CAP is capacity utilization rate, actual relative to trend real GDP,
        UZ is degree of unionization of the work-force,
        TC is transport costs of government assisted and free migrants as a ratio to the foreign nominal wage,
        $RGNE$ is real national expenditure,
        UMS is unexpected monetary shocks,
        AMG is anticipated monetary growth,
        F is United Kingdom,
        A is Australian,
        t is current year,
        L is lagged values, i.e. earlier year(s).

Details of the construction of the variables can be found in the appendix at the end of this chapter and in Pope and Withers (1990). The expected direction of influence of the variables on Australian real wages is indicated by positive and negative signs. Most of the signs in our wage equation follow standard economic theory, but the natural rate of increase (to be lagged 15 years) needs elaboration. Following Easterlin (1961), natural increase affects labor supply with a lag equal to the average labor market entry age; this leads us to predict a negatively signed coefficient on the natural rate. On the other hand, Hall (1963) and Kelley (1968) convincingly demonstrate lags approximately of this duration in macroeconomic demand and savings variables. Such effects could plausibly increase the derived demand for labor, and hence wages.

We turn now to our results. Table 12.1 reports Two Stage Least Squares estimation of the model(s) and Table 12.2 the steady state or long-run effects of migration derived from these equations. Our main concern is with the long-run effects of migration on real wages, the dynamics of which in our models are

$$\Psi_j = (\Omega_{1j} + \Omega_{2j}) / (1 - \Lambda_j) \tag{5}$$

where Ψ is the steady-state multiplier of changes in net migration on real wages

Ω is regression coefficients of the net migration rate t, $(t-1)$

Λ is regression coefficient of Australian real wages $(t-1)$

j is equation number

If international real wage convergence came through labor flows then we might expect the Australian long-run multipliers to be negatively signed.

First, observe Table 12.1. Abstracting from the migration rate (discussed elsewhere) the contemporaneous/short-term effects of variables generally support our predictions of the direction of their impact. The unemployment rate is the exception. However, this term is insignificant in equation 12.13 and may be poorly measured. From the results, rises in the utilization rate put upward pressure on real wages, as did rises in productivity; both the variables were significant. Greater union representation in the workplace appears to have led to some pressure on wages too, its coefficient being positive and significant. The natural rate of increase also enters the equations with a positive sign suggesting that long-past demographics could lift the derived demand for labor while also increasing labor supply – the sign on the natural rate's coefficient reflecting the net impact of such forces, controlling for the other included variables. While not shown in Table 12.1, deleting the natural rate from our equations made little difference to the findings reported above.

What, most importantly, of the long-run effects of the net migration rate on Australian real wages? Can we confirm Figure 12.8, where, following an increase in the former, the new equilibrium real wage is lower than before? Or, are the off-setting demand-side forces given tentative support? In this latter case real wages might not fall and could even rise as a consequence of migration, at least in the presence of the factors mentioned above.

The long-run multipliers reported in Table 12.2 offer support for the latter supposition. These are all positively signed. So not only do the raw data on wages show no convergence, but going behind these to control for the variables in equations (1) to (4) does not alter the picture. Two minor qualifications should be mentioned. First, only in equation 12.11 is the

Table 12.1 Migration and the determinants of Australian real wages, 1861–1913
(Two Stage Least Squares estimates)

	Equation number		
	12.11	*12.12*	*12.13*
Explanators:			
Real wages (*t*–1)	0.560	0.556	
	(5.113)	(8.215)	
Log real wages (*t*–1)			0.625
			(5.698)
Net migration rate (*t*)	0.004	0.002	–0.742 E–3
	(1.796)	(1.867)	(–0.313)
Net migration rate (*t*–1)	–0.001	–0.002	0.002
	(–0.712)	(–1.416)	(1.134)
Natural rate of increase (*t*–15)	0.002	0.001	0.001
	(3.673)	(5.134)	(3.023)
Unemployment rate (*t*)	0.005	0.006	0.002
	(2.857)	(4.838)	(1.356)
Unionization rate (*t*)	0.002	0.005	0.002
	(2.383)	(4.954)	(1.739)
Productivity (*t*–1)	0.359		
	(1.620)		
Log productivity (*t*–1)			0.183
			(2.149)
Capacity utilization rate (*t*)		0.002	
		(4.780)	
Constant	0.92	0.063	0.042
	(2.595)	(2.206)	(0.506)
$\bar{R}^2$	0.974	0.984	0.978
LM (1) test for serial correlation	0.943	0 .214	1.840

Table 12.2 Migration real wage steady-state multipliers, Ψj

Equation (j)	Estimate of long-run effect	t ratio
12.11	*0.006*	*2.406*
12.12	*0.003*	*1.591*
12.13	*0.003*	*1.066*

Source: Table 12.1.

long-run multiplier statistically significant. Second, in that equation the positive effect is very small: a doubling of Australia's net migration rate in the years before the First World War generates a less than 1 percent rise in Australian real wages. None the less, this conclusion is important, for in Australia's case for this period it rules out a simple view of wage convergence across international labor markets through Australian labor factor flows.

Table 12.3 Migration and the determinants of Australian real wages, 1861–1913
(Ordinary Least Squares estimates)

Explanators:	Equation number		
	12.31	*12.32*	*12.33*
Real wages (*t*–1)	0.664	0.644	
	(6.297)	(2.811)	
Log real wages (*t*–1)			0.716
			(7.263)
Net migration rate (*t*–1)	0.921 E–3	–0.660 E–3	0.001
	(1.404)	(0.986)	(1.324)
Natural rate of increase (*t*–15)	0.001	0.001	0.001
	(3.010)	(3.161)	(2.534)
Unemployment rate (*t*–1)	0.778 E–3	0.002	0.441 E–3
	(0.562)	(1.543)	(0.297)
Unionization rate (*t*–1)	0.002	0.004	0.937 E–3
	(1.518)	(2.321)	(0.807)
Productivity (*t*–1)	0.364		
	(1.991)		
Log productivity (*t*–1)			0.151
			(2.051)
Capacity utilization rate (*t*–1)		0.990 E–3	
		(2.073)	
Constant	0.095	0.096	0.056
	(2.765)	(2.810)	(0.802)
	0.975	0.978	0.979
LM (1) test for serial correlation	2.166	1.605	1.591

Some readers might feel that our econometric modeling could be stream-lined, made simpler. We have used Two Stage Least Squares because, otherwise, coefficients can be biased by the two-way interaction (simultaneity) between the dependent variable and variable(s) employed as explanators. This problem disappears if the explanators are all *predetermined* – that is, predate the dependent variable. The hypothesis becomes that only *past* values of net migration (and other variables) affect *current* real wages. The Ordinary Least Squares estimates reported in Table 12.3, however, do not lead us to alter the conclusion of the preceding paragraph. From Table 12.3 the net migration rate (*t*–1) is positive albeit statistically insignificant.

One further experiment was tried. Instead of including the separate sources of Australia's work-force growth – i.e., the net migration rate and the Australian natural rate of increase lagged fifteen years – these variables were simply replaced by Australia's work-force to give a stock measure. Such a specification might be thought to more directly capture the vertical axes of Figure 12.8. But for both Two Stage Least Squares and Ordinary Least Squares estimates the tenor of the previous results still stands. Just as long-run multipliers of wages with respect to net migration were small but *positive*, so were the steady-state multipliers of wages with respect to the Australian work-force.

A more valid concern in this modeling is that a productivity term has been included as a surrogate for the effects of capital stock expansion, technological change, scale economies, and terms of trade effects. These are the major longer-run counter-balancing factors to wage convergence outcomes at the Australian end, enunciated above. Each was predicted as increasing real wages in this period. Certainly, we find here that a positive and significant coefficient is obtained on productivity.

However, also entering separate labor supply variables and testing for their influence while controlling for the set of productivity determinants in this way may not fully capture their labor supply influence. These labor variables, too, could influence productivity through worker quality effects and worker quantity effects, the latter being a negative direct influence through diminishing marginal product of labor. Thus our productivity variable may still bias the model against finding a negative labor supply effect.

If the capital, scale and technology effects could be separately specified along with labor supply, the elusive negative relation might well emerge, holding these other factors constant. Data does not permit this. Nevertheless, the interesting point for the present is that these other factors were not constant and that an outcome obtains of non-convergence of Australian real wages, despite high levels of immigration. It is these other factors that evidently dominate the observable trend movement in Australian real wages over the period. Counterfactually, in the absence of diminishing returns, there might have been even higher real wages. The effects of diminishing returns coming from international labor mobility (or natural increase) was not itself sufficient in this period to dominate real wage trends for Australia.

DID MIGRANTS AFFECT PAY RELATIVITIES FOR SKILL?

International migration may not have played a discernible role in any UK–Australian wage convergence before 1914, but this does not necessarily mean that labor flows between countries left the relative wages of different categories of labor unaffected. Take an example: suppose Australia received a substantially larger share of its inflow in one category of labor, say skilled workers, than did other alternative destinations, then subject to differences in the size of the work-forces of the two labor categories in the countries – and subject to other influences on wages for categories – migration could lower the relative wage of skilled workers in Australia and lower it relative to other destinations of UK emigrants. Did anything like this happen?

Skill composition ratios for major destinations are available. Australian recorded data on migrant characteristics are poor until after the Second

World War. However, the fact that early emigrants were overwhelmingly British (Figure 12.2) provides a way around the problem, because British documents provide considerable data on levels and composition of British Isles' emigrants for each of the major destination countries (USA, Canada, Australasia). These data are given in annual statistical returns for the Board of Trade and are incorporated in UK Parliamentary Papers. They are available for the years from 1876. The data provide region of origin, country of destination, broad age category, sex and, last and most importantly, occupation. It is the latter that can be used to derive skill measures of UK emigrants for each of the major destination countries (USA, Canada, Australia). The common classification possible is a grouping into four skill categories: skilled, semi-skilled upper and lower, unskilled. The basic content of these categories is:

I   Skilled: professional, technical and skilled trades;
II Semi-skilled upper: clerical, commercial, financial and administrative;
III Semi-skilled lower: agricultural workers and industrial operatives;
IV Unskilled: laborers, domestic staff.

As can be seen, the classification system corresponds broadly to an education or training ranking which seems economically defensible. But it is not without problems of interpretation and implementation. The semi-skilled upper category, of statistical necessity, embraces both managerial and clerical occupations, and the semi-skilled lower category includes all agricultural workers, including laborers. Ideally, managerial workers would be classified as skilled and rural laborers as unskilled, but this is not possible from the data source. The classification system possibly biases the skill distribution. For the sub-periods where greater disaggregation is possible, it is found that the effects of this bias, relative to the local work-force skill distribution, serve to understate the migrant skill contribution and increasingly so over time. The data limitations therefore make our measure a conservative estimate of migrants' contribution.

It might be noted that the occupation given in the data is usual or last occupation prior to embarkation. This may not translate into intended or actual occupation upon arrival. Yet economically it is strongly arguable that the degree of skill in the usual occupation is still quite indicative of the likely ability, and hence broad labor productivity, of workers after their arrival. Some particular quirks of the data should also be mentioned. One problem is the need to include in skills to 1911 young persons over twelve. From 1912 skill data refer to persons eighteen years and over. While no doubt in this early period relatively more young persons under eighteen were indeed in the work-force, the 1912 change marks a discontinuity in the data. (Also, 1912 data were presented for nine months.) Further, in terms of country of destination, the Board of Trade data refer jointly to Australia and New Zealand ("Australasia") until 1912. The obligation to use Australasian data

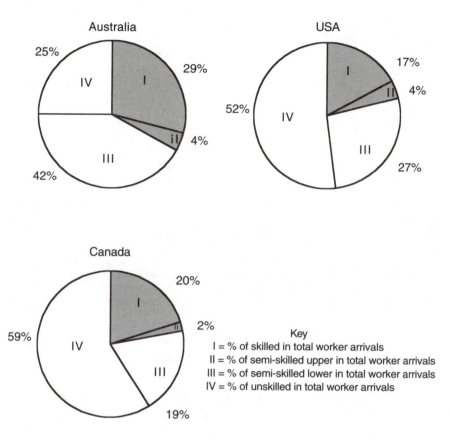

Figure 12.9 Skill composition of arrivals, 1877–1913
Source: See appendix at end of chapter.

until 1912 probably biases the migrant skill estimates down, if, as post-1912 data show, New Zealand would actually have attracted a smaller share of skilled and white-collar urban workers and a greater share of rural workers.

Figure 12.9 shows the skill composition of emigrants from the British Isles to Australia, the United States and Canada. If recording bias was small among reporters (emigrants) and recorders (Board of Trade), then these data depict quite strong differences between labor flows to the main nineteenth-century destinations. Australia obtained the highest quotient of human capital, the highest ratio of "skilled" to "unskilled" labor arrivals. In the four decades or more leading up to 1913 unskilled worker arrivals accounted for one-quarter of all male workers from the United Kingdom to Australia. In the case of the United States the figure was double this, 50 percent, whilst for Canada it was 60 percent.

Figure 12.10 Australian and US pay relativities for skill

If we were to make a simple prediction of relative wage convergence across receiving countries, then it would be that wages for skill versus unskilled would fall in Australia and rise in North America. Figure 12.10 provides evidence of this – virtually a perfect cross of the United States and Australian series. (Our Australian data, Fahour 1987, terminates in 1900. Apparently no comparable long-run wage data for skill is available for Canada.)

A deficiency with our analysis above is, of course, that we have not controlled for other factors that could have influenced the outcome. In short, it is a preliminary or suggestive result. What we do below is to attempt to track the effects of UK emigration on Australian wages for skilled/unskilled workers, controlling for these other factors. In doing this our model draws on a combination of economic theory and history:

$$\left(\frac{W^S}{W^{NS}}\right)_t = f\left[\left(\frac{W^S}{W^{NS}}\right)_{t-1}, \left(\frac{ML^S}{ML^{NS}}\right), CAP, UNI, PSBR\right] \qquad (6)$$

$$+ \qquad\qquad - \qquad - \quad + or - \quad -$$

where $\left(\dfrac{W^S}{W^{NS}}\right)$ is Australian skilled to unskilled wage ratio: skilled is represented by carpenters' wages, unskilled by laborers' wages;

$\left(\dfrac{ML^S}{ML^{NS}}\right)$ is relative skilled to unskilled UK arrivals: skilled covers categories I and II, unskilled, III and IV numbers;

CAP is Australian capacity utilization rate;
UNI is Australian unionization rate;
$PSBR$ is Australian public sector bias rate.

The model is one of explaining the Australian skill relativity in wages in terms of immigration skill composition, controlling for other relevant variables – namely capacity utilization, unionization and industrial structure. A few of these variables require fuller elaboration. First, capacity utilization can be assigned a negative effect on wage relativities. As the economy shrinks below its output potential unskilled workers tend to be the first dismissed. We view this as a trade cycle effect on the composition of labor hire. Second, consider the unionization variable. The story of Australian unionization has not yet been satisfactorily told. To some extent Australian unionization patterns followed the British system. Craft (skilled) unions were, it is often believed, dominant in Australia, so increased unionization of the work-force would exert upward pressure on skilled workers' wages relative to those of the unskilled worker. This view is now seriously being questioned. The alternative view is that there is no adequate quantitative history of Australia's unions, their membership, distribution and bargaining clout. New quantitative work (Quinlan and Gardiner 1990, and forthcoming) points to much greater strength of unskilled unions than previously thought; thus, whilst union pressure from both "craft" and unskilled workers' unions could press average real wages upwards (as confirmed by Table 12.1), the effect of unionization on relative wages for skill could be positive or negative.

One further variable needs to be explained: our public sector bias rate. As mentioned earlier in the chapter, Australia's public sector labor and capital commitments were large by international comparison. Australian governments chased foreign labor and capital for infrastructure development needs. Could this have imparted a bias in favor of unskilled labor? Construction works before 1914 were "pick and shovel" jobs requiring more brawn than skill. The bias rate used below is the ratio of Australian public capital spending to Australian GDP to allow for this sectoral or industry structure effect.

Our results are reported in Table 12.4. With the exception of the public sector bias rate – the variable is itself insignificant – the signs attached to the coefficients of the explanators are consistent with our a priori theorizing. (In the case of unionization, the sign matches with the new, not old, view.) In

Table 12.4 Migration and the determinants of Australian relative wages, 1877–1900 (Ordinary Least Squares estimates)

Explanators:	Equation number	
	12.41	12.42
$W^S/W^{NS}(t-1)$	0.360	0.434
	(1.717)	(2.419)
$ML^S/ML^{NS}(t)$	−1.304	−0.503
	(−3.326)	(−3.344)
CAP (t)	−0.016	−0.006
	(−2.504)	(−2.589)
UNI (t)	−0.148	−0.026
	(−1.715)	(−1.295)
PBSR (t)	−0.682 E−2	
	(−0.511)	
Constant	4.760	1.667
	(2.982)	(3.028)
$\bar{R}^2$	0.861	0.867
LM (1) test for serial correlation	0.249	1.632

Note: See text for variable definitions.

equation 12.41 the lag term and control variables are significant at or above the 10 percent level and our central variable, (ML^S/ML^{NS}), is highly significant in both equations. This gives cause for believing that the numbers and skills of British arrivals affected pay relativities in the Australian labor market. This, of course, implies no economic irrationality on the part of skilled (or unskilled) British emigrants to Australia if the present value of their expected net earnings streams to retirement in Britain were below that anticipated in Australia. Moreover, if this is accepted, then the presence of biased coefficients through the simultaneous effects of relative wages on relative quantities of the two categories of labor is remote (emigrants from the UK were far more motivated by real wages in different economies than pay relativities at their destination). Finally, from Australia's viewpoint, entrants with above-average skills contributed to the build-up of Australia's human capital and future economic growth (Withers 1989).

The effect of relative supply of migrant skills upon the wage relativity in Australia is, in this case, just as predicted by the standard neoclassical economic theory, despite there actually being some other variables omitted from this analysis, particularly on the supply side. Presumably these have washed out. There is some suggestive evidence for this. In earlier work Withers (1977: 137) found that the migrant skills pattern for Australia in this period much more closely duplicated the pattern of skills in the overall domestic work-force than that for UK emigration and US immigration relative to their local work-forces. Hence the ability to identify a (relative) labor supply effect differs from the situation above for the absolute labor supply effect where the variables that could not be separately identified (e.g. technology, capital inflow) worked in the opposite direction to the labor supply effect, so leaving isolation of the labor supply effect there on absolute wages, holding all else constant, as problematic.

CONCLUSIONS

The case for wage convergence between Australian workers and their British cousins in the years down to 1914 is in some doubt – at least through the lens of Feinstein, Thomas and Fahour's *wage* series. (National income *per capita* might provide a more complicated story on account of the fall in Australian farm *incomes* in the 1890s.) As is well known, ultimately Australian workers did lose their standard of living edge, but not in this period. McLean and Pincus (1983) have engendered a debate on the Australian standard of living, saying the retardation may not have been as great as is commonly assumed. But this debate refers more to a later period and to a claimed need to adjust per capita income measures for improvements in living standards not well reflected in standard national accounts.

Our main purpose in this chapter has not been to resolve this question regarding Australia's ultimate drop down the real income rankings, but to explore the links between migration and wages, although the latter informs aspects of the former. Specifically, our research suggests that mass migration did not discernibly drive down the Australian real wage rate in this period (as consideration of labor supply effects alone imply). Rather, shifts in the demand for labor occasioned by the rising immigrant population and underpinned in the longer run by scale economies, technology, capital inflow and improved terms of trade ameliorated, indeed reversed, the force of such a tendency.

We found strong evidence supporting the hypothesis that the migrant skill mix of British arrivals affected Australian pay relativities for skill. However, it is possible to identify labor supply influences upon wages at the relative wage level. While offsetting influences mask and mute the average real wage effect of immigration in Australia in this period, this chapter does find clear evidence that the distinctive skill mix of arrivals to Australia (quite different from North America) did significantly influence the Australian pay relativities for skill, producing a domestic convergence or narrowing of the relativity structure over much of the period.

It may be that late-nineteenth-century Australia is a particular case, and that the absolute and relative wage experience may be different for other times and places. Other chapters in this volume provide insight into these questions. But our interpretation of Australia's experience argues that neoclassical theory needs to include other influences in order to obtain a more accurate view of migration and wages in the late nineteenth century.

APPENDIX

Australian capacity utilization rate: real GDP/trend, where the trend is fitted for sub-periods by a regression spline technique described in Vishwakarma (1987).

Australian gross migration: Crowley (1951).

Australian industry structure (Stoikov) index (1910/11 + 1.000): employment by industry from N. G. Butlin (1964: 174, Table 40); annual figures between census bench-marks linearly interpolated. From 1891, Butlin and Dowie (1969).

Australian migrant skills index: Withers 1989; BIR 1991.

Australian net migration: CBCS 1913.

Australian nominal gross domestic product ($A millions): N. G. Butlin (1987a: 133, column ANA 64); N. G. Butlin (1987b: 229–30); M. W. Butlin (1977); ABS (1991).

Australian GDP price deflator: Vamplew et al. (1987: 219).

Australian nominal wages ($A): Fahour (1987); Endres (1984); Macarthy (1980: 56–76); Withers et al. (1985). From 1907 average annual manufacturing earnings data from CBCS (1937).

Australian pay relativities: Fahour (1987: data file). Series is of carpenters/ urban unskilled.

Australian population: ABS (1974).

Australian real gross national expenditure: N. G. Butlin (1962); M. W. Butlin (1977).

Australian transport costs: unassisted (basic) passage cost per adult from Colonial and State *Statistical Registers*; *The Times*; *Manchester Guardian*; *Daily Telegraph*; *Morning Post*; DIEA archival material; Maritime Museum (Sydney) P & O Fleet Records; air fares from Qantas Airways (Sydney) archives. Government outlays per assisted arrivals are based on data from nineteenth-century Colonial Treasurers' *Reports* (see Pope 1976: 245–7).

Australian Unemployment Benefits: Podger (1979); DSS (1991).

Australian unemployment rate (percent): Barnard et al. (1977).

Australian unionization rate: extrapolated on the basis of Buckley (1970: 314–15).

Australian work-force and employment (thousands): Withers et al. (1985) and corrigenda: 203–4.

Foreign unemployment rate (percent): Feinstein (1972: Tables 125–7).

Foreign wages and prices: foreign wages based on UK nominal wages, in (i) Feinstein (1972, and 1990: 612), with prices from Feinstein (1972: Table 65, and 1991: Table 6.4); (ii) Thomas (forthcoming: Appendix I-1).

US pay relativities: Williamson and Lindert (1980: Appendix D).

Australian Net Capital Stock: Clark (1970).

BIBLIOGRAPHY

Abramovitz, M. (1961) "The Nature and Significance of Kuznets Cycles," *Economic Development and Cultural Change* 9: 225–48.
—— (1968) "The Passing of the Kuznets Cycle," *Economica* 35: 349–67.
—— (1979) "Rapid Growth Potential and Its Realization: The Experience of the Capitalist Economies in the Postwar Period," in E. Malinvaud (ed.) *Economic Growth and Resources*, Vol. 1, London: Macmillan.
—— (1986) "Catching Up, Forging Ahead, and Falling Behind," *Journal of Economic History* 46: 385–406.
Akerman, S. (1976) "Theories of Migration Research," in H. Rundblom and H. Norman (eds) *From Sweden to America; A History of the Migration*, Minneapolis: University of Minnesota Press.
Allen, R. (1990) "Real Incomes in the English Speaking World, 1878–1913," Discussion Paper, No. 90-32, Department of Economics, University of British Columbia.
Alston, L. J. and Hatton, T. J. (1991) "The Earnings Gap Between Agricultural and Manufacturing Laborers, 1925–1941," *Journal of Economic History* 51: 83–99.
Anderson, M. (1971) *Family Structure in Nineteenth Century Lancashire*, Cambridge: Cambridge University Press.
—— (1990) "The Social Significance of Demographic Change: Britain 1750–1950," in F. M. L. Thompson (ed.) *The Cambridge Social History of Britain*, Vol. II, Cambridge: Cambridge University Press.
Arellano, M. (1987) "Computing Robust Standard Errors for Within-Group Estimators", *Oxford Bulletin of Economics and Statistics* 49: 431–4.
Australia, Bureau of Statistics (1974) *Demography*, Canberra.
—— (1991) *Australian National Accounts*, Canberra.
—— Bureau of Immigration Research (1991), *Australian Immigration Consolidated Statistics*, Canberra.
—— Commonwealth Bureau of Census and Statistics (1913 and earlier issues) *Shipping and Overseas Migration of the Commonwealth of Australia for the Year 1912*, Melbourne.
—— (1937) *Production Bulletin No. 30, Summary of Australian Production Statistics*, Canberra.
—— Department of Immigration and Ethnic Affairs, Canberra, files (various dates).
—— Department of Social Security (1991) *Annual Report*, Canberra.
—— (1912) *Commonwealth Parliamentary Debates*.
Bade, K. J. (1985) "German Emigration to the United States and Continental Immigration to Germany in the Late Nineteenth and Early Twentieth Centuries," in D. Hoerder (ed.) *Labor Migrations in the Atlantic Economies. The European*

and North American Working Class during the Period of Industrialization,
Westport, Conn.: Greenwood Press.

—— (1987) "Labor Migration and the State: Germany from the Late Nineteenth
Century to the Onset of the Great Depression," in K. J. Bade (ed.) *Population,
Labor and Migration in Nineteenth and Twentieth Century Germany,* Lea-
mington Spa: Berg.

Baganha, M. I. B. (1990) *Portuguese Emigration to the United States, 1820–1930,* New
York: Garland.

Baily, S. L. (1983) "Italian Immigrants in Buenos Aires and New York," *American
Historical Review* 88: 281–305.

Baines, D. E. (1986) *Migration in a Mature Economy. Emigration and Internal
Migration in England and Wales, 1861–1900,* Cambridge: Cambridge University
Press.

—— (1991) *Emigration from Europe, 1815–1930,* Basingstoke: Macmillan.

—— (1993) "Population, Migration and Regional Development," in R. F. Floud and
D. McCloskey (eds) *The Economic History of Britain Since 1700,* Vol. II, 2nd edn,
Cambridge: Cambridge University Press.

—— (1994) "European Emigration, 1815–1914. Looking at the Migration Decision
Again," *Economic History Review* 47 (forthcoming).

Bairoch, P. (1988) *Cities and Economic Development. From the Dawn of History to
the Present,* London: Mansell.

—— (1990) "The Impact of Crop Yields, Agricultural Productivity and Transport
Costs on Urban Growth between 1800 and 1910," in A. D. Van De Woude, A.
Hayami, and J. De Vries (eds) *Urbanization in History. A Process of Dynamic
Interactions,* Oxford: Clarendon Press.

—— and Goertz, G. (1986) "Factors of Urbanization in the Nineteenth Century
Developed Countries: A Descriptive and Econometric Analysis," *Urban Studies*
23: 285–306.

Baldwin, R. E. (1956) "Patterns of Development in Newly Settled Regions,"
Manchester School 24: 161–79.

Barciela, C. *et al.* (1989) *Estadisticas Historicas de España: Siglos XIX–XX,* Madrid:
Fundación Banco Exterior.

Barnard, A., Butlin, N. G., and Pincus, J. J. (1977) "Public and Private Sector
Employment in Australia, 1901–1974," *Australian Economic Review* 1: 43–52.

Barro, R. J. (1991) "Economic Growth in a Cross Section of Countries," *Quarterly
Journal of Economics* 106: 407–43.

—— and Sala-I-Martin, X. (1991) "Convergence across States and Regions,"
Brookings Papers on Economic Activity 1: 107–82.

Baumol, W. J., Blackman, S., and Wolff, E.N. (1989) *Productivity and American
Leadership: The Long View,* Cambridge, Mass.: MIT Press.

Becker, G. S. (1971) *The Economics of Discrimination,* Chicago: University of
Chicago Press.

Bengtsson, T. (1990) "Migration, Wages and Urbanization in Sweden in the
Nineteenth Century," in A. D. Van De Woude, A. Hayami and J. De Vries (eds)
Urbanization in History. A Process of Dynamic Interactions, Oxford: Clarendon
Press.

Bernard, W. S. (1982) "A History of U.S. Immigration Policy," *Immigration,*
Cambridge, Mass.: Belknap Press.

Bertram, G. W. (1963) "Economic Growth in Canadian Industry, 1870–1915: The
Staple Model and the Take-off Hypothesis," *Canadian Journal of Economics and
Political Science* 29: 162–84.

Bideau, A., Dupâquier J., and Biraben, J-N. (1988) "La mortalité de 1800 à 1914," in

J. Dupâquier (ed.) *Histoire de la population française*, Vol. 3, Paris: Presses universitaires de France.

Bodnar, J. (1985) *The Transplanted; A History of Immigrants in Urban America*, Bloomington: Indiana University Press.

Boehm, E. A. (1979) *Twentieth Century Economic Development in Australia*, 2nd edn, Melbourne: Longman Cheshire.

Borjas, G. J. (1985) "Assimilation, Changes in Cohort Quality and the Earnings of Immigrants," *Journal of Labor Economics* 3: 463–89.

—— (1990) *Friends or Strangers? The Impact of Immigrants on the U.S. Economy*, New York: Basic Books.

—— (1991) "Immigrants in the U.S. Labor Market: 1940–80," *American Economic Review* 81: 287–91.

—— and Freeman R. B. (eds) (1992) *Immigration and the Workforce*, Chicago: University of Chicago Press.

Bourbeau, R. and Legare, J. (1982) *Evolution de la mortalité au Canada et au Qébec 1831–1931*, Montreal: les Presses de la Université de Montreal.

Bowley, A. L. (1899) "The Statistics of Wages in the United Kingdom during the last Hundred Years, Part III: Agricultural Wages – Ireland," *Journal of the Royal Statistical Society* 42: 395–404.

Boyer, G. R., Hatton T. J. and O'Rourke, K. "The Impact of Emigration on Real Wages in Ireland, 1850–1914," Centre for Economic Policy Research Discussion Paper No. 854, London: CEPR, December 1993.

Brattne, B. (1973) *Bröderne Larsson. En Studie i Svensk emigrant agent verksamet inder 1880 talet*, Uppsala: Almqvist & Wiksell.

Brettell, C. B. (1986) *Men who Migrate, Women Who Wait. Population and History in a Portuguese Parish*, Princeton: Princeton University Press.

Briggs, J. W. (1978) *An Italian Passage; Immigrants to Three American Cities, 1890–1930*, New Haven, Conn.: Yale University Press.

Briggs, V. M., Jr. (1984) *Immigration Policy and the American Labor Force*, Baltimore: Johns Hopkins University Press.

Buckley, K. D. (1967) "A New Index of Engineering Unemployment 1852–94," *Economic Record* 43: 108–18.

—— (1970) *Amalgamated Engineers in Australia, 1852–1920*, Department of Economic History, RSES, Australian National University, Canberra.

Bunge, A. E. and Garcia Mata, C. (1931) "Argentina," in I. Ferenczi and W. F. Willcox (eds) *International Migrations*, Vol. 2, New York: National Bureau of Economic Research.

Bunle, H. (1943) *Mouvements migratoires entre la France et l'étranger*, Paris: Imprimerie Nationale.

Burda, M. C. (1993) "The Determinants of East–West German Migration: Some First Results," *European Economic Review* 37: 452–61.

Butlin, M. W. (1977) *A Preliminary Annual Data Base, 1990/01 to 1973/74* (Research Discussion Paper 770–1), Sydney: Reserve Bank of Australia.

Butlin, N. G. (1946) "An Index of Engineering Unemployment, 1852–1943," *Economic Record* 22: 241–60.

—— (1962) *Australian Domestic Product, Investment and Foreign Borrowing*, London: Cambridge University Press.

—— (1964) *Investment in Australian Economic Development, 1861–1900*, London: Cambridge University Press.

—— (1987a) "Australian National Accounts," in W. Vamplew (ed.) *Australians: Historical Statistics*, Sydney: Fairfax, Syme & Weldon.

—— (1987b) "Our 200 Years: Australian Wealth and Progress Since 1788: A

Statistical Picture," in *Commemorative Bicentenary Diary*, Brisbane: Queensland Newspaper Ltd.

—— and Dowie, J. A. (1969) "Estimates of Australian Workforce and Employment, 1861–1961," *Australian Economic History Review* 9: 138–54.

Cairncross, A. K. (1949) "Internal Migration in Victorian England," *Manchester School* 17: 67–87.

Camps y Curia, H. (1992) "Population Turnover and the Family Cycle: The Migration Flows in a Catalan Town during the Nineteenth Century," *Continuity and Change* 7: 225–45.

Canada, Commissioner of Immigration (various years) *Sessional Papers*.

—— Department of Agriculture (1882) *Annual Report*, Ottawa: Sessional Paper 11.

—— Department of Colonization (1930) *Annual Report*, Ottawa: Table 5.

—— Decennial Census (various years).

—— Department of Immigration and Colonization (1922) *Annual Report*.

—— Department of Immigration and Colonization (1928) *Annual Report*.

Carlsson, S. (1976) "Chronology and Composition of Swedish Emigration to America," in H. Rundblom and H. Norman (eds) *From Sweden to America; A History of the Migration*, Minneapolis: University of Minnesota Press.

Carpi, L. (1972) *Dell'emigrazione italiana all'estero nei suoi rapporti con l'agricoltura, coll'industria e col commercio*, Firenze: Civelli.

Carré, J-J., Dubois, P., and Malinvaud, E. (1972) *La croissance française*, Paris: Seuil.

Carrier, N. H. and Jeffery, J. R. (1953) *External Migration. A Study of the Available Statistics, 1815–1950*, London: Her Majesty's Stationery Office.

Chambers, E. J. and Gordon, D. F. (1987) "Primary Products and Economic Growth: An Empirical Measurement," in D. McCalla (ed.) *Perspectives on Canadian Economic History*, Toronto: Copp Clark Pitman Ltd.

Chatelain, A. (1971) "L'attraction des trois plus grandes agglomérations françaises: Paris – Lyons – Marseilles en 1891," *Annales de Démographie Historique*: 27–41.

—— (1976) *Les migrants temporaires en France de 1800 à 1914*. Lille Villeneuve-D'Asc: University of Lille III.

Chenais, J-C. (1986) *La transition démographique. Étapes, formes, implications économiques*, Paris: Presses universitaires de France.

Chevalier, L. (1950) *La formation de la population parisienne au XIX siècle*, Paris: Presses universitaires de France.

Chiswick, B. R. (1978) "The Effect of Americanization on the Earnings of Foreign-Born Men," *Journal of Political Economy* 86: 897–921.

Chmelar, J. (1973) "The Austrian Emigration, 1900–14," *Perspectives in American History* 7: 275–378.

Cinel, D. (1982) *From Italy to San Francisco: The Immigrant Experience*, Stanford, Calif.: Stanford University Press.

Clark, C. (1970) "Net Capital Stock," *Economic Record* 46: 449–66.

Clark, P. (1987) "Migration in England during the Seventeenth and Early Eighteenth Centuries," in P. Clark and D. Souden (eds) *Migration and Society in Early Modern England*, London: Hutchinson.

Coats, R. H. (1931) "Canada," in I. Ferenczi and W. F. Willcox (eds) *International Migrations*, Vol. 2, New York: National Bureau of Economic Research.

Collins, B. (1982) "Irish Emigration to Dundee and Paisley during the First Half of the Nineteenth Century," in J. M. Goldstrom and L. A. Clarkson (eds) *Irish Population, Economy and Society. Essays in Honour of the Late Ken Connell*, Oxford: Clarendon Press.

Coward, J. (1982) "Birth Under-Registration in the Republic of Ireland during the

Twentieth Century," *Economic and Social Review* 14: 1–27.

Crafts, N. F. R. and Thomas, M. (1986) "Comparative Advantage in UK Manufacturing Trade 1910–35," *Economic Journal* 96: 629–45.

Cross, G. S. (1983) *Immigrant Workers in Industrial France: The Making of a New Laboring Class*, Philadelphia: Temple University Press.

Crotty, D. (1966) *Irish Agricultural Production: Its Volume and Structure*, Cork: University College Press.

Crowley, F. K. (1951) "British Migration to Australia: 1860–1914, A Descriptive, Analytical and Statistic Account of the Immigration from the United Kingdom," Unpublished D. Phil. thesis, University of Oxford.

Daily Telegraph (Sydney: various dates).

Dales, J. (1966) *The Protective Tariff in Canada's Development*, Toronto: University of Toronto Press.

Darby, M. R. (1976) "Three and a Half Million Workers Have Been Mislaid: Or an Explanation of Unemployment 1934–42," *Journal of Political Economy* 84: 487–93.

David, P. A. (1974) *Technical Choice, Innovation and Economic Growth*, Cambridge: Cambridge University Press.

Davidson, B. (1987) "Agriculture," in W. Vamplew (ed.) *Australians: Historical Statistics*, Sydney: Fairfax, Syme & Weldon.

Davie, M. R. (1947) *Refugees in America,* New York: Harper.

Davis, L. E. and Huttenback, R. A. (1986) *Mammon and the Pursuit of Empire: The Political Economy of British Imperialism*, Cambridge: Cambridge University Press.

Della Paolera, G. (1988) "How the Argentine Economy Performed During the International Gold Standard: A Reexamination," Unpublished Ph.D. thesis, University of Chicago.

de Long, J. B. (1988) "Productivity Growth, Convergence, and Welfare: A Comment," *American Economic Review* 78: 1138–54.

—— (1992) "Productivity Growth and Machinery Investment: A Long-Run Look, 1870–1980," *Journal of Economic History* 52: 307–24.

—— and Summers, L. (1991) "Equipment Investment and Economic Growth," *Quarterly Journal of Economics* 106: 445–502.

Depoid, P. (1942) *Les naturalisations en France (1870–1940)*, Paris: Imprimerie Nationale.

De Vries, J. (1984) *European urbanization, 1500–1800*, London: Methuen.

—— (1990) "Problems in the Measurement, Description and Analysis of Historical Urbanization," in A. D. Van De Woude, A. Hayami, and J. De Vries (eds) *Urbanization in History. A Process of Dynamic Interactions*, Oxford: Clarendon Press.

Díaz-Alejandro, C. F. (1970) *Essays on the Economic History of the Argentine Republic*, New Haven, Conn.: Yale University Press.

—— (1985) "Argentina, Australia and Brazil Before 1929," in G. Di Tella and D. C. M. Platt (eds) *Argentina, Australia and Canada: Studies in Comparative Development, 1870–1965*, London: Macmillan.

Di Comite, L. (1986) "Aspects of Italian Emigration, 1881–1915," in I. A. Glazier and L. De Rosa (eds) *Migration across Time and Nations*, New York: Holmes & Meier.

Dirección General de Inmigración (1925) *Resumen Estadístico de Movimiento Migratorio en la Republica Argentina, Años 1857–1924*, Buenos Aires: Republica Argentina, Ministerio de Agricultura.

Dirección General de la Estadística de la Nación (1938–40) *La Población y el*

Movimiento Demografico de la Republica Argentina, Buenos Aires: Republica Argentina, Ministerio de Hacienda.

Dunlevy, J. A. and Gemery, H. A. (1977) "The Role of Migrant Stock and Lagged Migration in the Settlement Patterns of Nineteenth Century Immigrants," *Review of Economics and Statistics* 59: 137–44.

—— —— (1978) "Economic Opportunity and the Responses of Old and New Immigrants in the United States," *Journal of Economic History* 38: 901–17.

Easterlin, R. A. (1961) "Influences in European Overseas Emigration before World War I," *Economic Development and Cultural Change* 9: 331–51.

—— (1968) *Population, Labor Force, and Long Swings in Economic Growth*, New York: National Bureau of Economic Research.

Easton, S., Gibson, W., and Reed, C. (1988) "Tariffs and Growth: The Dales Hypothesis," *Explorations in Economic History* 25: 147–63.

Eckaus R. (1961) "The North–South Differential in Italian Economic Development", *Journal of Economic History* 21: 285-317.

Edelstein, M. (1981) "Foreign Investment and Empire 1860–1914," in R. Floud and D. McCloskey (eds) *The Economic History of Britain Since 1700*, Vol. 2, Cambridge: Cambridge University Press.

—— (1982) *Overseas Investment in the Age of High Imperialism*, New York: Columbia University Press.

Eichengreen, B. J. and Gemery, H. A. (1986) "The Earnings of Skilled and Unskilled Immigrants at the End of the Nineteenth Century," *Journal of Economic History* 46: 441–54.

—— and Hatton, T. J. (1988) "Interwar Unemployment in International Perspective: An Overview," in B. J. Eichengreen and T. J. Hatton (eds) *Interwar Unemployment in International Perspective*, Boston: Kluwer Academic Publishers.

Eltis, D. (1983) "Free and Coerced Transatlantic Migrations: Some Comparisons," *American Historical Review* 88: 251–80.

Endres, A. (1984) "Colonial Workforce Aggregates: Estimates from Colonial Censuses, 1828–1901," *Source Papers in Economic History*, No. 3, Canberra: Department of Economic History, Australian National University.

Erickson, C. (1972) "Who were the English and Scottish Emigrants in the 1880s?," in D. V. Glass and R. Revelle (eds) *Population and Social Change,* London: Arnold.

—— (1981) "Emigration from the British Isles to the U.S.A. in 1831," *Population Studies* 35: 175–98.

—— (1989) "Emigration to the U.S.A. from the British Isles: Part I," *Population Studies* 43: 347–67.

—— (1990) "Emigration to the U.S.A. from the British Isles: Part II, Who were the English Emigrants?," *Population Studies* 44: 21–40.

Estevadeordal, A. (1992) "Comparative Advantage at the Turn of the Century," Unpublished paper, Cambridge, Mass.: Harvard University.

Fahour, A. (1987) "Australian Wage Determination 1850 to 1982," Unpublished honors thesis, Melbourne: La Trobe University.

Faini, R. (1991) "Regional Development and Economic Integration," in J. da Silva Lopes and L. Beleza (eds) *Portugal and the Internal Market of the EEC*, Lisbon: Banco de Portugal.

—— and Venturini A. (1993) "Trade, Aid and Migrations," *European Economic Review* 37: 1–8.

—— —— 1994 "Migration and Growth: The Experience of Southern Europe," Centre for Economic Policy Research Discussion Paper 964, CEPR: London.

Federico, G. and Toniolo G. (1991) "Italy," in R. Sylla and C. Toniolo (eds) *Patterns of European Industrialization*, London: Routledge.

Feinstein, C. H. (1972) *Statistical Tables of National Incomes, Expenditure and Output of the UK*, London: Cambridge University Press.

—— (1990) "New Estimates of Average Earnings in the United Kingdom, 1880–1913," *Economic History Review*, 2nd series, 43: 595–632.

—— (1991) "A New Look at the Cost of Living, 1870–1914," in James Foreman Peck (ed.) *New Perspectives on the Late Victorian Economy: Essays in Quantitative Economic History, 1860–1914*, Cambridge: Cambridge University Press.

Ferenczi, I. and Willcox, W. F. (1929) *International Migrations*, Vol. 1, New York: National Bureau of Economic Research.

—— —— (1931) *International Migrations*, Vol. 2, New York: National Bureau of Economic Research.

Ferrie, J. P. (1992) "Geographic Mobility of European Immigrant Arrivals at New York, 1840–1860," presented to the National Bureau of Economic Research/DAE Conference, Cambridge, Massachusetts, March.

Firestone, O. J. (1958) *Canada's Economic Development, 1867–1953*, London: Bowes & Bowes.

—— (1960) "Development of Canada's Economy, 1850–1900" in *Trends in the American Economy in the Nineteenth Century, Income and Wealth*, Vol. 24, Princeton: Princeton University Press.

Fishlow, A. (1966) "Productivity and Technological Change in the Railroad Sector, 1840–1910," in *Output, Employment, and Productivity in the United States after 1800*, New York: Columbia University Press.

Fitzpatrick, D. (1980) "The Disappearance of the Irish Agricultural Labourer, 1841–1912," *Irish Economic and Social History* 7: 66–92.

—— (1984) *Irish Emigration 1801–1921*, Dublin: Economic and Social History Society of Ireland.

Flam, H. and M. J. Flanders (eds) (1991) *Heckscher–Ohlin Trade Theory*, Cambridge, Mass.: MIT Press.

Flinn, M. (1981) *The European Demographic System, 1500–1820*, Brighton: Harvester.

Ford, A. G. (1962) *The Gold Standard, 1880–1914: Britain and Argentina*, Oxford: Clarendon Press.

—— (1971) "British Investment in Argentina and Long Swings, 1880–1914," *Journal of Economic History* 31: 650–63.

Foreman-Peck, J. (1992) "A Political Economy of International Migration, 1815–1914," *Manchester School* 60: 359–76.

Friedlander, D. and Roshier, R. J. (1966) "A Study of Internal Migration in England and Wales: Part I," *Population Studies* 19: 239–79.

Fridlizius, G. (1979) "Sweden," in R. Lee (ed.) *European Demography and Economic Growth*, London: Croom Helm.

—— (1990) "Agricultural Productivity, Trade and Urban Growth during the Phase of Commercialization of the Swedish Economy, 1810–70," in A. D. Van De Woude, A. Hayami and J. De Vries (eds) *Urbanization in History. A Process of Dynamic Interactions*, Oxford: Clarendon Press.

Gallaway, L. E. and Vedder, R. K. (1971) "Emigration from the United Kingdom to the United States, 1860–1913," *Journal of Economic History* 31: 885–97.

——, Vedder, R. K., and Shukla, V. (1974) "The Distribution of the Immigrant Population in the United States: An Economic Analysis," *Explorations in Economic History* 11: 213–26.

Garden, M. (1988) "L'évolution de la population active," in J. Dupâquier (ed.) *Histoire de la population française*, Vol. 3, Paris: Presses universitaires de France.

Geary, P. and C. Ó Gráda (1985) "Immigration and the Real Wage: Time Series Evidence from the United States, 1820–1977, Discussion Paper 71, Centre for Economic Policy Research, London.

Gerardi, R. E. (1985) "Australia, Argentina and World Capitalism: A Comparative Analysis 1830–1945," Transnational Corporations Research Project, Occasional Papers no. 8, Faculty of Economics, University of Sydney (May).

Gerschenkron, A. (1952) "Economic Backwardness in Historical Perspective," in B. F. Hoselitz (ed.) *The Progress of Underdeveloped Areas*, Chicago: University of Chicago Press.

Giusti F. (1965) "Bilanci Demografici della Popolazione Italiana dal 1861 al 1961", *Annali di Statistica* 8: 17.

Gjerde, J. (1985) *From Peasants to Farmers: The Migration from Balestrand, Norway to the Upper Mid West*, Cambridge: Cambridge University Press.

Goldin, C. (1993) "The Political Economy of Immigration Restriction in the United States, 1890–1921," National Bureau of Economic Research Working Paper 4345, National Bureau of Economic Research, Cambridge, Mass.

Gould, J. D. (1979) "European Inter-continental Emigration, 1815–1914: Patterns and Causes," *Journal of European Economic History* 8: 593–679.

—— (1980a) "European Inter-continental Emigration. The Road Home: Return Migration from the USA," *Journal of European Economic History* 9: 41–112.

—— (1980b) "European Inter-continental Emigration: The Role of 'Diffusion' and 'Feedback'," *Journal of European Economic History* 9: 267–315.

Green, A. G. (1993) "The Political Economy of Immigrant Selection in Canada, 1896 to 1930," Queen's University: unpublished.

—— and Green, D. (1993) "Balanced Growth and the Geographical Distribution of European Immigrant Arrivals to Canada, 1900–1912," *Explorations in Economic History* 30: 31–59.

—— and Sparks, G. R. (1991) "A Macro Model of Canada, 1870–1939," Unpublished paper, Ontario: Queen's University.

—— and Urquhart, M. C. (1976) "Factor and Commodity Flows in the International Economy of 1870–1914: A Multi-Country View," *Journal of Economic History* 36: 217–52.

—— —— (1987) "New Estimates of Output Growth in Canada: Measurement and Interpretation," in D. McCalla (ed.) *Perspectives on Canadian Economic History*, Toronto: Copp Clark Pitman Ltd.

Greenwood, M. J. (1975) "Research on Internal Migration in the United States: A Survey," *The Journal of Economic Literature* 13: 397–433.

—— and McDowell, J. M. (1986) "The Factor Market Consequences of U.S. Immigration," *Journal of Economic Literature* 24: 1738–72.

—— and Thomas, L. B. (1973) "Geographic Labor Mobility in Nineteenth Century England and Wales," *Annals of Regional Science* 7: 90–105.

Griliches, Z. (1967) "Distributed Lags: A Survey," *Econometrica* 35: 16–49.

Habakkuk, H. J. (1962) *American and British Technology in the Nineteenth Century: The Search for Labour-saving Inventions*, Cambridge: Cambridge University Press.

Haines, M. R. (forthcoming) "The Population of the United States, 1790–1920," in S. Engerman and R. Gallman (eds) *The Cambridge Economic History of the United States*, Vol. 2.

Hall, A. R. (1963a) "Some Long Period Effects of the Kinked Age Distribution of the Population of Australia 1861–1961," *Economic Record* 39: 43–52.

—— (1963b) *The London Capital Market and Australia 1870–1914*, Canberra: The Australian National University.

—— (ed.) (1968) *The Export of Capital from Britain 1870–1914*, London: Methuen.

Handlin, O. (1951) *The Uprooted*, Cambridge, Mass.: Harvard University Press.

Hanes, C. (1991) "Migration and Earnings in the Late Nineteenth Century," Paper presented to the Historical Labor Statistics Conference, University of Kansas, Lawrence, Kansas (July).

Hannon, J. U. (1982a) "Ethnic Discrimination in a Nineteenth Century Mining District: Michigan Copper Mines, 1888," *Explorations in Economic History* 19: 28–50.

—— (1982b) "City Size and Ethnic Discrimination: Michigan Agricultural Implements and Iron Working Industries, 1890," *Journal of Economic History* 42: 825–45.

Harley, C. K. (1988) "Ocean Freight Rates and Productivity, 1740–1913: The Primacy of Mechanical Invention Reaffirmed," *Journal of Economic History* 48: 851–76.

Harris, J. R. and Todaro, M. P. (1970) "Migration, Unemployment and Development: A Two Sector Analysis," *American Economic Review* 60: 126–42.

Hatton, T. J. (1993) "A Model of UK Emigration, 1870–1913," Centre for Economic Policy Research, Discussion Paper 771, Centre for Economic Policy Research: London.

—— and Williamson, J. G. (1991a) "Wage Gaps between Farm and City: Michigan in the 1890s," *Explorations in Economic History* 28: 381–408.

—— —— (1991b) "Integrated and Segmented Labor Markets: Thinking in Two Sectors," *Journal of Economic History* 51: 416–17.

—— —— (1992a) "What Explains Wage Gaps between Farm and City? Exploring the Todaro Model with American Evidence, 1890–1941," *Economic Development and Cultural Change* 40: 267–94.

—— —— (1992b) "International Migration and World Development: A Historical Perspective," Discussion Paper 1604, Harvard Institute of Economic Research, Cambridge, Mass.

—— —— (1993) "After the Famine: Emigration from Ireland 1850–1913," *Journal of Economic History* 53: 575–600.

—— —— (1994) "What Drove the Mass Migrations from Europe in the Late Nineteenth Century," *Population and Development Review* (forthcoming).

Hayami, Y. and Ruttan, V. W. (1971) *Agricultural Development: An International Perspective*, Baltimore: Johns Hopkins Press.

Higgs, R. (1971) "Race, Skill and Earnings: American Immigrants in 1909," *Journal of Economic History* 31: 420–9.

Hill, P.J. (1975) *The Economic Impact of Immigration into the United States*, Chicago: Arno Press.

Hochstadt, S. (1981) "Migration and Industrialization in Germany, 1815–1977," *Social Science History* 5: 445–68.

Hohenberg, P. (1974) "Migrations et fluctuations démographiques dans la France rurale, 1836–1901," *Annales: Économies. Sociétés. Civilisations* 29: 461–97.

—— and Lees, L. H. (eds) (1985) *The Making of Urban Europe, 1000–1950*, Cambridge, Mass.: Harvard University Press.

Hollingsworth, T. H. (1970) "Historical Studies of Migration," *Annales de Démographie Historique* 7: 87–96.

Houston, R. A. and Withers, C. W. J. (1990) "Population Mobility in Scotland and Europe, 1600–1900: A Comparative Perspective," *Annales de Demographie Historique* 27: 285–308.

Howard, D. S. (1943) *The WPA and Federal Relief Policy*, New York: Russell Sage Foundation.

Hutchinson, E. P. (1981) *Legislative History of American Immigration Policy:*

1798–1965, Philadelphia: University of Pennsylvania Press.

Hvidt, K. (1966) "Danish Emigration Prior to 1914. Trends and Problems," *Scandinavian Economic History Review* 14: 158–78.

—— (1975) *Flight to America. The Social Background of 300,000 Danish Emigrants*, New York: Academic Press.

IEERAL (Instituto de Estudios Económicos sobre la Realidad Argentina y Latinoamericana) (1986) "Estadísticas de la Evolución Económica de Argentina 1913–1984," *Estudios* 9: 103–84.

Irish Commission on Emigration and other Population Problems (1954) *Reports*, Dublin: Eire.

Jerome, H. (1926) *Migration and Business Cycles*, New York: National Bureau of Economic Research.

Jones, M. A. (1992) *American Immigration*, 2nd edn, Chicago: University of Chicago Press.

Kamphoefner, W. D. (1976) "At the Crossroads of Economic Development: Background Factors Affecting Emigration from Nineteenth Century Germany," in I. A. Glazier and L. de Rosa (eds) *Migration Across Time and Nations*, New York: Holmes & Meier.

Karlstrom, U. (1985) *Economic Growth and Migration During the Industrialization of Sweden: A General Equilibrium Approach*, Stockholm: Stockholm School of Economics.

Kelley, A. C. (1965) "International Migration and Economic Growth: Australia, 1865–1935," *Journal of Economic History* 25: 333–54.

—— (1968) "Demographic Change and Economic Growth: Australia 1861–1911," *Explorations in Economic History* 5: 207–77.

Kenwood, A. G. and Lougheed, A. L. (1983) *The Growth of the International Economy, 1820–1980*, London: Unwin Hyman.

Kero, R. (1974) *Migration from Finland to North America in the Years between the United States' Civil War and the First World War*, Turku: Institute for Migration, Annales Universitatis Turkuensis, Ser. B-Tom. 130.

—— (1991) "Migration Traditions from Finland to North America," in R. J. Vecoli and S. M. Sinke (eds) *A Century of European Migrations 1830–1930*, Urbana: University of Illinois Press.

Kerr, D. and Holdsworth D. W. (1990) *Addressing the Twentieth Century*, Vol. 3 of Historical Atlas of Canada, Toronto: University of Toronto Press.

Keyfitz, N. (1950) "The Growth of Canadian Population," *Population Studies* 4: 47–63.

Keyssar, A. (1986) *Out of Work: The First Century of Unemployment in Massachusetts*, Cambridge, Mass.: Cambridge University Press.

Kindleberger, C. P. (1964) *Economic Growth in France and Britain, 1851–1950*, Cambridge, Mass.: Harvard University Press.

Kirk, D. (1946) *Europe's Population in the Interwar Years*, Geneva: League of Nations.

Klein, H. S. (1983) "The Integration of Italian Immigrants into the United States and Argentina: A Comparative Analysis," *American Historical Review* 88: 306–29.

Köllman, W. (1969) "The Process of Urbanization in Germany at the Height of the Industrialization Period," *Journal of Contemporary History* 4: 59–76.

—— (1971) "Les mouvements migratoires pendant la grande periode d'industrialisation de la Rhenanie–Westphalie," *Annales de Démographie Historique* 18: 87–120.

Korol, J. C. (1991) "Argentine Development in a Comparative Perspective," *Latin American Research Review* 26: 201–12.

Krajlic, F. (1985) "Round Trip Croatia, 1900–14," in D. Hoerder (ed.) *Labour*

Migrations in the Atlantic Economies. The European and North American Working Class during the Period of Industrialization, Westport, Conn.: Greenwood Press.

Krichefsky, G. (1945) "Quota Immigration, 1925–1944," Immigration and Naturalization Service, *Monthly Review* 2: 156–9.

Kuznets, S. (1958) "Long Swings in the Growth of Population and in Related Economic Variables," *Proceedings of the American Philosophical Society* 102: 25–52.

—— (1966) *Modern Economic Growth*, New Haven: Yale University Press.

—— and Rubin, E. (1954) *Immigration and the Foreign Born*, Occasional Paper 46, New York: National Bureau of Economic Research.

Landes, D. (1969) *The Unbound Prometheus*, Cambridge: Cambridge University Press.

Langewiesche, D. and Lenger, F. (1987) "Internal Migration: Persistence and Mobility," in K. J. Bade (ed.) *Population, Labor and Migration in Nineteenth and Twentieth Century Germany*, Leamington Spa: Berg.

Laux, H-D. (1989) "The Components of Population Growth in Prussian Cities, 1875–1905 and their Influence on Population Structure," in R. M. Lawton and R. Lee (eds) *Urban Population Development from the Late-eighteenth to the Early-twentieth Century*, Liverpool: Liverpool University Press.

Lawton, R. (1989) "Population Mobility and Urbanization: Nineteenth Century British Experience," in R. M. Lawton and R. Lee (eds) *Urban Population Development from the Late-eighteenth to the Early-twentieth Century*, Liverpool: Liverpool University Press.

—— and Lee, R. (1989) "The Framework of Comparative Urban Population Studies in Western Europe, c1750–1920," in R. M. Lawton and R. Lee (eds) *Urban Population Development from the Late-eighteenth to the Early-twentieth Century*, Liverpool: Liverpool University Press.

Leamer, E. E. (1984) *Sources of International Comparative Advantage*, Cambridge, Mass.: MIT Press.

Lebergott, S. (1964) *Manpower in Economic Growth: The American Record Since 1800*, New York: McGraw-Hill.

—— (1992) "Historical Unemployment Series: A Comment," *Research in Economic History*, Vol. 14, Greenwich, Conn.: JAI Press.

Lee, C. H. (1979) *British Regional Employment Statistics, 1841–1971*, Cambridge: Cambridge University Press.

Lee, E. S., Miller, A. R., Brainerd, C. P. and Easterlin, R. A. (1957) *Population Redistribution and Economic Growth, United States, 1870–1950*, Vol. 1, Philadelphia: American Philosophical Society.

Lee, J. (1973) *The Modernization of Irish Society 1848–1918*, Dublin: Gill & Macmillan.

Lee, R. (1979) "Germany," in R. Lee (ed.) *European Demography and Economic Growth*, London: Croom Helm.

Leff, N. H. (1992) "Economic Development in Brazil, 1822–1913," First Boston Working Paper Series FB-92-02, Columbia University.

Lewis, W. A. (1954) "Economic Development with Unlimited Supplies of Labour," *Manchester School of Economic and Social Studies* 22: 139–91.

—— (1978) *The Evolution of the International Economic Order*, Princeton, N.J.: Princeton University Press.

Lindert, P. H. (1978) *Fertility and Scarcity in America*, Princeton, N.J.: Princeton University Press.

Livi Bacci, M. (1969) "I fattori demografici dello sviluppo economico," in G. Fua (ed.)

Lo sviluppo economico in Italia, Vol. III, Milano: Franco Angeli.

Lower, A. R. M. (1930) "The Case Against Immigration," *Queen's Quarterly* 37: 557–74.

Lucas, R. E. (1988) "On the Mechanics of Economic Development," *Journal of Monetary Economics* 22: 3–42.

Lucassen, J. (1987) *Migrant Labor in Europe, 1600–1900. The Drift to the North Sea*, London: Croom Helm.

Macarthy, P. (1980) "Wages in Australia, 1891 to 1914," *Australian Economic History Review* 10: 56–76.

McCloskey, D. N. (1970) "Did Victorian Britain Fail?," *Economic History Review* 2nd series, 23: 446–59.

MacDonald J. S. (1963) "Agricultural Organization, Migration and Labour Militancy in Rural Italy," *Economic History Review* 2nd series, 10: 61–75.

McDougall, D. M. (1961) "Immigration into Canada, 1851–1920," *Canadian Journal of Economics and Political Science* 27: 162–75.

—— (1971) "Canadian Manufactured Commodity Output, 1870–1915," *Canadian Journal of Economics* 4: 21–36.

McGouldrick, P. and Tannen, M. (1977) "Did American Manufacturers Discriminate Against Immigrants before 1914?," *Journal of Economic History* 37: 723–46.

McInnis, R. M. (1992) "Infant Mortality in Late Nineteenth Century Canada," Paper presented to Seminar on Child and Infant Mortality, International Union for the Scientific Study of Population, Montreal, October.

MacKinnon, M. (1993) "New Evidence on Canadian Wage Rates, 1900–1930," Unpublished paper, McGill University.

Mackintosh, W. A. (1939) *The Economic Background of Dominion–Provincial Relations*, Appendix III of the Report of the Royal Commission on Dominion–Provincial Relations, Ottawa: King's Printer (Carleton Library reprint, 1964).

McLean, I. W. (1990) "Notes on Growth in Resource-Rich Economies," Unpublished paper, Harvard University (March).

—— and Pincus, J. (1983), "Did Australian Living Standards Stagnate Between 1890 and 1940?," *Journal of Economic History* 43: 193–202.

McPhee, E. T. (1931) "Australia – Its Immigrant Population," in W. F. Willcox (ed.) *International Migrations*, 2 vols, New York: National Bureau of Economic Research.

Maddala, G. S. (1977) *Econometrics*, New York: McGraw-Hill.

Maddison, A. (1982) *Phases of Capitalist Development*, New York: Oxford University Press.

—— (1991) *Dynamic Forces in Capitalist Development*, New York: Oxford University Press.

—— (1992) "Explaining the Economic Performance of Nations 1820–1989," Unpublished paper, Canberra: Australian National University.

—— (1993) "Standardized Estimates of Fixed Capital Stock: A Six Country Comparison," in R. Zoboli (ed.) *Essays on Innovation, Natural Resources and the International Economy*, Milan: Montedison.

Magnussen, O. and Sigveland. G. (1978) "Migration from Norway to the U.S.A. 1866–1914: The Use of Econometric Methods in Analyzing Historical Data," *Scandinavian Journal of Economics* 80: 34–52.

Manchester Guardian, The (various dates) Manchester.

Mankiw, N. G., Romer, D. and Weil, D. N. (1992) "A Contribution to the Empirics of Economic Growth," *Quarterly Journal of Economics* 107: 407–37.

Marchand, O. and Thélot, C. (1991) *Deux siècles de travail en France*, Paris: Presses universitaire de France.

Margo, R. A. (1990a) "Unemployment in 1910: Some Preliminary Findings," in E. Aerts and B. J. Eichengreen (eds) *Unemployment and Underemployment in Historical Perspective*, Proceedings of the 10th International Economic History Congress, Leuven: Leuven University Press.

—— (1990b) "The Microeconomics of Depression Unemployment," Working Paper 18, National Bureau of Economic Research, December.

—— (1993) "Employment and Unemployment in the 1930s," *Journal of Economic Perspectives* 7: 41–59.

Marr, W. L. (1977) "The United Kingdom's International Migration in the Inter-War Period: Theoretical Consideration and Empirical Testing," *Population Studies* 31: 571–9.

—— and D. G. Paterson (1980) *Canada: An Economic History*, Toronto: Macmillan of Canada.

Massey, D. S. (1988) "Economic Development and International Migration in Comparative Perspective," *Population and Development Review* 14: 383–413.

Mauco, G. (1932) *Les étrangers en France, leur rôle dans l'activité économique*, Paris: Armand Colin.

Mitchell, B. R. (1978) *European Historical Statistics, 1750–1970*, New York: Macmillan.

—— (1983) *International Historical Statistics: The Americas and Australasia*, Detroit: Gale Research.

— and Deane, P. (1962) *Abstract of British Historical Statistics*, Cambridge: Cambridge University Press.

Moch, L. P. (1983) *Paths to the City. Regional Migration in Nineteenth Century France*, Beverly Hills: Sage.

Moe, T. (1970) *Demographic Developments and Economic Growth in Norway 1740–1940: An Econometric Study*, Ann Arbor: University Microfilms.

Mokyr, J. (1983) *Why Ireland Starved. A Quantitative and Analytical History of the Irish Economy, 1800–1850*, London: Allen & Unwin.

Molinas, C. and Prados L. (1989) "Was Spain Different? Spanish Historical Backwardness Revisited," *Explorations in Economic History* 26: 385–402.

Morawska, E. (1985) *For Bread with Butter. The Life Worlds of East Central Europeans in Johnstown Pennsylvania, 1890–1940*, Cambridge: Cambridge University Press.

Moreda, V. P. (1987) "Spain's Demographic Modernization, 1800–1930," in N. Sanchez-Albornoz (ed.) *The Economic Modernization of Spain, 1830–1930*, New York: New York University Press.

Morning Post, The (various dates) Melbourne.

Nelson, R. R. and Wright G. (1992) "The Rise and Fall of American Technological Leadership," *Journal of Economic Literature* 30: 1931–64.

New South Wales, *Statistical Register* (various issues) Sydney.

—— *Report* (various dates) Sydney.

Newton, M. P. and Jeffery, J. R. (1951) *Internal migration*, General Registry Office, Studies in Medical and Population Subjects, No. 5, London: Her Majesty's Stationery Office.

Nilsson, F. (1973) *Emigrationen från Stockholm till Nordamerika, 1880–93*, Upsalla: Studia Historica Upsaliensis.

Noiriel, G. (1984) *Longwy, immigrés et prolétaires, 1880–1980*, Paris: Presses universitaires de France.

—— (1992) *Le creuset français, histoire de l'immigration XIXe–XXe siècle*, Paris: Seuil.

Norman, H. (1976) "Causes of Emigration. An Attempt at a Multivariate Analysis," in H. Rundblom and H. Norman (eds) *From Sweden to America. A History of the Migration*, Minneapolis: University of Minnesota Press.

—— and Rundblom, H. (1985) "Migration Patterns in the Nordic Countries," in D. Hoerder (ed.) *Labor Migrations in the Atlantic Economies. The European and North American Working Class during the Period of Industrialization*, Westport, Conn.: Greenwood.

—— —— (1988) *Transatlantic Connections. Nordic Migration to the New World after 1800*, Oslo: Norwegian University Press.

Norrie, K. and Owram D. (1991) *A History of the Canadian Economy*, Toronto: Harcourt Brace Jovanovich.

North, D. C. (1958) "Ocean Freight Rates and Economic Development 1750–1913," *Journal of Economic History* 18: 537–55.

Nugent, W. (1992) *Crossings. The Great Trans-Atlantic Migrations, 1870–1914*, Bloomington: Indiana University Press.

Nurkse, R. (1954) "International Investment Today in the Light of Nineteenth-Century Experience," *Economic Journal* 64: 744–58.

O'Connell, P. (1993) "Puts and Calls on the Irish Sea: An Option Theory Model of Emigration," Mimeo, Department of Economics, Harvard University (September).

Offer, A. (1989) *The First World War: An Agrarian Interpretation*, Oxford: Clarendon Press.

Ó Gráda, C. (1975) "A Note on Nineteenth Century Irish Emigration Statistics," *Population Studies* 1: 143–9.

—— (1988) *Ireland Before and After the Famine: Explorations in Economic History, 1800–1925*, New York: Manchester University Press.

—— (1991) "New Evidence on the Fertility Transition in Ireland, 1880–1911," *Demography* 28, 535–48.

—— (1994) *Ireland 1780–1939: A New Economic History*, Oxford: Oxford University Press.

—— and Walsh, B. (1993) "Irish Emigration: A Survey of Research Findings," Unpublished paper, University College Dublin.

O'Rourke, K. (1991) "Rural Depopulation in a Small Open Economy: Ireland 1856–1876," *Explorations in Economic History* 28: 409–32.

—— and Williamson, J. G. (1992) "Were Heckscher and Ohlin Right? Putting the Factor-Price-Equalization Theorem Back into History," Discussion Paper 1593, Harvard Institute of Economic Research, Cambridge, Mass. (May).

—— , Taylor, A. M., and Williamson, J. G. (1993) "Land, Labor and the Wage-Rental Ratio: Factor Price Convergence in the Late Nineteenth Century," Discussion Paper 1629, Harvard Institute for Economic Research, Cambridge, Mass.

Ostergren, R. A. (1986) "Swedish Migration to North America," in I. A. Glazier and L. De Rosa (eds) *Migration Across Time and Nations*, New York: Holmes & Meier.

Palairet, M. (1979) "The 'New' Immigration and the Newest; Slavic Migration from the Balkans to America and Industrial Europe Since the Late Nineteenth Century," in T. C. Smout (ed.) *The Search for Wealth and Stability. Essays in Economic and Social History Presented to M. W. Flinn*, London: Macmillan.

—— (1987) "The Migrant Workers of the Balkans and their Villages," [18th century to the Second World War] in K. Roth (ed.) *Handwerk in Mittel-und Südosteuropa. Mobilität, Vermittlung und Wandel im Handwork des 18. bis 20. Jahrhunderts*, Munich: Sudosteuropa-Gesellschaft.

P & O Ltd, Fleet Records, Maritime Museum, Sydney (various dates).

276

Podger, A. (1979) "Data Appendix," in R. Mendelsohn, *The Condition of the People*, Sydney: Allen & Unwin.

Pollard, S. (1981) *Peaceful Conquest: The Industrialization of Europe 1760–1970*, Oxford: Oxford University Press.

Pope, D. H. (1968) "Empire Migration to Canada, Australia and New Zealand, 1910–1929," *Australian Economic Papers* 7: 167–88.

—— (1976) "The Peopling of Australia," Unpublished Ph.D. thesis, Australian National University (June).

—— (1981a) "Modelling the Peopling of Australia, 1900–1930," *Australian Economic Papers* 20: 258–81.

—— (1981b) "Contours of Australian Immigration 1901–30," *Australian Economic History Review* 21: 29–52.

—— (1985) "Some Factors Inhibiting Australian Immigration in the 1920s," *Australian Economic History Review* 25: 34–52.

—— (1987) "Population and Australian Economic Development 1900–1930," in R. Maddock and I. W. McLean (eds) *The Australian Economy in the Long Run*, Cambridge: Cambridge University Press.

—— (1988) "Did Australian Trading Banks Benefit from Scale Economies and Branch Networks in the Nineteenth Century?," Working Papers in Economic History No. 111, Australian National University, Canberra.

—— (1990) "Australia's Payments Adjustment and Capital Flows Under the International Gold Standard, 1870–1913," Working Papers in Economic History No. 141, Australian National University, Canberra.

—— and Withers, G. (1990) "Do Migrants Rob Jobs from Locals? Lessons from Australian History," Working Paper in Economic History No. 133, Australian National University, Canberra.

—— —— (1993) "Do Migrants Rob Jobs from Locals? Lessons from Australian History," *Journal of Economic History* 53: 719–42.

Pounds, N. G. (1985) *An Historical Geography of Europe, 1800–1914*, Cambridge: Cambridge University Press.

Poussou, J-P. (1970) "Les mouvements migratoires en France et à partir de la France de la fin du XVe siècle au debut du XIXe siècle: approches pour une synthèse," *Annales de Démographie Historique* 17: 11–71.

—— (1989) "The Population Increase of French Towns between 1750 and 1914 and its Demographic Consequences," in R. Lawton and R. Lee (eds) *Urban Population Development from the Late-eighteenth to the Early-twentieth Century*, Liverpool: Liverpool University Press.

Price, C. (1987) "Immigration and Ethnic Origin," in W. Vamplew (ed.) *Australians: Historical Statistics*, Broadway, N.S.W.: Fairfax, Syme & Weldon.

Prost, A. (1966) "L'immigration en France depuis cent ans," *Esprit* 34: 532–45.

Qantas Airways Ltd, Sydney, files (various dates).

Queensland, *Statistical Register* (various issues) Brisbane.

Queensland, Colonial Treasurer, *Report* (various dates) Brisbane.

Quigley, J. M. (1972) "An Economic Model of Swedish Emigration," *Quarterly Journal of Economics* 86: 111–26.

Quinlan, M. and Gardiner, M. (1990) "Researching Australian Industrial Relations in the Nineteenth Century," in G. Patmore (ed.) *History and Industrial Relations*, Sydney: Australian Centre for Industrial Relations Research and Training, University of Sydney.

—— —— (forthcoming) *Australian Trade Unions, Structure, Strategy, Growth, 1825–1925*, Oxford: Oxford University Press.

Rabut, O. (1974) "Les étrangers en France," *Population* 29 (special issue): 147–60.

Ratti, A. M. (1931) "Italian Migration Movements from 1876 to 1926," in I. Ferenczi and W. F. Willcox (eds) *International Migrations*, Vol. 2, New York: National Bureau of Economic Research.

Ravenstein, E. G. (1885) "The Laws of Migration," *Journal of the Royal Statistical Society* 48: 167–227.

—— (1889) "The Laws of Migration," *Journal of the Royal Statistical Society* 52: 241–301.

Redford, A. (1976) *Labor Migration in England, 1800–50*, 3rd edn, Manchester: Manchester University Press.

Reher, D. S. (1989) "Urban Growth and Population Development in Spain, 1787–1930," in R. Lawton and R. Lee (eds) *Urban Population Development from the Late-eighteenth to the Early-twentieth Century*, Liverpool: Liverpool University Press.

—— (1990) *Town and Country in Pre-industrial Spain, Cuenca, 1550–1870*, Cambridge: Cambridge University Press.

—— (1990) "Mobility and Migration in Pre-industrial Urban Areas. The Case of Nineteenth Century Cuenca," in A. D. Van De Woude, A. Hayami and J. De Vries (eds) *Urbanisation in History. A Process of Dynamic Interactions*, Oxford: Clarendon Press.

Richardson, H. W. (1972) "British Emigration and Overseas Investment, 1870–1914," *Economic History Review* 2nd series, 25: 99–113.

Ringrose, D. R. (1983) *Madrid and the Spanish economy, 1560–1850*, Berkeley: University of California Press.

Romer, P. M. (1986) "Increasing Returns and Long-Run Growth," *Journal of Political Economy* 94: 1002–37.

Rondhal, B. (1972) *Emigration Folke Emflyttning och Sasongarbete i att Saguvarksdistrikt i Sodra Haslinghand, 1865–1910*, Stockholm: Almqvist and Wiksell.

Sanchez Alonso, B. (1988) "La Emigración Española a la Argentina, 1880–1930," in N. Sanchez-Albornoz (ed.) *Españoles Hacia America: La Emigración en Masa, 1880–1930*, Madrid: Alianza Editorial.

—— (1990) "Una Nueva Serie Anual De La Emigración Española 1882–1930," *Revista de Historia Economica* 8: 133–70.

Schofield, R. S. (1970) "Age-specific Mobility in an Eighteenth Century Rural English Parish," *Annales de Démographie Historique* 17: 261–74.

Schrier, A. (1958) *Ireland and the American Emigration, 1850–1900*, Minneapolis: University of Minnesota Press.

Semmingsen, I. (1960) "Norwegian Emigration in the Nineteenth Century," *Scandinavian Economic History Review* 8: 150–60.

—— (1972) "Emigration from Scandinavia," *Scandinavian Economic History Review* 20: 45–60.

Sharlin, A. (1986) "Urban–Rural Differences in Fertility in Europe during the Demographic Transition," in A. J. Coale and S. C. Watkins (eds) *The Decline of Fertility in Europe*, Princeton, Princeton University Press.

Sicsic, P. (1991) "Labor Markets and Establishment Size in Nineteenth Century France," Unpublished Ph.D. thesis, Harvard University.

—— (1992) "City–Farm Wage Gaps in Late Nineteenth Century France," *Journal of Economic History* 52: 675–95.

Simon, J. L. (1989) *The Economic Consequences of Immigration*, Cambridge, Mass.: Blackwell.

Simon, M. (1967) "The Pattern of New British Portfolio Foreign Investment, 1865–1914," in J. H. Adler (ed.) *Capital Movements and Economic Development*, London: Macmillan.

Sinclair, W. A. (1976) *The Process of Economic Development in Australia*, Melbourne: Longman Cheshire.

Skelton, O. D. (1913) "General Economic History, 1867–1912," in A. Shortt and A. G. Doughty (eds) *Canada and its Provinces*, Vol. 9, Edinburgh: T. and A. Constable.

Snell, J. G. (1979) "The Cost of Living in Canada in 1870," *Histoire sociale* 12: 186–91.

Solow, R. (1957) "Technical Change and the Aggregate Production Function," *Review of Economics and Statistics* 39: 312–20.

South Australia, *Statistical Register* (various issues) Adelaide.

——, Colonial Treasurer, *Report* (various dates) Adelaide.

Staehle, H. (1950–1) "Statistical Notes on the Economic History of Irish Agriculture 1847–1913," *Journal of the Statistical and Social Enquiry Society of Ireland* 18: 444–71.

Stokvis, P. (1992) "Dutch Transnational Migration, 1880–1920," Unpublished paper, Historisches Seminar Symposium, Hamburg.

Swierenga, R. P. (1976) "Dutch International Migration and Occupational Change: A Structural Analysis of Multinational Linked Files," in I. A. Glazier and L. de Rosa (eds) *Migration Across Time and Nations*, New York: Holmes & Meier.

—— (1991) "Local Patterns of Dutch Migration to the United States in the Mid-Nineteenth Century," in R. J. Vecoli and S. M. Sinke (eds) *A Century of European Migrations, 1830–1930*, Urbana: University of Illinois Press.

Tasmania, *Statistical Register* (various issues) Hobart.

——, Colonial Treasurer, *Report* (various dates) Hobart.

Taylor, A. M. (1991) "Patterns of Factor Migration to Australia, 1870–1914," Mimeo, Department of Economics, Harvard University, Cambridge, Mass. (April).

—— (1992a) "Argentine Economic Growth in Comparative Perspective," Unpublished Ph.D. thesis, Harvard University.

—— (1992b) "External Dependence, Demographic Burdens and Argentine Economic Decline After The *Belle Époque*," *Journal of Economic History* 52: 907–36.

Tederbrand, L-G. (1972) *Västernorrland och Nordamerika, 1875–1913*, Uppsala: University of Uppsala.

Temin, P. (1966) "Labor Scarcity and the Problem of American Industrial Efficiency in the 1850s," *Journal of Economic History* 26: 277–98.

Thernstrom, S. (1973) *The Other Bostonians: Poverty and Progress in the American Metropolis, 1880–1970*, Cambridge, Mass.: Harvard University Press.

Thistlethwaite, F. (1960) "Migration from Europe Overseas in the Nineteenth and Twentieth Centuries," 11th Congress International des Sciences Historiques, *Rapports*, Upsalla.

Thomas, B. (1954) *Migration and Economic Growth. A Study of Great Britain and the Atlantic Economy*, Cambridge: Cambridge University Press.

—— (ed.) (1958) *Economics of International Migration*, New York: Stockton Press.

—— (1972) *Migration and Urban Development. A Reappraisal of British and American Long Cycles*, London: Methuen.

Thomas, D. S. (1941) *Social and Economic Aspects of Swedish Population Movements*, New York: Macmillan.

Thomas, M. (forthcoming) *The Edwardian Economy: Structure, Performance and Policy*, Oxford: Clarendon Press.

Tilly, L. A., and Scott, J. W. (1978) *Women, Work and Family*, New York: Holt, Rinehart & Winston.

Times, The (various dates) London.

Todaro, M. P. (1969) "A Model of Labor Migration and Urban Unemployment in Less Developed Countries," *American Economic Review* 59: 138–48.

Tomaske, J. A. (1971) "The Determinants of Intercountry Differences in European

Emigration, 1881–1900," *Journal of Economic History* 31: 840–53.

Tugault, Y. (1971) "L'immigration étrangère en France: une nouvelle méthode de mesure," *Population* 26: 691–705.

—— (1974) "Les migrations internationales," *Population* 29 (special issue): 115–23.

Turner, M. (1987) "Towards an Agricultural Price Index for Ireland 1850–1914," *Economic and Social Review* 18: 123–36.

Tyrrell, I. (1991) "American Exceptionalism in an Age of International History," *American Historical Review* 96: 1031–55.

United Kingdom, Board of Trade (various dates) *Journals* and *Annual Reports*.

United States, Bureau of Immigration (1920–31) "Intended Future Permanent Residence of Aliens Admitted and Last Permanent Residence of Aliens Departed, by States and Territories," in *Annual Report of the Commissioner General of Immigration to the Secretary of Labor*, Washington, D.C.: United States Government Printing Office.

—— (1920–34) "Intended Future Residence of Aliens Admitted and Last Permanent Residence of Aliens Departed, by States and Territories," in *Annual Report of the Secretary of Labor*, Washington, D.C.: United States Government Printing Office.

——, Department of Agriculture (USDA), Bureau of Agricultural Economics (1943) "Farm Wage Rates, Farm Employment, and Related Data," Washington, D.C.: United States Government Printing Office.

——, Department of Commerce, Bureau of the Census (various years) "Immigrant Aliens Admitted and Emigrant Aliens Departed: by Country of Last or Future Permanent Residence," in *United States Statistical Abstract*, Washington, D.C.: United States Government Printing Office.

—— (1934) "Immigrant Aliens Admitted and Emigrant Aliens Departed: by Sex and Age; and Illiteracy of Immigrants," in *United States Statistical Abstract*, Washington, D.C.: United States Government Printing Office.

—— (1937) "Immigrant Aliens Admitted and Emigrant Aliens Departed, Fiscal Years 1934 to 1937: by Principal Occupations, Sex, and Age Groups," in *Annual Report of the Secretary of Labor*, Washington, D.C.: United States Government Printing Office.

—— (1941) "Immigrant Aliens Admitted: by Sex, Age, Occupation, Illiteracy, and Amount of Money Brought; Emigrant Aliens Departed: by Sex, Age, and Occupation," in *United States Statistical Abstract*, Washington, D.C.: Government Printing Office.

—— (1946) "Population, Internal Migration, 1935–1940, Economic Characteristics of Migrants," in *Sixteenth Census of the United States: 1940*, Washington, D.C.: United States Government Printing Office.

—— (1975) *Historical Statistics of the United States, Colonial Times to 1970*, Part I, Washington, D.C.: United States Government Printing Office.

——, Department of Labor (1933–40) *Annual Report of the Secretary of Labor*, Washington, D.C.: United States Government Printing Office.

——, Immigration Commission (1910) Reports, Washington, D.C.: United States Government Printing Office.

Urquhart, M. C. (1993) *Gross National Product, Canada, 1870–1926*, Kingston and Montreal: McGill–Queen's Press.

—— and Buckley, K. A. H. (eds) (1965) *Historical Statistics of Canada*, Cambridge: Cambridge University Press.

Van Vugt, W. E. (1991) "Welsh Emigration to the U.S.A. During the Mid-nineteenth Century," *Welsh History Review* 15: 545–61.

Vamplew, W. (1987) *Australians: Historical Statistics*, Sydney: Fairfax, Syme and Weldon.

Vázquez-Presedo, V. (1971–6) *Estadísticas Historicas Argentinas*, 2 vols, Buenos Aires: Ediciones Macchi.

Vecoli, R. J. (1986) "The Formation of Chicago's 'Little Italies'," in I. A. Glazier and L. De Rosa (eds) *Migration Across Time and Nations*, New York: Holmes & Meier.

Vedder, R. K. and Cooper, D. (1974) "Nineteenth Century English and Welsh Geographic Labor Mobility: Some Further Evidence," *Annals of Regional Science* 8: 131–9.

Viazzo, P. P. (1989) *Upland Communities. Environment, Population and Social Structure in the Alps since the Sixteenth Century*, Cambridge: Cambridge University Press.

Victoria, *Statistical Register* (various issues) Melbourne.

——, Colonial Treasurer, *Report* (various dates) Melbourne.

Virtanen, K. (1979) *Settlement and Return. Finnish Emigrants in the International Overseas Migration Movement*, Turku: The Migration Institute. Migration Studies, C5.

—— (1985) "Finnish Migrants (1860–1930) in the Overseas Migration Movement," in D. Hoerder (ed.) *Labor Migrations in the Atlantic Economies. The European and North American Working Class during the Period of Industrialization*. Westport, Conn.: Greenwood.

Vishwakarma, K. (1987) "A New Method of Identifying the Turning Point of Business Cycles," Discussion Paper, Melbourne: School of Economics, La Trobe University.

Wakefield, E. G. (1849) *A View of the Art of Colonization*, London: John W. Parker.

Walker, M. (1964) *Germany and the Emigration, 1816–85*, Cambridge, Mass.: Harvard University Press.

Wallis, J. J. (1989) "Employment in the Great Depression: New Data and Hypotheses," *Explorations in Economic History* 26: 45–71.

Walsh, B. (1970) "Marriage Rates and Population Pressure: Ireland 1871 and 1911," *Economic History Review* 2nd series, 23: 148–62.

Weber, A. F. (1967) *The Growth of Cities in the Nineteenth Century. A Study in Statistics*, 2nd edn, Ithaca: Cornell University Press.

Weir, David R. (1992) "A Century of U.S. Unemployment, 1890–1990: Revised Estimates and Evidence for Stabilization," *Research in Economic History* 14, London: JAI Press.

Western Australia, *Statistical Register* (various issues) Perth.

——, Colonial Treasurer, *Report* (various dates) Perth.

Whitney, W. G. (1968) "The Structure of the American Economy in the Late Nineteenth Century," Unpublished Ph.D. thesis, Harvard University.

Wicksell, K. (1882) *Om utvandringen: Dess betydelse och orsaker*, Stockholm: Albert Bonniers Forlag.

Wilkinson, M. (1970) "European Migration to the United States: An Econometric Analysis of Aggregate Labor Supply and Demand," *Review of Economics and Statistics* 52: 272–9.

Williams, J. H. (1920) *Argentine International Trade Under Inconvertible Paper Currency, 1880–1900*, Cambridge, Mass.: Harvard University Press.

Williamson, J. G. (1974a) *Late Nineteenth-Century American Development: A General Equilibrium History*, Cambridge: Cambridge University Press.

—— (1974b) "Migration to the New World: Long Term Influences and Impact," *Explorations in Economic History* 11: 357–90.

—— (1982) "Immigrant-Inequality Trade offs in the Promised Land: Income Distribution and Absorptive Capacity Prior to the Quotas," in B. Chiswick (ed.) *The Gateway: U.S. Immigration Issues and Policies*, Washington, D.C.: American Enterprise Institute.

—— (1986) "The Impact of the Irish on British Labor Markets During the Industrial Revolution," *Journal of Economic History* 46: 693–720.

—— (1990) *Coping with City Growth During the British Industrial Revolution*, Cambridge: Cambridge University Press.

—— (1992) "The Evolution of Global Labor Markets in the First and Second World Since 1830: Background Evidence and Hypotheses," DAE Working Paper 36, National Bureau of Economic Research, Cambridge, Mass. (February).

—— (1993) "Economic Convergence: Placing Post-Famine Ireland in Comparative Perspective," Keynote address read before the Annual Conference of the Economic and Social History Society of Ireland, University College Dublin (September 10–12).

—— (1994) "The Evolution of Global Labor Markets in the First and Second World Since 1830: Background Evidence and Hypotheses," *Explorations in Economic History* (forthcoming).

—— and Lindert, P. H. (1980) *American Inequality: A Macroeconomic History*, New York: Academic Press.

Winter, J. M. (1985) *The Great War and the British People*, London: Macmillan.

Withers, G. (1977) "Immigration and Economic Fluctuations: An Application to Late Nineteenth-Century Australia," *Australian Economic History Review* 17: 131–49.

—— (1987) "Labour," in R. Maddock and I. W. McLean (eds) *The Australian Economy in the Long Run*, Cambridge: Cambridge University Press.

—— (1989) "The Immigration Contribution to Human Capital Formation," in D. Pope and L. Alston (eds) *Australia's Greatest Asset: Human Resources in the Nineteenth and Twentieth Centuries*, Sydney: Federation Press.

——, Endres, A. and Perry, L. (1985) "Australian Historical Statistics Project, Labour Statistics," with corrigenda to "New Composite Estimates of Selected Long Run Labour Series, 1861–1984," *Source Papers in Economic History*, No. 7, Canberra: Department of Economic History, Australian National University.

Wolff, E.N. (1991) "Capital Formation and Productivity Convergence Over the Long Term," *American Economic Review* 81: 565–79.

Work Projects Administration (1946) *Final Report on the WPA Program, 1935–43*, Washington, D.C.: United States Government Printing Office.

Wright, G. (1990) "The Origins of American Industrial Success, 1879–1940," *American Economic Review* 80: 651–68.

Wrigley, E. A. (1990) "Brake or Accelerator? Urban Growth and Population Growth before the Industrial Revolution," in A. D. Van De Woude, A. Hayami and J. De Vries, (eds) *Urbanization in History. A Process of Dynamic Interactions*, Oxford: Clarendon Press.

—— and Schofield, R. S. (1981) *The Population History of England: A Reconstruction*, London: Arnold.

Zelinsky, W. (1971) "The Hypothesis of the Mobility Transition," *Geographical Review* 61: 219–49.

Zevin, R. B. (1992) "Are World Financial Markets More Open? If so Why and With What Effects?," in T. Banuri and J. Schor (eds) *Financial Openness and National Autonomy*, Oxford: Oxford University Press.

Zubrzycki, J. (1953) "Emigration from Poland in the Nineteenth and Twentieth Centuries," *Population Studies* 6: 248–72.

—— (1956) "Patterns of Peasant Migration with Special Reference to Eastern Europe," *REMP Bulletin* 4: 73–87.

Zunz, O. (1982) *The Changing Face of Inequality: Urbanization, Industrial Development and Immigration in Detroit, 1880–1920*, Chicago: Chicago University Press.

INDEX